Greenhouse Gardener's Companion

Greenhouse Gardener's Companion

**GROWING FOOD AND FLOWERS IN
YOUR GREENHOUSE OR SUNSPACE**

Shane Smith

FULCRUM PUBLISHING
GOLDEN, COLORADO

Copyright © 1992 Shane Smith
Book Design by Ann E. Green, Green Design
Cover Illustration by Joyce Kitchell, Copyright © 1992
Chapter Opening Illustration by Carolyn Crawford, Copyright © 1992
Illustrations on pages 11, 13, 26, 32, 43, 48, 49, 60, 71, 82, 115, 127, 128, 150, 151, 153, 163, 341, 374, 443, 459, 471 by Heidi L. Herndon, Copyright © 1992
Illustrations on pages 156, 202, 215, 225, 227, 233, 234, 238, 242, 247, 249, 252, 261, 279, 304, 329, 383 by Shane Smith, Copyright © 1992

Library of Congress Cataloging-in-Publication Data

    Smith, Shane.
       Greenhouse gardener's companion : growing food and
    flowers in your greenhouse or sunspace / Shane Smith.
           p.   cm.
    Includes bibliographical references and index.
    ISBN 1-55591-106-4
       1. Greenhouse gardening—Handbooks, manuals, etc.
    2. Sunspaces—Handbooks, manuals, etc.   I. Title.
    SB415.S663   1992
    635.98'23—dc20   92-53031
                                           CIP

Printed in the United States of America

0 9 8 7 6 5 4 3

Fulcrum Publishing
350 Indiana Street, Suite 350
Golden, Colorado 80401-5093

Dedicated to my wife,
Paige, who always had an encouraging word,
loving patience, a smile
and hug when I needed it most

Table of Contents

Acknowledgments

Without the efforts of these people who gave the precious gift of their time, I could never have finished this book. I want to thank Sharon Gaus, who helped me to see from a different point of view and enabled me to say what I really meant to say (so many adverbs, so little time); Claus Johnson, for his sharp eye that sees what others miss, his humor and his wit; Don Mason, who could dissect a sentence like a surgeon while brightening up the day; and Jim Weis for his photographic assistance. Thanks also to Whitney Cranshaw for his bug advice. Thanks to the people of Cheyenne and the volunteers of the Cheyenne Botanic Gardens, who are the best at making greenhouse dreams come true. I also want to thank Bob Baron, Jay Staten, Linda Stark and David Nuss, who never gave up on this book; the many good friends I am blessed with, for their words of encouragement; and my parents, for their love, strength, support, trust and advice through it all.

Greenhouse Gardener's Companion

Introduction

Breathe in. The air is rich, humid, fragrant and full of life—warm on your face. It's comfortable. What is it about a greenhouse or sunspace that feels good to almost everyone? It's more than just stimulation of the senses. It goes deeper, further back. The tropics were the womb of human life, and the greenhouse is a connection to our origins. The tropics cradled our earliest developments; there we learned the basics of living on the planet. In returning the tropics to our temperate climates, perhaps we can remember some of those lessons.

It is interesting that the term "greenhouse effect" is used to describe the overheating of planet earth because of our mismanagement of the environment. There is another greenhouse effect with more positive connotations. It is the greenhouse effect that gives you a warm, sunny room to relax in; the effect of a fragrant plant in full bloom whose aroma fills the senses; the effect of a fresh-picked salad in winter; the effect of home-grown colorful bouquets of flowers on a cold, dreary day.

I have always been intrigued by what goes through our minds when we garden or, perhaps more importantly, what doesn't go through our minds during that spe-

Greenhouse enjoyment is not limited by age.

3

A greenhouse is like a tropical island—a warm and comfortable place surrounded by outside cold.

cial time when working with plants. When I'm working in the sunroom with the plants, the day's worries aren't nearly as important as they were earlier. It is cleansing or, as a good friend says, like mental floss. Another friend says gardening is refreshing ... like taking a nap. Whatever you want to call it, gardening is a therapeutic activity. Having a greenhouse enables you to enjoy this therapy on a daily basis in any season.

Gardening to me, and probably to many of you, is an important therapy. A good, growing greenhouse can provide you with wonderful things, such as fresh food, flowers and exercise, but above all, the unexpected gift of therapy.

Gardening teaches us much about the natural world. When you place an ecosystem within glass walls, the greenhouse becomes a metaphor for the earth and can teach us much about how the planet works.

Gardening is said to be both a science and an art. The thing that makes gardening an art is that nobody knows exactly what will happen in a garden. Often, long-held ways of growing a particular plant are tossed out for new ways that work equally well. As a botany instructor once explained to me, "Plants don't read the books and sometimes do as they please." This unpredictability is what makes it fun and makes you a pio-neer as a greenhouse or sunspace gardener. Even so, there is still much to share about growing in a greenhouse. On the other hand, there is still much to learn. If you are like most gardeners, you will retain the pio-neering spirit and try different things while also growing the "tried and true."

My goal in writing this book is to produce a resource that any greenhouse gardener can use. I have not forgotten solar green-houses in this book, as they are

A greenhouse garden provides the perfect mix of creativity, light exercise and a feeling of really producing something of value that everyone can enjoy.

discussed throughout, but I also feel that the lines have blurred between solar-heated and conventional types of greenhouses as more energy-conserving glazings and heating systems have developed and are more commonplace. I have included growing techniques for any greenhouse or sunspace regardless of their temperature, size, shape, orientation or other inherent characteristics.

Years ago, I believed that the only noble purpose for a greenhouse garden was to grow food. I still believe that growing food crops in home greenhouses is very important, especially with the safety and quality of our food coming under increasing scrutiny. I have also come to revere the food for the mind that ornamental plants provide. When food and flowers are grown together, there is a wonderful, serendipitous effect of flavor, color and fragrance.

Bouquets in a flower store or the fruit you buy in the grocery have often traveled further than you will in 20 years. The United States now imports more fruits and vegetables than it exports. The

Growing your own food year-round in a greenhouse eliminates the problems of pesticides and additives that are often associated with store-bought produce (see Chapter 10).

majority of our cut flowers are grown overseas. Producing food and flowers in a home greenhouse is empowering. Even more importantly, it is fun.

As you read this book, the first thing you will find is that growing plants in a greenhouse is different from growing them outside. Yes, there are similarities, but sometimes there are just enough similarities to get a person in trouble. A greenhouse or sunroom is a unique agricultural environment. It is not more difficult to grow in a greenhouse, just different. In a greenhouse, space is limited and light, humidity, temperature and the atmosphere are all different from the

outside climate. As a result, gardening techniques, pest controls and timing are also different. A year-round greenhouse garden still has four seasons with which to be concerned, but as you might have guessed, these seasons are also different.

It is my goal to give you the information you need whether you want to grow a few plants or turn your sunroom into a plant factory. In running the Cheyenne Botanic Gardens since 1977, I have had the opportunity to test a wide variety of horticultural practices and plants. I have had a home greenhouse for a number of years. Over the past 14 years, I have worked with a number of home and commercial greenhouses and have visited with growers from coast to coast as a consultant. It is my hope that the advice and experiences written here can shorten the learning curve so the time you spend gardening in a greenhouse or sunroom is enjoyable.

There can be a whole world contained in a greenhouse if only you gather up some soil, water and a seed.

"The best way to do something is to do it."

—Joseph Standing Eagle

The
Greenhouse
Environment

1

The Greenhouse Environment

Every greenhouse or sunspace is different, and even the same greenhouse has big changes in its environment from season to season and from day to day. Where you live and your particular outside climate also affects the environment within your greenhouse or sunspace. The first step in understanding your particular greenhouse environment is to learn not only to look but also to see and feel what is going on. Look at the shadows and where they fall. Feel the difference between being in the center of the greenhouse and being against a wall. Watch the changes as the days get longer in spring and shorter in fall. Everything is changing. Every minute something is happening. A cloud maneuvers in front of the sun, and the temperature drops. Water the plants, and it can quickly feel steamy and tropical ... or cool and clammy. Each cloud, storm, hot spell or cold spell is part of the environment.

The basic principle of a greenhouse is as old and uncomplicated as the practice of placing a glass lantern over a plant to protect it from the elements. I can imagine the delight of some farmer, back in time, when the idea of protecting a plant with a lantern came to him. How pleased he must have been when he came out after a frosty night to find the plant still alive. The glass creates a totally new environment within its walls, extending the productive life of the plant. It's like creating an earth within an earth or an ecology within an ecology.

The simplicity of light and glass creates a wonderful semiautonomous system. If you have a solar-heated greenhouse, the simplicity of heating by the same light that you grow with is even more spectacular. The things that create the greenhouse environment are usually determined by the building's structural design. So, if that has been done well, all that's needed is a certain amount of fine-tuning and timing on your part to make it an effective year-round growing, productive place.

I have always leaned toward simplicity in what is required to maintain a good growing environment (simple pleasures for simple minds). It is incredible to see all the gizmos and thingamabobs that you can install in a greenhouse to automate everything. It gets to the point where you are no longer an involved participant of this garden (which makes for a poorly tended garden). But if the cost doesn't scare you away first, then think about the prospects of these things breaking. When I am tempted by greenhouse gizmos, I always ask myself if it makes life more simple or more complicated. I am not totally against some of the gizmos available, but as with all things you can spend your money on, keep a wry eye on the gizmos and remember the beauty in simplicity.

Everyone who spends time in a greenhouse becomes a bit of biologist and ecologist. But when you get into it, you can also plan on becoming an entomologist (bug person), olericulturist (vegetable grower), pomologist (fruit grower), floriculturist (flower grower) and horticulturist (general gardener). You are the conductor of a biologi-

cal symphony in this little microcosm of a planet called greenhouse. So, grab your baton, maybe even put on some good music and let's begin to talk about what makes the plants grow, and I mean really grow well, producing wonderful things for you in your greenhouse.

Let's begin with the basics. The basis for plant growth is the conversion of light into energy (sugar). This is called photosynthesis. But it takes a lot more than simply the plant and some light to make photosynthesis. The major requirements for photosynthesis are: (1) light, (2) carbon dioxide (CO_2), (3) temperature generally between 32° F (0° C) and 100° F (38° C) and (4) water.

If any one of these environmental elements is less than optimum, the whole growing process may be slowed.

LIGHT

Simply put, when light hits the surface of the leaf, the energy of the sunlight combines with carbon dioxide (CO_2) in the air and water from the soil. By means of photosynthesis, these elements are converted into oxygen and sugar. The oxygen is given off into the air as a component of water vapor, and the sugar is oxidized (burned) in the plant to provide all the energy the plant needs for growth. What do plants do at night? The major plant activity at night is the burning of these sugars in the plant, which is known as respiration. So think of photosynthesis as a way for plants to make plant energy, and respiration as a way for plants to use that energy. Photosynthesis and respiration are almost opposite of each other ... yet they fit so well together.

An approximate measurement of one foot candle.

Measuring Light in the Greenhouse

Plants require certain minimal quantities of light for proper growth. These quantities are commonly measured in footcandles (fc). A footcandle is a unit of illuminance equal to the direct illumination on a square foot of surface a foot from a standardized source called an international candle. I know it's an odd definition, but it becomes easier to understand once you work with it. The main thing here is being sure your plants get enough light. You can buy instruments that measure footcandles in greenhouse supply catalogs for $70 to $120, which is expensive just to measure how much light comes inside your greenhouse. If you want to get a rough idea of the footcandles coming into the green-

house, you can try this method. It is not 100 percent accurate, but it will give you a ballpark figure.

Vegetables need at least 1,000 fc for proper growth. Usually houseplants can get by with much less.

To give you a feel for things, here are some approximate footcandle values.

Footcandle Values	
Light Source	**Footcandles** (approximate)
Starlight	.00011
Moonlight	.02
Overcast daylight	1,000.00
Direct sun	10,000.00

Measuring Footcandles

1. Find a 35mm camera with a built-in light meter. Automatic types won't work.
2. Set the ASA (film type) at 200.
3. Set the shutter speed at 1/125 of a second.
4. Aim the camera at the light source (your greenhouse glazing).
5. Dial the F-stop to the proper photo exposure.
6. If your F-stop reads: Your greenhouse light is:

If your F-stop reads:	Your greenhouse light is:
2.8	32 fc
4	64 fc
5.6	125 fc
8	250 fc
15	1,000 fc
22	2,000 fc

Every plant has its own preferred level of light, but for growing tall vegetables and cut flowers, the maximum photosynthesis occurs around 2,300 fc for tall plants and 1,300 fc for short, bushy ones. The range for many ornamental blooming plants is slightly lower and varies much more. Houseplants generally prefer much lower levels.

The interesting thing about plants is that sometimes you can increase one of the requirements in the photosynthesis reaction to make up for a deficiency in another. For example, if you have a low-light situation, you can increase the CO_2 in the atmosphere, raise the temperature, as long as it's not past 85° F (29° C), or space the plants further apart.

Fertilizer commercials or hydroponics enthusiasts will tell you that fertilizer is the most important need that plants have. Wrong. Light and temperature are the primary factors in creating plant growth in most home greenhouse situations.

Crops compete for light if planted too closely, and nobody wants a fight in the greenhouse. Like people, plants can get unruly in a crowded situation. When plants are too close together, they will grow slowly; the leaves will often become yellow, elongated and spindly; and the plants won't produce much in the way of leaf, flowers or fruit. Even when plants are not crowded, they can be short on light. This is usually a result of the greenhouse design. Often, solar greenhouses or sunspaces have little or no glazing on the roof. This creates low-light problems in the late spring and summer, which can be helped only by the addition of skylights in the roof or supplemental lighting (see Sun Substitutes, p. 17).

A low-light situation can be helped substantially by painting interior surfaces white or lighter colors. Dark interior surfaces can rob the plants of their light by absorbing it. In contrast, surfaces painted white or similar colors will reflect light to the plants (see Increasing Reflective Surfaces, p. 22).

Shading can cause low-light problems and must be given some thought. For example, when you grow a bed of vining tomatoes, all 6 feet (1.8 m) high, you'll have a

Seedling with adequate light (left); symptoms of low-light conditions (right).

dense canopy of leaves 6 feet (1.8 m) deep. It would require much more than 1,000 fc to penetrate the canopy to maintain proper growth. The leaves at the center would be receiving far less than the original 1,000 fc. In this instance, the plants could use 2,000 fc or more for optimum growth and general contentment. So, as a general rule, taller plants with many leaves require higher light levels.

Symptoms of Low-Light Conditions

1. Slow growth
2. Spindly, slender growth and elongation of stems
3. Yellowing of lower leaves
4. Growth of softer, succulent and sometimes larger leaves
5. Plants bend drastically toward light source (this is called phototropism)

Glazing

The history of greenhouse glazings began with thin sheets of mica, alabaster and talc laid over a hole in the earth. Before glass technology became well developed, small cold-frame season extenders were made of oiled paper, much in the same way we use flexible plastics today.

Now we have a wide array of choices, including glass, vinyl, fiberglass, polycarbonates, acrylics and polyethylenes. They vary in cost, ease of application, solar performance and longevity. The choice can be confusing, and to make things more bewildering, researchers are continually developing additional "new and improved" glazings. If you are building a greenhouse, refer to greenhouse design and construction books in the Helpful Books appendix. Before you buy glazing material, be sure that it is sold specifically for use in the sun over many years without losing its clarity. Many plastics break down rapidly when exposed to the sun's ultraviolet light, eventually limiting the amount and quality of light entering the greenhouse. Following are some things to think about when choosing greenhouse glazing.

Best of all, before you reglaze or build a greenhouse, have a long visit with your glazing salesperson or contractor and refer to as many books as you can dig up covering the design and building of greenhouses. See the Helpful Books appendix.

Triple-glazed polycarbonate glazing.

WHERE IS MY TAN?

When I was in high school, I applied for my first job in a greenhouse. To my surprise, I was hired. I thought that this job would be fun and relaxing. What could be better than working around good-smelling plants, occasionally watering them and maybe even getting a tan? Unlike a home greenhouse, this was a production enterprise and that meant hard work.

Tips for Choosing Glazing

1. *Fire resistance.* Some plastics are incredibly inflammable, including some acrylics, polyethylene and fiberglass. I have seen fiberglass burst into flame. Polycarbonate is more flame resistant.
2. *Hail resistance.* If you live in an area with a high incidence of damaging hail, you must check out the ability of glazing to withstand an onslaught.
3. *Guaranteed life span.* Plastic glazings can last anywhere from 1 to 20 years. Glass can last indefinitely, at least until it breaks from a rock, stray baseball or hailstone. Read the written guarantees. If it's not in writing, it's not guaranteed.
4. *Energy efficiency.* Some acrylics, polycarbonates and glass are available in double and triple thicknesses, which greatly increase their energy efficiency. Also, there are new glass glazings available with added films and coatings that hold in radiant heat and even turn reflective to the sun on very hot days.

Unfortunately, my job consisted mainly of hauling hundreds of pounds of dirt around in a big wheelbarrow and endless hours of boring transplanting of spring bedding plants. On top of that, I didn't even get a tan. The glass or glazing materials on most greenhouses filter out most of the tanning rays. Even though it wasn't my dream job, it was about as good a job as anyone in high school could find. I learned the finer points of how to not tip over an overly full wheelbarrow and became an excellent transplanter. Also, I learned how to nurse my new blisters, calluses and sore back. I have since learned that working in a home greenhouse is much more fun and rewarding than working in a commercial production-oriented greenhouse. I have also learned that there is nothing healthy about a tan.

Because greenhouse glazings absorb most of the ultraviolet light from the sun, don't expect to get a glowing bronze tan while working in your greenhouse. Ultraviolet light produces tans and is usually what makes plastic-based glazings degrade over the years. In a way, ultraviolet does the same thing to our skin. It causes premature aging after repeated tannings and burnings. Don't despair. People who work in their home greenhouse seem to have more color in their face (though not a dark tan) and a healthier, happier look. Is it the glazing or the lifestyle?

GLAZING AND PLANT GROWTH

Let's look at how glazings affect plant growth. According to Colorado State University research, most glazings developed for greenhouses allow satisfactory growth. A marked difference, however, has been noted between clear glazings, such as clear glass, and those that are not crystal clear, such as those that diffuse the light in a transparent way. Plants seem to grow better under glazing materials that are not visibly clear. Don't get confused: It seems that glazing materials that diffuse light let in about as much total light as clear materials. The difference is that they scatter the light beams over a broader area, resulting in a more even distribution of light without sharp shadows. When light is scattered, plant leaves that are not in the direct path of the sun can still receive increased lighting. Under clear glazings, any leaf not in the direct path of the sun is in a

shadow and receives substantially less light, which may result in less plant growth.

The diffused light is also helpful for solar greenhouses with thermal mass components, such as rock, concrete or passive solar storage materials (water barrels), and tends to moderate the temperatures of such structures. Fiberglass is one of the best diffusers of light; polyethylenes, polycarbonates, acrylics and glass follow roughly in that order. This is not to say that fiberglass is the best glazing, because there are many other considerations (such as heat loss, durability, fire resistance, aesthetics, strength and cost) that may make other glazings much better choices. How much more will plants grow in diffused light? That's hard to say. It's not enough to alter a choice if the glazing meets most other considerations.

Photoperiodism

Photoperiods are not the art of teaching your plants to pose for glossy spreads in the garden tabloids. Rather, it's the length of the day or night that influences plant growth. The plant's response to the length of the day or night is called photoperiodism. The amount of light and dark periods can change how plants grow, when they flower and fruit and whether seeds germinate or cuttings develop roots.

Usually the term photoperiod is applied to the flowering/fruiting response. In many garden books, plants are listed as long-day plants (which flower when days are long), short-day plants (which flower when days are short) or day-neutral plants (which aren't influenced by photoperiods). Day-neutral plants respond to other aspects, such as levels of maturity and cold or warm temperatures.

Scientists have found that it is not the length of the day that triggers photoperiodism but the length of uninterrupted darkness. A long-night (or short-day) plant, for example, can be thrown off schedule if the night period is interrupted by light: This would simulate a short-night (long-day) situation. I know it sounds confusing, but fortunately, photoperiodism need only be taken into account when growing a few ornamental crops such as asters, chrysanthemums, poinsettias, snapdragons and Christmas cactus (for more information, see these specific plants discussed in Chapter 8, A Closer Look at the Plants). There are a few vegetable crops that are affected by photoperiodism. Most onion varieties sold in temperate regions will bulb only with short nights (long days), though varieties have been developed for areas in the Deep South with its warmer winters that bulb with longer nights (shorter days). Also, many strawberries are dependent on day length and won't produce during the winter, when they are naturally dormant. A few day-neutral strawberries have been developed that aren't affected by day length. Look in the catalogs that offer extensive lists of strawberry varieties that are called day-neutral types. These are generally the best types to attempt in a greenhouse (although strawberries aren't known for their high yields in greenhouses).

Fortunately, most vegetables aren't influenced by the length of the night or day. Rather, it is a matter of maturity. For example, when a tomato plant grows for a period of time and reaches a certain level of maturity, it flowers and fruits regardless of the length of the day or night.

SUN SUBSTITUTES

Nothing can take the place of that most precious star, our sun. But for those short winter days or for greenhouses with poor light, there are ways to extend the light through the wonders of electricity (and money). I remember an old-time horticulturist who was fond of saying, "I can grow you a big crop of bananas above the Arctic Circle in winter … if you give me enough money." With the input of heat and the wide assortment of grow lights available today, I'm sure he could grow those bananas, but they would cost at least 50 bucks a fruit.

The nice thing about the sun is that it's made up of a rainbow of colors. For photosynthesis, the most important colors in the spectrum of sunlight are red and blue. Years ago, a common problem with supplementary lighting was that artificial light was often deficient in at least one of the colors that plants needed. Over the past few de-cades, researchers have begun to tinker with the manufacturing pro-cess, resulting in lights that can grow plants very well.

Supplementary lighting is gen-erally used on a small scale for propagating seedlings or to illumi-nate large areas. Three types of lights can be used for growing plants: incandescent, fluorescent and what's known in the trade as high-intensity discharge (HIDs).

Incandescent Lights. Incandes-cent lights run very hot compared with the other types of grow lights, and their output is relatively weak when it comes to growing plants. Incandescent lights are best used

For flowering plants, vegetable plants and seedlings, a fluorescent light needs to be within 3 to 4 inches (8 to 10 cm) of the plants for satisfactory growth.

to trigger photoperiods. By just flashing on an incandescent light in the middle of the night, you can confuse certain sensitive plants into thinking a night was short rather than long. Generally, this is not a recommended practice, because photoperiod-sensitive plants need a long period of uninterrupted darkness to trigger their reaction (usually flowering). For more detail on this, see Chapter 8, A Closer Look at the Plants, to find out if a photoperiod is important to your crop.

While incandescents radiate much of the red spectrum of lights, they lack in the bluish colors and are not good choices for growing. There are, however, special incandescent grow lights that have been altered to give off both red and blue wavelengths. They do an acceptable job of growing plants but generate a high level of heat for the amount of light they emit. They also consume a lot of electricity when compared with the amount of light you get.

Fluorescent Lights. Fluorescent lights are what most offices use for a light source. They are the familiar long, white tubes. When you go to the store (preferably one that specializes in lighting), you'll find two main choices in fluorescent light bulbs: warm white (which emit

more of the red wavelengths) and cool white (which emit more of the blue wavelengths). The terms warm and cool relate only to the wavelength spectrum, not the temperature of the bulbs (all fluorescents run cool to the touch). Usually the cool-whites are more commonly found, but warms are available.

As with incandescent lights, specially formulated widespectrum fluorescent bulbs for growing plants give off a nice combination of the blue and red spectrums. Of course, these special fluorescent grow lights cost $15 to $20. The regular cool-white and warm-white bulbs cost only $3 to $5 and can do a bang-up job of growing plants if you use a combination of them. They'll save you a fair amount of money.

Because of the low cost of both purchasing and operating the fluorescent bulbs, they are a favorite choice of growers. Before you set out to install the fluorescent bulbs all over the place, there is one important thing to consider. Fluorescent lights work best for only short-growing plants, such as seedlings or plants that grow a foot or two high. Fluorescents are not appropriate for growing a 6-foot tomato vine or a similar tall light-loving plant. Fluorescent lights need to be at least 3 to 4 inches from the top of the plant (especially those that need high-intensity light, such as vegetables and cut flowers). Only at this close range can these lights really make a difference in providing enough footcandles of light intensity to do a good job.

I find the best use of fluorescents is in germinating seedlings. A system can easily be set up in a basement or other area of your house, freeing up precious greenhouse space for growing the crops to maturity. I use about two tubes for every 10 inches (25 cm) of planting width. When you set up your germinating bench, it will be very helpful to hang the fluorescent lights from a pulley or chain so you can adjust it as your plants start to grow, always keeping the distance of 3 to 4 inches (8 to 10 cm) above the tops of the plants. It's important to remember that fluorescents do lose their intensity over time, so it's a good idea to replace them every 300 or 400 hours to maintain maximum brightness.

Please use extreme caution when you set up your electrical connections so you don't end up with the deadly combination of electricity and water. This is especially true with fluorescents because the lights are sitting so close to your plants and thus closer to the watering can.

High-Intensity Discharge Lamps (HIDs). If the name high-intensity discharge lamps sounds like we're getting down to some serious lighting, you're right. HIDs, as they are affectionately known to official lighting guys, are the same as street lamps glowing faithfully every evening right down the street.

These lamps include mercury vapor, sodium vapor and metal halide lights. They give off by far the brightest light, and while they are efficient in terms of electricity usage (in comparison to the amount of light they give off), they are also relatively expensive to purchase. The bulbs cost anywhere from $45 to $95. It doesn't stop there. You'll also need what's known as a ballast (to give the lamp its correct voltage), reflectors and other important electrical materials needed to make it all work. So, to get just one light to work in your greenhouse, it'll end up costing you between $175 and $275. One light (depending on the type) consumes between 400 and 1,000 watts of electricity. The big question with the wattage is whether your house can handle that kind of additional drain on your circuit breakers before they blow. Be sure to consult an electrician in both the planning and installation of HIDs.

If they still sound like something you might want in your greenhouse, there are some other things that you should know. First, some HID lights can be quite noisy and not the kind of thing you would want buzzing in your sunspace, especially if you like to spend time relaxing there. These lights can also become hot. This is both good and bad, good in that they will actually help in winter heating your greenhouse and not so good if your greenhouse is already too hot. Also, the hot lamps can be dangerous if someone gets too near them. Often the HID lights are big, especially when you have a reflector as part of the apparatus (about the size of a large salad bowl). Because of the size, they're usually mounted in the eaves of the home greenhouse. HID lights aren't to be turned on and off on a whim, because they won't restart immediately. They need to cool off for anywhere between 2 and 20 minutes before they will be able to glow properly again.

If all these points haven't discouraged you from getting an HID light, then read on for a brief discussion of what types are available out there. The four main types of HID bulbs on the market are mercury vapor lights, low-pressure sodium lamps, high-pressure sodium lamps and metal halides. Of these, the most commonly available and best lamps for greenhouse use are the high-pressure sodium and the metal halides.

High-pressure sodium. These lamps are similar to the yellowish street lights that have taken the place of the old bluish-colored mercury vapor lamps (high-pressure sodium lamps are more energy efficient). The high-pressure sodium lamps do an excellent job of growing plants and even aiding them to flower and produce fruit, even though they give off that sickly yellow cast. They are highly efficient in terms of wattage per footcandle, and the bulbs are very long-lived, up to 24,000 hours (which is equivalent to around 5 years of use). A single 400-watt high-pressure sodium HID can provide around 1,000 footcandles to a 22-square-foot (2-square-meter) area. A 1,000-watt bulb can give 1,000 footcandles to a 66-square-foot (6-square-meter) area.

Metal halides. These give off a quality of light that, unlike any other artificial light, appears to the human eye to be very similar to sunlight. They have a great balance of the spectrum for photosyn-thetic activity. And, like sunlight, they also produce ultraviolet light, which can damage the eyes and possibly give you a bit of a tan or even a burn if you're working under them for a long time. It's not a bad idea to wear sunglasses and protective clothing when working under these lights. The metal ha-lides are not as energy efficient as the high-pressure sodium lamps, but they are about equal in effi-ciency to a fluorescent (which still isn't bad). A 1,000-watt bulb will light approximately 70 square feet (6.5 sq. m) at 1,000 footcandles. Metal halides require some cau-tion because if they are wired incorrectly or accidentally bumped, they can explode. They are not a good do-it-yourself project. Be-cause of this, many are required to have a protective glass covering.

Talk to some experts in the lighting field to help assist you in deciding which type of light to use. It would also help to visit with (or hire) an electrician before you get started.

INCREASING REFLECTIVE SURFACES

In the dark corners of your greenhouse, sufficient light may be lacking. Your plants will be telling you by the way they grow (elongating and bending toward the light). Shady areas are almost unavoidable in most any type of greenhouse or sunspace, but they are more common in solar-heated greenhouses and sunspaces, which usually have glass or glazing only on one side. Shadows are also created by shelves and benches and around water drums in solar greenhouses. You can deal with these shady areas by placing shade-loving plants in these spots, or you can try bouncing light into these areas with reflective surfaces.

When we think of reflective surfaces, usually we envision me-tallic mirrored surfaces such as aluminum foil or the like. While mirrored surfaces do reflect a more accurate likeness of adjacent im-ages, they are not the best light reflectors. Aluminum reflectors are silver-gray in color. This color is halfway between the color white and black. Believe it or not, alumi-num reflectors can and do absorb some light.

By far the best reflector in a greenhouse is the color white. The more white surfaces in your green-house (except for glazing and ther-mal mass), the better your plants will grow. This means getting ahold of some high-quality gloss or semigloss white paint for the walls, the benches and even the floor, if possible, to help reflect light.

Using fiberglass barrels as a water thermal storage system can also allow light to pass through the containers.

There are those of you with beautiful rock surfaces or exposed wood in your greenhouse who are saying to yourselves, "No way." I can understand a reluctance to paint over a beautiful natural surface, so if this is your situation, you may want to look at installing more overhead glazing if you don't already have some or think about the supplementary light option here.

For those of you who have solar greenhouses, paint everything white except for surfaces that you'll want to absorb solar heat (such as water barrels or rock walls). Paint the sides of your raised beds, trellising, potting bench and anything else to bounce around that precious sunlight (don't get carried away and paint your seedlings or family pets!). Semigloss or gloss exterior latex paint is a good choice. Epoxy paint is even better. You might also consider light-colored rock if you have a gravel floor.

Another solution to low-light greenhouses is to spread white rock on the outside of your greenhouse, which will actually reflect more light into the structure (snow does this too). This has been a

Snow is a good winter light reflector.

successful practice with many greenhouses in areas that have cloudy winters.

If you have a solar greenhouse with oil drums (or the like) along the north wall, you've probably noticed that area becoming a shady spot in the summer. One solution is to place a white curtain over the barrels in the summer to reflect more light. This will help keep the greenhouse cooler in the summer. When cool weather returns, take the curtain down.

CARBON DIOXIDE (CO_2)

As I mentioned earlier, carbon dioxide in the air is essential to photosynthesis. The normal level of carbon dioxide in the air is about 300 parts per million (ppm), or .03 of 1 percent of the air we breathe. Because about 50 percent of a plant is made of carbon (and all that must come from the air), you can see that plants have quite an appetite for CO_2. Much of the CO_2 normally occurring in the air comes from animals (everything from bacteria to humans), the burning of fossil fuels and the decomposition of organic matter. It is partially what you are breathing out of your lungs right now as you respire. Plants love you for your kind words and attention, but they also love you for your body—well, at least for your high CO_2-laden breath.

When CO_2 is scarce, plant growth slows. But when the supply of CO_2 increases beyond the normal 300 ppm (up to a certain point), plant growth increases.

When plants are in a sealed environment such as a greenhouse, they can actually deplete the supply of CO_2 in the air. This is exactly what happens in a greenhouse in winter when the doors are sealed tight. The level of CO_2 has been seen to drop from 300 ppm to 100 ppm by noon on an average winter day. This can slow plant growth by 68 percent—not a pleasant thought. This phenomenon occurs only in winter greenhouses when there is no outside ventilation and the structure is sealed to the outside. CO_2

depletion is less in attached greenhouses where there are people, gas stoves and pets, all producing extra CO_2.

Depletion of CO_2 is also less in greenhouses with soils high in organic matter because of the billions of microbes breathing in that black pulsing-with-life, humus-rich soil. But depletion may still occur because, by nature, our new sunspaces and solar greenhouses are tight structures. What does a CO_2-deficient plant look like? Well, that's the big problem. It's almost impossible to see a CO_2 deficiency, because the only symptom is slower growth. You won't see any telltale signs in the crop you are growing. There is equipment available to measure CO_2 amounts in the air, but it's expensive and hard to obtain.

CO_2 Enhancement

Early greenhouse operators in Europe quickly discovered that when they added a mulch composed of manure, peat moss, sawdust and straw around plants, they saw an increased crop production. Around the early 1900s, scientific experiments proved that CO_2 was created during the decomposition of organic materials in the soil. It was not until the late fifties and early sixties that researchers worked with levels higher than the normal ambient (300 ppm) amounts. Enhancing CO_2 levels from a depleted greenhouse atmosphere of 100 ppm all the way to 1,500 ppm resulted in significant yield increases. Since the sixties many commercial greenhouse growers have been enhancing the CO_2 levels in winter greenhouses to 1,200–1,500 ppm, with a yield increase of 10 to 30 percent. It's like fertilizing the plants through the air. It is thought that anything above 2,000 ppm is a wasted effort, and continuous exposure to levels of 5,000 ppm may be a problem to human health.

Ventilation for More CO_2 to Your Plants

The amount of carbon dioxide supplied to the plant from the atmosphere depends upon the level of CO_2 at the leaf surface, or even more precisely, the CO_2 level at the cell surface on the leaf. In still air, a leaf can draw out most of the CO_2 at the cell surface, thus creating an envelope of CO_2 deficiency around the leaf. When there is no turbulence, CO_2 replenishment is slow. A lack of turbulence can be a common problem in the winter greenhouse, triggering carbon di-

STILL AIR

In still air, a leaf can draw out most of the CO_2 at the cell surface, creating a deficiency. Turbulent air solves this problem.

oxide deficiencies even though there is plenty of the gas in the air.

Turbulent air around a leaf disperses this envelope of low carbon dioxide concentration, replenishing the air adjacent to the leaf with an ample supply of CO_2, so there is something good about wind. Research in the Netherlands by P. Gaastra in 1963 showed that the rate of photosynthesis can be increased by as much as 40 percent with no change in atmospheric CO_2 when the wind velocity increases from 10 to 100 centimeters (4 to 40 inches) per second.

So, for better greenhouse plant growth, keep the air constantly moving around during the day, especially in winter, when your windows are closed. In winter I set up a small fan to stir up the air. In larger greenhouses, a cheap Casablanca-style ceiling fan works great, especially if you can control the speed of the paddles. It seems to work best if you run the fans on days with good light (partly cloudy days or sunny days). When the day is dark, cool and cloudy, it can be uncomfortable to have the fans on and there is less photosynthesis. I tend to turn the fans down or off.

One final note on greenhouse turbulence. There is no need to stir the air up for carbon dioxide during the night, because plants don't use CO_2 in the dark.

Increasing Carbon Dioxide

Commercial growers are able to increase the level of CO_2 by burning propane or natural gas. It has also been increased by burning kerosene and less commonly from the release of CO_2 from pressurized tanks of liquid CO_2, which vaporize the gas in the air. The burning of fossil fuels for CO_2 requires special burners (called CO_2 generators) because the normal exhaust would contain carbon monoxide, sulfur and fluorides, which are poisonous to plants and humans.

Because most of us can't afford a CO_2 generator or the fuel to run one, there are alternatives for the home greenhouse grower. These include decomposing organic matter in your soil or as a mulch, raising animals in the greenhouse (rabbits) and burning homemade ethanol. Being inflammable, ethanol can be dangerous. It is also unsafe because greenhouse structures can be quite inflammable (especially those with plastic glazings). Raising animals in a greenhouse can cause offensive odors and added trouble. Manure from unclean cages and pens emits ammonia gas, which in high concentration may cause some damage to plants.

So, that leaves the option of having a high level of organic matter in your soil. This is by far the most simple solution to the problem of having a CO_2 deficiency. Also, it is helpful if your greenhouse is attached, benefiting from the natural CO_2 levels of your household air.

Let's look at some specifics when it comes to organic matter and the level of CO_2 in your greenhouse air. When compost is mixed into the soil as an amendment or as a mulch, it produces CO_2. Few people have the room to compost in their greenhouse, but when it is done, it not only produces CO_2, it can also give off heat. As it breaks down, a compost pile can easily run above 100°F (38°C), which can even help to heat a greenhouse in winter. The New Alchemy Institute in East Falmouth, Massachusetts, has constructed an experimental composting greenhouse, in which half of the greenhouse is set aside for composting and can be loaded from the outside. Inside, a significant increase in CO_2 (as high as 650 ppm) has been noted, and in addition, the compost contributes a major amount of heat to the greenhouse. Other recent experiments by compost pioneers have been able to raise CO_2 levels in greenhouses to as high as 800 ppm to 2,000 ppm. Danish growers have achieved CO_2 levels up to a whopping 5,000 ppm (almost too high for humans to be comfortable in) just with the addition of a manure, peat and straw mulch, applied at a rate of 200 tons (181.4 metric tons) per acre in their greenhouses. Well, it's unlikely any home greenhouse owner will import 200 tons of compost into a greenhouse. But if you have the situation of gardening in your greenhouse with raised beds (which I prefer over small containers), then you can actually increase the level of CO_2 substantially. One of the best ways to add CO_2 (and fertilizer nutrients) to your greenhouse atmosphere and soil is to add some good old homemade compost.

COMPOSTING FOR PLANET EARTH AND THE HOME GREENHOUSE

I have some strong feelings about the way we Americans have always thrown so much away with little thought about recycling. For years I've had a compost pile in my backyard, and I'm always amazed at how much it returns to me in beautiful dark compost for both my outside garden and my greenhouse. I had a friend recently buy his wife a garbage disposal as a birthday present. I realized for the first time that the thought of needing a garbage disposal had never occurred in our household. That was because our compost pile served that purpose so very well. Besides, garbage disposals break and get silverware stuck in them, causing all kinds of trouble; a compost pile never breaks and rarely eats your silverware.

Setting Up for Composting

Among questions some of you creative thinkers may have is: Why not put a compost pile in my greenhouse? I suppose there is no real problem to that idea except that it can use up valuable space perhaps better used by the growing plants. So unless you have a large greenhouse, I would suggest that you compost outside and then use the finished product inside your greenhouse.

Composting can be done in a dug-out trench in fancy barrels sold by garden supply companies or in homemade areas set aside with cinder blocks or fencing. You may want to check out books that cover the subject more thoroughly. It doesn't matter what you compost in. It is more important that you get in the habit of doing it.

The first thing you should do to get into the practice of composting is to set a bucket with a lid next to your kitchen trash can and then get into the habit of filling it with appropriate kitchen scraps (soon to be greenhouse fertilizer).

I want to simplify the process of composting for those of you who have had little previous luck with composting and for you newcomers to the idea of composting.

What Not to Compost

1.   Meat or meat by-products. It makes for a greasy pile that attracts flies and the neighbor's dogs.
2.   Any salty foods, such as pickles or potato chips. Salt (sodium chloride) is not good for soil.
3.   Anything that has been treated with herbicides.
4.   Compost starters. Research shows that this stuff doesn't get your compost working any better than a shovelful of manure or plain old dirt. Save your money.
5.   Your mother-in-law's cooking. It would insult her greatly.

Now the question is: What can go into a compost pile? Well, most anything that was once growing or part of a living thing is fair game. Virtually any kitchen scrap, from coffee grounds to potato skins. What I want you to do is to set up a two-category classification system in your mind that labels everything you would commonly throw into a compost pile. Category one is what we will call the green list. The green list would include anything that is green and all kitchen scraps, coffee grounds, fresh garden waste, and manure. In general, it includes everything that is high in nitrogen. Even though human hair is often brown, it must go into the green category, which is good to know if you've just given the kids haircuts.

The second category is what I call the brown list. This includes everything that is brown (except coffee grounds and hair, which are on the green list), such as straw, sawdust and any plant refuse or organic matter that has turned brown (leaves, tan grass clippings, etc.) These are things that are relatively low in nitrogen (compared to our green list of ingredients). Before I give you the method to turn these ingredients into compost, I must first give you the basic compost rules. These rules apply to the care and feeding not just of your compost pile but also of the microscopic critters that are the workhorses, turning your pile into good stuff. If you keep them happy, the pile is a success. The mark of success is that the compost pile heats up and begins to break down into a material that looks more like good, rich dirt.

Compost Rules

1.   The smaller the ingredients, the better your compost will be. The compost critters can work faster with smaller stuff. You can make your ingredients smaller by just attacking them with a sharp-edged shovel on the ground before you throw them in. Or you can go all out by obtaining a shredder/grinder. The basic goal is to get the ingredients to around 3 or 4 square inches (19 to 26 sq. cm). You should know that I never chop up my kitchen scraps (they're usually small enough), but I do attack a corn stalk with a shovel before adding it to the compost pile.

2.   Compost needs to breathe oxygen to do the job well. Actually, it's the microscopic organisms that need to breathe. If they can find some oxygen to breathe, then they can happily eat up the raw materials into a good soil amendment. You can get your compost pile to breathe by turning the pile every two weeks or so (less often in winter, as the pile usually is more dormant then). Another method to allow air into the compost as an alternative to turning is to poke holes into it with an old broomstick. There is even a special tool developed to poke holes into the compost, which I have found to work well, known as a compost aerator. It's a short metal pole with two wings that fold up as you poke it into your pile. When you pull it out of your pile, the metal wings open and fluff and add air to your pile. It is readily available in many garden catalogs and is not very expensive.

3.   Compost piles get thirsty. The microscopic critters need to get a drink of water every so often in order to do the job of composting well. Now, don't get carried away and drown them. The pile needs to be wet like a wrung-out towel is wet. That means moist, not dripping wet. So an occasional watering is helpful to a good pile if it hasn't rained in a while. If it is raining too much, you might want to consider a tarp to protect the pile temporarily.

Now that we have our rules, let me give you a recipe for making some first-class compost.

The Compost Recipe

1. Combine by volume 1 part brown stuff to 1 part green stuff (see p. 29).
2. Mix the ingredients (there is no need to layer it) so that there is not a high concentration of either in any one place in the pile.
3. Allow it to breathe and maintain moisture.
4. To get the pile to go through the winter, it needs to be at least a few square yards in size. If not, no big deal. It'll get going again come spring.
That's all.

The Compost Troubleshooter

Problem	Solution
Pile doesn't heat up.	Check moisture; add more green material.
Pile smells bad.	Add air holes or turn the pile.
Pile slow to break down.	The pieces you have added may be too large—chop them up or shred them. Or it may be too cold outside—be patient, things will speed up when it heats up.

Positive Results of Composting for Your Greenhouse

You are greatly reducing your impact on the local landfill, and you are also going to end up with an excellent fertilizer for your greenhouse. It is best to add about 2 to 3 inches (5 to 8 cm) of compost to your greenhouse soil about once a year. You have also added a material that will give off a fair amount of CO_2 to your greenhouse air, which will help increase the rate of plant growth. For more information on fertilizers, see Chapter 9, Getting to the Roots.

HUMIDITY

Did you know that all plants have small openings in their leaves? Through these openings gases such as CO_2 and oxygen pass. Also, because plants don't use all the water they take up, a large amount of water vapor comes out through these openings. Vapor is also in the greenhouse air from water that has hit the soil or walkways and evaporated. All this vapor combines to make up what is called humidity. Relative humidity is the term most often used to quantify the invisible water vapor in the air. More simply it tells us how wet the air is. Relative humidity can be measured by a hygrometer, an inexpensive instrument. Hygrometers can be found in scientific instrument catalogs. With a hygrometer, humidity is often expressed as a percentage of the maximum moisture the air can hold at a given temperature and pressure. Hot air can hold more moisture than cold air. When warm air holding much water comes in contact with a cold window, the water vapor condenses. That is how you get condensation or drips on the cold windows. The colder the windows the more condensation.

The Water Must Go Somewhere

In the winter greenhouse, there is little air infiltration from the outside, so heat is retained and relative humidity is often high. Most plants grow best at relative humidities between 45 and 60 percent. But something to consider besides how well plants grow is the higher incidence of diseases in higher humidities. Studies show that humidity over 80 percent fosters rapid development of various forms of leaf mold and fruit flower and stem diseases. Disease problems become worse if the high humidity occurs at night. This is a good reason to avoid late-afternoon watering.

Another problem associated with high humidity is the formation of condensation. This happens when warm, humid air moves along a

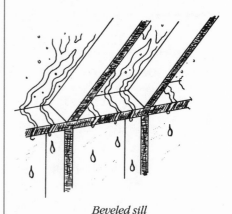

Beveled sill

cooler surface, causing the vapor to transform into water droplets on the cold surface. You will see condensation on glazing, walls and doors and dripping from the roof like rain, giving the illusion of a little weather system cruising through the greenhouse. Condensation on glazing can block incoming solar heat and light, which can be a problem in solar-dependent greenhouses or in greenhouses that already have low light. The condensation will also drip onto sills. If these droplets continually land on wood surfaces, you will soon see some serious structural rot problems. I recommend beveling any wood surface that could hold water (this alone can add years to the life of a greenhouse). With double or triple glazings, always try to get a tight seal between the glazing and the frame to minimize condensation in this vulnerable place. Many new plastic glazings have been treated with a surface coating that helps to prevent droplets from forming. There are also materials that you can spray on glazings to achieve similar results. These products help but do not cure the condensation problem.

Conventionally heated greenhouses have fewer problems with high humidities compared to solar-heated greenhouses. However, even though active heating burns off some of the humidity, they are not im-mune to condensation problems. With high humidity, condensation is just a fact of life in winter greenhouses. Probably the one thing you can do is minimize your watering. It's rare to see a home greenhouse that isn't overwatered to some extent. That is usually the root of the problem, because all that water has to go somewhere and a good proportion of it ends up causing problems. Please read Knowing When to Water (p. 54) in this chapter, and ask yourself before you grab for the hose, "Do I really need to water?"

Wood in the Humid Greenhouse

One thing you can do when you are in the process of building or rebuilding a greenhouse is to be sure any exposed wood surface in the greenhouse has been treated to prevent rot. Be careful here because some materials that prevent wood rot also prevent the growth of plants and may be harmful to your health. Use either wood sold as landscape timbers or treat the wood yourself with a material that contains copper naphthenate types of wood preservatives. Some brand names include Cuprinol and Copper 8 Quin Olinolate. You should avoid any wood preservatives that are made up of creosote, pentoxide or pentachlorophenal (also known as penta) because they are toxic to plants.

I'll never forget a woman I met years ago who had built a beautiful freestanding greenhouse that was heated by an artesian hot spring. Sounds heavenly, doesn't it? She understood that the humidity would cause her wood to rot so she applied the common wood preservative pentachlorophenal. After she was well into growing, winter came on. With the cold temperatures, condensation formed on the wood, causing the penta chemical to leach into the droplets that eventually found their way onto the plants, causing their death. It was a sad wipeout before winter was over. The only solution at that point was to recoat all the wood with a plant-safe material.

Lumberyards also sell pressure-treated lumber, which is a long-lived wood in moist situations. The one type of lumber recommended for landscaping and bed construction is wood treated with chromated copper arsenate (CCA). It has been touted as being safe; however, it is brewing a lot of controversy. The copper, chromium and arsenate all have toxic properties, but many manufacturers claim that this stuff won't leach out of the wood in quantities that are harmful. Some

studies have shown potentially harmful levels of leaching, which could be absorbed by the plant when used in construction of raised beds. There is less concern over leaching when this lumber is used structurally. To make things even more confusing, all CCA-treated wood is not the same. Some manufacturers claim that their lumber is safe but are quick to point out that certain other brands are not. Hopefully, in the future there will be some good research to clear away the controversy.

One way to help prevent leaching from CCA-treated raised beds is to line your lumber on the soil side with plastic film (be sure not to line the bottom of the bed—this could create drainage problems).

To further confound those considering purchasing CCA-treated lumber, there is the long-term problem of disposal. If burned, it produces toxic fumes. Because leaching is a problem, the treated lumber is not a good choice for landfills.

If you do use CCA-treated lumber, take precautions. When sawing it, wear rubber gloves and a dust mask, doing all of your cutting outdoors and disposing of all sawdust in a bag in the trash. Also change your clothes when finished and wash them separately. When buying pressure-treated lumber, check that it is indeed treated with

CCA. Most, but not all, treated lumber is treated with CCA. There should be a label stapled to each piece of lumber showing "CCA-C" or "CCA oxides." If the treated lumber doesn't say CCA, you have no assurance of purchasing the right stuff. You may even be purchasing something that is more hazardous. Avoid purchasing any lumber that is noticeably dusty or looks like it has sawdust on the surface.

Some alternatives to CCA-treated lumber for raised beds include redwood or cedar. You can even use regular old pine if you don't mind replacing it in a few years. You might also consider using concrete, rock or cinder blocks in construction of raised beds.

Help for High-Humidity Problems

Here are some things you can do to minimize problems with high relative humidities.

1. *Circulation.* Circulate the air even when the greenhouse is sealed to the outside in winter. This produces more uniform temperatures, reduces humidity, promotes better use of CO_2 and even helps keep the bugs and diseases down.

2. *Water early in the day.* This will help prevent evening humidity problems, which are the most severe as far as plant diseases are concerned.

3. *Water only when needed.* All too often people overwater in greenhouses. Excess water increases humidity problems and is not good for roots (see Knowing When to Water, p. 54).

4. *Ventilate to the outside.* Whenever the outside temperature is warm enough, ventilate the moist air to the outside. This can also be done when the greenhouse is running hot, even if it is not warm outside. In a solar greenhouse, this practice is not recommended if you are heading into a long, cool cloudy spell of weather.

5. *Use air-to-air heat exchangers.* This is a fancy (and not cheap) piece of equipment that trades warm, moist air for cool, dry air. During the exchange process, the cool, dry air is heated by the exiting warm, moist air, thus minimizing heat loss while dumping out the wet air. For more information, you should talk to an architect.

Low Humidity

Low humidity in a greenhouse with many plants is a rare occurrence because people tend to overwater and because a greenhouse or sunspace is a relatively sealed environment from which it is hard for moisture to escape. Most greenhouses or sunspaces containing a number of plants will not have this problem because the plants will naturally increase the humidity. But low humidity could occur when too much outside venting is going on. It could also be a problem when you are growing just a few plants in a sunspace.

While high humidity is not good for plants, neither is extremely low humidity. Fortunately, if this is happening to your greenhouse, it is easy to remedy. Humidity may be increased easily by simply watering the floor. In the living-room-type sunspaces, this may not be possible. Humidity can also be increased if you are using a swamp-type air conditioner, which will help cool the greenhouse while adding moisture to the air. Swamp air coolers do not work very well in naturally humid areas of the country. The drier your air outside is, the better a swamp cooler works. There are also commercially available humidifiers that would pro-

vide the best solution in living-room sunspaces with low humidity.

One place that plants love high levels of humidity is the area in which you are germinating seeds and trying to root cuttings. Here you will see much benefit from regular misting with a special misting hose nozzle available from most greenhouse supply catalogs and gardening supply companies.

TEMPERATURE

The optimum high temperature range for most greenhouse plants is around 85° F (29° C), although there are always exceptions. If the temperatures are running into the high nineties or higher, then you will see a slower plant growth and even an inability for fruiting crops to set fruit. It may also cause flowers to drop. That's where proper ventilation comes in.

The optimum low temperature range for most greenhouse plants is between 50° and 60° F (10° and 15° C). When it gets cooler, you will also see problems similar to what happens when it's too hot (slow growth, poor fruit set and blossom drop). It can also stress plants that are native to the tropics.

Plant growth requires heat. Temperature controls the rate of water and nutrient uptake, photosynthesis and even the plant's cell division. Each plant has different optimum temperature requirements, and different growth stages have different optimums. Seedlings often benefit from warmer temperatures; mature plants will not. For instance, many plants in the cabbage family require cool temperatures to mature properly.

The solar greenhouse often allows little control over the minimum temperature, so you are at the mercy of how good a design you have and/or the outside weather. For heated greenhouses, there is a high degree of temperature control, and you can adjust the climate to the type of plants you are growing with a simple turn of the thermostat. Later in this book I discuss the specific temperature requirements of many plants for you to use in setting the temperature.

Solar Greenhouse Heating Checklist

If you have a solar greenhouse and you are having unusually cold temperatures, you should review this checklist to be sure you have done everything properly in the construction of your greenhouse. If you have a heated greenhouse, you can reduce the need for heat and your heating bills by applying some of these solar greenhouse basics to make your greenhouse more energy efficient.

1. *Insulation.* Can you insulate the north wall of your greenhouse? If you live in a sunny area, you may also consider insulating the east and/or west walls.
2. *Insulated foundation.* The foundation of your greenhouse should not be a heat sink. Is your foundation's perimeter insulated with only 2 inches (5 cm) of foam board insulation? Insulation should extend down to at least 2 feet (.6 m) in cool areas. If you live in gardening zone 3 or less (as determined by the USDA), you should consider having even deeper foundation insulation. Foam-board insulation is set vertically adjacent to and outside of your greenhouse foundation. What if your greenhouse is without a foundation? Consider placing vertical insulation in the ground around your greenhouse anyway by just trenching it in.

3. *Double or triple glazing.* This is a must for an energy-efficient greenhouse and essential for any solar greenhouse. Of course, glazing should be tightly sealed, free of dust or dirt and not yellowing (which is common to many older plastic glazings).

4. *Sealed to the outside.* Vents and doors must be weather-stripped, and cracks must be caulked and checked for wear every year. I usually do an inspection for any potential air leaks in fall before the cold weather comes. I always find an area that needs some sealing up.

5. *Thermal storage.* This is the use of rock water or other thermal mass to store the solar heat that comes into the greenhouse. Water is by far the most efficient way to store heat in the greenhouse. Solar greenhouses are notorious for their accumulation of black 55-gallon (208-liter) drums of water placed along the north wall to store the sun's heat. They are cheap and efficient. Many owners of heated greenhouses have also installed containers of water to increase heating efficiency. It's easy to use a water drum as a support for a plant or soil table.

6. *Air-lock entry.* If you use your greenhouse door to the outside with any frequency in wintertime, you should have an air-lock entry. This is a two-door setup with a little space between them so that when you open the door, you won't get a blast of freezing air onto your poor little plants. It will also save you an immense amount of energy in heating your greenhouse. If you have a solar greenhouse, an air-lock entry is almost essential unless the greenhouse is attached to your house and you never use your door to the outside when it's cold.

7. *Site orientation.* If you have a solar greenhouse, you had better hope it's oriented in the correct direction. If it's not, I guess that there isn't much you can do about it now. A solar greenhouse should face within 20° of true south.

8. *Night curtain.* This is a curtain that your greenhouse can wear at night like a blanket to prevent excess heat loss. This is an option that I view with a bit of skepticism. That's because these devices are costly, have a lot of problems with reliability and are not easy to find. The farther north you live, the more they may make sense. An extra layer of glazing might be a better choice. For some extra winter

insulation, you might want to try some greenhouse bubble insulation. This is similar to the bubblelike plastic used as a packing material, but is clearer and stronger. It is attached with an adhesive spray and can be removed again when the extra insulation is not needed. By the way, a light evening snow on the glazing is a great nighttime insulator and is free. Always wait until morning to knock the snow off unless you have concerns about the weight of the snow on your greenhouse structure.

Weather Information

Even though your greenhouse is protected from the elements, the weather does have some impact. If you watch the weather, you can make some preemptive energy-saving decisions for your greenhouse. For instance, if you hear that you're in for a few days of cool, cloudy winter weather and it's still sunny out, then it might make sense to let your greenhouse heat up a bit. Solar greenhouses with thermal mass storage such as water drums are excellent at holding heat. Any greenhouse holds some heat.

When the weather is hot, I often look forward to a cool night when I may leave an exhaust fan on all night. It seems as if the greenhouse runs cooler for a few days.

Tools to Measure the Climate

The important tool for measuring the greenhouse and sunspace climate is a good high/low thermometer. This will tell you what the low was last night and what the high temperature was for the day in your greenhouse. It's fun to have two high/low thermometers, one for outside and one for inside the greenhouse to compare the difference. This is even more important for solar-heated greenhouses, where you can track the performance of the structure.

There are different types of high/low thermometers on the market. They run from $11 to $40 and are available in hardware stores and garden and greenhouse supply catalogs. Starting with the cheapest, the four main types are:

Dial-type thermometers. These high/low thermometers run around $13 and are made of a cheap plastic. They are not known for their accuracy, but you can't beat the price.

Mercury thermometers. Two types are available through catalogs and even in some hardware stores. One type has a button you use to reset the highs and lows. I've found that these don't last very long. However, the mercury high/ low thermometers that you reset with a small magnet have been dependable for me. Mercury high/ low thermometers run around $30.

Digital thermometers. These are usually available from electronic supply houses and greenhouse supply catalogs. They give you a great digital readout to the nearest tenth of a degree. How's that for accuracy? The digitals run anywhere from $30 to $40. Some are available that give you not only the

high and low temperatures but also an outdoor reading all in one unit. I've come to really like these thermometers. It does take a bit of study of the operating instructions and practice before you feel comfortable using them, but they are not as bad as programming your VCR. If the digital thermometers ever stop functioning, be sure to check the batteries.

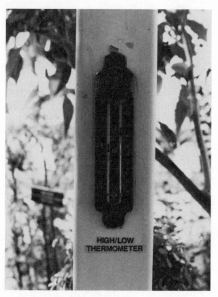

High/Low thermometer

PLACEMENT OF THE HIGH/LOW THERMOMETER

It is important that you not set your thermometer or the sensors of the digital thermometers in direct sunlight, or you'll get some crazy readings. The best way to set a thermometer in your greenhouse

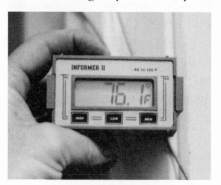

Digital thermometer

is to build a little sun shelter that has plenty of air circulation around it and is painted white. With the digital, you need to set the sensor (which is a metal piece at the end of a plastic cord) out of the sun. If your thermometer receives any sunlight directly, it will give you an unusually high reading.

OTHER CLIMATE-MEASURING TOOLS

There are many instruments to measure the relative humidity. Most are not known for being real accurate, but they are adequate for giving you a ballpark figure that will help you determine how moist your air is. These range in price from $10 to $30. For a super accurate measurement of the humidity, you will need what is known as a sling psychrometer and a conversion chart to interpret what it reads. Generally the simple, cheap and less accurate ones work fine for the needs of a home greenhouse.

There are thermometers that are developed especially for measuring the soil temperature. This can be helpful in determining how well a compost pile is working or deciding if your climate is suitable in winter for warm-loving plants.

There are meters on the market that will tell you how moist your soil is, but I have always found that my finger in a pot works even better.

Most carbon dioxide–measuring units are quite expensive. There are cheaper, expendable detectors that take a sample of air in a tube and indicate the level of your greenhouse carbon dioxide by turning colors. A kit with two tubes is around $20. Extra tubes are available for around $5 each.

Most of these tools are available through good gardening or greenhouse gardening catalogs (see Mail-Order Supplies appendix). Some may also be found in hardware stores or other supply stores.

Predicting Weather

If you have a solar-heated greenhouse or a greenhouse with little or no supplementary heat, the weather can have a real impact on the indoor climate. A good tool for these greenhouses is a weather radio. The federal government has set up a series of low-powered radio stations that play taped weather information 24 hours a day. About 85 percent of the U.S. population lives within range of one of these stations. Radio Shack stores commonly sell radios that broadcast on a special radio band, not on AM or FM frequencies. You can use these radios to help you make decisions about heating or ventilating solar greenhouses. For example, if it is a sunny winter day and the temperature inside the greenhouse has risen to 95° F (35° C) and is still climbing, you can tune in to the weather radio for an up-to-date prediction for your area. If the weather is predicted to turn cold and cloudy, you might want to let your greenhouse run a little hot for a short while to store up some heat for the coming cool weather. If the weather is predicted to stay clear and sunny, you should probably go ahead and ventilate the greenhouse to help let in some cool, dry air while letting out the humid, wet air that winter greenhouses are notorious for. Of course, this approach is assuming that the weather predictions are going to be correct. Remember the old saying "Only fools predict the weather."

Years ago, I was working in a greenhouse in Wyoming that needed a lot of buttoning up before it could survive the winter. Wyoming is a place where you can get fall weather ranging from a tornado to a blizzard to a heat wave. So far this fall it had been crystal-clear warm days with cool nights, but no sign of winter. I had an 88-year-old friend named Howard who kept saying, "We're gonna have a rough, early winter." My weather radio kept saying, "Warm days ahead." So I kept putting off the task of caulking the vents and weather-stripping all the doors, vents and windows for winter. One day Howard said, "It's gonna storm tomorrow!" I just smiled at Howard and kept working on other projects outside, without a shirt in the warm sun. The folks at the weather office kept saying, "Warm days ahead."

That night it clouded up.

Most of the 3 feet of snow we received the next day was still on the ground in early spring. It was cloudy for 12 straight days. Howard just smiled but never said, "I told you so." It was a rough winter, and I found that caulk just doesn't go on right when it's cold. Moral: Don't put all your eggs in just one weather forecaster. Sometimes the weather does what it wants to do, no matter what our satellite-aided, scientific weather people say is going to happen. Also, if you have a Howard living near you, listen to him, too.

Soil Temperatures

Soil temperatures are more crucial than air temperatures even though the latter usually has a lot

Soil thermometer

to do with the temperature of your soil. The warmth of the soil is something we're not commonly aware of because we live our days surrounded by air. Most of us, anyway.

When soil temperatures are below 45° F (7° C), roots grow much slower and have a harder time taking up water and nutrients. When the sun comes out and air temperatures begin to heat up immediately after a cool period, you may see plants wilting even though there is ample moisture in the cold soil. This is because of the slow water uptake by roots in the cool soil even though the air is rapidly warming. That's why you must be careful not to overwater in the winter, because the plants could be wilting just because they have cold feet. Check the soil moisture before you grab for the watering can.

Research has shown that if soil temperatures are kept around 65° F (18° C), the winter air temperature can drop 10° F (6° C) without any loss in yield. This is especially true with fruiting crops. Many researchers believe that the great results obtained by heating the soil are due not just to the effects of temperature but also to the effects of faster organic matter decomposition (that occurs with warmer temperatures, which creates more CO_2), increasing the rate of photosynthesis.

There is a special thermometer with a 5-inch (13-centimeter) probe that is made to measure your soil temperatures. These run around $8 to $10. Soil thermometers are a great help in discovering environmental differences and in just seeing the relationship between air temperature and the soil. You'll find you will soon get a feel for little microclimates within your greenhouse that you can plan for accordingly. It is also helpful to keep records of your soil and air temperatures to see the general trends and the relationship to the outside weather.

When people learn that warm soil helps to increase plant growth, they immediately start scheming on ways to heat up the soil. In earlier times, people used the heating qualities of decomposing manure to heat cold frames. They placed an 8-inch (20-centimeter) layer of raw manure about 1 foot (.3 m) below the top of the soil. This manure would heat the soil that covered it for a few weeks until the manure cooled off. On top of the soil, above the manure, they started their seedlings in containers for later outside transplanting. Planting seeds directly into soil that has heating manure in it would eventually cause over-fertilization, especially when the roots reached the raw manure. But containers sitting on top of this heated soil did fine.

Many people have set up beds with warm-water pipes hooked to solar or conventional hot-water collectors running through them. This is fine, except that it can make it difficult to work beds with a shovel.

For large growing beds, one of the easiest ways to heat up your soil is to water your beds with warm (not hot) water. This is a great help to plants in winter, when the temperature of the tap water is often quite low, and can be accomplished by just installing a hot-water faucet and mixing valve in your greenhouse plumbing.

Many industrious greenhouse gardeners often preheat water by irrigating from a black metal drum

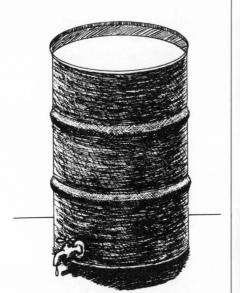 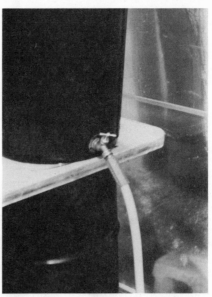

Attach a spigot to a black 55-gallon (208 l) drum or plastic trash can to warm up water temperature for winter irrigation. Place the drum in a high location to use gravity flow for water pressure.

or trash can with a spigot on the bottom placed in a sunny spot. Sometimes the drum is plumbed into the cold-water line. It is set in the sun, where it will warm up from the solar action of the sun shining on the drum. Thus, instead of having ultra-cold winter water coming out of the hose, you can gain a few precious degrees of warmth from the sun. Some people have had good luck with using broken recycled hot-water heaters (with good tanks). The insulation is stripped off, and the tank is painted black. You could also use a solar heating panel that is designed to run water through.

When it comes to starting seedlings and growing things in smaller pots, you can use electric heating mats or cables. These are thermostatically controlled rubberized mats or wires that heat up to a preset temperature. If your greenhouse is a solar-heated structure or if you are just running your greenhouse on the cold side, a heating mat can be a great thing to have for starting seedlings. Potted plants that require warmer temperatures can also be set on top of an electric heating mat.

Please don't jury-rig your own heating mat from old electric blankets or heating pads for arthritis unless you like the feeling of 110 volts going through your body. Instead, check a garden or greenhouse supply catalog for a ready-made, waterproof heating mat or heating cables. The mats are preferred for their durability over the short-lived cable heaters. Mats, being better, are of course more expensive, running around $70 to $100. You'll also need a thermostat for around $65 to $80. Cables run as cheap as $15 all the way up to $60, depending on the length and quality of cable you find for sale.

Cooling the Greenhouse and Sunspace

I don't know why it is, but it seems that from my experience one of the most common problems home greenhouse gardeners have is that of overheating in summer. I see more problems with overheating than I do with freezing or greenhouses running too cool. When a greenhouse runs too hot, it can cause many problems, not only with your deodorant but also with your plant's health. A hot greenhouse may reduce a plant's ability to flower, fruit and even resist bugs and disease.

Unfortunately, the origin of the overheating problem is rooted in the basic design of the greenhouse and a poor design for ventilation.

While this book is not a greenhouse design book, the problem of overheating is so common I need to spend some time discussing it. First, what is considered overheating? As I said earlier, it is different for different plants, but to generalize, I would say that a hot greenhouse is anything above a range of 85° to 100° F (29° to 38° C). To continue my generalization, if it is a plant that you grow for its fruit (yes, even tomatoes) or is native to the tropics, then it can probably better withstand temperatures on the high side. If it's a vegetable you are growing for leaf or root or is native to the more-temperate regions, then it probably cannot tolerate the higher range of temperatures and prefers to grow on the cooler side of the high range.

VENTILATION

One of the best ways to correct overheating is to be sure you have an optimal ventilation system. It's best to establish a natural cross flow of air with both high and low vents. The high vents should be placed on the side of your greenhouse that is opposite your prevailing summer winds, if possible. The high vents should be around 15 percent larger (in total square footage) than your low vents. A rule of thumb for sizing ventilation in solar or attached greenhouses is to have the total venting area (both high and low) equal to 25 to 30 percent of the total area of glazing. For freestanding or conventionally heated greenhouses, the number is less, around 20 percent of the total glazing. If you have a good exhaust fan that really moves the air, these numbers can be lowered.

Be sure your vents are insulated and built tight. Any vent doors to the outside should be well constructed and able to be opened any day of the year (especially in regions where they say, "If you don't like the weather, just wait a few minutes and it'll change"). When your vents to the outside are closed you don't want to have them leaking air during cold gusts of winter, so be sure that they're insulated, weather-stripped and sealed tight to the outside.

Opening and closing the vents may be automated by using commercially available electric and nonelectric motors. The nonelectric types are triggered by the heat of the sun. As the temperature rises, the piston on the vent opener pushes the vent open. The nonelectric types run anywhere between $20 and $80. The more expensive ones can push more weight for heavier vents. The electric vent openers are controlled by a thermostat to open and close the vents automatically. These run around $140.

If just having proper ventilation is still not doing the job of cooling your greenhouse, then it's time to consider installing a fan. The first rule for a greenhouse fan is to place it high: You get a much more efficient job of ventilation that way. Aim it so that it exhausts the air rather than blowing it in. This creates a negative pressure so that cool air will enter through the other lower vents to replace the exhausted warm air. Try to get the air to travel across the full length of the greenhouse before being exhausted to the outside. This means to separate the exhaust fan as far as possible from where the air enters the greenhouse. If the exhaust fan is too close to the air entry vent, then you can short-circuit the ventilation, and a good part of your greenhouse will continue to run hot.

There are some good greenhouse fans (usually in kit form) available in greenhouse supply catalogs that run around $150 to $600, including thermostat. I have also had good results using fans found at garage sales by rigging them up in my high vent. If you want to hook up your own thermostat, you need one that is set for cooling, not for heating. Talk to a supply company that deals in heating and cooling thermostats. Fans are sold by size and by how many cubic feet per minute (CFM) of air that they move. If you want to get scientific about your fan selection, you can do a little calculation to find out what fan size (based on CFMs) that your particular greenhouse needs. A fan in a hot greenhouse needs to be able to move all the cubic feet of air in your structure every 1 1/2 to 2 minutes. To figure this out, you need to calculate the volume of your greenhouse. Multiply the length by the width by the average height. Then multiply this volume by .7, and you have the typical cubic feet per minute needed by your greenhouse. For example, a typical 8 by 12 by 10 foot (2.4 by 3.6 by 3 m) greenhouse needs to have a fan that can move 670 CFMs. A simple way to calculate the needs of a solar greenhouse is to figure 5 to 8 CFM per square foot of south-facing glazing. (Use 5 CFM for areas with dry, cool nights; use up to 8 CFM for climates with humid, warm nights.)

Another way to cool down your greenhouse is to use the cooling effects of evaporation. This is the same cooling effect that we feel when wind blows across

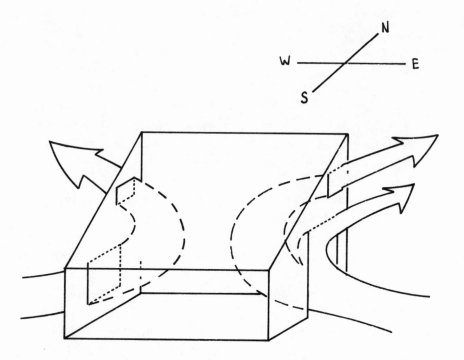

Low and high vents on each end wall can promote good ventilation. Exhaust fans placed in higher vents greatly increase efficiency.

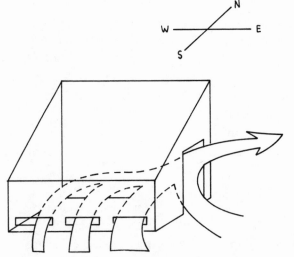

Summer ventilation in attached solar greenhouses. Notice how the west side of the greenhouse needs another exhaust area to provide efficient ventilation.

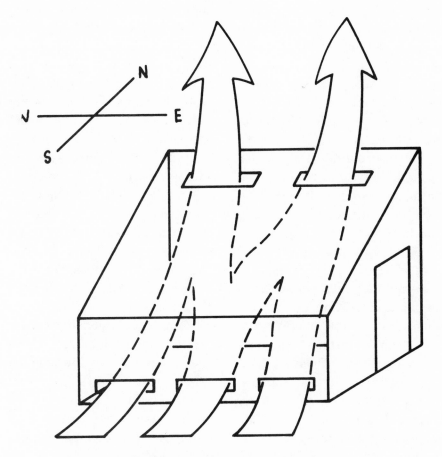

Ridge vents help promote a good flow of air.

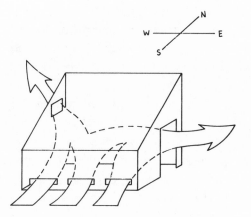

This shows a more balanced ventilation. An exhaust fan placed up high increases efficiency of ventilation.

sweaty skin. As water evaporates, it cools the air around it. Unfortunately, if you live in a humid part of the world, the air is already wet and evaporation just doesn't work very well, thus evaporative cooling is not as effective. But in most places, you can cool down a greenhouse considerably by just watering down the floors. When the air moves across the wet floor, the water evaporates for a cooling effect.

A fine mist near an air-intake vent is also a way to increase evaporation (and cooling) in a greenhouse. Misting nozzles are commonly available in supply catalogs. A fog is even finer than a mist, and commercial growers are turning more and more to sophisticated (and very expensive) man-made fog units. These are way out of the range of most home greenhouse owners. Misting, fogging or watering the floor may not be possible in the living-room type of sunspaces, where you should consider using either an evaporative swamp cooler or a traditional air conditioner.

If you live in a relatively dry locale, you can use an evaporative swamp cooler, which works best for the money. A swamp cooler operates on the evaporative principle (which causes cooling). In humid climates, swamp coolers are less effective, especially when the relative humidity rises above 75 percent. At 90 percent outside relative humidity, evaporative cooling hardly works at all. You can buy swamp coolers at large department stores starting at $450. You can often find used ones much cheaper. Swamp coolers have fibrous pads that require regular cleaning or replacement. They may also need to be either plumbed into a water source or regularly filled with water. They have the advantage of using much less electricity than traditional air conditioners.

Commercial greenhouses often use an evaporative cooling system known as a pad and fan system, which works like a big swamp cooler. At one end of the greenhouse, water is dripped through a thin fibrous pad in front of an intake vent to the outside. An exhaust fan at the opposite end pulls outside air through the wet pad, cooling the air, and the cooled air flows across the length of the greenhouse until it's exhausted to the outside.

If you live in a humid part of the world and money is no object, you can always consider installing a regular air conditioner. Unfortunately, they are expensive to run. The price may not bother you when you are faced with the prospect of a hot, humid greenhouse. Some of us will do (or pay) anything to keep our cool.

SHADING TO COOL THE GREENHOUSE

When all else fails to cool off a hot greenhouse, you can always put something up between the greenhouse and the sun. That could be accomplished by hanging commercially available shade cloth over the outside of the glazing or by directly treating the glazing surface. Check out greenhouse supply catalogs for either shade cloth or glazing treatments.

If you want to treat the surface, there are commercial greenhouse shading compounds available from greenhouse suppliers. This is a paintlike material that is usually white and is sprayed or splattered onto the glazing. It is a temporary solution that usually lasts one summer. It can easily be removed and seems to come off quite readily after a few frosts. There are many shading compounds available on the market, so check with a local commercial greenhouse supplier because they can vary in life span and effect. Before you apply anything to your glazing surface, be sure to check the warranty (or talk to the manufacturer) on your par-

ticular type of glazing, as some plastic glazings may be permanently damaged by something (including shading materials) applied to their surfaces.

One good low-budget trick to cool off funky ragtag-type greenhouses is to just splatter some muddy water on the surface of the glazing. This works especially well for cold frames but may scratch plastic glazings.

A more handsome and less damaging way to shade your greenhouse is to use a shade cloth. These are cloths that are loosely woven to allow some sun in and are usually made out of some type of vinyl or polypropylene mesh. They can be found in varying degrees of densities for heavier or lighter shading, depending on your needs. These can be placed on the outside or inside of your glazing, but they work best when placed on the outside. They can be installed on a roll shade so you can move them up and down, or you can tie them down to the surface. Commercially available shade cloth is usually treated to not break down in ultraviolet light (so it lasts a number of years). If you are creative and short on dollars, you could also rig up less permanent solutions by using cheesecloth, burlap or an old sheet. Shading can also come from deciduous trees, sunflowers, pole beans and grapevines planted outside of your greenhouse glazing.

No matter what you do, you should keep in mind that while shading may help cool off your greenhouse, it will also slow down the growth of some plants. This is especially true of most vegetables and also many flowering plants. In defense of shade, there are also many other plants that might prefer the shadier space. You need to decide what kind of crops you want to grow before you put your whole greenhouse in the shadows.

It is important to not use shading as an alternative for poor summer ventilation if you can possibly correct the ventilation problem. When you have good ventilation, you can use shade cloth only in the areas where special plants may need it; for example, setting aside a small area with shade cloth hanging above for shade-loving plants. This leaves the rest of your greenhouse for the option of growing sun-loving plants. Since this book is about growing primarily food and flowers, you'll find that the majority of the food and flowering plants prefer bright growing conditions. Besides, it's always nice to have your options open.

WATER

Everyone thinks that they are good at watering. But this is where most people make the biggest mistakes in growing plants. Usually the problem lies in overwatering.

Variables Affecting Watering

1.   The amount of sunshine that plants receive. More sun equals a need for more water.

2.   The amount of outside venting. The more you vent to the outside, the more water your greenhouse will probably need.

3.   Different plants have different watering requirements. For example, cactus need less water than most plants. Small seedlings and seeds that haven't yet germinated need a steady water supply. Seedlings should not be dripping wet but constantly moist.

4.   Clay soils and soils very high in organic matter need less water than do sandy soils. Get your soil tested to find out what type you have. Check your county agent for instructions.

Testing Soil for Watering

The first step in watering is to use your fingers instead of your eyes. You can feel the moisture level in a bed or a pot easily by just poking your finger into the soil surface an inch or so. With a little experience you'll be able to tell when a plant needs water. For larger growing beds, you may want to try the ball method of testing the soil for moisture. This is especially good for people new to greenhouse gardening. First, dig 1 inch under the surface and grab a handful of soil. Form a ball out of this soil with your hands. Then try to toss the ball from hand to hand.

If the ball ...   is powdery dry and won't form a ball
Then ...   water.

If the ball ...   falls apart easily when tossed
Then ...   water.

If the ball ...   falls apart but not easily
Then ...   don't water. Maybe tomorrow.

If the ball ...   doesn't fall apart
Then ...   don't water. Wait a few days.

If the ball ...   doesn't fall apart and water can be squeezed
                     out in droplets
Then ...   you got carried away and overwatered. Hold
                     off a while and try to perfect your technique.

When using the ball method, be aware that soils high in sand tend to fall apart more easily than other soils, so also take into account how wet it feels. Experience is the best teacher, and over time you will get a real feel for it.

In the soil, there are small, open air pores that are important to roots. Beside needing to take up water, roots also need to breathe. When you water, all those air spaces are filled up. Since roots can't come up for air like whales do, when you overwater, the poor little roots suffocate. When roots suffocate, one of the common symptoms is often wilting, which creates an irresistible urge among greenhouse gardeners to ... you guessed it. Greenhouse gardeners with the most frequent overwatering problems are people living in dry western climates because they are so used to watering their outside garden on a regular basis. When you come in the greenhouse, remember even though it works outside, it may not work inside.

Greenhouses use less water than an outside garden because they are closed systems and have less evaporation. You might even say greenhouses are water efficient.

So what are the variables that we must look at when deciding how often and how much to water?

Knowing When To Water

Rule Number One: Don't water out of habit! Always check the soil before you water. Wilting suggests that you are too late in watering. But few people realize that it might also be a symptom of overwatering. In cooler greenhouses, plants may wilt because the air is cold. So, wilting is not a dependable indicator of when to water. But it is a symptom that should not be ignored. If the soil is dry and the air is hot, then by all means, go ahead and water! But if

---

Symptoms of Overwatering

1. Bluish green mold growth on the soil surfaces.
2. Increased seedling or plant diseases and poor germination.
3. Increased number of slugs feeding on leaves (see Chapter 10, When Things Go Wrong).
4. Slower growth.
5. Leaves that turn yellow and fall (can be normal for this to occur occasionally). If several leaves turn yellow at the same time, the most likely cause is overwatering, cold drafts or air pollution (from a heater vent or burner).

you are only watering when you see wilting plants, then you are using the too-late approach.

As a general rule, water very little or not at all on cloudy, cool days. There is usually no need for it, except for seedlings, which need constant moisture, especially if they are on bottom heat. When you water, always try to do it in the morning to prevent evening condensation on the leaves, which can lead to disease problems. Also, the greenhouse tends to need less water in coldest winter months than other times of the year. During periods of prolonged cold, cloudy weather, I have gone more than a week without a major watering. Except for seedlings, it is always better to do less frequent, heavier waterings than to get in the habit of frequent light waterings. Frequent light waterings can pose a problem because excess salts (that occur naturally and from fertilizers) are never drained out of the soil. These salts can accumulate and reach toxic levels if not occasionally leached out of the pot or below the root zone with a heavy watering.

Hand Watering

Hand watering is probably the most practical way for most greenhouse owners to water. By the term "hand watering," I mean using both a watering can or holding a water hose. Watering cans are helpful for watering small dry spots or an occasional water-hungry potted plant. It is important to obtain a high-quality watering can with a nozzle that lets the water out like a gentle rain. Whether you are using a watering can or a hose, be careful about the force of water coming out so hard that it knocks down seedlings or young plants. This can injure plants and open them up to disease or even snap their stems. Watering-can nozzles should also be removable for cleaning and for times when you don't need them.

When you need to do a major watering, a watering can may be a tedious way to go about it. It is probably much better to use a hose. The first step is to purchase a good rubber hose. Keeping it off the ground will help prevent the spread of disease. You can purchase hose winders at your local hardware or garden center to help keep the hose tidy. Or you can also use an old tire rim to wind up the hose.

The type of hose nozzle is important in greenhouse watering. A good nozzle is one of the most important equipment purchases for your greenhouse. Much of this is personal preference, but to head you in the right direction, I would suggest that you have a couple of specific nozzles on hand.

The two types of nozzles I would recommend are a misting nozzle and a water-breaker nozzle. A misting nozzle produces a fine mist and is ideal for small seedlings or light winter watering. One brand name that is commonly available is Fogg-it. It is used by professional growers and is made of brass. It is available in different mist amounts, such as "heavy mist," which puts down around 4 gallons (15 l) of water per minute, to a minimum of "super fine mist," putting out around 1/2 gallon (1.9 l) of water per minute. You may want to have an assortment of these nozzles for different situations. These nozzles run around $5 each. If you have only one Fogg-it nozzle, I would suggest the "fine mist" nozzle. It puts out around 1 gallon (3.8 l) per minute and is great for seedlings.

Another favorite nozzle is the water-breaker nozzle, which is commonly found in garden catalogs. These are good for watering pots or beds. They are nice because they put out a fair amount of water, but the stream is soft and won't knock down plants.

When you water from a hose, it is helpful to have some type of

hose extension handle made of aluminum. They are available in many different lengths, but I have found that a shorter length of around 16 to 24 inches (41 to 61 cm) works best in the greenhouse.

A shut-off valve at the base of the extension handle is also very helpful. Then, while you are watering, you can turn off the water for short periods without running back to the faucet. Shut-off valves will help prevent overwatering and enable you to put water only where you want it. You will find both plastic and brass shut-off valves for hoses. Of course, the brass types are both better and more expensive. Be sure when you have finished watering that you turn off the main hose valve at the faucet. If you use only your hose shut-off valve, leaving the main valve on for long periods of time, you can

Clockwise from upper left: mist nozzle, brass shut-off valve, water breaker nozzle, brass fan sprinkler with aluminum extension handle.

cause your hose to burst, creating leaks and other big wet problems.

When you are watering, try to keep the water off the leaves. Water the soil, not the plants. Try to avoid splashing mud, and be especially gentle with seedlings; a hard spray can bury seedlings forever and even knock down mature plants. Water thoroughly and as infrequently as possible: When you do water, soak the beds well. Stop when puddles begin to form.

Never let the soil in your beds or pots completely dry out (except for cactus and other special plants). Besides the obvious stress that wilting causes plants, dry soil increases the concentration of fertilizer salts that naturally accumulate in the soil. This will cause the tips and margins of leaves to burn.

When watering pots and containers, stop when the water comes out the bottom. If the soil in your container has dried out considerably, you may want to try the water-twice method. The first watering will immediately run out the bottom. It will have caused the soil to expand and contact the sides of the pot, but the soil will have absorbed little water. So, now when you do the second watering, it will soak into the center of the soil mass, finally getting water where the plant needs it.

If you don't have the time or energy, there are systems you can set up to automatically water your greenhouse. These involve timers and extensive plumbing and are usually drip-irrigation systems. They're great if you're going to be away for a while, but if it is a warm time of year, you may need an automatic ventilation system too. When I leave town for a few days, I usually just hire a neighborhood youngster or ask a friend to watch things. Come on now, and get your friends involved! Trade them some fresh flowers or produce from the greenhouse or sunspace harvest!

I generally don't advocate using automatic watering systems for day-to-day watering, because it takes the fun out of greenhouse gardening. Watering is an important job and one that should not be left to a computer or a timer. If you are a gizmo nut, you can probably install an automatic system for $200 to $400 and possibly even cheaper if you are mechanically inclined in plumbing techniques. Check a greenhouse supply catalog for more information on automatic systems. Another alternative is to use the now commonly available black leaky pipe drip system. It works like a soaker hose and can be easily laid under the plants.

Water Quality

In rare instances, people run into water-quality problems caused by pollutants or salts in the water. The quality of water varies greatly from region to region and is affected by both nature and people. It is the human factor that causes most problems because people often don't respect or maintain their water at a high-quality level.

Water is classified as either hard or soft. Hard water is high in minerals, usually calcium or magnesium carbonates. Dishwashing and laundry soaps work best in soft (low-mineral) water. People often soften hard water chemically for washing, but beware! Plants don't grow well in artificially softened water. Water softeners usually raise the sodium content in the soil, which causes poor soil structure and poor drainage. It would be best to plumb your greenhouse with water that has not been run through a water-softener system.

Generally, chlorine is no problem, but if you suspect an unusually high level, just let some water sit in a bucket overnight and most of the chlorine will disappear. Usually, the amount of chlorine that it would take to harm plants would probably harm you first and wouldn't be suitable to swallow.

Fluoridated water in high amounts can occasionally be harmful. Fluoride is also added to many towns' water supplies to help prevent tooth decay. In many parts of the country it occurs naturally in the water. Horticultural research has shown that fluoride may cause some leaf tip burning, especially if your soil pH is below 6.5. Tip burn can also be caused by a high soil pH, overfertilization or a high level of salts. If you suspect the possibility of fluoride injury, be sure your water and soil are in the range between 6.7 and 7.3 pH. For more explanation of pH, see Chapter 9, Getting to the Roots.

Unless you live in an area where acid rain is a problem, rainwater may be a good alternative to tap water. But winter collection may pose a bit of a problem in cold areas. You'll have to be creative.

Droughts seem to occur somewhere in our country each year. Some have been so severe that the growing of gardens both outside and in the greenhouse has been threatened. When water resources are scarce because of droughts, many people have turned to gray water. Gray water is wastewater from sinks, laundry, bathtubs and showers. As much as 80 gallons (303 l) a day can be reused from a household of four. Please use extreme caution when using gray water and consider the following if you choose to use it in the greenhouse.

To transfer gray water to storage or to deliver it directly to your greenhouse, water may be caught in buckets from disconnected sink traps, or a more sophisticated system may be installed. Unfortunately, you may be breaking the law, as many areas have local ordinances against reusing water because of safety concerns. If you are concerned about usage, check with local authorities. I don't want you to break the law. If the quality of your water turns out to be a real problem, the only solution is locating another water source. Capturing rainwater is always a good way to go before you get into using gray water.

Water Temperature

In winter, most people don't like to be splashed with cold water ... and neither do plants. It slows their growth and lowers the soil temperature tremendously. Water is considered cold when it is below 43° F (6° C). The ideal water temperature for plants is between 65° and 80° F (18° and 27° C); above 80° F (27° C) is usually too hot.

Using Gray Water

1.   Avoid laundry water that contains bleaches, boron (Borax) and high sodium detergents. Because most detergents contain some sodium, it's usually best to forget laundry water unless it says on the package the detergent is safe for this use. If not, be on the safe side, and use only the rinse water.

2.   Dilute gray water by 50 percent with tap water or rainwater when possible.

3.   Devise a sand and gravel filter to remove lint, grease or other impurities. Even a double layer cloth bag around the end of a hose makes an adequate filter.

4.   Use mild, simple soaps. Castile soaps work well.

5.   Wash and rinse all produce before consuming. For an extra measure of safety soak vegetables in a few drops of chlorine per gallon of water before you eat them.

6.   Never, never drink this water.

Some Options on How to Raise
Water Temperature in Winter

1.   Plumb in domestic hot water from your home hot-water heater.
Be sure to have it run through a mixing valve with cold water.
2.   Plumb a faucet into the side of a black 30- or 55-gallon (113-
or 208-liter) metal drum. The drum must sit in the sun (to use solar
heating) in a high location to use gravity flow for your pressure
(see p. 44).
3.   Set a coil of black plastic tubing up against your north wall,
which receives winter sun. Connect one end of the tubing to your
house plumbing and put a valve on the other end for watering.
Using solar energy this will warm up the water a few degrees.

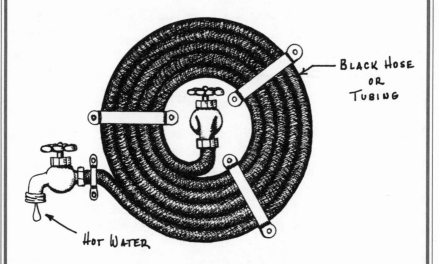

BLACK HOSE
OR
TUBING

HOT WATER

Coiled black plastic tubing can increase water temperature through solar heating.

4.   Look into commercially available solar water-heating systems. A company by the name of Zomeworks carries the only one
I've heard of for greenhouses. It's called Big Fin. For more
information, write to Zomeworks, P.O. Box 712, Albuquerque,
NM 87103.

*Interior
Design
2*

Interior Design

When planning a new greenhouse, people are often preoccupied with design of the exterior, and the inside design is a result of afterthoughts rather than good, solid planning. The inside design is as crucial as the structure itself. Greenhouse space is always limited, so most decisions are made to use space efficiently.

Your own personal preference as to how much space is dedicated to growing versus how much will be used for living space is usually your first important decision. I can't imagine any greenhouse that doesn't have at least a few chairs for enjoying the space and ambience. For many people, plants are just a small touch of green to a bright glass-walled living room.

The main idea is to mix living and plant-growing space in a way that not only is beneficial for creating a comfortable greenhouse to live in but also will gain you the most out of the area you have set aside for plants.

COMFORT

Rule number one in designing the interior is to provide for comfort. If working and getting around your greenhouse or sunroom is an uncomfortable chore, you won't take as good care of the plants. I have noticed that greenhouse gardeners tend to take better care of their plants if the greenhouse is attached to the house rather than freestanding in the yard. Why? Because it is more uncomfortable to first put on shoes and a jacket to go out to the greenhouse instead of deciding to pull a weed while talking on the phone or noticing the plants need water while walking from the kitchen to the living room. Comfort also comes into play when you design beds. It is always more comfortable to have plants growing in raised beds or on a table rather than on the floor.

SAFETY

A major concern in the greenhouse is safety. Electricity is often used in greenhouses: running fans, vent openers, automated watering systems, heat mats for seedlings and pots, and heaters. Unfortunately, electricity does not mix with water, and there is always water roaming around wherever you find plants. No one should have a shocking experience in a greenhouse or sunroom. Special care should be taken when using electricity to prevent any possible contact between water and electrical connections. Any electric outlets installed in your greenhouse should be a ground fault interrupter type, which can help prevent any possible electric shocks. They usually have a little red and black button on the outlet. Be sure to have a licensed electrician install them.

Gas heaters should be properly vented to prevent air pollution, which could harm both you and the plants. Any heater should be placed far enough away from the wall or any combustible material to prevent accidental fires. Fiberglass and many other plastic glazings are extremely inflammable. Plastic flats and pots can literally explode into a blaze, so be careful with any flame in a greenhouse. Another good reason to go with solar heat!) It is a good idea to have a smoke detector and a small fire extinguisher in your greenhouse. Both are commonly available in hardware or department stores.

Any fans in a greenhouse that are within reach of children should have protective screens to keep out little fingers.

Pesticides, fertilizers and sprayers should be placed in an area where children can't get to them, and they should never be left sitting out in a greenhouse. You should always be concerned with safety when handling pesticides and fertilizers. The best precaution is to follow the directions on the label. See Chapter 10, When Things Go Wrong, for more information on the handling of chemicals.

DEFINING THE AREAS

While some people have sunspaces that are used mainly for living areas, most people are going to want to grow a few plants. My preference is to use as much of the greenhouse for growing as possible, but I always like a place where I can sit and enjoy the space, watch the plants grow and just soak up the environment of a green growing place.

Sitting in a greenhouse in the winter is one of the best cures for cabin fever, which usually sets in sometime after Christmas. But where is the best place to sit? Where is the best place to grow? Does it matter? Well, yes, it matters to some extent, especially if your greenhouse is solar heated.

Solar Greenhouse Interior Design

Because solar greenhouses have limited amounts of glass or glazing, the light is also limited. In temperate northern climates during winter months, the sun never gets very high in the southern sky (northern sky if you live south of the equator). When the winter sun is low, shading caused by interior objects may be a problem. Any tall object placed toward the southern half of a solar greenhouse in winter will cause shading. This can

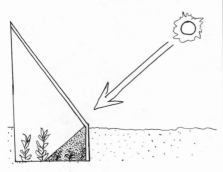

Shading at winter sun angles in a pit greenhouse.

reduce the yields of vegetables and many flowering plants. So be sure that solar water storage such as 55-gallon (208-liter) drums or any other nonplant furniture is not placed to the south of growing beds with plants that require high levels of light.

INTERIOR SURFACES

Because of the constant problem of low light in solar greenhouses, it's important that all light entering the greenhouse be used either for plant growth or for heating dark-colored solar collectors or passive solar storage (usually water drums). The best way to utilize light that does not directly strike these surfaces is to bounce (or reflect) this light where plants or solar collectors can catch it. This is best done by painting walls, ceilings, floors and even the sides of raised beds white. If you live in an area that experiences cloudy winters and you want to grow vegetables in your solar-heated greenhouse, then this can make a big difference (see Increasing Reflective Surfaces, p. 22).

THERMAL MASS

If you don't have a solar greenhouse, then you might be confused by the term "thermal mass."

This is what is used to collect and store the sun's energy. Usually it is water held in metal containers (either 30- or 55-gallon [113- or 208-liter] drums or 5-gallon [19-liter] oil tins), or it may be plastic tubes. There are other types of containers for storing water. Some people may be using rock as a thermal storage, but water is much more efficient. It is most efficient when placed in a metal container such as a drum, as opposed to plastic (or fiberglass). This is because metal is quicker at transferring the sun's heat to the water and it also radiates heat faster than plastic or concrete water containers. Still, if it is a choice between metal or plastic water containers or no water as thermal mass, I would use the plastic. Plastic tubes provide a much better-looking thermal mass container and are only 10 to 15 percent less effective than a comparable metal container.

For solar greenhouses wider than 18 feet (5.5 m), drums painted black on the side facing out and white facing in provide thermal water storage, plus result in more heat gain when the sun is shining.

Most solar-heated greenhouses have water storage for solar heat and moderate temperatures, usually located along the north wall. However, there is one exception: If your greenhouse is much wider than 18 feet (5.5 m), it may be wise to place some thermal mass (water drums) along the south wall too. This will help create more-even temperatures across the width of your greenhouse. If you do this, thermal mass along the south face of the greenhouse should be in small containers such as 30-gallon (113-liter) drums laid on their side to minimize winter shading. Any water drums placed on the south side of a solar greenhouse should be painted half black and half white, with the white half on the north side of the thermal mass container and the black half on the sunny side (toward the glazing).

In the summer in a solar greenhouse, the thermal mass storage along the north wall can be a very shady area. Light can be increased by hanging a white curtain over your mass containers to bounce and reflect more light to plants.

The effect of water as a thermal mass enables the greenhouse to collect the day's heat and then radiate it back into the greenhouse at night. If you've ever been in a solar greenhouse with water containers, then you probably noticed that even on a sunny day the containers did not feel all that warm to the touch. Many people wonder how it can work if it is not warm. Actually it works pretty well, and here's how. When using water as a thermal mass, you are not particularly trying to get the water extremely hot. Rather, you are after gaining a good difference between the day and night temperature. By having the water temperature rise even just a few degrees (no matter how cool it feels to the touch), it can be translated into thousands of calories or BTUs (a term for heat measurement) of heat for the greenhouse space. Besides, think how warm your fingers are from normal body temperature. If those water containers felt hot, then the greenhouse would probably be unbearably hot for both you and the plants.

Having water storage in your greenhouse also will help in another way. If for some reason your greenhouse space becomes incredibly cold and the temperature gets down to freezing, then there is an added benefit of having water containers. What occurs near the freezing point of water is what chemists call the "latent heat of water." This is a reaction in which water actually gives off heat as it starts to form ice crystals. I know it sounds odd that when water is about to freeze, it gives off heat. Ask your local chemistry teacher for verification if you don't believe me. This is the same reason that fruit growers turn on a sprinkler system when their crop is threatened with frost. The droplets of water on the leaves give off enough heat to protect the plants until the sun rises. The same is true with water in a greenhouse threatened with frost. The water in drums or other containers will help prevent the temperature from going below the freezing point, thus protecting your plants. This can come in handy for people with 100 percent solar-heated greenhouses, and it can even be helpful for conventionally heated greenhouses, especially if your heater goes out or something else goes wrong that causes the temperature to drop to freezing.

I have worked in many a solar greenhouse that has been saved by its water mass. Once I had a recording thermometer that produced a graph of the temperature. I set it in a solar greenhouse on the high plains of Wyoming, which had a lot of 30- and 55-gallon (113- and 208-liter) metal drums filled with water. It was winter, and the predicted low for the night was -30° F (-34° C). The wind was blowing 15

to 20 miles an hour. I figured these conditions would be a challenge for any solar greenhouse to survive without frost. When I returned in the morning, the plants looked fine, with the exception of some slight frost damage to some plants near the window. I was surprised to see on the thermometer graph that the temperature had been bouncing up and down slightly off of 32° F (0° C) most of the night. It was evident to me that it was the water as thermal mass that had protected the greenhouse that night.

Water as Thermal Mass for Nonsolar Greenhouses

Owners of conventionally heated greenhouses often investigate ways to conserve energy. Common sense usually steers people toward the obvious solutions, such as weather-stripping vents and doors; another common practice is to add some winter insulation to the north walls. An easy solution is to add a layer of glazing, usually a plastic film, to the inside of the outer glazing. But, many wonder about using water drums.

The answer is yes, using water as thermal mass can help moderate both high and low temperatures in

Tops of fiberglass barrels used for thermal mass can serve as shelves.

the greenhouse. I usually recommend that people try using them to hold up benches or tables for plants or as the base to a small potting bench. While there is no hard research on this, I suggest that you try some experimenting around, and you'll find that it can help reduce heating costs. With every greenhouse being different, it would be hard to tell you how many to put in your greenhouse, but for an average greenhouse of 8 by 10 feet (2.4 by 3 m) I would try at least three 30-gallon (113-liter) drums or two 55-gallon (208-liter) drums filled with water and sealed. It is best to place these drums to the north side of a greenhouse.

Where would you ever find drums for using as thermal mass? Check your local oil companies, junkyards, army surplus stores and construction contractors. New barrels are best, but old ones can work fine as long as they weren't used to store toxic waste. Drums are usually reasonable in cost. Always try to use drums with sealable lids to prevent evaporation. Fill the drums with plain old water within 2 inches (5 cm) of the top (to allow for expansion). There are chemicals you can put into the drums that will slow rusting, but I have never used them. I have seen drums last well over 10 years without any signs of rust. It is important, however, not to set metal drums directly on dirt, as this will cause quick corrosion of the metal. The drums should be set on concrete, wood or brick for a long life. If you are interested in obtaining the much more ornamental (but less effective) plastic (or fiberglass) drums, check the Solar Components Corporation listed in the Mail-Order Supplies appendix. There may be others who carry the product, but they are the only ones I can find who carry plastic water storage units.

If you use the plastic storage tubes, you may need to occasionally add an algicide to the water to prevent the unsightly buildup of green scum. The algicide commonly used for spas, hot tubs and swimming pools works fine in controlling algae. Many people wonder about increasing the solar heating effectiveness of the clear fiberglass tubes by adding dyes to the water. I have not found an increase in efficiency high enough to warrant the addition of colorings unless it is for aesthetic reasons. When left clear, they usually take on a pleasant bluish green color.

RAISED BEDS

You have some options of where and how to grow plants. One of my favorite ways to grow plants is in raised beds. A raised bed is usually made out of wood and filled with soil or other appropriate growing medium. Raised beds may also be built of brick, concrete or recycled material. I have found that growing in raised beds allows for excellent root production and is especially well suited for food crops and cut flowers. Raised beds are also good for growing long-lived plants, such as perennial herbs, and tropical fruiting plants, such as citrus and figs. Of course, these plants will also grow satisfactorily in pots that are suited to the size of the plant, but I have seen people have better luck with a raised-bed planting. Many greenhouse growers like to mix both types of planting schemes, having a combination of potted plants and plants growing in a raised bed or two. By having a raised bed, you do not eliminate the possibility of placing potted plants on top, using it like a table some times of the year and then directly planting in the soil of the raised bed another time.

Gardening in raised beds is by far more comfortable than reaching down to a bed made at ground

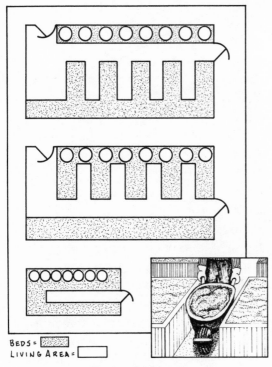

BEDS =
LIVING AREA =

Peninsular layouts

There are a number of ways to lay out a raised bed. The peninsular system uses space most efficiently, with the main aisle running north-south or east-west. The width of the raised bed should be comfortable for you to reach across, usually 3 1/2 feet (1 m), providing access from both sides. For one-sided access (such as a bed up against a wall), don't make the beds any wider than 2 1/2 feet (.8 m). Again, bed and aisle width really depend on what is comfortable for you. Think about the size of your wheelbarrow and the route you must take to carry soil to the beds. The old-fashioned three-point, one-wheel wheelbarrow has the advantage of being able to roll down narrower aisles.

Another option for many greenhouse gardeners is to raise the beds by lowering the walkway. This leaves the top of your raised beds at grade level. This option is out for those of you who already have a greenhouse with a concrete slab for a floor ... unless you're good with a jackhammer. This also

level. Ground beds have the disadvantage of getting trampled as people walk through. A raised bed, even a few inches off the ground, can work wonders in keeping big feet off of your plants; of course, a low raised bed won't stop cats, dogs or curious kids. Up to a point, the higher the raised bed, the less you have to stoop to garden. I have found that a 24-inch-high (61-centimeter-high) bed is about perfect for most people. Another advantage of a raised bed is that the soil also acts as thermal mass, complementing other thermal storage.

requires that you have installed some type of floor drainage, or you'll be walking in water.

Some growers prefer a raised-raised bed. This is like having a raised bed on stilts usually built out of wood, but other materials may work as well. Usually the bed is a minimum of 1 foot (.3 m) deep. The main advantage here is to create storage space under the bed for things like pots, hoses, garage sale accumulations and other junk (just what you need, huh?). If you attempt this kind of bed, be sure that your soil area has some holes in the bottom for drainage. Also check into your particular ground-water conditions before you get going on this type of walkway.

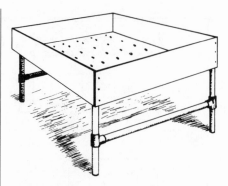

Raised-raised bed allows under table storage capacity.

the price. To get a little longer life out of these materials, you can staple some plastic to the interior sides. Never put plastic sheets on the bottom of any bed, because they will cause drainage problems. Before you get started using any wood in building a greenhouse bed, please see Wood in the Humid Greenhouse (p. 33), where treated lumber is discussed.

Constructing Raised Beds

There is no right way to construct raised beds. There are, however, methods and materials that make the bed last much longer. These are usually limited only by your budget and your imagination. For example, new lumber, landscape timbers, brick, cinder blocks, stone, concrete and old tires can all be made into acceptable raised beds. Materials that are famous for being short-lived are plywood and scrap lumber, but you can't beat

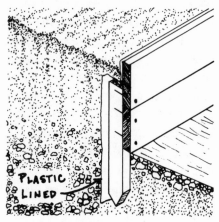

Use support stakes in the construction of raised beds.

Create a place to sit on the side of a raised bed for working and for comfort.

To prevent rust, use galvanized nails or, better yet, the brass-colored deck screws. In building wooden raised beds, you should sink vertical support timbers (treated four-by-fours are best) or metal stakes on the side of the bed. This will anchor the bed, keeping it from moving as you fill it with soil.

If you want to maximize the light your plants receive, you can really help things along by painting the sides of your raised beds white. A gloss or semigloss exterior paint will enhance the photosynthetic light throughout the greenhouse or sunspace.

A 1-by-6-inch (2.5-by-15-centimeter) board laid on top of the perimeter of the bed makes a nice seat for people and a good place to set pots. If you don't do this, people will tend to sit on the edge of your beds anyway ... unless you place cactus there.

You can also make nice beds out of reinforced concrete or cinder blocks, although cinder blocks are a bit on the wide side, taking up much growing space.

GROUND BEDS

Obviously, ground beds are easier to construct than raised beds. Basically you just go in there and rework the soil, and you are on your way. It is usually helpful to have some kind of barrier, even a two-by-four staked into the ground, to keep out wayward feet.

The advantage of a ground bed over a raised bed is that it allows you to grow taller plants. This can be helpful because it is easy to let a greenhouse tomato, cucumber or ornamental plant get extremely tall. For instance, it is not uncommon for a healthy greenhouse tomato variety to grow 10 feet (3 m) high, which is a major concern if you have a low-clearance roof.

DRAINAGE

All flower pots should have drainage in the bottom. Without it, the soil will become waterlogged and sour. It eventually means certain death for a plant. The same is true for any raised bed. All water needs to go somewhere when you water a raised bed. Unless you are gardening on a space shuttle, all water eventually succumbs to gravity and goes down.

If you are in the process of designing a greenhouse or sunspace and plan to have raised beds, I recommend that you not pour a solid slab of concrete on the floor. You can take advantage of the natural drainage of the soil if you can limit the concrete just to the walk paths and leisure areas, leaving dirt over which to build your raised beds (see Aisles and Floors for other options, p. 80). This gives water a place to go downward into the soil.

Unfortunately, most greenhouses and sunspaces have already been built on a concrete slab. No, you don't have to get out the jackhammer and start chopping away at the concrete. You do need to think a little more about the drainage of your raised bed. There should be small weep holes in the bottom of your beds where

they touch the floor so water can escape. It is also important to fill the bottom 3 inches (8 cm) or so with 1 to 2 inches (2.5 to 5 cm) of gravel to help promote drainage (see Filling Soil Beds below).

Once you have established good bed drainage, you will need to think about floor drainage, which is often overlooked in sunspaces. If your greenhouse or sunspace does not already have floor drainage, that can cause problems and it is hard to install. All that you can really do is to not overwater. As mentioned in Chapter 1, The Greenhouse Environment, overwatering is a common mistake made by novice greenhouse gardeners. If floor drainage becomes a major problem, you may want to grow plants only in pots that have saucers to catch the water.

Filling Soil Beds

If you plan to do your gardening in a soil medium, here's how to fill your beds (for more about soil and plant nutrition, see Chapter 9, Getting to the Roots). First, you need to determine the quality of the soil you plan to use. This is best done with a professional soil test. You can find out how to get your soil tested by checking with your local county agricultural extension agent. There are also many home soil-test kits on the market that work well. In general, try to use rich top soil. Never use soil found near heavily trafficked highways or streets, because it is often high in toxic lead.

You should always strive for a well-drained soil in a greenhouse or sunspace. This is determined by finding out through your soil test if your soil is clayey or sandy. A less scientific way to make this determination is to use the feel method of testing. Wet a tablespoon of soil and rub it between your thumb and fingers. If it feels gritty, it's probably a sandy soil. If it feels only slightly gritty, it is probably a mix of sand and clay. And if it feels plasticlike and smooth, it probably leans more toward clay. (If it feels really slimy, you probably grabbed a slug.) A large number of hard dirt clods may indicate a clay soil.

Soils that are on the sandy side tend to drain best. Clay soils are notorious for drainage problems that can lead to a salt buildup and water-logging—both can hurt the growing of plants. But a good soil should have some ability to hold water. This is best achieved by relying on decomposed organic matter rather than on high clay content.

If you must deal with a soil high in clay for inclusion in a raised growing bed, you can reduce its impact by mixing in enough sand to make it drain well. You can add up to one-third sand to a heavy clay dirt for a good growing bed soil. If you are building a greenhouse over soil extremely high in clay, you may want to consider drainage tiles under the greenhouse. Talk to a good contractor or engineer for more details. On second thought, forget the engineer. You can't afford that solution.

If your soil test indicates that your soil is high in salts, you may want to find another source. Also, if the test indicates that the soil is low in certain nutrients, you will have to add material to correct this.

DEPTH OF FILL

For good plant growth, you should try to have a depth of about 1 1/2 feet (.5 m) or more. Less depth works, but it tends to produce some growing problems and plant stress. If your greenhouse bed sits on dirt rather than concrete, then you can work the planting soil below the ground level to give yourself a good area for root growth.

Begin filling the bottom with 3 inches (8 cm) or so of gravel, 1 to 2 inches (2.5 to 5 cm) in diameter, to help promote drainage. Then add 2 inches (5 cm) of coarse sand or pea gravel. Many gardeners place a fine mesh nylon or plastic screening on top of the sand and gravel. This is not essential but it does help maintain good drainage for many years. On top of the screen or gravel is your soil mix (see Chapter 9, Getting to the Roots, for details on how to make a good soil mix).

FANS AND VENTS

As mentioned in the previous chapter, fans and proper ventilation are important to the cooling of the greenhouse and CO_2 absorption by the leaves. Unfortunately, overheating as a result of undersized cooling systems is an all-too-frequent-problem affecting greenhouses and sunspaces. But fans are good not only for cooling. By stirring up the air in wintertime, you can also help reduce the incidence of disease and pests.

When you are designing the placement of your cooling fans and winter fans, be sure to think about where the fans should be placed. You don't want to have them interfering with tall plants or the movement of people. Also, give some thought to safety, in terms of water mixing with the electrical parts and people with the moving blades. The same kind of consideration should be given to the windows and shutters that open for ventilation.

Screens

Screens not only can help in keeping a low, accessible fan or vent safe, they can also keep critters out, like birds and the neighbor's dog or cat. Galvanized hardware cloth is a good material to keep most things out. You may also want to keep out bugs. Window screen can help somewhat with this job. Researchers have recently introduced a microfine screen that can supposedly keep out even the smallest insect while letting a fair amount of air through. It is not available to home greenhouse gardeners as of yet, but it may be available someday soon. Check with a commercial greenhouse supply company for more information.

PLANTS IN CONTAINERS

You have two options when growing plants in a greenhouse: raised beds or containers and pots. There are lots of choices for containers, including plastic pots, clay pots and a whole array of things that can be recycled into a pot for growing plants. When your greenhouse is set up with raised beds, you have your options wide open. You can grow in the beds themselves, or you can use the bed as a table and set containers directly on top of it. Be sure to set the pot in a saucer, or the roots may grow out of the hole in the bottom of the pot and anchor into the raised bed. This has happened to me. I usually suspect that this has happened when I find a walloping big plant growing in a little pot sitting on some soil. When I try to pick it up (to no avail), I quickly learn how it got so big.

My personal preference is to use raised beds for growing vegetables and cut flowers and to use pots for foliage plants, ornamental plants and specialty plants such as cactus and orchids. The raised bed provides for more root development for the cut flowers and vegetables than a container will.

This does not mean that if you aren't set up with raised beds, you can't grow these plants. They are just a bit more difficult, especially when it comes to growing large plants. Of course, this can be overcome by using larger pots or tubs.

When you grow plants in containers, be sure the soil mix is rich and well-drained and that there are drainage holes in the bottom of the containers.

Making Your Own Potting Mix

When using containers to grow plants, many people become interested in mixing up their own soil. There are, however, many good soil mixes available at reasonable prices. But if you are determined to make your own, here are some tips.

First, using just plain old soil from the outside garden is usually not a good choice for the container. Outside garden soil often has a lot of weed seeds and possibly even some devastating diseases in it. This can be overcome by sterilizing the soil. You do this by heating the soil to between 150° and 180° F (65° and 82° C) for 30 minutes. Garden soil can also be low in organic components, which help the soil to hold water and nutrients in the tight confines of a pot. The addition of peat moss may help this. Again, never use soil found near heavily trafficked highways or streets. It is often high in toxic lead. (See p. 397 for a recipe for potting soil.)

Sizing Pots

The biggest mistake is usually made not in the type of pot but by using too large a pot. People think that they are doing the plant a favor by giving it a lot of room. But if the plant doesn't grow fast enough to use all of the space, trouble can occur. An oversized pot can become waterlogged easily, and then the plant can suffer from lack of air (yes, roots need to breathe too). The soil can also become sour, causing problems to the plant's health. When you are up-potting a root-bound plant, it is usually best not to jump to a size any bigger than 1 or 2 inches (2.5 or 5 cm) larger than the original pot.

Many houseplants do well in a root-bound state for quite a while. Oftentimes, the problem is just one of needing repotting with some new soil. You do this by knocking off a fair amount of the old soil, adding some new, virgin potting soil and putting the plant back in the same pot.

Vegetables in Pots

Vegetables can also be grown in pots quite well. There are some things that you can do to make vegetables survive and thrive in pots. Be sure that the future size of the vegetable is in balance with the pot size. A vegetable plant that is too big for its pot will create a stress situation that can lead to bugs and disease. If you are growing a tomato variety that is known to get up to 5 feet (1.5 m) tall, you're asking for trouble if you plant it in a 6-inch (15-centimeter) pot. It would do much better in a 5-gallon (19-liter) pot.

Often you can choose to grow bushy varieties of vegetables instead of vining types, which tend to get large. For instance, bush beans do better in pots than pole beans; determinate (bushy) tomatoes do better than indeterminate (vining) types; bushy squash do better than vining squash.

Why not break all the rules of convention and try mixing flowers, vegetables and even herbs all in the same pot? Don't be afraid. It works fine, and it can create an interesting collection of food and flowers. Take care not to consume any inedible or poisonous flowers or plants.

When you are growing veggies in pots, watch for more-frequent wilting, and make a good effort to supply the nutrient needs of the plants. Excess nitrogen as well as nitrogen deficiencies are common in plants growing in pots. Get on a regular schedule of fertilizing (see

Chapter 9, Getting to the Roots, for more information).

Plastic Versus Clay

There are two main types of plant containers on the market these days. They are plastic pots and clay pots. They both have advantages and disadvantages. Let's look at the advantages of both. Clay pots are heavier, drain better (because they are porous) and have a natural appearance. Plastic pots are lighter, unbreakable (if dropped) and easier to clean, need less watering and come in many different colors and shapes.

Now let's look at the dis-advantages of clay and plastic pots. Clay pots are breakable, more ex-pensive and harder to clean, may create water stains on surfaces where they are placed and need more water than plastic pots. Plastic pots risk overwatering problems, are easier to tip over because of their light weight and appear more artificial than clay pots. Re-search has shown that plants growing in white or light-colored plastic pots have significantly slower growth when compared to those grown in dark-colored pots. This is because the white or light-colored pots let light through to the roots, which confuses them,

and thus you end up with an unhappy plant.

I use both types, although I tend to prefer clay pots. Because overwatering is so common in greenhouses, clay can tolerate the water more. I also like the way clay looks. For plants that need con-stant moisture, I like to use plastic pots. I always try to find terra-cotta-colored plastic pots. When it comes down to a decision be-tween plastic or clay pots, I usually use what I have available to me at the time. If I am feeling real lazy, it is usually what is closest.

The Hole in the Bottom

A donut isn't a donut without its hole. The same is true for a plant pot. It must have the all-important drain-age hole or it isn't worth using. The water, fertilizer and salts that can accumulate in the soil need to drain out the bottom. It often helps to place a piece of broken clay pot or a large rock over the hole to prevent the dirt from spilling out. Of course, to prevent the water from coming out of the hole and spilling all over everything, you must use a saucer under the pot.

Recycled Materials or Pots

Pots don't have to be of the store-bought variety. You can make pots out of all kinds of recycled materials. I have seen pots made out of everything from old tires to milk jugs, and they work just as well as the kind that you buy. Whatever you use, just be sure it has a hole in the bottom.

HANGING POTS

Hanging pots for growing either food or flowers are a good way to utilize the air space of your greenhouse. Hanging pots also add a nice element of design to a greenhouse. Hanging pots don't have to be just flowers or foliage plants. You can also hang vegetables, herbs or other interesting combinations.

If you have a solar-heated greenhouse that tends to the cold side, you can take advantage of the warmer climes of the upper reaches of the sunspace by putting a few hanging baskets up high. If a basket is in a position that is hard to water, try rigging it up on a pulley so that you can lower it for watering and grooming and then pull it back up to the warmer reaches of the greenhouse. Be careful, though. In summer it may be too hot up high, and you may want to keep the hanging pot a little lower.

AISLES AND FLOORS

There are a number of ways to deal with aisle and floor space. Each material has its special attributes: My favorite is brick, but let's look at how each one stacks up.

Wheelchair Access

Wheelchairs vary between 2 and 3 feet (.6 and .9 m) in width. They need a diameter of about 5 1/2 feet (1.7 m) for a turnaround. For complete access, you should replace stairs into the greenhouse with ramps, which should not rise

Brick floors and wide aisles make the greenhouse space functional and attractive.

Options to Walk Upon

Material	Comments
Dirt:	Gets muddy; may harbor disease and insects.
Wood boards:	May harbor slugs and insects. Rots and is hard to clean. Bare feet may pick up splinters.
Brick:	Easy to clean and has a pleasing look. Somewhat porous and drains excess water well. You can create some interesting patterns with the way you lay the brick. Will store some solar heat.
Gravel and rock:	Use only pea-size gravel with some "fines" (a rock guy's term) to stabilize it. Drains well. Great on hot days; it can be watered down and cools the greenhouse as the water evaporates. Not good for barefooted humans. Cheap to buy and easy to install. Harder to roll wheelbarrows and wheelchairs, though not impossible.
Concrete:	If the whole floor is a concrete slab, plan for water drainage, preferably built in, if possible. Easy to clean. Grayish white color reflects for photosynthesis. Don't paint floor black for solar heat storage, because it will be too hot come summertime. Concrete walkways are preferred over concrete slabs that cover the whole floor (see Raised Beds, p. 70).

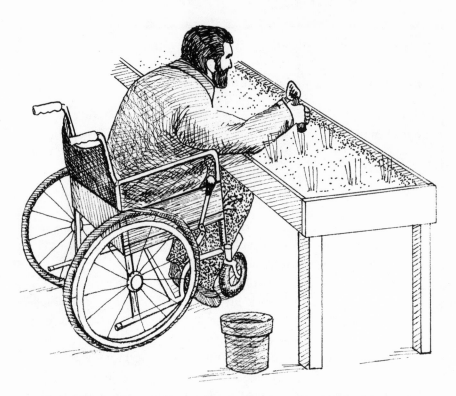

Allow at least two feet of clearance under growing tables for wheelchair access.

faster than 1 foot per 10 feet (.3 m per 3 m) in length. For wheelchair access to growing beds, it is nice to be able to position the chair so that it's facing a bed or growing table with an underneath clearance for the knees of 2 feet (.6 m) rather than having to pull up alongside. The gardener's legs are then under the bed or table, which provides an easy front reach from the wheelchair rather than an uncomfortable twist to the side to reach plants. Gravel flooring makes it difficult to roll wheelchairs. Remember, being handicapped does not mean being "unable." Gardening is an art and adventure that can be enjoyed by many people with a variety of abilities. Even if you are not challenged by a handicap, please consider making your greenhouse more accessible. You, yourself, could be only a moment away from being beset with a handicap. Wouldn't it be nice to continue to garden in your greenhouse?

PROPAGATION BENCH

Everything has to start somewhere, and having a special area in which to start seeds and cuttings is helpful to the overall scheme of a good growing greenhouse or sunspace.

The location of a propagation area or propagation bench (as the commercial greenhouse operators call it) can be just about anywhere. It doesn't even have to be in your greenhouse. In fact, it is a good idea to not take up good well-lit growing areas for this purpose, unless you have a sizable greenhouse with space to spare. Through the wonders of grow lights, bottom heaters and automatic misting systems, you can have a semiautomatic setup anywhere. I must admit, however, I prefer having a propagation bench right in my greenhouse. A good place to locate one is in a back corner. In solar greenhouses, a northwest or northeast area is best.

What do you need for a good propagation bench? Well, it depends on your pocketbook and how many plants you hope to start at any given time. Let's begin with the basics. One of the most important things needed to start seeds or cuttings is bottom heat. Seeds or cuttings benefit greatly from a steady source of heat from below, making germination and root growth take off at a phenomenal rate.

A variety of electric bottom heaters for plant propagation are on the market and available through a number of garden and greenhouse catalogs. As with many things in life, generally the more expensive ones are the better ones. I have had bad luck with the cable-type bottom heaters, which are just a plastic-lined wire that heats up. The cable heaters have never lasted for more than a year for me before they corrode or just quit working, although there are some new types of cable bottom heaters that are claiming to be more durable.

I've always found the best way to get bottom heat for a propagation area is to use the mat types, which come complete with an adjustable thermostat. Prices for mats with thermostats begin at around $70 and go up from there. These types come with a remote probe on the thermostat. For the most accurate results, it is important that you place the probe in a pot that has the same type of soil that you usually use in other pots on the mat. (Be sure to set the potted probe on the mat.) It is helpful to occasionally check the temperature of your soil in some of the pots on the mat. All too often I have found that the mats run hotter than the thermostat indicates, causing some damage to my plants and making them dry out too fast. If your mat runs hotter than the thermostat indicates, turn it down accordingly.

Any type of bottom heat should be set to keep your soil temperature at around 75° F (24° C) for faster germination or rooting. Keep an eye on things; if it gets too hot, your plants will dry out or burn up, and if it is too cool, germination will slow considerably.

New to the business of propagation are little self-contained plastic propagation units that have built-in bottom heaters. Some water themselves with a capillary mat that feeds moisture to the plants from a reservoir. Others are just a plastic tray with a clear plastic top to maintain a high humidity. Some even come with built-in thermostatically controlled bottom heaters. These can be a good way to start and can take the mystery out of setting up the propagation environment. After a while you may want to construct your own for more size.

Another helpful component of a propagation area is to maintain high humidity. This can be done in the labor-intensive way of misting your plants by hand a number of times a day. An easier way is to set up an automated misting system. Check a good greenhouse supply catalog for the many options. If you're not a plumber, you may want to get some help installing this type of system (although if you're a handy person, it's not too difficult to set up yourself). I have had good luck with a commonly available system called Mist-A-Matic, which turns the mist on and off to match the rate of water evaporation from the propagation area. The last time I looked, the Mist-A-Matic system cost around $190. There are other acceptable misting systems, usually triggered by a timer, which produce an intermittent mist.

A mist system involves a solenoid valve, some plastic plumbing pipe and some mist nozzles. A good greenhouse catalog usually does a fine job of explaining the options available for setting up an automated mist system.

A final option to a propagation area is lighting. This is needed only if you locate your propagation in a low-light area. Usually this can be accomplished with an array of common cool-white fluorescent lights (see Fluorescent Lights, p. 19). Remember two things when using fluorescent lighting for growing or starting plants. (1) Safety. Be care-

Mist-A-Matic is a simple control for an intermittent misting system.

Summary for Setting Up
a Propagation Bench

Location: In bright but not direct sun; not taking up precious growing space if possible.

Bottom heat: Preferably thermostatically controlled. Try to maintain cuttings or germinating seedlings around 75° F (24° C).

Humidity: Constant 80 percent or higher relative humidity. Maintained best by misting system set up with timer or based upon leaf evaporation. Can also be maintained by using clear plastic covers over plants or by frequently misting plants by hand.

Lighting: Fluorescent lights work great for seedlings when placed within 1 inch (2.5 cm) of the tip of the seedling. Regular cool white work fine for growing seedlings. For propagating cuttings, light can be less intense. Without artificial lights for seedlings, use bright sunny spot. For cuttings, find bright spot, but not direct sun.

Moisture: If possible, plumb a water spigot nearby for easy access, or set up an automatic misting system.

ful of mixing water with electricity. You might want to check with an electrician for help in installation. (2) Distance. You must keep the lights close to the growing or germinating plant. A minimum of 3 inches (8 cm) is best. This means the light must be adjustable (with chains or the like) to stay close to the top of the growing plant. Fluorescent lights are a great addition to a propagation setup, if you do it right. If you have a lot of natural light, you probably don't need them. Your plants will tell you if you do. If you see them growing in an elongated fashion, it's a sure sign of light deficiency.

In spring I like to utilize much of the greenhouse space for starting seedlings for outside. When this occurs, any part of your greenhouse can become a propagation area. I often set trays of seedlings on raised beds, tables, benches, floors and solar storage barrels. Then the only trick is keeping the environment warm and the seedlings moist (but not too moist).

POTTING AREA

A potting area is a nice but not essential component of a greenhouse. Like the propagation bench, it doesn't have to be in the greenhouse proper. Many people locate one in their basement, tool shed or garage. All you really need is a good tabletop where you can work with soil mixes. This is where you pot-up, transplant or prune plants. It's a work area that will get dirty (what do you expect when you work with dirt?). A potting area is easy to build using plywood painted with a heavy-duty exterior deck paint or, better yet, covered with galvanized sheet metal. All you really need is a small area to work in, usually a minimum of 18 inches by 18 inches (46 cm by 46 cm) square (larger is even better), but the size is up to you and the space you have to work in. I prefer to have a vertical back and sides to catch the soil from falling on the floor.

For true luxury, it is nice to have a sink adjacent to the potting area, but this is not a requirement. If you do have a sink for greenhouse use, be sure to install a dirt trap in the drain. With all the dirt "accidently" going down the drain, a dirt trap will save hiring a plumber when you plug up the drain. A dirt trap is a small container under the sink that catches all of the stuff that shouldn't go down the drain. Every so often you must remove a small paillike container and clean it out. I must admit, this is a smelly job that I would rather avoid. Still,

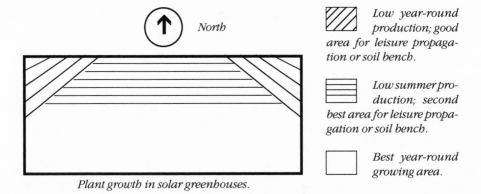

North

Low year-round production; good area for leisure propagation or soil bench.

Low summer production; second best area for leisure propagation or soil bench.

Best year-round growing area.

Plant growth in solar greenhouses.

it is better to clean your dirt trap every once in a while than to have your sewer professionally cleaned out or, worse, to have your lawn dug up when your sewer plugs up beyond repair. A plumbing shop usually sells these traps, and if you are good at plumbing, they are not too hard to install. If you are not an adept plumber, hire a real one. If you don't have a dirt trap, just be careful about what you let go down the drain. Try placing a screen in the drain to catch rocks and other debris.

If you locate the potting area in your greenhouse, as with the propagation area, don't put it in a prime growing area (with good light qualities). It is better to put it in a darker area where plants wouldn't do well anyway. In a solar greenhouse use the northeast or northwest corner for nongrowing activities such as a potting area.

SHELVES FOR GROWING

Shelving can help create extra growing space for potted or containerized plants. Shelves can be attached to the wall, or if space permits, they can be set up temporarily over a raised bed for extra room to start seedlings. They may also be hinged onto the side of raised beds to swing out into an area previously used for living or into an area where aisles are wide enough, as long as there is still enough room to walk or waltz through.

For solar greenhouses or other greenhouses short on natural light, be sure to paint the shelves white. The shelves may create some shade below, possibly cutting out light for lower plants, but usually there is not a noticeable difference. Glazing materials that diffuse the light help to minimize shade problems (see Glazing, p. 14).

MIXING GARDEN AND LEISURE SPACE

Many people like to use their greenhouses or sunrooms primarily as a living space, with furniture, hot tubs and just a few plants. Other people want the greenhouse for gardening and can't see wasting any space for just sitting around. I like a good mix in a greenhouse: a place to sit and a garden to enjoy. I like a greenhouse that is a mix of comfort, a place where I can relax and read the paper with a year-round garden close at hand, producing fruits, flowers, herbs and spices. It sounds like heaven to me … and it is!

If you're like me and prefer a mix of leisure and garden, try not to use up the best growing areas of your greenhouse for leisure. Always locate the living or leisure areas in the shadier spots in a greenhouse. In the solar-heated greenhouse, the best places for leisure tend to be the northwest and northeast areas. Sometimes the north wall is also a shady place, depending on your greenhouse or sunspace design.

If you are going to use your greenhouse leisurely or socially in the evening, include overhead lights, not for growing, but rather for seeing at night. Consider a dimmer switch for your light to create varying moods. If you go for real romantic lighting, please be careful with candles, because some glazings are quite inflammable. How about a stereo or extension speakers for music (botanists often say that plants like classical and jazz)? What a great place to visit with friends!

PLAN IT WELL

No matter how the inside of your greenhouse ends up, it's a good idea to try drawing it out on paper first. It is much cheaper to make your mistakes on paper before you get into major interior design.

*Plant
Layout
3*

Plant Layout

In winter the greenhouse is an ecological island surrounded by cold on all sides. It is a world of its own, and year-round it undergoes changes in its ecology. The more you experience the interactions among the plants, the soil, the insects, the sky and yourself throughout the seasons, the more complex and fascinating the relationships appear. Look closely and with some extra patience to see what's happening. There are many microenvironments within the greenhouse. These are easy to identify and can help you in setting out plants in the optimal spot for healthy growth. The best way to learn about the differences is to be incredibly observant from season to season.

The greenhouse environment changes through the seasons. These changes in the growing environment are mainly the result of changes in temperature and light intensities throughout the year. The seasonal changes are especially profound in solar-heated greenhouses or greenhouses that are run cool in winter. It is true to a lesser extent with conventionally heated greenhouses that maintain the same temperatures in winter as they do in summer.

There are three distinct seasons in a greenhouse with respect to temperature and light. The first two are the summer season and the winter season. The third season is actually two: fall and spring. These two are considered as one because they are the season of transition and they have similar light and heat characteristics.

THE SUMMER SEASON IN SOLAR-HEATED SUNSPACES

The summer season is (of course) hotter than any other time of year. For solar greenhouses, the summer has the worst light penetration, which is contrary to what

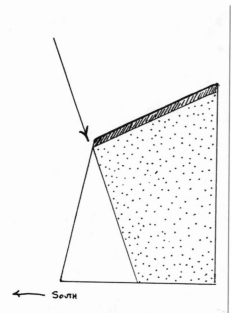

Summer sun in a solar greenhouse without overhead glazing provides limited light.

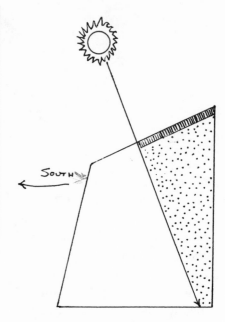

Summer sun in a solar greenhouse with some overhead glazing creates better light penetration.

many people think of summer: a bright, well-lit time of year. Though the days are longer and brighter, the light penetration is reduced because most solar greenhouses (or solar-heated sunspaces) have steep south angles to their glazing. Sun penetrates best when it comes through the glazing in a perpendicular manner. The more perpendicular the light is, the less reflection there is off the glazing. Because solar greenhouses are designed to let in winter sun at a perpendicular angle, it compromises the quality of light in the summer. Often this can work to an advantage because it can

also lessen the amount of incoming heat in summer.

Solar Greenhouses without Overhead Glazing

If your solar sunspace has little or no glazing on the roof, you can find yourself short on light in the summer. Vegetables, herbs and flowering plants grow best in bright areas. This requires that in the summertime you move all of your plants to the first 2 feet (.6 m) adjacent to the south glazing. If you don't want to be so limited in the summer and wish to grow light-loving plants (including most vegetables and flowers), you might want to consider installing three or four skylights in the roof of your sunspace. Of course, you can always grow shade-loving houseplants in the summer. You can also offset the effects of shade by painting surfaces of the interior white, as mentioned in the previous chapters, but there is no substitute for good old natural sunlight, unless you invest in fancy grow lights.

In the summer season, you will also find a lack of light in solar greenhouses against the north wall as the sun gets to a steeper angle. Day by day, you will see the shadow climb down the wall and out into the greenhouse space. It's almost like a walk-in sundial or calendar. I know people who make marks on the floor signifying where the shadows hit on winter and summer solstices. All spaces in the summer greenhouse are warm, but of course it gets hotter toward the roof.

THE SUMMER SEASON IN NONSOLAR GREENHOUSES

Those of you with freestanding or nonsolar-heated greenhouses with glass on four sides don't have to worry about lack of summer light. Because of the angles and quantity of glazing on your greenhouse, instead of worrying about a lack of light, you will have to cope with having too much light, which may cause excess heating in the space.

Longer Summer Days

The most obvious thing that occurs in summer is that the sun stays up longer. This increases the growth of plants (and bugs, which can always be counted on). All greenhouses begin to grow plants at full speed, so changes in plants (and bug populations) will happen at a rapid clip. The plants in solar greenhouses or sunspaces don't capitalize on the longer days quite as well as those in other greenhouses. Often this is because there is an east or west solid wall that prevents direct sunlight from entering early in the morning and late in the day. Because some diffuse light enters into solar greenhouses, they still benefit somewhat from the longer day.

THE SPRING AND FALL SEASONS

The spring and fall seasons in a greenhouse are a compromise of the best attributes found in the summer and winter. It is a wonderful time to grow in a greenhouse because the environment is easier to adjust to what plants prefer … not too cold or too warm. Both spring and fall seasons have good light penetration, coinciding with good temperatures. I often see the plants in my greenhouse thriving in the spring and fall.

THE WINTER SEASON

In winter, the angle of the sun is usually quite good, especially for solar greenhouses. Unfortunately, it is also the time when the days are short and the temperatures are cold. In many places it is also a cloudy time of year.

In winter, there are cold temperature microclimates up against windows, where it can be much colder than your thermometer tells you. Be careful when placing plants close to windows during cold spells. I know many a greenhouse gardener who has lost a favorite plant with this practice. In the winter, growth is slowed, especially on plants that are grown for their fruits and flowers. Many plants seem as if they are almost hibernating, while others prefer the cool temperatures. A friend of mine calls them the "zerex plants" (named after the car antifreeze) in

honor of their ability to weather the cold; check Chapter 8, A Closer Look at the Plants, to see if your favorite plant passes the antifreeze test. In general, plants grow slower in the winter, mainly because of the short days and cool temperatures.

In solar greenhouses during the winter season, your north wall goes from being a very shady spot (as it was in summer) to being a very sunny, warm spot.

Another change you'll notice is that when its real cold outside, there is often a gigantic increase in relative humidity. Your greenhouse may feel almost like a rain forest. This is when you need to ask yourself if you truly need to water. As you get close to Christmas, 'tis the season of overwatering, fa la la la la. In greenhouses that are seriously overwatered, it almost rains on you, as the condensation drips incessantly from the ceiling. So, be careful. Try to ventilate the water-laden air to the outside if you get a warmer day among the cold days of winter.

THE EFFECT OF PLANTS UPON PLANTS

The plants themselves also create change in the greenhouse environment. Tall plants cause shading; overcrowding of plants causes competition for limited light, water and nutrients. Research shows that plants growing adjacent to one another can have both positive and negative effects on each other. This can be as simple as competition for light, water and nutrients, or one plant can actually give off substances that help or hurt other plants. Sometimes researchers don't know what is causing the effect, but they know there sometimes may be an effect.

The presence of plants also has a major impact on the humidity. Even more tangible are the changes in smells from the flowers, leaves and herbs. There are other things you feel in a greenhouse too, things that are hard to describe ... but you know something special is going on.

In laying out crops within the greenhouse, it is important to use the differences in the environment to your advantage. This results in having healthier plants that grow faster, and your fruit and vegetables will have a bigger harvest.

Often when I am gardening in a greenhouse, I can almost hear plants speaking to me: "Help, I'm in the wrong place, and it has put me under incredible stress!" How can I hear a plant say such a thing? Is it that I have a good imagination?

Nope. Just look for a plant that appears to be out of sorts. What you see is a plant that is unduly attacked by bugs or disease. Think of yourself when you are under stress. That's when you are most susceptible to catching colds, your energy is low and usually everything is harder than it should be. The same is true with plants.

For example, when you grow a plant that prefers warm night temperatures above 55° F (13° C) but your greenhouse consistently remains lower, you will likely see symptoms of its stress. It will be losing leaves, leaves will be turning yellow or you'll see increased disease and/or insect damage. In this case, by moving the plant to a warmer area, its health is easily restored and the plant will forgive your innocent mistake.

The best environment for a plant is usually determined by its native environment on the planet. Where possible, I will try to help you by listing its preference when you look up specific crops in Chapter 8, A Closer Look at Plants. For example, most of our favorite houseplants are native to tropical forest floors—down where it is naturally shady and warm. These plants have learned to survive on low light and warm temperatures, which is similar to the environment of our homes. Many houseplants might suffer slightly from the higher light levels of the greenhouse.

A greenhouse can't provide a perfect environment for all the plants you may want to grow, but it can help, and you can always make special adjustments. Greenhouses and sunspaces by nature are conducive to growing a wide variety of plants. A greenhouse is a subtropical or tropical type of environment. That's great because this is where many of our food crops come from. It is also the native environment of many of our favorite greenhouse flowering plants. This logic tells us that the plants (with some exceptions) that are the most difficult to grow are often those native to colder, more-temperate climates, such as the ones that you see growing outside your window (I'm assuming that you live in a temperate climate). That is because these plants often need a winter to trigger proper growth. For example, it's almost impossible to grow apple trees in a greenhouse, because they need a winter in order to flower and produce fruit. Of course, you could grow a dwarf apple tree in a pot and carry it outside to give it a fix of winter, or just leave the windows open in winter, but why bother?

When people walk into my 80°

F (27° C) greenhouse in the middle of a Wyoming winter storm, they can't believe that it feels so tropical. I tell people, "It's a lot like a few hundred square feet of Hawaii." In fact, who needs a winter vacation to warmer climates when you have a greenhouse? You don't tan very well in a greenhouse, because glazings filter out most of the ultraviolet tanning rays, but think of that as one less thing to worry about. It is still very nice to sit out in your greenhouse on a cold winter day. But, let's get back to crop layout.

LOOKING FOR MICROCLIMATES IN A GREENHOUSE

When you are trying to grow a plant out of place, you can always attempt to change the immediate environment to suit the needs of the plant. You can do this either by taking advantage of an existing microclimate or by creating one. Perhaps the word "microclimate" is new to you. Let me give you an example. If you are growing a plant that likes it warm, you can set it near the heater. If a plant likes it on the cool side, you can set it near a cold window. You create a microclimate when you grow cactus successfully by not watering it as much as other plants. Learn the microclimates in your greenhouse so you can use them to your advantage. Again, you have to be observant.

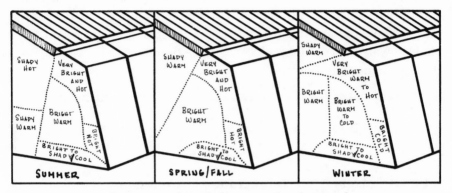

Microclimates vary through the seasons in solar greenhouses.

Rules for the Greenhouse Microclimate

Here are some rules that apply to the greenhouse microclimates (I know that they may sound simplistic, but stop and think about it as you look at your greenhouse, and think how you could use these rules to your advantage):

1. Hot air rises; cool air drops.
2. Shade has less light intensity than sunny areas.
3. On sunny summer days, it is very hot near the glazing, and the closer to the glazing the plant is, the more light intensity there is on it.
4. On cool winter nights, it is much cooler next to the glazing.
5. Plants near thermal mass (such as water drums in solar greenhouses) feel more-even temperatures with fewer night fluctuations.
6. In solar greenhouses, the area near a north wall is brighter and warmer in the winter and shadier and cooler in the summer.

Different types of vegetables have different environmental requirements, so now it's a matter of plugging the plants' needs into the appropriate microenvironments. But remember, these microenvironments vary seasonally. Let's look at these changes graphically. (For more specific information on growing each plant, see Chapter 8, A Closer Look at the Plants.) Your greenhouse may vary depending on interior and exterior design and local climates, but in general this is what happens.

Crop Light and Temperature Requirements for Edible Plants

Crop	Light	Temperature	Comments
Banana	Bright	Warm to hot	Depending upon the variety, they can grow 7 to 25 feet (2 to 7.6 m). Will cause a lot of shading. Grows fast when hot, very slow when cold.
Beans	Bright to very bright	Warm to hot	Will tolerate some shade. Pole beans, when trellised, cause shading. Seeds need 65° F (18° C) soil temperature to germinate well. Fava or broad beans prefer the cool temperatures and also need trellising. Don't grow favas in summer—they hate the heat.
Beets	Bright to very bright	Cool to warm	May go to seed if temperature nears 32° F (0° C) and then rises again.

Crop	Light	Temperature	Comments
Broccoli	Shady to bright	Cold to warm	Will flower fast and pro-pude small heads if consistently warm to hot.
Brussels sprouts	Shady to bright	Cold	Poor quality if consistently warm to hot. Get tall toward maturity and may cause shading.
Cabbage	Bright to very bright	Cold to warm	May go to seed if temperature is below freezing for a long period.
Carrots	Shady to bright	Cool to warm	Do not tolerate crowding.
Cauliflower	Shady to bright	Cold to warm	Will flower fast and produce small heads if consistently warm to hot.
Celery	Shady to bright	Cool to warm	Likes many months of consistent cool temperatures. Will often go to seed before it matures in warm summer temperatures.
Cherimoya	Bright	Cool to warm	Grows 15 to 20 feet (4.6 to 6 m) tall and will cause shading. Will not tolerate temperatures below freezing.
Chicory	Shady to bright	Cold to warm	Not good in hot areas.

Crop	Light	Temperature	Comments
Chinese cabbage	Shady to bright	Cold to warm	Flowers rapidly in warm to hot conditions.
Citrus	Bright	Cool to warm	May get tall (depending on variety) and cause shading. No frost toleration.
Coffee	Shady to bright	Cool to warm	Grows up to 10 feet (3 m). May cause shading after a few years of growth. Will not tolerate frost.
Collards	Shady to bright	Cold to hot	Can grow tall and cause shading. Well adapted to solar greenhouses, except in summer.
Cucumber	Bright to very bright	Warm to hot	Needs nights above 50° F (10° C).
Eggplant	Bright to very bright	Warm to hot	Needs nights above 50° F (10° C).
Endive	Bright	Cold to cool	Poor quality with warm conditions.
Fig	Bright	Cold to warm	Grows 15 to 30 feet (4.6 to 9 m) tall. Will cause shading. Will tolerate light frost and some shade. May lose leaves in winter allowing more winter sun underneath.
Garlic	Shady to very bright	Cool to warm	Will tolerate diverse greenhouse conditions.

Crop	Light	Temperature	Comments
Herbs	Shady to bright	Cold to warm	Will tolerate diverse conditions.
Kale	Shady to bright	Cold to warm	Poor quality with warm to hot temperatures.
Kohlrabi	Bright	Cool to warm	Enlarged stem (edible portion) cracks with hot temperatures.
Leeks	Bright	Cool to warm	Will go to seed if temperature goes below freezing and then returns to warm.
Lettuce	Shady to bright	Cool to warm	Will go to seed with consistent warm to hot temperatures.
Mustard greens	Shady to bright	Cool to warm	Will go to seed with consistent warm to hot temperatures.
Okra	Bright to very bright	Warm to hot	Will not grow in cool, shady spots. May get tall and cause shading. Needs warm temperature.
Onions	Bright	Cool to warm	Will not bulb in winter but are good for greens year-round.
Parsley	Bright to shade	Cool to warm	Will often go to seed folowing winter.
Parsnips	Bright	Cool	Plants that overwinter may go to seed.
Peas	Shady to bright	Cool to warm	Warm to hot temperatures will reduce yield.

Crop	Light	Temperature	Comments
Peppers	Bright to very bright	Warm to hot	Prefer warm temperatures in young ages. Will overwinter if temperatures remain above 40° F (5° C), but grow best above 50° F (10°C).
Radish	Shady to bright	Cool to warm	Consistent warm temperatures cause top growth and flowering. Poor taste in warm to hot temperatures.
Rutabaga	Shady to bright	Cool	Poor quality with warm to hot temperatures.
Spinach	Shady to bright	Cool to warm	Consistent warm to hot temperatures cause rapid flowering and short production period.
Squash	Bright to very bright	Warm to hot	Requires nights about 50° F (10° C). Winter squash varieties need trellising and cause shading. Summer squash generally stays bushy.
Sweet potato	Shady to bright	Warm to hot	Needs hot temperatures for a long period. May get viny and cause shading.
Swiss chard	Shady to bright	Cool to warm	May flower in spring if winter temperatures go below freezing.

Crop	Light	Temperature	Comments
Tomatoes	Bright to very bright	Hot	Will tolerate short periods of hot temperatures. Vining tomatoes cause shading. Little or no production below 50° F (10° C).
Turnips	Shady to bright	Cool	Warm to hot temperatures cause cracking and produce poor eating quality.
Water-melon	Bright to very bright	Warm to hot	Requires nights above 50° F (10° C). Needs trellising, which causes adjacent shading.

Crop Light and Temperature Requirements for Selected Cut Flowers

Crop	Light	Temperature	Comments
Alstro-meria	Bright	Cool to warm	Needs trellising. Flowers at temperatures above 50° F (10° C).
Carnation	Bright	Cool to warm	Needs trellising.
Chrysan-themum	Bright	Cool to warm	May get tall and cause shading. Needs specific night length to flower. Flowers need temperatures above 50° F (10° C).

Crop	Light	Temperature	Comments
Rose	Bright	Warm to hot	Will not grow well if temperatures go below 40° F (5° C). Can get tall and cause shading. Will not tolerate shade well.
Snap-dragon	Bright	Cool to warm	Tall varieties need trellising and may cause shading.
Stock	Bright	Cool to warm	A good winter-spring plant. Don't start before July 10 or after February 15 or plants may not flower. Some varieties are tall and will cause shade.
Sweet pea	Bright	Cool to warm	Usually needs trellising and may cause shading. Poor growth in hot temperatures.

If you don't see your favorite plant listed above, it is probably a plant that is commonly grown in a pot, can be easily moved to accommodate its needs and doesn't greatly affect the microclimate. See Chapter 8, A Closer Look at the Plants, for information on the above plants as well as many plants not listed in this chart.

SPACING THE PLANTS

The space between plants is something that can dictate their overall health. A lot of competition for light, water and nutrients can occur when plants are too close. In a greenhouse, most competition between plants is for the available light. When plants are placed too close together, the results are usu-

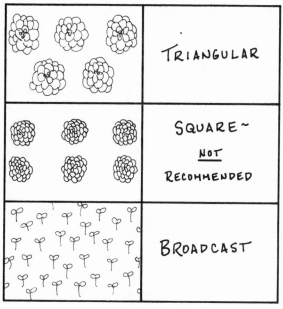

Crop layouts

ally poor: If it's food you're growing, you see decreased yields; if you're growing flowering plants, your chances for quality flowers are slim. The key to proper spacing for seedlings is not sowing the seed too closely. If things do come up too thick, then you have to be ruthless and get to the job of thinning. This is where new gardeners often fail. They can't bring themselves to pull up (and kill) baby plants. If this describes you, wait until you are in a bad mood, after paying the bills or having a domestic argument. It does wonders for your thinning abilities, and when you are done, you'll find yourself to be in a much improved mood. This is called horticultural therapy (a side benefit of growing in a greenhouse or sunspace). If you are doing some transplanting, then you need to be sure you are giving each plant enough room as you set out the new plants.

Normal spacing can change depending on light. For instance, if you are growing a plant that prefers a bright light but you are trying to grow it in a spot with some shade, try to increase the space around the plant so that it can take advantage of as much indirect light as possible. How far do you space a plant? Check in Chapter 8, A Closer Look at the Plants, and if familiar with the plant, think about how big it usually gets. Often it's just a matter of common sense. If the leaves of two plants overlap, then chances are there is some competition for space and light.

Don't get greedy. There are only so many plants you can grow in a greenhouse. After that, if you are still interested in growing more plants, consider adding more greenhouse space to your structure, or wait until spring, when you can go wild with more plants outside.

TRELLISING

You can get a lot more use of your limited space in a greenhouse by growing plants up a vertical trellis. Of course, you can't grow just any plant up a trellis, but a good number can be grown in this manner for more efficient use of space.

Trellises can be made out of almost any material and are limited only by your imagination. You can buy new materials for trellising: nylon net (sold at garden centers), fencing materials such as chicken

Tomato cages make great trellises for ornamentals.

wire, other types of woven fencing or redwood lattice.

Find creative options for using recycled materials for trellising. I once made a great trellis out of recycled driver's-license plastic found in an alley behind the motor vehicle building. The plastic punch-outs had been used, leaving me with a perfect material for trellising. Old fencing or string is also easy to recycle into trellis material. To be sturdy, support posts should be laid deep into the ground. Nail, staple or wire the materials together. I always feel that the best trellises are those that can be set up and taken down as needed. If you are using old twine, it might be best to discard the twine after each season because it may harbor disease that could reinfest next year's planting.

When you set up trellising for most crops, I have found that it is usually best to run the trellis on a north-south axis. This minimizes shading, because the sun is usually in the southern portion of the sky, especially in winter. An east-west axis is best used only in areas where shading is not a problem, such as against a solid wall or along the north wall.

Trellises can be fun to put up and can become elaborate or creative if you wish. Trellises can be laid out in a serpentine form (who

Arched trellising provides good support for cantaloupe.

says they have to be straight?) or made into an arch or tunnel. You could almost call these trellises arbors. With these arbors you can create great effects and new microclimates to work with. I often grow shade-loving plants under or behind these elaborate trellises.

The best trellis I ever made was a walk-under tunnel. Up the trellis, I grew several cantaloupe plants. On either side, as you walked through the tunnel, you saw a virtual wall of ripening cantaloupes, which are almost impossible to grow outside in my part of Wyoming because of the short, cool

growing season. Each fruit's flower had been hand-pollinated and then slung into recycled nylon stockings to support the weight of the fruits on the trellis. It was both beautiful and impressive. If you are growing a heavy-fruited plant, the idea of using nylon stockings and slinging the fruit will prevent the fruit from pulling the whole vine off of the trellis. Tie a part of the stocking to the trellis and then slip the developing fruit into the stocking. The stocking will expand with the fruit.

Some plants, such as cucumbers and vining (indeterminate)

tomatoes, can easily grow up a single string. This works only when you prune off most all the side suckers. It requires that you are knowledgeable about proper pruning of suckers, or you can do more harm than good (see tomatoes and cucumbers in Chapter 8, A Closer Look at the Plants). What you do is tie the top of the string to the ceiling and the bottom to a stake (or loosely to the base of the plant) and then as the plant grows, you wind it carefully around the string, taking care to not strangle the stem. For further information on this type of trellising refer to specific discussions of cucumbers and tomatoes in Chapter 8, A Closer Look at the Plants.

Some plants take to trellising well because they have tendrils that grow out and physically grab onto the trellis to help them hold on. But many other plants that benefit from trellises don't have tendrils and will need your help in using the trellis. You'll have to weave the plant through or tie it to the trellis as it grows. When you are attaching a plant to a trellis, pole or any other plant support, try to use a soft piece of cloth, string or strap, and tie it loosely to avoid cutting and injuring the plant.

Growing vegetables vertically enables you to get more yields out of less space and can be done with some unlikely candidates. New Zealand spinach and summer squash

---

Plants Suitable for Trellising

Edible Plants	**Flowering Plants**
Cantaloupe	Bougainvillea
Cucumber	Golden Trumpet Vine
Grape	some Jasmines
New Zealand spinach	Mandevilla
Peas	Mina lobata
Pole beans	Morning-glory
Summer squash	some Nasturtiums
Tomato	Passionflower
Watermelon	Plumbago
Winter squash	Sweet pea
	Thumbergia

are never trellised in the outside garden, but in the greenhouse, trellising can stretch space like you never imagined. New Zealand spinach may be gently tied up to a trellis made of chicken wire or fencing. I've been able to get phenomenal yields on a 4-foot (1.2-meter) trellis when grown in this fashion. Summer squash may be wound up a string, as it grows in much the same manner as tomatoes. However, you need to be extremely careful to not break the stem when you attempt this. Underneath the vertical growing summer squash, I have been able to grow more shade-loving vegetables, such as lettuce. As you can imagine, these techniques can often increase the productivity of a small space.

Horizontal Trellises

Most trellises are set up vertically, but many cut flowers benefit from a horizontal type of trellis. I make this kind of trellis with welded wire "fencing," the type often used by cement masons for concrete reinforcement, or any other type of fencing that has at least 3-inch-square (8-centimeter-square) openings in it. To set it up, place four 4-foot-tall (1.2-meter-tall) stakes (or more, if needed) in the flower bed, one in each corner. Then at a level

of about 10 inches (25 cm), attach the fencing material horizontally to each post. If the plant tends to get tall, such as greenhouse snapdragons, you will need to add another tier of horizontal fencing at 20 to 24 inches (51 to 61 cm) high. You can add more tiers if needed. This allows for a bed of cut flowers to grow straight without unsightly bends in the stems. If you are growing just a few cut flowers in a pot, you don't need such elaborate trellising. In potted plants you can just use some small stakes or small flower cages, which look like miniature tomato cages placed in the pot to keep the plant growing straight.

Horizontal trellising

STAKING

I often find that when you are growing plants inside a greenhouse or sunspace, the growth is a bit softer. This makes plants a bit more floppy. You'll often find plants falling over or developing a serious lean. If you are having this problem, you can help these plants look and grow better by staking them. The stoutness of the stake is determined by the size of the plant that needs staking.

Stakes can be made out of all kinds of recycled materials, including old sticks and pipe. Or you can buy stakes at your local garden center. My favorite store-bought stakes are made out of plastic-coated (usually green) metal rod. These are nice because they fit right into the natural colors of the greenhouse and are less noticeable. More commonly available are bamboo stakes, which also look natural but have less strength than the plastic-coated metal rods.

Bamboo works fine for staking smaller plants. If you have enough room, you can grow your own bamboo in the greenhouse. It provides excellent stakes, but be careful because it can become invasive in the bed, taking over any free space it can find in a very short time.

Be sure to bury the stake as deeply as possible to give your plant a good anchor. When you have your stake in place next to the plant, use soft string or a cloth strip to tie the plant to the stake. A tight string may strangle the plant over time as the diameter of the plant increases. When you put a stake in the ground for support, be careful not to damage any large fleshy roots that might be growing near the base of the plant.

PLANTING PATTERN FOR VEGETABLES IN WIDE BEDS

Certain crops grow much more efficiently when laid out in a triangular pattern in the bed. With a triangular layout, there is usually less wasted space than with square layouts. Another efficient layout is to just broadcast the seed much like a lawn (although not as thick as a lawn). I find this works great for leafy and root vegetable crops. This method leaves you with a solid bed of the plant with no wasted space. The broadcast method works best, however, when you don't sow too thickly and are diligent about thinning. If you skip the thinning job, you can forget having decent vegetables to har-

Appropriate Layout for Wide-Bed Vegetable Planting in the Greenhouse

Crop	Distance Between Plants	Mature Height	Layout
Beans, bush	6 feet (1.8 m)	10 inches (25 cm)	TRI
Beans, fava	4 inches (10 cm)	4 feet (1.2 m)	TRE
Beans, pole	4 inches (10 cm)	5 to 12 feet (1.5 to 3.6 m)	TRE
Beets	4 inches (10 cm)	10 inches (25 cm)	BRO
Broccoli	1 1/2 feet (.45 m)	2 feet (.6 m)	TRI
Brussels sprouts	1 1/2 feet (.45 m)	3 to 4 feet (.9 to 1.2 m)	TRI
Cabbage	1 foot (.3 m)	1 foot (.3 m)	TRI
Cantaloupe	3 feet (.9 m)	10 feet (3 m)	TRE
Carrots	1 1/2 inches (3.8 cm)	10 inches (25 cm)	BRO
Cauliflower	1 foot (.3 m)	15 inches (38 cm)	TRI
Celery	10 inches (25 cm)	1 foot (.3 m)	TRI
Collards	1 foot (.3 m)	3 to 4 feet (.9 to 1.2 m)	TRI
Cucumber	2 feet (.6 m)	10 to 15 feet+ (3 to 4.6 m+)	* %
Eggplant	1 1/2 feet (.45 m)	2 1/2 feet (.8 m)	TRI
Garlic	4 inches (10 cm)	8 inches (20 cm)	**
Kale	1 foot (.3 m)	1 foot (.3 m)	TRI
Kohlrabi	8 inches (20 cm)	1 foot (.3 m)	TRI
Lettuce	6 inches (15 cm)	10 inches (25 cm)	**
Onion, bulbs	5 inches (13 cm)	14 inches (36 cm)	TRI
Onion, greens	3 inches (8 cm)	1 foot (.3 m)	BRO
Parsley	1 foot (.3 m)	1 foot (.3 m)	TRI
Peas	5 inches (13 cm)	1 to 7 feet (.3 to 2 m)	TRE
Peppers	1 foot (.3 m)	2 1/2 feet (.8 m)	TRI
Radish	1 1/2 inches (3.8 cm)	6 to 8 inches (15 to 20 cm)	BRO
Spinach	5 to 8 inches (13 to 20 cm)	10 inches (25 cm)	**
Squash, summer	2 to 4 feet (.6 to 1.2 m)	2 1/2 feet (.8 m)	*
Squash, winter	4 to 5 feet (1.2 to 1.5 m)	10 to 15 feet+ (3 to 4.6 m+)	TRE
Swiss chard	1 foot (.3 m)	1 foot (.3 m)	TRI
Tomatoes, bush	2 feet (.6 m)	2 1/2 feet (.8 m)	TRI
Tomatoes, vining	2 to 3 feet (.6 to .9 m)	6 to 12 feet (1.8 to 3.6 m)	* %
Turnips	5 inches (13 cm)	10 inches (25 cm)	**
Watermelon	4 feet (1.2 m)	10 to 15 feet+ (3 to 4.6 m+)	TRE

TRE=Trellis TRI=Triangular BRO=Broadcast
*=Trellis or Triangular **=Triangular or Broadcast + =May grow taller, the roof is the limit.
% =Requires stake, especially when grown in a triangular layout.

Note: Heavy fruits such as watermelon, cantaloupe and winter squash will need a sling to support the developing fruit. Slip the developing fruit at baseball size into the end of a recycled nylon stocking. Tie the open end of the stocking to the trellis. Without a sling, the fruit may rip the whole vine off the trellis as it gets heavy. For more detail see Chapter 8, A Closer Look at the Plants.

Mixed plantings can greatly increase yields in limited growing areas.

vest. Refer to the following chart for the best method of laying out greenhouse vegetable plants.

HOW HARVESTING CAN AFFECT CROP LAYOUT

Some crops are harvested only one time, when they are mature. Examples include cabbage and carrots. Once they're harvested, that's it. You need to start over again. But other crops, such as Swiss chard, spinach or leaf lettuce, may be harvested many times, leaving the plant in the ground to continue growing between pickings. When planting vegetables in the greenhouse, always consider which category each crop fits into. Then, in the easy-to-reach places, plant the crops that are harvested many times. As you might have guessed, in the harder-to-reach places, put those plants that are harvested only once.

This type of layout will prevent some trampling of crops and compacting of your soil as you reach into the bed for harvesting.

MIXED PLANTING

Who says that each bed or area of bed has to be planted with all the same plant? With our seemingly logical minds and need for organization, this is the way most of us plant. Besides, that is the way we see farmers do it. But, it ain't necessarily so. You can mix it up. What does that mean? Well, if you are growing vegetables, you can cultivate a mixture of plants in one area, such as carrots with lettuce and an occasional broccoli plant (a good combination for winter growing).

It can be even a broader mix, including herbs, flowers, subtropical plants and vegetables. Why would you even want to mix things up like this? Here are some reasons: When two totally different plants grow next to each other, they compete less than two alike plants growing side by side, so you can plant more crops per square foot. For example, growing carrots next to lettuce: The carrot has a deep root system and the lettuce has a shallow one, so there will be less competition for water and nutrients. Because both plants can tolerate some partial shading, there is no competition for light.

Another reason for mixed planting is to take advantage of a slow-growing plant, squash, for example. While the squash plant is young, the space around it that will be taken up eventually may be used by a quick crop of radishes. By the time the leaves of the squash have matured, the radishes will be gastronomic history. This adds up to closer spacing, and closer spacing means higher total yields per square foot.

Mixed plantings help prevent disease infestation. Diseases are usually specific to plant families and often won't cross over to affect different families. A cabbage disease, for instance, usually won't affect the tomato family but could spread to broccoli, which is in the same family as cabbage (cole crop family). When a bed is interplanted with different crop families, disease infestation is limited and an epidemic is prevented.

Insects prefer constant and similar stimuli from plants, such as taste and smell. When a bed has many different plants growing in it, pests move much slower in their feeding because the stimuli are being constantly altered as they jump from plant to plant. Also, some plants, such as garlic and other herbs and plants with strong-smelling leaves, may repel certain insects and frustrate pest attacks. Now, this doesn't mean that you can totally control bugs by mixing your plantings, but it can slow their onslaught considerably.

The symbiotic effects of mixed plantings is beginning to be confirmed by research: Plants may secrete something that benefits adjacent and different plants. But secretions may also have negative effects. The research generally is still sketchy, and most information available is based on nonscientific observations or old tales. Please don't lose any sleep over planting combinations you have chosen for your greenhouse. It may be worthwhile to observe closely any repeated positive trends when you mix up your plantings. Keeping records and notes on your greenhouse can help you learn some of these trends.

Mixing up your plantings also has its disadvantages. You will

Radishes are in and out of the bed before squash plants take over the space.

often have to harvest each plant at a different time. This makes it harder to renew the soil and replant after a harvest without disturbing the other crop's root systems. Also, it's sometimes more difficult to see when a crop is ready to harvest, so you may have vegetables sneaking past their prime harvest time before you notice them.

If you are mixing flowers with vegetables, you should make a point of never mixing in any plant that could have poisonous plant parts. They could be inadvertently harvested (along with your vegetables) and possibly consumed. See specific flower crops in Chapter 8, A Closer Look at the Plants, for a discussion on poisonous plants.

An integrated bed has a wilder look to it, which some enjoy but others have trouble getting used to—especially those who prefer organized-looking gardens.

It is harder but not impossible to attempt mixed plantings in pots, tubs and other containers. It does help, however, to use a larger container with room for more than one plant.

So, with these negatives, should you mix up your plantings or not?

The answer is sometimes yes and sometimes no. It's a matter of what you want to grow, space considerations, and above all, personal preferences.

I like to do it here and there, but not all the time. I especially like to mix flowers and herbs with vegetables in my growing beds. It adds to the overall beauty of the greenhouse. My attitude has changed about gardening as a result of some experiments with mixed plantings. I've decided that a garden doesn't have to be a picture of perfect order. I've even played around with some controlled chaos by taking a handful of selected seeds and randomly spreading them into a prepared bed. Later, I thin them out to the proper distances. This random pattern of different plants often becomes a very productive (wild-looking) bed. On the whole, however, an organized style of integrated planting, combining triangles, trellises and broadcast plantings, is easier to manage, especially when you are new to gardening.

To maximize the benefits of an integrated planting, try to mix plants from different families, but be sure they are all able to do well in the same microclimate. Also, avoid mixing physically similar plants. For instance, you'll have better results mixing a root crop with a leafy crop, such as onions with lettuce, than mixing two leafy crops, such as lettuce with spinach. Try mixing crops sown in a broadcast style with triangle-layout crops, or trellis crops with broadcast crops.

By mixing flowers and herbs with your vegetables, you not only will add to the beauty of the greenhouse, but the flowers will provide a backup food source for beneficial insects and may repel harmful pests (see Chapter 10, When Things Go Wrong). Some flowers are edible and will be a great mix in a vegetable bed. Above all, be cre-

Broadcast planting mixed with triangular planting.

ative with mixing up your plantings; experiment and have fun.

Although mixing plantings is helpful, when you are laying out the plants in your greenhouse, you should be sure to also think about the effects of crops shading each other, planting at the proper time and selecting the proper varieties for your greenhouse.

Crop Rotation

Crop rotation, an old practice, is still important when you are planting in the same bed season after season. You might think that you will remember what you have grown in each area as time goes on, but I can almost guarantee you that you won't. This is where good record-keeping is important so you can remember what has occurred in each area over time.

Whenever possible, try to wait a year or two before planting the same crop in the same place. It also helps to avoid vegetables of the same plant group in the same place year after year. Why do this? It is good preventative medicine against major diseases that can accumulate in soil over time. You can help reduce the buildup of disease organisms by adding healthy amounts of organic matter to the soil between crops or a minimum of once a year (see Chapter 9, Getting to the Roots).

Crop Maturity

You'll find that crops will generally have different maturity times (often called "days to harvest") than specified on packets of seed or in catalogs. To better time your planting and harvesting, especially in winter, allow a 20 to 30 percent longer period than listed for crops to reach the harvest stage. For fall and spring greenhouse crops, add 10 to 15 percent more time to the days to harvest. Now, don't feel bad about the slower growth in fall, spring and winter; it's still not bad compared to zero growth outside.

Rotating crops creates fewer disease problems and healthier soil.

Basic Crop Families

This guide will help you plan integrated crop plantings and crop rotation season to season. Always try to cross-mix the groups wherever possible.

Cabbage Family
(Cole Crop or Crucifers)

Broccoli	Kale
Brussels sprouts	Kohlrabi
Cabbage	Mustard
Cauliflower	Nasturtium
Chinese cabbage	Radish
Collards	Rutabaga
Cress	Stock
	Turnips

Onion Family
(Alliums)

Chives
Leeks
Onions
Scallions
Shallots

Legume Family

Beans (soy, bush, garbanzo,
    broad, fava, wax, lima, pole)
Cowpeas
Peas
Sweet peas

Beet Family

Beets
Spinach
Swiss chard

Carrot Family

Anise	Caraway
Carrots	Celery
Coriander (cilantro)	Dill
Fennel	Parsley

Tomato Family

Angel's-trumpet
Eggplant
Nicotiana
Peppers
Petunia
Potato
Tobacco
Tomatoes
Salpiglossis
Datura

Cucumber Family

Melons	Cantaloupe
Cucumber	Pumpkins
Squash (summer and winter)	
Watermelon	

Selecting
the Right
Plants

4

Selecting the Right Plants

In earlier chapters, we have looked extensively at the environment and even the microenvironments of the greenhouse. Selecting the right plant and the right variety of plant can make a huge difference in your chance for success or failure. The first question many people ask is "Where do you get the best seeds?" You will find seed racks in almost every grocery and hardware store (especially in spring) along with the traditionally more extensive seed racks found at garden centers. I use seed racks only when I am pressed for time and can't wait the 3 or more weeks to order from a catalog. For the most part, I prefer ordering from catalogs for the following reasons:

Advantages of Ordering from Catalogs

1. *Freshness.* The seed is usually fresher and comes directly out of being in a proper storage situation, which results in better germination.

2. *Selection.* A good catalog will offer many more varieties to choose from than a seed rack. For instance, a seed rack will have only 3 or 4 tomatoes to choose from. One catalog I often use commonly offers more than 20 varieties! A better selection means I can have a better chance at finding a variety well suited to my greenhouse.

3. *Description.* Many catalogs do a good job of giving you a detailed description of the varieties they carry. This will often include the plant's physical characteristics as well as the diseases to which the plant may have a resistance.

When you are ordering seeds or plants for your greenhouse, be sure to specify when you want them sent to you. Many catalogs assume that you'll be using the seeds or plants for the outside garden and automatically send them in spring. Be aware of having any plant shipped in the middle of winter (when it could freeze) or in the middle of summer (when plants will get scorched). When plants arrive by mail, don't hesitate to rescue them from the box and give them the care they need. Usually instructions will be included. It takes a few weeks for the plants to get over the shock of transcontinental travel.

When you order vegetable seeds, take the listed number of days until harvest with a big grain of salt. If you do a little comparison for the same variety of seed, you will find that these figures are usually different in different catalogs. Look at the days until harvest numbers like the E.P.A. mileage figures on new cars: Use them for comparison, don't believe them literally. Like Ronald Reagan used to say when negotiating with the Soviets, "trust but verify." The numbers are good for comparing things in the same catalog. Over time, you will figure out how long each crop will take. Read Chapter 7,

Scheduling, to help you along.

Even though I prefer to use catalogs, I have learned that they are not all created equal. I have found real discrepancies in price, service and selection. It pays to do some comparing. If you find that you are disappointed with a plant or seed you received from a catalog, most of the time you can get a refund or credit toward something else. I have yet to find a catalog in the seed and plant business that hasn't gone to extremes to please me if I feel like I have been had.

To enable you to use a catalog as a learning experience and to fully understand what is being offered, read the first few pages of the catalog with a sharp eye. Here, you will often find a shorthand guide (using a little symbol or letter) that is keyed to certain characteristics of the plant. Once you understand these notations, you can learn a lot more about a variety in question.

For a listing of catalogs providing essentials for the greenhouse, please refer to the Mail-Order Supplies appendix. A few companies charge for a copy of their catalog (what nerve!), while most of the others will have you on their mailing list long after you are dead and gone. I find reading a new seed and plant catalog as entertaining as a good book. Each one has its own personality. Some read like the *National Enquirer* or *Ripley's Believe It or Not*. Some are snooty, and others are unabashedly aimed toward the upwardly mobile. Over the years, gardening catalogs become like an odd collection of friends that invade your mailbox from December through spring.

It is easy to get the ailment my friend Sharon Gaus calls seed-catalog burnout. The main symptoms include being overwhelmed by all of the choices in the catalog and the sometimes uncontrollable desire to grow everything and anything. The severity of seed-catalog burnout increases with the number of mailing lists you are on. The cure? First, get yourself off the mailing lists of the catalogs that you absolutely have no interest in. It will help you and helps reduce the solid waste in landfills that originates in your mailbox each day. When you request a catalog, ask that they not sell your name to any other catalog or mailing list.

Second, when you are looking at a catalog, try to keep in mind exactly what you need. If something strikes your fancy, ask yourself, "Where will it grow?" "Is there room for it in my greenhouse?" And, if it is a food crop, "Who will eat it?" A good rule to avoid seed-

catalog burnout is: When in doubt, don't order it.

SELECTING VEGETABLE VARIETIES

Selecting the best plant variety or crop for greenhouse food production will help maximize yields in your greenhouse. This decision may seem easy and unimportant at first thought, but it is one of the most important factors in how much food you are going to grow. Let's say you wanted to grow some greens, such as spinach. Well, spinach is a fine plant to grow in the winter greenhouse, but if you instead made the decision to grow Swiss chard in the same place, you could quadruple your yields. The reason? Spinach bolts (goes to seed) with warm, sunny days. I have had spinach bolt on me in only 5 weeks of growth. Bolting ends the productive life of the plant because it quits producing edible leaves. The best thing to do is pull it up and start over. Swiss chard rarely goes to seed (unless you give it a frost), so it produces abundantly for many seasons, if not years. Swiss chard is a relative of spinach and tastes similar to it. When cooked, they are impossible to tell apart. Many people even prefer Swiss chard to spinach. But there are those of you who still won't eat it over spinach. No problem. Grow spinach, and put up with less of a harvest (but at least give chard a try first).

If you are really concerned with a productive food-producing greenhouse, then you need to think about every crop and how it grows before you decide to plant it. By their nature, some plants just produce more edible food than others. For example, compare cauliflower to cabbage. Virtually the whole cabbage plant is edible, every last leaf. Cauliflower produces many leaves that are tossed out, leaving a small edible head. Imagine two equal-sized plots of land, one growing cabbage and the other cauliflower. The total poundage of food in the cabbage plot will be much greater than that from the cauliflower plot.

Another example: Compare peas to beets. Peas require space to grow many leaves before you can harvest the small, round sweet pea. Beets, on the other hand, are almost 100 percent edible. The greens, or tops, are excellent when cooked like spinach. And, of course, the roots are edible. There is little waste. With a crop of peas, the vines, leaves and roots are all thrown out (or composted). Hence, with peas, less food per growing space is produced than with beets.

So, if you are after high yields, you may want to give the crop some thought.

Don't get me wrong. I'm not trying to talk you out of growing peas or any other crop. Peas are one of my favorite things to grow and eat in a greenhouse. I only want to get you to think about these plants in a different light. If the price of fresh food were to skyrocket, or in emergency or survival situations, these considerations might become very important.

Sometimes, it all comes down to the taste buds, old habits and what people are used to. What good is a bushel of greenhouse-grown radishes if nobody likes radishes? Be sure you plant only what will be consumed.

To be economical, avoid growing food in a greenhouse that can be stored easily or purchased cheaply. Why grow potatoes when they can be purchased cheaply and keep great in your root cellar? Instead, get the most value out of your greenhouse by growing the more expensive and perishable crops.

I wish I could just give you a list of what will do best in your greenhouse and send you on your way. The trouble is, every greenhouse is different. It depends on where you live and the orientation and construction of your greenhouse or sunroom. No one variety will work for everyone's greenhouse. Also, plant varieties change rapidly, with old varieties being dropped and replaced by new ones. Whenever possible, I will list specific varieties of plants that I have found to perform the best over a wide variety of circumstances. Most of these plants are listed in Chapter 8, A Closer Look at the Plants.

To best complement these plant recommendations, it is my hope that you will learn to understand the special qualities of your greenhouse. Discover its personality. Then you can make better decisions about which varieties will do best for you.

PLANTS FOR THE SOLAR-HEATED AND COOL WINTER GREENHOUSE

When it comes to selecting plants for the greenhouse, usually the greenhouse that runs cool in winter and the solar-heated greenhouse have more exacting requirements. A greenhouse that constantly runs a minimum of 60° F (15° C) at night can grow most any crop year-round without much problem, as long as the light, soil and water requirements are correct. But a greenhouse that gets down to the 40s or even the 30s (0° to 9° C) requires some special consideration. It helps to start subscribing to the good seed catalogs. While you look through the many selections, keep the following considerations in mind.

Selection For Heat Tolerance

Whenever your greenhouse is above 85° F (29° C) in the winter or above 90° F (32° C) in the summer, it's too hot for maximum plant growth. Above these temperatures, plant growth usually slows, blossoms will not set fruit and many edible leafy plants and root crops will go to seed prematurely. Surprisingly, in areas with sunny winters you can often have as much of a problem with high temperatures in the winter as you do in summer. The best way to deal with warm temperatures in an attached greenhouse in winter is to ventilate into your house ... and to grow plants that can tolerate warm winter temperatures.

Leafy crops are usually best grown in the cooler months of the year. A greenhouse in an area with sunny winters may be too hot for good production of many leafy and root crops. To minimize any

Instead of bolting as above, a more heat-tolerant variety of lettuce will produce harvests over longer periods.

problems, you can do a little research in the seed catalogs for plants that can thrive in a hotter situation. Just look for plant descriptions that say "heat tolerant, heat resistant or slow to bolt." I usually can find a selection of lettuce and spinach (and occasionally radishes) with this type of notation. Another solution is to grow substitute crops, such as New Zealand spinach or Swiss chard, which are perennial in the greenhouse and will produce quality greens for many years regardless of the temperature, as long as it is above freezing.

Other plants may not bolt or go to seed but respond to overheating in other ways. For example, yields of peas drop drastically with hot daytime temperatures. However, certain pea varieties are tolerant of heat as well as being cold hardy. All it takes is some close investigation of the seed catalogs.

Vegetables in the Cold Greenhouse

Some people prefer to not heat their greenhouses in the winter, while others with solar greenhouses don't have to worry about heating, because they can let the sun do most of the work. Either way, if you have a greenhouse that consistently has cold night temperatures and you want to grow things, there are some great options.

When it comes to vegetables in the icebox greenhouse, it is best to stick to plants that are grown for their roots or leaves, with the only exception being peas and plants in the cole/cabbage family, such as broccoli, cauliflower and kohlrabi. Some of these plants can even tolerate temperatures below freezing.

For years I had a greenhouse that would get down to 25° F (-4° C), when outside it would be -25° F (-31° C). I was still able to grow vegetables by sticking to plants that can tolerate some frost. In fall, before it got cold, I would start spinach, French sorrel, Swiss chard, lettuce, broccoli, chives, top-set onions, radishes and carrots. I also grew some herbs, including rosemary, fennel, dill and cilantro, which all grow great in the cold. In the dead of winter, I could still count on a tasty leafy salad and a few herbs even with ice in the watering can. I even grew a few pansies and snapdragons, which are also incredibly cold tolerant.

If you plan to grow vegetables in a cold greenhouse, select varieties that have a relatively short number of days until harvest. This can mean a shorter wait for you. But don't expect your plants to be harvested in the number of days listed on the seed packet. It will take quite a few more days with the cold temperatures and short days of winter. Another thing you should know about plants that have a short number of days until harvest is that they may often be smaller or lower-yielding plants. This is especially true when compared to the longer-maturing varieties. But it is still worthwhile to grow quicker-maturing varieties in the cold greenhouse because it might be a choice of a smaller harvest compared to none at all.

NITRATE IN THE COOL WINTER GREENHOUSE

Leafy vegetables such as spinach and lettuce, when grown in a cool winter greenhouse, can accumulate high levels of nitrate. At high levels, nitrate can be dangerous to infants and pose potential health problems to children and adults. The nitrate is taken up by the roots from the soil. When there is adequate light, the nitrate is a beneficial fertilizer that is quickly converted into plant proteins. When there is low light in the greenhouse accompanied by cool temperatures, the nitrate is not converted into protein and instead accumulates in the leaf. The nitrate accumulation increases when the soil is rich in nitrogen.

The folks at the former New Alchemy Institute in East Falmouth, Massachusetts, did some excellent research into this problem. They recommended some ways to minimize nitrate in greens grown in cool winter greenhouses. First, select the right varieties. New Alchemy found that certain varieties take up less nitrate than others. Green ice lettuce (found in Burpee and Park seed catalogs) takes up 20 to 40 percent less nitrate than the greenhouse bibb variety Diamante. Researchers also found that the romaine lettuce variety

Winter Density and bibb varieties Jeanette, Cantille and Sabrina had 12 to 15 percent less nitrate. Second, plan your harvest according to the calender. The researchers found that nitrate levels were highest near the winter solstice but much lower on crops harvested in the warmer, sunnier month of March.

New Alchemy further recommended that you:

Tips to Avoid Nitrate Accumulation in Edible Plants in Winter

1. Avoid the application of nitrogen fertilizers to greenhouse greens in the darker winter months.
2. Harvest later in the day on sunny afternoons, especially after a few consecutive clear days.
3. Harvest the older, more mature outer leaves first.
4. Set the harvested plants (roots and all) in water for 24 to 48 hours before eating.
5. Grow other edible crops in the winter besides just greens.

Unfortunately, the New Alchemy Institute, after 22 years of working on food, energy, water, waste and small farming issues, is no longer in business. In its day, New Alchemy sparked a new environmental awareness and demonstrated the importance of the home greenhouse. They helped people to do more with less while treading on our planet in a lighter, less destructive way. Fortunately, the institute produced and nurtured not only ideas but many good people who have moved on to private and public projects. These people continue to have a positive impact on how we treat the land and our environment.

Selection for Fruit and Vegetable Shape and Size

When a plant grows vertically, it can make better use of often unused air space. If you are growing vegetables or flowers, vertical growing might mean more of both for you to enjoy. Because the growing space in a greenhouse always seems to be limited, it is sometimes wise to grow vining or vertically growing varieties as opposed to bushy varieties. When it comes to vegetables, there are many types that grow either bushy and low or tall and vining. These include peas, beans, cucumber, squash, melons, figs and bananas. Tomatoes are also included in this list, but horticulturists have a special vocabulary for them that might pose some confusion. Bushy tomatoes are called "determinate" because they grow to a determined height and then the main leader on the plant quits growing. Tomatoes that grow tall and viney are called "indeterminate." That is because they can grow indeterminately, given the right growing conditions.

Bushy vegetable varieties can fit into special places in the greenhouse or sunroom, like next to a knee wall with little headroom. But one of the best places to use bushy varieties is in pots. The tall vining varieties grown in a pot might quickly get out of balance, with too much top supported by a small, limited root system. This will cause the plant to wilt at the slightest provocation. It will be under constant stress, which is an invitation to every bug and disease in the area. This type of plant stress can be avoided—just make sure that the pot or container corresponds to the size of the mature plant. I have had great luck growing bush beans in hanging baskets. I like to grow bushy determinate tomatoes in 1- to 5-gallon (3.8- to 19-liter) pots with great yields.

Determinate and indeterminate tomatoes

Bush varieties grow well by a knee wall.

Play around with bushy vegetable varieties in pots, and you'll see that it works great.

Selection for Disease Resistance

The inherent high humidity of greenhouses and intensive plant production can bring conditions that promote plant diseases. The best defense against disease is to maintain healthy plant growth. But you can also help things out by selecting varieties that show some tolerance or resistance to a particular disease problem. Again, this is where you need to really study the seed catalogs and look for any listed "resistant to diseases." Before you start, it is important to make every effort to identify your disease problem. Begin by reading Chapter 10, When

Things Go Wrong. There are also many good books on plant diseases as well as good resources through your local university. Your county agricultural extension agent can also be helpful in identifying a particular disease problem.

Many plants show variability in their resistance to diseases. I had a problem with powdery mildew affecting squash and cucumbers. Powdery mildew is a white powdery fungus growth that covers the leaves and slows growth. I went back to the catalog and found varieties that were listed as resistant to powdery mildew. By just changing varieties, I was able to see about an 80 percent decrease in the disease without doing anything else to control it.

You should know, however, that the degree of resistance may vary a good deal, from totally resistant to slightly resistant. Don't be surprised if you are growing a variety that is listed as resistant to a certain disease and still see evidence of it. The variety may be only more tolerant than other varieties. That is something that isn't specialized in the catalogs. Usually you have to find out for yourself.

You may discover that some varieties have some resistance to a disease, even though it is not listed as such in the catalogs. For this reason, don't put all your eggs in one basket. Try to grow more than one variety of a particular crop, and nature's genetic diversity will work for you. This is how you learn what works and what doesn't. Good record-keeping is also helpful in determining what worked well and what was mediocre. Don't be lazy about record-keeping. It's not hard and will provide you with valuable information not available anywhere else.

Selection for Insect Pest Resistance

Plant varieties that exhibit resistance to insect pests are more rare than those resistant to disease. The better catalogs will tell you about their resistance, but usually you have to learn on your own. You will find that some plants are naturally more resistant to bug attacks. For instance, I used to grow a light-green Grand Rapids lettuce variety called Slo Bolt. It was a good producer in winter, spring and fall, but it was often attacked by aphid and white fly. I switched to two newer, related varieties, Green Ice and Royal Green. They were darker green, and I found that the bugs were less attracted to the darker green lettuce varieties. For some reason the bugs just loved the color of the lighter green plants. The change made a huge difference in my bug problem.

Don't expect that just by changing varieties you will totally eliminate a bug problem, but it can make a deciding difference. Again, keep records. There may be other reasons for a crop's insect tolerance besides just the color of the leaf. Be observant. Watch the changes year to year among the varieties to be sure a change in bug infestation is truly because of a change in varieties and not because it might have been a bad year for bugs (yes, bugs can have good years and bad years).

GREENHOUSE VARIETIES

There have been many vegetable and flower varieties that have been developed especially for commercial greenhouses that sometimes are offered in regular retail seed catalogs. These greenhouse varieties have been selected for high productivity under ideal conditions of light and temperatures in a totally controlled energy-intensive environment. Often these varieties exhibit the characteristics of disease resistance, high yields, vining growth, bolt resistance (lettuce) and resistance to physiological disorders (i.e., fruit cracking on tomatoes). In the case of cucumbers, some varieties don't require pollination to set fruit.

In good catalogs, these varieties are usually flagged with a statement such as "For greenhouse production" or "For forcing." Forcing is a common term used to describe greenhouse growing that forces the plant to grow out of season. I always thought it was a term that sounded like cruelty to plants. Two catalogs that commonly list greenhouse varieties are Stokes and Johnny's (see the Mail-Order Seeds appendix). When you are reading these catalogs, you might, for instance, find a greenhouse cucumber (sometimes called a European Forcing Cucumber) that does well in cooler temperatures and is tolerant to powdery mildew. Here is where you apply what you know about your greenhouse environment and your greenhouse's specific problems with diseases in order to select the right variety.

You might also be able to get ahold of a wholesale catalog that commercial growers use, or even buy some seed off of a local commercial greenhouse grower. Greenhouse varieties are available for only a limited number of crops right now. Hopefully, in the future, people will show the seed companies that there is a large demand for these varieties. Maybe then they'll start breeding a whole slew of crops specifically for the greenhouse and even the solar-greenhouse environment.

Here are plants that you may find available in a catalog that have been developed for greenhouse growing. Vegetables: certain herbs, cucumber, lettuce, peppers and tomatoes. Flowers: alstromeria, aster, calceolaria, carnation, chrysanthemum, cineraria, cyclamen, freesia, gerbera, ranunculus, rose, snapdragon and stock.

CROPS THAT NEED WINTER

Why not grow native wildflowers, asparagus, rhubarb, cherries, peaches, pears, apricots, currants and raspberries in your greenhouse? There are a couple of problems here. First, these crops are usually grown outside and the cold of winter is required for them to grow normally. Without the winter cold treatment, they would not produce properly. Also, these crops require an appreciable amount of space and produce for only a relatively short time. Depending on where you live, these crops may do just fine outside and, unfortunately, won't do much better inside unless you live where summer frosts are common.

But there are those of us who wish we could be eating fresh rhubarb or peaches in the winter. Well, with some effort there are ways to pull it off, although I'm not sure if it is worth it. You can sometimes fake a winter, or force a crop, as horticulturists put it. Different crops and varieties have different chill requirements, and these can be imitated artificially. One way to do this is to go outside in midwinter or early spring, carefully dig up the plants (you may need a pick for the frozen soil) and transplant them inside for late-winter harvests. The half-winter treatment is usually enough to ensure proper production. The wintertime transplanting method is, of course, much harder with an 8-foot (2.4-meter) peach tree, but it can be done with dwarf varieties in moveable containers on rollers.

These winter-loving temperate crops warrant further experimentation and development. There is some good potential for growing crops such as asparagus and rhubarb in winter greenhouses. In the South, plant breeders have developed varieties of temperate crops that require less chilling to produce. Look through some small regional southern plant catalogs to find these low-chill requirement plants.

VIVE LA DIFFÉRENCE

As you gain more experience in the greenhouse, you will find it is rare for the same variety that you grew outside to do well inside. The extra yields of vegetables and flowers make the reward well worth selecting plants especially suited to the greenhouse environment. The inside garden and the outside garden are two different and special worlds and for the most part should be treated as such.

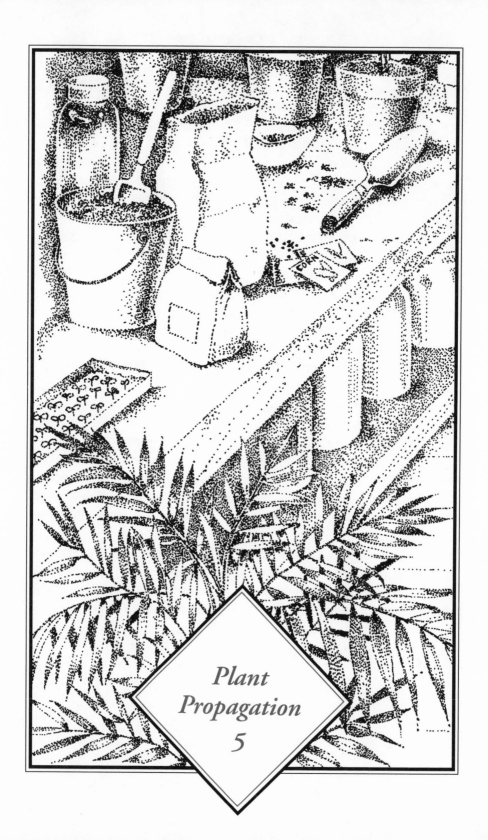

*Plant
Propagation
5*

Plant Propagation

I'm always amazed at the incredible selection of goods when I walk into a big supermarket. Now we have hypermarts, which are even bigger and have most any commodity a person could ever need or want. With this luxury of selection, we become even more disconnected with where things come from. "Where did it come from?" is a most important question we all should be asking more often.

I remember asking a little girl where she thought her french fries came from. She said, "France." Eggs? "The egg factory." Pineapple? "A pine tree." She said that bananas came from the store. It's a healthy thing to wonder where things originate. It is even healthier to be directly involved in the creation of things that are important to us.

Plants grow from seeds or spores; from cuttings, grafting or divisions from existing plants; or from runners that spread new plants from above or below the ground.

Your ability to start plants in your greenhouse is the heart of good gardening skills. Starting your own plants provides the greatest reward of any gardening activity you undertake. After all, what can be more satisfying than becoming involved in the process of creating new life?

If you never become good at starting your own plants, you are stuck with the task of always buying them. This can become expensive, and you will be forever dependent upon others for your plants.

There are simple tricks you can use in the greenhouse for starting and establishing plants that can result in better efficiency. For example, rather than wasting precious bed space waiting for seeds to germinate, use another area for starting seedlings. Many greenhouse growers propagate seedlings in the basement under lights or on top of thermal mass water drums in solar-heated greenhouses.

When seedlings are ready to plant out, 4 to 6 weeks later, you can transplant them into a bed the very same day you rip out an old planting. It is like hitting the ground running.

In this chapter we will discuss the art of starting seeds and starting plants directly from the mother plant, using cuttings or divisions.

SEED PROPAGATION

Seeds come from the plant flower. Pollination fertilizes the egg within the flower, and the results of this sexual reproduction are seeds. Seeds are truly amazing self-contained units. They are new genetic individuals. Within each seed is an embryonic plant and a food reserve to get the plant going until it can provide for itself: a nice little complete package.

The first step for the gardener is to obtain new high-quality seeds.

Older seeds produce lower-quality plants with less vigor. They are slower to germinate, and a lower percentage of older seed germinates at all. They may also be more susceptible to disease. How long do seeds stay viable? Every species is different. If the seeds are stored properly, you can count on 3 to 4 years for most vegetables, but onions and beets are usually good only for a couple of years. Tomatoes, peppers, watermelon, cucumber and cantaloupe can stay viable for 5 years or more. Most flower seed can be stored for around 3 years if done properly. The fresher the seed, the better the germination and plant vigor. If possible, avoid storing seeds for more than one season by ordering no more than you will use. To help determine the proper amount to order, refer to the following list of the number of seeds per ounce. It is easy to see that a little amount of seed can go a long way.

These seedlings will soon be ready for transplanting.

Number of Seeds Per Ounce

Ornamentals and Herbs	Approx. No. of Seeds per Ounce	Vegetables	Approx. No. of Seeds per Ounce
Ageratum	130,000	Beans	120
Alyssum	90,000	Broccoli	10,000
Basil	20,000	Brussels sprouts	8,500
Begonia	2,000,000	Cabbage	7,500
Browallia	120,000	Cantaloupe	1,000
Calceolaria	640,000	Carrots	15,000
Calendula	3,000	Cauliflower	10,000
Carnation	14,000	Celery	70,000
Chives	22,000	Chinese cabbage	16,000
Cineraria	100,000	Collards	9,500
Coleus	100,000	Cucumber	1,000
Coriander	19,000	Eggplant	6,000
Cosmos	5,000	Kale	8,500
Dahlia	2,800	Kohlrabi	8,000
Dill	6,300	Lettuce	20,000
Fennel	8,000	Okra	550
Geranium	6,200	Onions	9,500
Impatiens	44,000	Peas	150
Lavender	25,000	Peppers	4,500
Marigold	10,000	Radish	2,500
Mimulus	700,000	Spinach	2,000
Nasturtium	175	Squash	250
Nicotiana	400,000	Tomatoes	10,000
Pansy	20,000	Watermelon	250
Parsley	19,000		
Phlox	14,000		
Rosemary	24,000		
Salpiglossis	125,000		
Snapdragon	180,000		
Stock	18,500		
Sweet pea	300		
Thyme	76,000		
Verbena	10,000		
Viola	24,000		
Zinnia	2,500		

Storing Seeds

Seeds are best stored in an airtight container such as a glass jar. Seeds like a place that is dry, dark and cool, close to freezing but not below 32° F (0° C). To maintain a dry atmosphere, I store seeds in glass jars with a teaspoon of dried milk to help absorb any possible moisture coming off the seeds. Put a label on the jar that tells you what is inside, and to be as organized as possible when you store seeds because they have a natural tendency to become disorganized. Try to keep similar seed in the same jar, each in its own envelope or packet. Don't mix this year's seed with last year's, so you can keep track of how old the seed is.

Hybrids

When you are looking through seed catalogs, one of the first choices you often will find is whether you want to grow hybrids or nonhybrids (sometimes called open-pollinated seeds). A hybrid is defined as the result of two genetically diverse parents. Nowadays it means more. Agricultural scientists have developed what is called the F1 hybrid. This hybrid is created by a long process of inbreeding two different parent lines

for a specific number of years. During the inbreeding, each parent line is kept separate. After the period of inbreeding, usually many years, the two lines are finally cross-pollinated. The resulting seed is the F1 hybrid seed. Where does the designation F1 come from? It is the First generation after the inbreeding is completed. When you see the word "hybrid" in a catalog or on a seed packet, it means F1 hybrid.

Why do seed companies go to all this trouble? Hybrids have some distinct advantages. They also have a few disadvantages. You should know about both.

Because you can't harvest your own seed from hybrids with acceptable results, you are forced to purchase new seeds each season. Seed companies love this—especially because the hybrids are more expensive, creating a higher profit margin. Farmers and professional greenhouse growers don't mind the higher-priced seed, because the extra yield of hybrids more than makes up for the cost.

There is much controversy about hybrids. Most of it is associated with the cost of the seed and the need to depend upon seed companies. There is also controversy surrounding the lack of use (and subsequent loss) of the old-fashioned varieties, whose genetic

Mail-Order Tips

As I mentioned in Chapter 4, Selecting the Right Plants, I prefer to acquire seeds from catalogs. I use the seed racks only when I am pressed for time and can't wait the 3 or more weeks to order from a catalog. Here are a few tips to keep in mind when ordering:

1. Let the company know if you don't want substitutes. Oftentimes you have your heart set on obtaining one particular variety, and if it's out of stock, you might not get what you want.

2. Experiment. Order a few different varieties of the same plant. In a short growing season it's helpful to test different varieties until you are sure which one has the best performance. Be wary of a new variety on the market; it may not be as good as your old standby. Test the new variety next to the old one. Don't give up on the tried and true until the new is well proven.

3. Carefully follow the ordering instructions. Read the fine print for hidden items such as shipping and packing costs and possible sales tax. Some catalogs may even offer free growing information or free test seeds, if you mark the right box.

4. Make a copy of the order. Having a duplicate will tell you if you received the full order or if unauthorized substitutions were made. I like to make special notes on my copy, including the page that each variety is found and where I plan to grow the plant.

5. Date the seed packets when they arrive. Many companies already have a date on the packet, but if not, do it yourself immediately after your seeds arrive. This will help you in future years to determine if the seed is too old to plant. Seeds older than 2 or 3 years may have a lower germination rate and less growing vigor.

If you are disappointed with a plant or seed you grew from a catalog, most of the time you can get a refund or credit toward something else. I have yet to find a catalog company that hasn't gone to extremes for dissatisfied customers.

Be sure to check out the extensive Mail-Order Supplies appendix in this book.

The Advantages of Using Hybrid Seed

1. Hybrids can have up to 25 percent higher yield.
2. Hybrid plants are physically uniform. This is advantageous for farmers who harvest with machines.
3. Hybrids show greater vigor and faster growth.
4. Hybrids may have special disease resistance.

The Disadvantages of Using Hybrid Seed

1. Higher cost. Hybrids are up to five times more expensive because they take longer and are more trouble to produce.
2. They often require a more exacting horticulture. When things aren't optimum, they suffer more than nonhybrid open-pollinated seeds.
3. If you save and grow seeds from an F1 hybrid plant, don't expect a similar plant in the next generation. The resulting plants in the second generation are usually much lower yielding, have less vigor and are quite variable in their physical characteristics. You don't know what you are going to get, and usually you'll lose all the advantages you had in growing the original hybrid.

---

makeup is more diverse. Some organizations have made wonderful efforts to maintain availability of the older seeds and those sometimes known as heirloom seeds. If you're looking for a hobby, I can't think of a better one than helping to preserve heirloom seeds. If you are interested in saving heirloom seeds, contact Kent Whealy at the Seed Savers Exchange, Rt. 3, Box 239, Decorah, IA 52101.

So, if a plant is sold as a hybrid, is it bad? No. Using hybrids is not a black-and-white issue. I have found a few hybrids that perform so well in the greenhouse that I routinely use them for various reasons. Sometimes I find a hybrid has the disease resistance that I am in need of, or a hybrid may have just proved to be better yielding. You will have to decide whether hybrids are worth it for you. If you are discouraged because you can't produce seed from your hybrid plant, you can always try reproducing the plant from cuttings as outlined later in this chapter. The best way to evaluate the worth of the hybrid is to compare it with nonhybrid varieties in your greenhouse.

Germinating Seeds

To germinate seeds, you must create a specific environment. Think about setting aside a special area for starting seeds within the greenhouse or even somewhere else in your house that has moderate temperatures and light. Good ventilation also helps. On the next page is a detailed list of what is needed for good germination.

Bottom heating pads provide more consistent temperature control.

PLANTING SEEDS

Starting plants from seed is by far the most common method of getting new plants. It is always amazing to see what can come from one little seed in a short time. Starting plants from seed is almost always cheaper than starting with plants. Sometimes it may be the only way to acquire a plant. In general, starting plants from seed is not hard to do. In fact, people often start too many seeds.

Vegetables are usually easier to start than flowers, often because many flowering plants have such small seed. There are many excep-

Seedlings in pots

Tips for Good Germination

1. *Disease-free soil and pots.* Many seedling diseases cause poor germination. Diseases can be borne on old, dirty pots. It's always a good idea to recycle, but if you are going to use an old pot, wash it well with some detergent and a little bleach. Old potting soil or garden soil can also harbor diseases. You can heat sterilize the soil (see Sterilized Soil for Starting Seeds, p. 144) to kill diseases before you use it. Even easier, you can start your seedlings in store-bought potting soil. See seedling diseases in Chapter 10, When Things Go Wrong.

2. *Moisture (for germination and seedlings).* Seedlings that are germinating usually need constant moisture, so keep the soil moist but not dripping wet. If the soil dries out even once, it might kill germinating seedlings. If your tap water is extremely cold in winter, you can speed germination by using warm water on the seedlings. Be careful of water pressure or nozzles that create a force so powerful that it blasts the seeds out of the soil. Gently mist seedlings with a spray, much like a light, gentle rain. Misting nozzles available at good garden centers or in catalogs are ideal for watering seedlings. In general, seedlings need a bit less water than do seeds, so cut back slightly once they germinate.

3. *Moisture (for seeds and cuttings).* High humidity and moisture are also beneficial to starting both seeds and cuttings. Mist the plants with a spray bottle a few times a day or set up a misting system. Many greenhouse catalogs offer misting systems (see Water for a discussion of misting systems, p. 52).

4. *Aeration.* Because seedlings need air to germinate, make sure the soil isn't constantly saturated. All containers in which you start seeds should have a drainage hole in the bottom.

5. *Soil temperature.* In the winter, many greenhouse gardeners have trouble germinating seedlings. This is often due to cold soil temperatures. Though plants vary in their temperature requirements, usually seeds have trouble germinating when the soil temperature is below 50° F (10° C). A temperature of 65° to 75° F (18° to 24° C) is optimum for germinating most seeds. Extreme high and low temperatures are harmful. In the cold season you can create

a microclimate of warmth by using heating cables or pads as discussed in chapters 1 and 2, The Greenhouse Environment and Interior Design. I prefer the pad-type bottom heaters. Unfortunately, they are the most costly to install. I have found that you get what you pay for when it comes to electric bottom heaters for germinating seedlings. Try checking the temperature of your soil with a thermometer to see if you really need to do something about it. A 10° F (6° C) variance can make a big difference in whether your seeds will germinate. An alternative to a bottom heater is to bring seedling trays inside your house to a warm sunny window or under a proper lighting scheme. After the seeds germinate, you can either move them back into the greenhouse or continue to grow them to a good transplanting size before you return them to the sunspace.

6. *Light.* Some seeds, often the tiny ones, need light to germinate. Check your seed catalog or packet instructions. Those that need light should be planted shallow in a well-lit area. Lettuce is one common vegetable that requires some light through the soil to trigger germination. Seedlings also need light to get a good start on life. If light is lacking, the seedlings have a great way of telling you about it; they will become extremely leggy and elongated. Some garden catalogs offer light benches for growing plants and starting seedlings. They are usually made of an array of fluorescent lights on adjustable hangers to accommodate the growing plant. You can always build your own light table for germinating seedlings. Place it most anywhere, except in prime greenhouse growing space, which should be used for growing the big plants (see Chapter 2, Interior Design). For best results, always place the light 2 to 3 inches (5 to 8 cm) above the top of the plant or the soil if you are germinating. Please remember to be careful about mixing water and electricity. Read more about supplemental lighting in Sun Substitutes (p. 17).

7. *Depth.* If seeds are planted too deep, they may run out of steam before they reach the surface. A general rule on seed planting is to place seeds at a depth 2 to 3 times their width. Small seeds have less food-energy reserves to push through to the surface, so plant them at correspondingly more-shallow depths. For shallow-planted seeds (small seeds), be extra careful that the soil surface doesn't dry out.

8. *Nutrients.* Seed germination requires little, if any, added nutrients. In fact, nutrients such as nitrogen can cause problems. Seedlings may benefit from a very diluted fertilizer, however high in phosphorus and low in nitrogen. When in doubt, don't do it—at least until the plant is starting to get six to eight leaves (see Chapter 9, Getting to the Roots).

tions, however. Native temperate-climate plants (many wildflowers) often benefit from a chilling treatment to mimic winter in order to break the dormancy in a seed. Six weeks of temperatures below 40° F (5° C) usually does the trick. Many tropical flowering plants can be difficult to start from seed, sometimes taking months to germinate or having exacting requirements. Many tropical plant seeds have a short period of viability before the seed loses its ability to germinate, so getting fresh seed is important.

Unless the plant is recommended to be directly sown into a bed, it is usually best to start the seed in an ideal propagating environment for later transplanting.

Seedlings can be germinated in many different types and sizes of flats.

Planting Requirement for Vegetables

Vegetable	Planting Method	Weeks to Transplanting	Soil Temperature for Germination
Beans	D	NA	W
Beans, fava	D	NA	C
Beets	TPS	3 to 4	C
Cabbage	TP	4 to 6	C
Cantaloupe	TPS	3 to 4	W
Carrots	TPS	4 to 5	C
Collards	TP	4 to 6	C
Celery	TP	7 to 10	M
Eggplant	TP	6 to 10	W
Garlic	B	6 to 10	M
Kale	TP	4 to 6	C
Kohlrabi	TP	4 to 6	C
Lettuce*	TP	5 to 8	C
Okra	TP	5 to 9	W
Onions	B and TP	4 to 14	W
Parsley	TP	6 to 10	C
Peas	TPS	5 to 10	C
Peppers	TP	8 to 11	W
Radish	D	NA	C
Spinach	TP	6 to 9	C
Swiss chard	TP	4 to 8	C
Tomatoes	TP	6 to 8	W
Turnips	TPS	4 to 8	C
Watermelon	TP	4 to 6	W

PLANTING METHOD

D–Best directly sown into bed and not transplanted.

TP–Transplant to save time and space.

TPS–Can be transplanted with extreme care. Will need to be thinned if directly sown in a bed.

B–Start from bulb.

*–Needs light to trigger germination.

SOIL TEMPERATURE FOR GERMINATION

C–Needs temperature of 45° to 75° F (7° to 24° C).

M–Needs moderate temperature of 60° to 75° F (15° to 24° C).

W–Needs warm temperature of 70° to 75°F (21° to 24° C).

For information on flower propagation, look for your plant of interest in Chapter 8, A Closer Look at the Plants.

Sterilized Soil for Starting Seeds

It's important that seeds get their start in soil that has been sterilized (also known as pasteurized) to kill any potential diseases or weeds that could cause problems to the germinating seeds. Most all commercial potting soil is sterile when you purchase it. Never reuse potting soil for starting seeds unless you go to the trouble of resterilizing it. You can sterilize soil by putting your soil in an oven-proof container 3 inches (8 cm) deep; set your oven for 200° F (93° C), and bake it. When a meat thermometer reads 180° F (82° C), you will have killed off most of the harmful diseases that would be a problem to your germinating seedlings. Avoid letting the soil get much hotter. If overcooked, the soil may release some toxic compounds (toxic only to plants) from the nitrogen in the soil, so keep an eye on the thermometer. Be forewarned: Baking soil does not smell very good, especially compared to what you usually bake in the oven. You can buy small soil sterilizers in many greenhouse supply catalogs, but they are not cheap. As you can see, it is often much easier to purchase some premanufactured potting soil for starting your seeds. It is not neces-sary to have sterilized soil in your bed or pot when you transplant the seedlings. There are ways to chemically sterilize soil, but it is dangerous because the chemicals are toxic. Avoid doing this. (See p. 397 for a recipe for potting soil.)

Containers for Starting Seeds

You can start seeds in most any container as long as it has holes in the bottom for drainage and is not deeper than 4 inches (10 cm). In spring, many garden centers sell plastic flats (also called trays), which are ideal for starting seeds. Commercial flats are usually 10 inches by 20 inches (25 cm by 51 cm). You can also use flowerpots or recycled materials for pots. I like to use old milk cartons cut in half, with holes poked in the bottom. Be sure to clean any recycled seedling pot, tray or flat. Use hot water and soap, and then dip it in bleach diluted in water and rinse well. If the container is brand new and has never had soil in it, cleaning is not necessary.

Fill the container with soil, and smooth out the surface. Where possible, sow seeds in rows rather than just scattering the seed. This slows diseases from spreading from plant to plant because it is harder for soil diseases to jump from row to row. It also enables you to plant more than one type of seed in one flat, but be sure to tag each row well. Use a small stick or board to make straight rows or minifurrows. I prefer to water the seedling container and let the water drain before I make the rows or plant the seed. Watering before planting will help prevent washing out the seeds in the dry soil mix. It also improves the seed to soil contact, which is helpful.

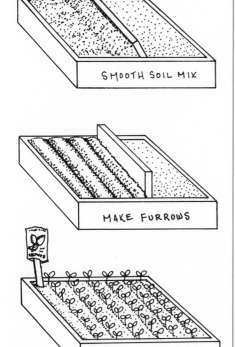

SMOOTH SOIL MIX

MAKE FURROWS

GROW IN ROWS

Sowing seeds in rows helps to minimize diseases.

Some other options for seedling containers are known as peat pots. These are completely biodegradable pots made from compressed and formed peat moss. They work fine but take up more space than seedling trays, at least initially. Besides the obvious environmental advantage, if you grow only one plant per pot, you can set the pot directly into the ground as long as the edges of the pot don't extend above the ground. This is a great way to lessen transplant shock because the roots are never disturbed. If you do use peat pots, keep a close eye on the watering because the soil in these pots tends to dry out more quickly than in other pots. Peat pots are relatively low-cost.

Another environmentally sound pot is none at all. Instead use what is sold as soil blocks. This requires a special tool that can turn your soil mix into a compressed block, a little less than 2 inches (5 cm) square, in which you directly plant the seed. By being compressed, the soil block stays together until it is time to transplant. Like the peat pot, soil blocks reduce the transplant shock but also need more water than conventional pots. Some growers have had problems with disintegration of the blocks, but others swear by

Tomatoes can be started in peat pots for easier transplanting.

them. Soil blocks take some getting used to and work better with a soil mix that holds together well. It might take some experimentation. Soil block tools run close to $20.

A number of plastic containers have been developed for transplanting seedlings. The most common are multiple-pot containers that bedding plants are sold in at a garden center. They are usually made of a cheap, thin, molded plastic and have drainage holes. They come in twelve-packs, six-packs (sounds like beer) and four-packs. Usually they fit perfectly in the standard commercial plastic 10-by-20-inch (25-by-51-centimeter) flat mentioned earlier. If you have recently purchased spring bedding plants in these plastic pots,

you may have some sitting around. They can be washed and reused for at least a few seasons before they start to split.

There are also reusable styrofoam trays with 24 to 40 cells per tray. These are good for starting seeds or for transplanting seedlings. Some come with a spongelike capillary mat, which the container sits upon. The mat wicks water to the cells for self-watering as long as you keep it wet. Both styrofoam and other types of plastic flats come with a clear plastic cover to help maintain humidity. If you use the cover, the seedlings will need little if any water. The styrofoam setups usually run around $10 and work quite well.

Sowing the Seeds

As you are sowing, be careful not to drop the seeds too close together or you'll create overcrowding, which results in spindly seedlings that are fighting for light. This makes a mess when it comes time to untangle this seedling riot. The distance between seeds can vary greatly depending upon the size of the seed. I usually leave a minimum of 1/3 inch (.8 cm) between the seeds.

Instead of poking the seed into soil to the proper depth, carefully

Well-cleaned six-packs can be reused many times for new seedlings.

spread more soil mix over the seeds. Add enough soil to reach the desired depth for the seed, twice as deep as the seed is wide. Some catalogs will instruct you not to cover the seeds at all, so follow their advice where applicable.

One tool I like to use, especially for small seed, is a seed sower, which looks like a small plastic trowel. I have a ratchet wheel that is turned with your thumb. This creates a vibration that bounces the seed out in an organized and controlled manner. It is sold in some catalogs as a Super Seed Sower® and usually goes for $6 to $10, which is well spent. When using this tool, you can sow tiny seeds more evenly by mixing the seeds with an equal volume (in comparison to the seeds) of granulated sugar.

There are also the more expensive electric seed sowers that use a battery to power a vibration to the tool that bounces the seeds out. I have found these imprecise and prefer the thumb-powered seeder. However, I know other greenhouse gardeners who love the electric seed sowers.

I have also had good luck using a sharp pencil with a slightly wetted tip, which I use to carefully pick up one seed at a time from a dry plate. The seed sticks to the pencil tip like a magnet. If everything works well, the seed drops off into the seedling soil when you ever-so-lightly brush the seed against the soil. You will need to clean the pencil tip and rewet it as needed. With a little practice, this can be a quick way to sow a small amount of small seeds.

To maintain high humidity, which seedlings love, many people slip the container into a clear plastic bag after planting. If you try this, your seeds will need very little water, so don't get carried away and overwater them. When the seeds begin coming up, immediately take the flat out of the bag and place it in a well-lit location. Keep a close eye: You don't want those seedlings short on light after they germinate, or they will become elongated and difficult to deal with.

How to Plant the Very Tiny Seeds

Some seeds of ornamental plants are so small that they are almost impossible to see with the naked eye. They might even resemble dust in the bottom of your seed packet. Don't despair. Here's how to deal with them:

1.   Use a small clean pot for sowing. Be sure the pot has drainage holes in the bottom.
2.   Fill the pot with virgin potting soil. Then firm the soil with your fingers.
3.   Mix the seed in the packet with a teaspoon of granulated sugar, close the packet and shake the mix of sugar and seeds.
4.   Open the packet and hold it over the pot. Tap the packet lightly to release the sugar/seed mixture evenly over the top of the soil (or use a seed sower as mentioned earlier).
5.   Do not cover the seed with soil. Lightly press the seed into the surface of the soil with the bottom of a dry spoon.
6.   Set the pot into a saucer filled with warm (not hot) water. The water will be absorbed automatically by the wicking action of the soil.
7.   Cover the top of the pot with a piece of glass, cling plastic wrap or a clear plastic bag to keep the soil moist and the air humid.
8.   Keep the saucer full of water.
9.   Place the pot in a very bright spot (not direct sun) where the temperature is above 65° F (18° C).

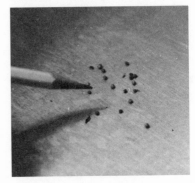

Sowing very tiny seeds

10. Remove cover and move to sunny spot as soon as the seeds have germinated.

After Germination

If the germinating plants begin to touch each other and look crowded, you may need to thin them out. It is best to thin by pinching or cutting out the excess seedlings with small pointed-tip scissors. If you pull out the plants, it will disturb and injure the remaining plant roots. After the plants get 4 to 5 leaves, it is time to transplant them into a small pot or directly into beds.

Direct Sowing and Thinning

Some plants don't take to transplanting well at all (check the chart on planting requirements, p. 143). When this is the case, it is better to sow the seed directly into the pot or bed where it will be growing to maturity. The biggest problem gardeners have with direct sowing is using too many seeds. This means you must thin out the seedlings. Failure to thin out seedlings is an amazingly common problem. Some people just don't have the heart to kill a seedling. After all, to thin out a bed of thick seedlings is killing plants. I admit it. I used to be guilty of not thinning my seedlings when they came up thickly. I would imagine the plants screaming and begging for another chance as I tossed them into the trash can. But without thinning, plants end up growing thick as a lawn and will never yield any harvest or flowers. No thinning, no harvest. Over the years, I've learned that sometimes you have to be ruthless to be a good gardener. If you aren't, you soon end up with a garden that you don't particularly like. With a little ruthlessness, you'll be surprised how much more you enjoy gardening.

If you have trouble being ruthless with the thinning job, try gardening after a bad day at work or immediately after driving in heavy traffic. Gardening after paying the bills or after domestic disagreements is also an excellent practice for the novice who lacks ruthlessness in the greenhouse. By being ruthless and taking some of your daily problems out on a bed that needs thinning, you'll end up with a better-looking greenhouse garden, and you may find that the day's problems seem less troublesome. You might even become a happier and more content person. That's called horticultural therapy, and it is part of the magic of gardening.

Think about thinning if your plants are starting to become elongated or if each single plant is touching its neighboring plant. Rather than thinning, you may just need to do some transplanting.

TRANSPLANTING

Transplanting seedlings rather than planting seeds directly into a bed is an easy way to conserve on space. Think about it this way. If you directly plant into a bed or the final pot where the plant will be growing, it could tie up the bed or pot space for 6 to 14 weeks. Instead, you can be using that space for mature producing plants, while your small seedlings are growing in a propagation area with an ideal environment until they are ready for transplanting.

Why waste precious bed space waiting for seed germination and initial growth? Admittedly, some crops can't tolerate transplanting, but whenever possible, do it. It requires a bit of planning—at least a month or two in advance. See Chapter 7, Scheduling, for help in planning. You must also be able to look at the space you are using to help predict when a bed or area will be freed up and readied for transplanting. It is ideal to have healthy-sized plants ready to place in a bed the same day old plants are removed. Before you put in new transplants you'll probably want to renew the soil with some amendments. Refer to Chapter 9, Getting to the Roots, for information on soil preparation.

Sometimes you will find that

When transplanting, handle seedlings by the leaves, not the stem.

you have more seedlings ready to transplant than you have room. You must either throw them out (ruthlessly, remember?) or try giving them to friends with greenhouses or sunspaces. When I am growing edible greens for later transplanting and end up with too many plants, I often let them continue growing in the flat. Later, I harvest the small leaves for eating. These "gourmet greens" are good eating. Don't try this with vegetables having nonedible leaves, such as tomatoes.

When to Transplant

Transplant your seedlings after the plants develop their second set of leaves. You'll notice that the first set usually looks quite different than the rest of the plant leaves. These leaves, botanically known as cotyledons, were originally part of the seed and function only to provide food reserves to the developing plant. Don't be surprised when, after a few weeks, they drop off.

Be careful not to let your seedlings remain too long in a small seedling flat or germinating pot. If a seedling is held too long and becomes crowded before it's transplanted, the stem might become hardened. On some plants this may spell disaster when you grow the seedling to maturity. The hardened stem can cause poor growth characteristics. This is particularly true of plants in the cole crop family (cabbage, broccoli, cauliflower) and peppers. You might notice it on other plants too. It is hard to give you an amount of time that is too long. To avoid stem hardening, make an effort to give the growing plant plenty of room by up-potting it as it becomes root bound and by occasionally fertilizing.

If you are a user of tobacco, be sure to wash your hands with soap and hot water before transplanting petunias, nicotiana, datura, browallia, peppers, eggplant and tomatoes. This will prevent your passing on the devastating disease tobacco leaf mosaic, which can be spread from

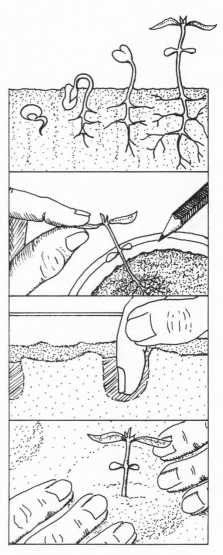

Transplant seedlings after they develop a second set of leaves.

your fingers to these plants. See Chapter 10, When Things Go Wrong, for more information.

Prior to transplanting the seedlings, water them in their original container. Dig deeply and gently. Remove one plant at a time. A sharp pencil makes an excellent transplanting tool to help ease out the roots. Get as much root as possible. Do not clean the soil off the roots, because this could cause damage to them. If you have a situation with many closely planted seedlings with their roots intertwined, place them in a bucket of water, which will loosen the roots' hold on each other. To prevent damage from drying, place the plants on a moist newspaper or towel. Never pull out more than you can transplant in a few minutes, because dry air will permanently damage the roots. Don't hesitate to discard spindly plants or those with poorly developed roots.

The best way to hold a small seedling is by its leaf. If you hold the plant by the stem, you can damage it with even slight pressure. Make a hole in the soil of the growing location (either another pot or bed) with a pencil or a dibble. A dibble is a small tool shaped much like a pencil but with a diameter two to three times that of a pencil. You can easily make dibbles out of dowels with different-shaped ends to ease transplanting.

Tuck all of the roots into the hole. Plant the seedling just slightly deeper than it was in the germinating container. Don't jam roots into a hole that is too shallow. Finally, replace soil around each plant, and use your fingers to gently firm it around the stem and roots. Be careful not to compress the soil too hard around the new seedling. Is the plant sitting upright? Yes? Good.

After transplanting, gently water the plants in their new spot. Be careful not to wash out or flatten them. Protect the seedlings from drafts or high temperatures.

Slugs love to munch on little seedlings. If you have a slug problem, you may want to put a slug trap near the seedlings for protection. Also check for aphids under the leaves and leaf tips; they love to congregate for feeding frenzies on new seedlings. (See Chapter 10, When Things Go Wrong, for help with these types of problems.)

GIVING PLANTS THE SLIP WHILE CLONING AROUND

An alternative to starting plants from seed is to use cuts from a

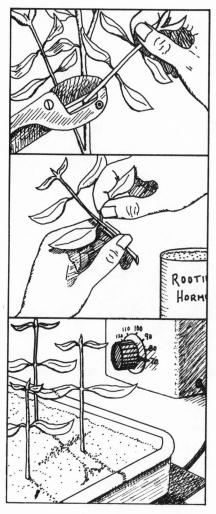

Plants can often be cloned (rooted) from cuttings. Success rates increase if you use rooting hormone and bottom heat.

with houseplants, but it also works great in starting certain vegetables and subtropical greenhouse plants.

When you start a plant from a slip of another plant, you are basically cloning the parent plant. Growing plants from cuttings is an easy way to get a new plant from an old plant. The resulting plant is an exact genetic duplicate of the original plant. It is usually faster than growing the plant from seed, and often it is much easier. It is also a cheap way to acquire more plants. I have propagated cuttings of a favorite tomato and European greenhouse cucumber with great success. Why even try to propagate vegetables from cuttings when they are easy to start from seed? It is a great way to create offspring from a hybrid vegetable that doesn't come true from seed. Also, it can save money. For example, European cucumber seed (a.k.a forcing or greenhouse cucumbers) is incredibly expensive.

Many plants are so easy to root that all you have to do is set a slip into a glass of water. A good example is coleus. Many other plants need a more exacting environment for rooting than placing in water, and some are easier than others to root into new plants. It's always fun to experiment with different plants to find out which

parent plant. Most everyone has witnessed someone rooting a cutting from a plant. Who hasn't seen an ivy, coleus or geranium in a glass of water happily growing roots? This practice is usually done

This rooted cutting is ready for potting.

are easiest to propagate.

The first step in taking a cutting is to select a healthy, disease-free parent plant. If this plant is showing any signs of disease, bugs or poor health, don't use it for cuttings. You'll just pass on the problems! The best place to take a cutting off a plant is from a tip. The tip doesn't have to be from the very top of the plant; it can also come from side branches.

To get started, gather a clean or new flowerpot (or any other appropriate container with drainage holes), rooting powder (available at garden centers for about $3), clean sand, peat moss, a plastic

bag, a sharp knife and a pencil. Fill the pot to a depth of about 4 inches (10 cm) with a one-to-one mix of sand and peat moss. Water the mixture. Place the pot on a saucer to catch the water that drains out of the bottom of the pot.

With a sharp knife, take a 3- to 5-inch-long (8- to 13-centimeter-long) stem cutting from the parent plant. If the cutting has any flowers or flower buds, remove them. Trim any large leaves off the lower end of the cutting; leave three or four smaller leaves toward the tip.

Dip the cut portion of the stem into your rooting powder and shake off any surplus. Rooting powder

This fig tree is newly potted from cutting.

contains a synthetic plant hormone that is based upon naturally occurring plant substances that help to stimulate the formation of roots. Rooting powder comes in different formulations for different types of plants. Additionally, rooting hormone usually comes mixed with a fungicide to prevent the cut portion of the stem from rotting.

An alternative to rooting hormone is to brew up some willow tea. Willow extract has been shown to have great root-promoting properties. To make it, steep many small willow twigs in hot water for 48 hours; then set your cuttings in this solution for 24 hours before placing them in the rooting soil. Water the cuttings daily with some willow tea. This willow method works but not as well as the rooting powder.

With a pencil, poke a hole about 3 inches (8 cm) deep into the sand/peat mix in the container. Place the cutting in the hole and firm the mix around the cutting so it stands upright. In one pot you can (and should) fit many cuttings. It is rare that every cutting will grow roots, so do a number of cuttings, and you'll be more likely to end up with healthy rooted plants. For instance, one 4-inch (10-centimeter) pot could hold up to 10 cuttings. Rooting can take anywhere from 4 weeks to 6 months, depending upon the plant. If the plant is forming callus tissue, still looks healthy but has no roots even after many months, don't give up the faith!

Place the pot or container in a warm, bright spot, but not in direct sun. A perfect spot is on a heating mat with a mist system (see Propagation Bench, p. 83). Keep the sand/peat mix consistently moist; it should never dry out. High humidity is a key in greatly speeding up rooting and preventing the leaves on these rootless stems from wilting. You can help to increase the humidity by placing a clear plastic bag loosely over the pot. There are also clear plastic domes available through some greenhouse and gardening catalogs and stores. Humidity levels can also be maintained if you can mist the cuttings on a daily basis when you don't have a misting system.

After 3 weeks or more, check your cuttings by gently pulling up on them. If they seem to move easily up out of the hole when pulled, they have not rooted. Check again in a couple of weeks. If they seem anchored and won't budge when lightly pulled, they may have roots. If you suspect your cuttings

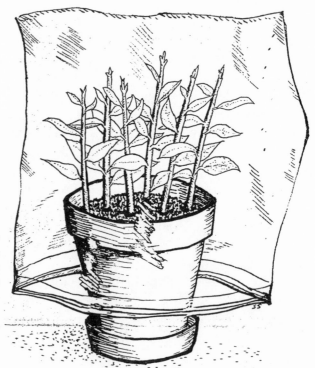

A plastic bag placed over cuttings helps to maintain high humidity when you do not have an automatic misting system. Mist regularly with a spray bottle. Cuttings can be placed in sand or perlite.

have rooted, carefully dig the plant out of the mix to see for sure. If not rooted, carefully replace it. If you see only a fleshy, whitish growth on the cut end but no roots, your plants have formed what is called callus tissue. The callus often, but not always, means roots will soon be forming. Replace the plant and wait a few more weeks.

If your cuttings are wilting, try to increase the humidity with more misting. If the wilting continues, consider pruning another large leaf toward the bottom of the stem or start over, using new cuttings with fewer leaves. If the bottom of the cutting seems to have rotted, toss it out because it will never root. Rotting may be an indication of not using rooting hormone or not covering the cut portion well enough with the powder.

If your cutting has a good set of roots, carefully transplant it into a small pot with new potting soil, taking care to not disturb the roots as you move it. After transplanting, keep the plant on the moist side for the first week or two and mist it often until the plant gets used to the real world.

Many, but not all plants, can be propagated from cuttings. Some easy plants to try include coleus, ivy, geranium, ficus, begonia and even tomato. Don't be afraid to try

most any plant after successes with the easier plants. Next thing you know, you'll have a plant production factory in full operation. When you really get good at rooting cuttings, you can even try your hand at propagating your favorite outside trees and shrubs in the same manner. The best time to take cuttings from outside plants is 5 to 6 weeks after the last frost. It is great to utilize your greenhouse to provide plants for your outside landscape.

As you gain experience, you may want to try rooting plants from just the leaf stems (petioles) and from the leaves themselves.

There is more to plant propagation than I can cover here. If you want to read more about propagating plants, two good books are *Plants Plus*, by George Seddon and Andrew Bicknell, published by Rodale Press, 1987, and *Secrets of Plant Propagation*, by Lewis Hill, published by Garden Way Publishing, 1985. These books can be ordered at a bookstore if they are not in stock, or check at your library or public botanic garden.

There is an inherent joy in starting your own plants. This is also a good way to perpetuate and pass around a special plant that may have been in the family for years. Plant propagation is a great family project for involving kids. Have fun!

Pollination

6

Pollination

In nature, flowers are pollinated by insects, birds, wind and even bats. In the greenhouse, we usually lack the natural pollinators that otherwise ensure adequate fruit or seed production. So humans must do the job of pollination. Pollination is comparable to conception, the first step in creating a new individual. We need to know about pollination primarily to get plants to produce fruits and occasionally for the production of seeds. Since the main reason greenhouse gardeners need to know about pollination is for the production of fruits, most of this chapter concerns itself with the growing of edible fruits rather than with ornamental plants.

flower is a plant's sexual reproductive part. Normally, the flowering response is triggered by maturity (common for vegetables) or by the length of the night (as discussed in Photoperiodism, p. 16). However, stress caused by the growing environment—low nutrient levels, too low or too high temperatures, wilting and competition—may sometimes induce premature flowering. Also, luxuriant amounts of nitrogen and water can sometimes delay flowering; this is often true with tomatoes. A greenhouse gardener should be concerned about when flowering takes place because a plant that flowers too early or too late often produces lower harvests.

WHY PLANTS FLOWER

Pollination is a primary step in a plant's reproduction cycle, which results in being a seed that grows into a new individual plant. But before pollination can take place, the plant needs to flower. The

FLOWER PHYSIOLOGY

In order to become a master pollinator in your greenhouse or sunspace, you need to first learn some simple flower physiology.

There are two major types of flowers. The complete flower con-

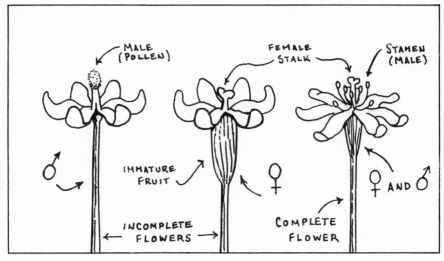

Incomplete and complete flowers require different methods of pollination.

tains both male and female parts. Some examples include tomatoes, peppers and eggplant. These types of flowers are the easiest to pollinate because the male and female parts often are adjacent to each other in the same flower.

The other flower type is (you guessed it!) the incomplete flower in which the male and female parts are in a different flower. Pollinating these flowers involves the physical transfer of the pollen from the male part in one flower to the female part in another (often using a small paintbrush to transfer the pollen).

ENVIRONMENTAL CONDITIONS FOR POLLINATION

Pollination is usually done most efficiently on bright days between 10:00 A.M. and 4:00 P.M. Optimally, it should take place at least once every other day. It's impossible to overdo it. Temperatures below 55° F (13° C) may damage the pollen and greatly decrease the number of fruits produced. This is why it is much more difficult to grow tomatoes in the middle of winter in a solar-heated greenhouse. Even though the plants may look fine, the poor little flowers just can't set on fruit when the nights are consistently cold. Temperatures above

90° F (32° C) can have the same
effect on the ability of flowers to
produce fruit. At certain times of
the year, your greenhouse may run
above and below these temperatures. Scheduling can make a big
difference on the ability of your
plants to grow their best. Adequate
ventilation and cooling in summer
is helpful for good fruit set. In the
cool winter greenhouse, you may
find it wise to grow fewer fruiting
crops and more leafy and root
types that don't need to produce
fruit (see Chapter 7, Scheduling).

WHAT AND HOW TO POLLINATE

Common Vegetables with Complete Flowers

Beans. Most common garden varieties will produce a good crop
without pollination. If you find
your variety is not setting fruit, try
changing to a more common variety. Runner beans are one exception; they need to be pollinated
and are not a good choice for
greenhouse growing because pollination is difficult.

Okra. Okra sets pods without being pollinated and produces a beautiful flower.

Peas. No pollination is required.

Tomatoes. An easy crop to pollinate. Use a long, thin stick about
1 1/2 inches (3.8 cm) long. A 1/4-
inch (.6-centimeter) dowel will do
fine. Tap the yellow blossoms gently and fruit generally will set if the
temperature conditions are correct. If you suspect that some of
your tomato plants have a disease,
always pollinate these plants last.
Electric vibrating gadgets are available to commercial growers that
work fine, but so does a stick …
and at a much lower cost. A large
greenhouse full of tomatoes can
be pollinated in a short time. One
or two light taps of your pollinating stick on each cluster of blossoms is sufficient.

*Tapping tomato blossom with a stick makes
pollination an easy task.*

Peppers. As done with tomatoes, tapping flowers will help fruit set, but pollination will often occur by itself if the temperatures are right.

Eggplant. Eggplants are more variable than other plants when it comes to fruit set. Some varieties don't seem to need pollination, while others do well with a good tap, much like tomatoes. If you are having a problem with eggplants setting fruit, try this method: Find a flower that is shedding a large amount of pollen (a yellow dust will fall from the flower when touched). Put your thumbnail under this flower and knock some pollen onto your nail. Touch the pollen on your thumbnail to the tip of the female element on each blossom. The female element is

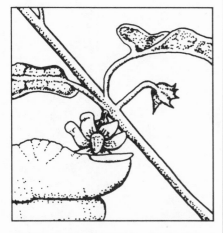

Eggplant pollination can be accomplished by tapping pollen onto thumb and transferring it to the female element of flower.

the green stalk in the center of the flower surrounded by the yellow pollen parts. Apply more pollen to your nail after pollinating about four flowers, and repeat the process on other blossoms.

Common Vegetables with Incomplete Flowers

Squash. First locate the male flower; it will have a thin stalk leading up to the flower base. Within the flower you will find a shorter stalk tipped with yellow powder (pollen). The female flower is easy to recognize if you look carefully. It has a little immature squash fruit just below the flower at the point where the petals are attached to the stem. If pollen is not transferred to the tip of the female element on the female flower, the little fruit will never grow and eventually will begin to rot from the tip. To get the best fruit set, pollinate the flowers as soon as they first open. There are a number of ways to transfer the pollen from the male to the female flower. Many gardeners use a small paintbrush. However, my favorite method requires no tools. Just pluck the freshly opened male flower, stalk and all. Then strip the petals off the stalk. You'll be left with a stalk tipped with yellow pollen.

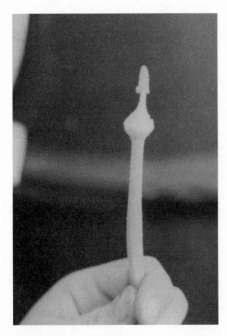

This male squash flower has had its petals removed; it can now be used to pollinate many female flowers.

Holding the bottom of the stalk like a wand, you can touch the pollen to the tip of the female element. With this method, there is usually enough pollen on one male flower to pollinate two or three female flowers. Also you can sometimes use pollen from one type of squash to pollinate another type, such as using a yellow squash to pollinate a green zucchini (this is not a good idea if you are growing the fruit only to harvest the seeds resulting from this pollination). Within days, you'll know if your pollination has worked. If it didn't,

you'll notice that the fruit will begin to rot from the blossom end. Pluck it and toss it out. There is an occasional problem of having only male flowers with no female flowers to pollinate. All you can do is wait for the females, which come later as the plant matures. If all you have are male flowers, you can do what many do in the southwest cuisine: Eat them (check out a southwestern cookbook). Also, you can see why flowers get pollinated—look for a bowllike indentation containing a small amount of clear liquid. This is the nectar. Taste it and see why bees are into pollinating.

We are just beginning to see a new type of summer squash that does not require pollination. It is so new at this writing that I've done only some limited testing. The first commercially offered variety is available from the catalog

A male squash blossom can be used to pollinate female flowers.

"The Cook's Garden," under the unromantic name of Type 1406. This zucchini will be perfect for the greenhouse if it really works. But early results with this particular variety do not look very promising. At least it is a start in the right direction. I hope there will be more for those growing under cover.

Cucumbers. Europeans have developed a cucumber specifically for greenhouse growing known as an European forcing cucumber. They don't need to be pollinated at all and yield great crops. For more information, read about cucum-

bers in Chapter 8, A Closer Look at the Plants. I recommend that you stick to these forcing greenhouse cucumbers. If you decide to grow the regular garden variety cucumbers in your greenhouse, they will need pollination in order to set fruit. The process is similar to the pollination of squash except that everything is much smaller. Some people may need tweezers. It is hard to pollinate cucumbers, but not impossible. The task requires some time and energy, so you might want to reconsider the benefits of the high-yielding European forcing cucumbers.

Female and male cucumber flowers

Melons. Melons and cantaloupe are also pollinated like squash, and like the cucumber, they have much smaller flowers. Look for the small, often fuzzy immature melon or cantaloupe behind the female flower. The male flower won't have the small fuzzy behind the petals. As with squash, transfer the pollen to the center of the female flower either by using a small paintbrush or by plucking the male flower stalk as explained with squash. Currently there are no varieties that do not need pollination; maybe someday that will change. So, if you want to grow melons or cantaloupe, you must get good at this because the fruit will not set if not pollinated.

Setting Fruit Artificially

Synthetic chemical hormones are available in a spray form that, when applied to blossoms, will often cause the fruit to grow even without pollination. These sprays work particularly well with tomatoes and not so well with melons and squash.

There have been reports of a much lower-quality of fruit (soft, misshapen fruit with poor color and storage characteristics) when they are triggered to grow artificially. In view of the quality risks and the always-present questions associated with using any synthetic chemicals on food, use of these chemicals should not replace pollination of blossoms.

Pollination of Tropical and Subtropical Fruiting Plants

The pollination of tropical and subtropical fruiting plants is a little trickier than the more common fruits and vegetables. With these plants, you will find the terms "self-fruitful" and "self-unfruitful." A self-fruitful plant is one that can set its own fruit either by providing its own pollen or by just automatically setting fruit without needing to be pollinated. Bananas are a good example of this. A self-unfruitful plant requires pollinating by another variety of the same plant, such as avocados. This means that you must grow two varieties and cross-pollinate the flowers by hand in order to get the fruit to set. This can take up a lot of greenhouse space. However, you can consider grafting a second variety onto a plant to accomplish this.

Oftentimes you can choose whether the plant is self-fruitful or self-unfruitful by just growing the right variety. For instance, many fig tree varieties need an insect pollination to set fruit. Some fig varieties, however, do not need pollination to set fruit. As you might have guessed, this is the type you want for a greenhouse. So, just selecting the right subtropical or tropical variety can make all the difference in whether you will ever get to harvest any fruits. Be sure to read the catalog descriptions well when you are purchasing any sub-tropical or tropical fruiting plants.

For more specific information on pollination of these plants, please refer to Chapter 8, A Closer Look at the Plants.

Trouble-Shooting Pollination Problems

Problem	Possible Causes
Poor fruit set:	Temperature above 90° F (32° C). Sudden cold or cool temperatures. Very dry air.
Blossom drop:	High temperatures. Cool temperatures. Low humidity and soil moisture. Nearby combustion fumes, generally a heater.
Misshapen fruit:	Incomplete pollination (not enough pollen transferred). Cool nights below 55° F (13° C).
Cracked fruit:	Alternating high and low temperature. Usually not due to pollination.
Low numbers of blossoms:	Too much nitrogen. Too cold.
Fruit rotting:	No pollination. Pollen used was not viable.
Immature shriveled fruit:	Usually with cucumbers; no pollination. Tiny mature cucumbers on the vine may cause this. Keep the vines well picked.

FINAL THOUGHTS ON POLLINATION

Pollination is one of the necessities of growing under cover and is something that greenhouse gardeners quickly get good at. I don't know why, but whenever I am engrossed in morning pollination, it seems that a bit of pollen always lands on my nose. Perhaps my nose is a magnet. It takes a while before a good friend will tell me there's something on my nose (only good friends tell you when you look bad). Over time I have decided that a bit of pollen on the end of the nose is an initiation rite for any serious greenhouse pollinator. So here's to some pollen on your nose too! Mohammed Ali, the boxer, likened his boxing to moving like a butterfly and stinging like a bee. In the greenhouse or sunroom, just move like a butterfly and pollinate like a bee.

Scheduling

7

Scheduling

In some respects, just having a greenhouse or a sunspace means that you can grow any plant any time you wish. If you can't grow a tomato in the off-season or a flower when it is snowing outside, then why go to all the trouble of having a green-house? The truth is you can grow most anything anytime of the year, but there are times when proper scheduling can make things work better, when plants respond best or when your greenhouse could consume less energy by timing the growth of your plants differently.

SCHEDULING TO CONSERVE ENERGY

If you schedule the growing of fruiting crops such as tomatoes to coincide with the warmer tem-peratures of March through Octo-ber, you will need very little supple-mentary heat to get a good crop. This is great if you are depending upon the sun for much of your energy (as in a solar greenhouse).

But if you have your heart set on growing a fruiting crop during the absolute coldest time of the year, usually November through February, then you will need to keep the temperatures above 50° F (10° C) just so the flowers will set fruit. In addition, you may have to consider supplemental lighting because of the shorter days of winter, especially if you live in an area with a cloudy winter. Some of you will want to pursue growing tomatoes in the dead of winter, and you'll do okay if the tempera-ture and light are acceptable. If not, don't be surprised to see some poor yields. So why fight it when instead you can schedule an edible plant that thrives in the cold winter months?

Everything depends upon what environment you maintain in your greenhouse. It's all a matter of fitting the right plant into the right environment at the right time. Even in a cold greenhouse, every single month (including the coldest ones!) can be filled with the activity of sowing, growing, and enjoying plants that produce both food and flowers, but only if you schedule them right.

SCHEDULING FOR THE BIOLOGICAL CLOCK

Many plants, mostly ornamental flowering plants, require certain day and night lengths in order to flower or respond in some other way (See Photoperiodism, p. 16). Remember, this is when a plant response is triggered by the length of the night. This tends to be more noticeable in ornamental plants than edible plants. For instance, it is hard to get a petunia to put on a lot of flowers in the wintertime. Garden-variety snapdragons grown in winter will often grow only leaves with no sign of flowers developing (unless you grow special greenhouse varieties). Seasonal timing may have other effects. For example, figs often drop their leaves for a few months in winter and go dormant.

In time, you start to notice that plants have their own schedules, no matter what you may want them to do. You will see that they continue to do certain things at specific times of the year. You learn to expect certain cycles in your plants after gardening in a greenhouse for a few years. In this chapter, I will try to shorten the learning curve and help you fit the right plant into nature's scheme of things. If everything goes right, you'll end up with a real orchestration of colorful flowers, herbs and food in concert with the environment and the biological clocks that tick within every plant. A growing and planting schedule that works right will bring you new wonders to enjoy every month.

Along with the selection of the right plants, the scheduling of your plants will enable you to put it all together.

SCHEDULING VEGETABLES

For the purposes of this chapter, I have split the year into two equal parts: The cool season, from mid-October through mid-March, and the warm season, from mid-March through mid-October. You will find that fruiting crops, those plants that produce an edible fruit (yes, tomato is a fruit), usually do their best in the warm-season months. These are times characterized by longer days, more light and warm to hot temperatures. Although fruiting crops are not efficient winter producers, if you want to grow them in the cool season, always try the warmer areas of the greenhouse (see Chapter 3, Plant Layout). The warmer your greenhouse is—up to 85° F (29° C) in the day and down to 65° F (18° C) at night—the better your fruiting crops will grow. If you plan to provide supplemental heat to your greenhouse to grow fruiting crops in winter, think about the possibility that you may be spending $10 on heat to get $5 worth of tomatoes.

Conversely, leafy and root-producing vegetables thrive in the cool-season greenhouse environment, when the night temperature might consistently drop below 50° F (10° C), but hopefully not below freezing. Lettuce, grown in place of tomatoes during the cool season, might produce $10 worth of lettuce for $5 worth of heat. In the case of a solar-heated greenhouse, it would be $10 worth of lettuce for the cost of free heat.

I'm not saying, "Don't grow fruiting crops in the cool season." I'm only trying to point out crops that will do better and what kind of environment will be needed. I usually rip out most of my fruiting crops in late September, but I often leave a few token tomatoes and peppers. They don't do much, but it's nice to have an occasional tomato from a plant that hardly produces more than four fruits all winter because of cool nights. Even if you don't start your tomato plants until February, you will still be eating fresh tomatoes about the time everyone else is just planting them outside.

Also, I am not saying, "Never grow leafy and root crops in the warm season." You can still grow many of those crops in the warm season, even though it's a more optimum time to be growing fruits. Growing would be much more efficient outside, however, where it is cooler in summer (compared to a greenhouse). Remember, think "efficient food production" for the greenhouse space.

STARTING PLANTS FOR OUTSIDE GARDENS

Millions of people spend millions of dollars every spring at their local garden center buying bedding plants and vegetable transplants for the outside garden. Now that you have a greenhouse, you can grow your own for very little money. Giving plants a head start in your greenhouse will greatly increase the food and flowers that you can produce outside. And, the farther north you live, the more important this becomes. Even a small greenhouse can produce hundreds of seedling transplants for outside, enough for you and your neighbors to enjoy.

Growing your own spring seedlings means you won't be buying them. Your homegrown plants are generally of better quality than store-bought transplants. I've come across many people with small greenhouses who sell their plants at local stores, swap meets and food co-ops for some extra spending money.

Getting Started

First, take two steps back to Chapter 5, Plant Propagation, for the basics in starting seeds.

When it comes to containers, I have had the best transplants when I grow the plants in a pot 1 1/2 to 2 inches (3.8 to 5 cm) square. Any container smaller than that can lead to a stunted root-bound plant. A wide variety of pots are on the market, along with a number of homemade options in which to grow transplants. The main thing is that the pots all have drainage holes in the bottom.

If you end up using a peat pot and plan on setting the whole pot into the ground, be sure to slash a few cuts in the side of the pot to help the roots escape. Additionally, check that the whole pot is buried under the ground. If any portion is above the soil surface after transplanting, a wicking action can occur that draws moisture from the pot into the air. I've come across quite a few peat pots that never decomposed in the garden soil because all the gardener did was pop them in the ground.

No matter what pot you use, pay special attention to watering. It is amazing how fast a seedling can dry out on a warm, sunny day in your greenhouse. Peat pots, soil blocks and clay pots will tend to dry out more readily than plastic containers.

Soil for the seedlings can be a homemade mix (see p. 397 for a recipe for potting soil.), or you can use commercially available potting soil.

As your seedling transplants grow, they will benefit from weekly feedings, beginning 4 weeks after germination. If you are transplanting from a germinating container, wait 2 weeks after the first transplanting. Houseplant fertilizer, the type mixed into water, works fine, but do not use full-strength fertilizer! Always dilute it by half the recommended rate. The best commercial fertilizers for seedlings are those that contain trace elements. Peters is one brand that contains trace elements. You can also use dilutions of manure tea, but be careful—it is hard to tell how strong the stuff is from batch to batch. If you see any leaf or tip burning or yellowing of the leaves, stop fertilizing and check the symptoms out in Chapter 9, Getting to the Roots. Please be careful here. Greenhouse gardeners have a natural tendency to love and overfertilize their plants to death. When in doubt, use less or none at all.

Warning: When growing transplants, keep your eyes open for aphids and other insect pests on the tips of plants and on the undersides of leaves. If you see them, follow the advice in Chapter 10, When Things Go Wrong.

SPRING TRANSPLANT SCHEDULE

One of the biggest problems people have when growing their outside garden seedlings in a greenhouse is scheduling. It is easy to start a plant too early or too late. If a plant is started too early, it suffers more from transplant shock when set outside and may also be rootbound and stunted. It is interesting to note that research has shown that a 1-gallon (3.8-liter) pot with a big blooming tomato plant will actually yield less than an 8-inch (20-centimeter) tomato transplant with a stem slightly wider than a pencil.

If a plant is started too late in spring, your transplant may not have developed enough roots to handle the stress of transplanting and may be late in producing food or flowers outside.

Garden centers tend to grow and sell ornamental plants that are in full bloom. It is almost torture to see these little plants in tiny pots, blooming their little hearts out. The commercial growers know that if they sold you the plant without blooms, it would transplant better and probably be healthier. But, they also know that most consumers prefer the blooming plants over the nonblooming. When you schedule your plants, don't worry if your ornamental transplants are not blooming in the pots before transplanting to the outside, unless you're trying to sell them.

It is disaster if your vegetables are blooming before transplanting. This messes up their internal clock and damages the total yield. Pluck the blooms off if you see a tomato or pepper transplant trying to bloom, and consider giving it a bigger pot and a later starting date next year.

For the best results refer to the Spring Transplant Schedule (p. 175).

Hardening Off

Young plants grown in a protective environment grow very rapidly. They also become tender, making them subject to substantial transplant shock, no matter how talented you are at transplanting. Some of this shock is just getting used to pure, unadulterated sunlight and wind. You can reduce this shock by putting your seedlings through an intermediate period to help them better withstand transplanting. This period is known as hardening off. For a week before transplanting to the outside garden, stop any fertilization. Also cut back slightly on watering, but don't let them wilt. Set your plants in direct sunlight outside the greenhouse during the day. You can also leave them out at night if the temperature will stay above 45° F (7° C). Take care. Plants will dry out much faster outside, so keep an eye on the watering.

While hardening off spring transplants is helpful, it should be noted that the plants that you purchase from a garden center are rarely hardened off. Many good gardeners don't do it either, but if you commonly experience transplant shock, then you might want to give it a try.

Whether you harden off the plants or not, shock can be reduced if you transplant to the outside garden on cloudy days and provide temporary protection from direct sun or wind with a piece of wood or cardboard. To reduce shock, the natural tendency for beginning gardeners is to water to the point of drowning the poor seedling. Yes, it needs water, but not a major flood. This is gardening, not mud wrestling. Too much water is stressful, especially if it goes on for a couple of days. Roots need oxygen, and if the soil is constantly muddy, no air gets under the soil surface.

Spring Transplant Schedule

ORNAMENTALS

Ornamental Crop	Number of Days to Germinate in Proper Environment*	Weeks from Seed Sowing to Setting Outside**
Ageratum	4	12 to 15
Alyssum	5	12 to 15
Aster	15	7 to 11
Begonia, fibrous	17	15
Celosia	10	6 to 8
Cleome	10	10 to 12
Coleus	10	7 to 10
Dahlia	5	10 to 12
Dianthus	5	5 to 8
Foxglove	9	9 to 13
Geranium	7	18 to 22
Globe amaranth	10	11 to 13
Impatiens	17	9 to 12
Kale, flowering	5	7 to 8
Lobelia	18	10 to 12
Marigold	6	6 to 10
Nicotiana	11	9 to 10
Pansy	7	9 to 12
Perennials, outside	5 to 20	12 to 20
Petunia	7	10 to 13
Portulaca	3	6 to 8
Salpiglossis	7	10 to 14
Salvia	15	8 to 14
Snapdragon	10	12 to 13
Stock	7	5 to 7
Zinnia	5	5 to 8

VEGETABLES

Vegetable Crop	Number of Days to Germinate in Proper Environment*	Weeks from Seed Sowing to Setting Outside**
Cucumber	4	3 to 4
Eggplant	7	7 to 9
Herbs	3 to 20	8 to 15
Lettuce	7	6 to 8
Melon	4	3 to 5
Onions	7	12 to 16
Peppers	7 to 20	11 to 13
Squash	4	3 to 4
Tomatoes	7	5 to 8

*The above chart assumes optimum germination conditions of constant temperatures around 65° to 70° F (18° to 21° C), consistent moisture levels, fresh seed and proper planting depth.

**Plants are usually set out before the last average frost date for your area. For every week that the night temperature runs 52° F (11° C) or lower, add an extra week. For every week that the night temperature runs above 70° F (21° C), subtract a week.

BRINGING PLANTS IN FROM THE OUTSIDE GARDEN

When you see fall bearing down on your beautiful outside garden, it is a common temptation to dig up and bring some plants into your greenhouse. There are some precautions you should take before you do this. First, check your plants over thoroughly for bugs; be sure to look on the underside of the leaves. If you find critters on your plants, it would be better not to bring them into your greenhouse.

But remember, varieties of plants suited to the outside garden may not be the best choice when it comes to the inside garden anyway. For instance, a tomato variety that does well outside may not do very well inside. Outside snapdragon varieties grow fewer flowers in the winter greenhouse when compared to snapdragon varieties bred for greenhouse culture. Conversely, European forcing cucumbers can be problematic when grown outside.

Of course, some plants take well to being brought into the greenhouse in fall. As a general rule, a big established plant such as a large, mature tomato plant will suffer a great setback when dug up outside for placement in the greenhouse. Smaller plants usually do much better, and annual flowers do better than perennials. If perennials are brought in for winter, most of them will refuse to bloom until they get a real taste of winter (which doesn't happen in the greenhouse). Try a few experiments with bringing in plants for the winter. You might find some exceptions to what I have said here and hopefully some successes.

THE SECRET TO GOOD WINTER GROWING

In the heart of winter, when days are short and cold, I've noticed that seedlings grow in slow motion, as if they were in molasses. Plants don't often perk up until late February. I've learned that if I want my greenhouse to look good in the middle of winter, action should be taken in late August through September. Plants need to get their root systems established

before the cool nights and short days set in around mid-October into November; this is especially true for solar-heated greenhouses or greenhouses running cooler in winter.

Plan out and start your winter crops in late August to early September. Procrastinators can even put it off until late September to early October, but after October the window of opportunity is about shut. The earlier you start your winter plants (no earlier than late August, however), the better. You may think this all sounds easy enough, but it isn't. The hard part is ripping out some of your summer greenhouse plants that have been thriving. I don't mean that you must rip everything out, but you have to make some hard decisions to make room for more appropriate crops for the cooler growing season, and you must do it before the end of October. It is always best to start pulling the summer plants that show higher levels of insect infestation or disease. Try to leave some of the healthier summer plants that are already growing in your warmer greenhouse microclimates. When you get an early start on plants for winter, they seem more able to tolerate the cold and continue to put on growth.

So, the secret to good winter growing is to get the special winter

A bed can be ripped out and replanted for future harvests.

food and flower crops started in late August through early September and be thinking about how you're going to make room for them.

SUMMER: WHAT TO DO WITH YOUR GREENHOUSE

Sometimes people aren't quite sure how to use their summer greenhouse. This can be a time when the greenhouse suffers at the expense of the manpower required in the outside garden. For people who live in northern areas with a short growing season, the summer greenhouse provides a place to grow crops that are hard to produce outside. Plants such as tomato, cantaloupe, melons and winter squash, which have barely come into production outside when the first frost attacks, produce abundantly in the greenhouse. All too often, people abandon the greenhouse in summer because of hot temperatures. This is unfortunate and the result of faulty design. It can be corrected, however, with proper ventilation, cooling systems and shading (see Chapter 1, The Greenhouse Environment).

So, in conclusion, what is the summer greenhouse good for? The summer greenhouse is where you continue growing your tropical edible crops, such as figs, citrus, banana and guava. It is the place to grow some of the more exotic perennial ornamental plants, such as angel's-trumpet, jasmine, bird-of-paradise, Amazon lily, croton, passionflower, chenille plant and gardenias. It is where you grow vegetables and herbs that will produce much earlier and in more abundance than outside (especially if you live in a short-season area).

Then again, you might find it easier to let much of your greenhouse rest during the summer and use it as a living area with just a few plants inside. With some shade cloth strung over the outside or summer plants providing shade, you can keep the temperature comfortable for sitting in a cool, quiet place, surrounded with shade-loving houseplants for a touch of green.

SCHEDULE FOR GROWING ORNAMENTAL FLOWERING PLANTS IN THE GREENHOUSE

Nothing is more frustrating than going to a lot of trouble trying to get a plant to bloom, only to end up with a plant that never blooms or, even worse, gets sick and struggles to live. This often has much to do with the scheduling. By changing the time of year you plant, you could end up with a prolific bloomer.

It is also frustrating to have big peaks and valleys in the blooming periods of your plants, where one month the greenhouse looks and smells great, only to be followed by a few months without any real show of flowers. It is all a matter of scheduling. After much experimentation, I have found trends when things seem to do best. I have included the following schedule so that you don't have to make some of the same mistakes I made. But this schedule is not perfect; you must do some fine-tuning so that it fits into your particular greenhouse environment. So be sure to keep your own records on how things do for you. Go ahead and make some notes right in this book where you can refer to them easily (yes, you have my permission to write in this book as long as it belongs to you).

Many plants that are perennials in a greenhouse are not listed in the following schedule, because their scheduling is not nearly so important and they can be grown most any time of the year.

Just because a plant is listed in the following schedule and you follow its timing does not mean you can assume success. Before you set out a desired plant, be sure you have read Chapter 4, Selecting the Right Plants, and look up the plant in Chapter 8, A Closer Look at the Plants, for more information in determining whether it will survive your particular situation.

On the following chart, grown warm refers to a greenhouse that has night temperatures consistently above 50° F (10° C). When the chart refers to grown cool, it is for a greenhouse with night temperatures that consistently run below 50° F (10° C). Of course, the cooler the greenhouse, the slower your plant will come into bloom.

Schedule for Year-Round Blooms in the Greenhouse or Sunspace

Note: All bloom dates are approximate. An asterisk (*) indicates that you should add 3 months or more if you propagate from seed.

Plants Started in December and January

Plant Name	Bloom Date Grown Warm	Bloom Date Grown Cool	Propagation
Begonia (tuberous)	April	May	Seed/tuber*
Calendula	March	April	Seed
Carnation	May	June	Seed/cutting*
Centaurea	April	May	Seed
Cyclamen	November	January (next)	Seed/corm
Geranium	June	June	Seed
Gloxinia	July	August	Seed/cutting*
Kalanchoe	December	February	Cutting

Plant Name	Bloom Date Grown Warm	Bloom Date Grown Cool	Propagation
Larkspur	May	June	Seed
Marigold (African)	April	May	Seed
Mina lobata	April	May	Seed
Nemesia	May	June	Seed
Nicotiana	March	April	Seed
Pansy	March	April	Seed
Petunia	April	May	Seed
Poppy	April	May	Seed
Primrose	December (next)	February	Seed
Ranunculus	April	May	Bulb
Salpiglossis	May	June	Seed
Snapdragon	April	May	Seed
Stock	April	May	Seed
Sweet pea	April	May	Seed

Plants Started in February and March

Bedding plants	May	June	Seed
Begonia (fibrous)	June	June	Seed/cutting*
Begonia (tuber)	June	July	Seed/tuber*
Carnation	June	August	Seed/cutting*
Christmas cactus	December	December	Cutting
Dahlia	July	August	Seed/tuber*
Fuchsia	June	July	Cutting
Geranium	June	June	Cutting
Jasmine	December	February	Cutting
Kalanchoe	December	February	Cutting
Larkspur	May	June	Seed
Maple, flowering	August	September	Cutting
Marguerite daisy	July	August	Cutting
Marigold	April	May	Seed
Mina lobata	April	May	Seed

Plant Name	Bloom Date Grown Warm	Bloom Date Grown Cool	Propagation
Morning-glory	May	June	Seed
Nicotiana	May	June	Seed
Petunia	April	May	Seed
Pineapple sage	October	October	Cutting
Poppy	May	June	Seed
Primrose	December	March (next)	Seed
Salpiglossis	June	July	Seed
Schizanthus	March	May	Seed
Snapdragon	May	June	Seed
Statice	July	August	Seed
Stock	May	June	Seed
Swan River daisy	June	July	Seed
Sweet pea	May	June	Seed
Zinnia	May	June	Seed

Plants Started in April and May

Aster	August	September	Seed
Begonia (fibrous)	September	November	Seed
Bougainvillea	October	December	Cutting
Centaurea	July	September	Seed
Cleome	July	August	Seed
Felicia	March	April	Cutting
Gardenia	August	September	Cutting
Globe amaranth	June	July	Seed
Kalanchoe	January	February	Cutting
Marigold	June	July	Seed
Marmalade plant	September	October	Cutting
Mina lobata	July	August	Seed
Morning-glory	July	August	Seed
Mullein	September	December	Seed
Nicotiana	June	July	Seed
Petunia	June	July	Seed

Plant Name	Bloom Date Grown Warm	Bloom Date Grown Cool	Propagation
Primrose	February	March	Seed
Salpiglossis	July	August	Seed
Schizanthus	July	August	Seed
Snapdragon	July	August	Seed
Swan River daisy	July	August	Seed
Zinnia	June	July	Seed

Plants Started in June and July

Aster	December	January	Seed
Azalea	April	May	Cutting
Browallia	December	February	Seed
Calceolaria	March	April	Seed
Calendula	October	November	Seed
Geranium	October	November	Seed/cutting*
Globe amaranth	October	November	Seed
Gloxinia	February	March	Seed
Impatiens	September	October	Seed/cutting
Larkspur	September	October	Seed
Pansy	December	January	Seed
Poinsettia	December	January	Cutting
Polka-dot plant	October	November	Seed
Poppy	September	October	Seed
Salpiglossis	October	November	Seed
Snapdragon	October	November	Seed
Statice	September	October	Seed
Stock	December	January	Seed
Sweet pea	November	December	Seed
Thunbergia	October	December	Seed
Zinnia	October	November	Seed

Plant Name	Bloom Date Grown Warm	Bloom Date Grown Cool	Propagation

Plants Started in August and September

Plant Name	Bloom Date Grown Warm	Bloom Date Grown Cool	Propagation
Ageratum	January	February	Seed
Anemone	January	February	Bulb/seed*
Browallia	January	March	Seed
Calceolaria	March	April	Seed
Calendula	December	January	Seed
Chenille plant	August (next)	September (next)	Cutting
Cineraria	February	March	Seed
Freesia	February	March	Bulb
Geranium	May	June	Seed/cutting*
Gerbera	January	February	Seed
Hyacinth	January	February	Bulb
Kale (flowering)	January	February	Seed
Larkspur	February	March	Seed
Lupine	April	May	Seed
Malope	April	May	Seed
Mimulus	November	December	Seed
Narcissus	December	January	Bulb
Nasturtium	January	February	Seed
Nemesia	December	January	Seed
Pansy	January	February	Seed
Polka-dot plant	January	February	Seed
Poppy	February	March	Seed
Primrose	February	March	Seed
Ranunculus	November	December	Bulb
Schizanthus	December	January	Seed
Snapdragon	December	January	Seed
Stock	December	February	Seed
Sweet pea	January	February	Seed
Tulip	January	February	Bulb

Plant Name	Bloom Date Grown Warm	Bloom Date Grown Cool	Propagation
Plants Started in October and November			
Aster	April	May	Seed
Begonia (fibrous)	March	April	Seed
Browallia	March	April	Seed
Calceolaria	May	June	Seed
Calendula	February	March	Seed
Chrysanthemum	March	May	Seed/cutting*
Cineraria	April	May	Seed
Freesia	March	April	Corm
Fuchsia	May	June	Cutting
Gardenia	December(next)	January(next)	Cutting
Impatiens	February	March	Seed/cutting
Larkspur	April	May	Seed
Nemesia	February	March	Seed
Pansy	March	April	Seed
Poppy	April	May	Seed
Ranunculus	January	February	Bulb
Schizanthus	February	March	Seed
Snapdragon	February	March	Seed
Stock	February	March	Seed
Sweet pea	April	May	Seed

Ornamental Flowers Best Suited
for the Winter Greenhouse

Stick to plants on this list if your night greenhouse temperature runs below 45° F (7° C) in winter:

ageratum	geranium	nasturtium
alyssum	gerbera	nemesia
amaryllis	hibiscus	pansy
anemone	hyacinth	petunia
angel's-trumpet	impatiens	pineapple sage
azalea	jasmine	poppy
bird-of-paradise	kalanchoe	primrose
bougainvillea	kale (flowering)	ranunculus
calendula	larkspur	shrimp plant
Christmas cactus	malope	snapdragon
cineraria	mandevilla	stock
cyclamen	maple (flowering)	sweet pea
freesia	marguerite daisy	thunbergia
	mullein	

Temperature in the Warm Winter Greenhouse

If you have a greenhouse or sunspace that can maintain night winter temperatures above 45° to 50° F (7° to 10° C) or warmer, then you are less limited as to what you can grow as long as you have the light required. Usually both cool-loving and warm-loving plants will do fine. If your night temperature tends to reach temperature higher than 60° F (15° C), however, it can limit the blooms of many plants.

An optimum night winter temperature that allows you to grow the most flowering ornamentals is 55° to 60° F (13° to 15° C). For information on the temperature requirements of specific crops, refer to Chapter 8, A Closer Look at the Plants.

VEGETABLE SCHEDULES

A vegetable production schedule is not as necessary if your greenhouse has supplementary heat and a good ventilation system and you wish to control the temperature to a consistent 70° F (21° C) during the day and 60° (15° C) at night. If this is the case for your greenhouse, you are making the climate accommodate the vegetable crop and can grow most any vegetable any time of the year.

Many people like to run their greenhouse or sunspace at cooler temperatures in winter, usually to save energy costs, while others with solar-heated greenhouses are at the mercy of the natural temperatures that their structure creates. In these situations you must fit the type of vegetable crop into the climate rather than fitting the climate to the plant. The following schedules can simplify the selection process for what will do best at what time of year, given different night temperatures.

These two schedules are designed for timing optimum growth and harvest of the vegetable crop. You can grow vegetables out of these optimum schedules in the cooler or unheated greenhouse, but the performance and yield may be lacking. One schedule is for a warmer greenhouse and one is for a cooler greenhouse.

P G H — Schedule Codes

The following schedules are coded like this: **P** designates a possible month to plant the crop. **G** indicates good months to be growing the crop toward maturity. **H** means the crop, if grown to maturity, could be harvested during these months. There are many variables involved in growing vegetables in a greenhouse that make it difficult to be totally accurate. But this general guide should help you in much of your planning.

Warm Greenhouse Vegetable Schedule

This chart applies to greenhouses that run winter night temperatures above 45° F (7° C) and to solar greenhouses that are in a climate that receives a winter monthly average of 45 percent or more of possible sunshine as listed by your closest National Weather Service office (see Average Percentage of Sunshine for Selected Locations appendix).

Crop	J	F	M	A	M	J	J	A	S	O	N	D
Beans, bush		P	PG	PGH	PGH	PGH	PGH	PGH	PGH	GH		
Beans, fava	PGH	PGH	PGH	PGH	H	H			P	P	PG	P
Beans, lima				P	PG	PG	PGH	PGH	GH	GH	H	
Beans, pole			P	PG	PG	PGH	PGH	PGH	GH	GH	H	
Beets	PGH	PGH	PGH	GH	GH	H		P	PG	PGH	PGH	PGH
Broccoli	PGH	GH	H						P	PG	PGH	PGH
Brussels sprouts	GH	GH	H					P	PG	PG	PG	GH
Cabbage	PGH	GH	GH	GH	H			P	PG	PGH	PGH	PGH
Cantaloupe				P	PG	PG	GH	GH	H	H		
Carrots	PGH	PGH	PGH	PGH	PGH	PGH	PGH	PGH	PGH	PGH	PGH	PGH
Cauliflower	GH	GH	H						P	PG	PGH	PGH
Collards	PGH	PGH	PGH	GH	GH	GH		P	PG	PGH	PGH	PGH
Cucumber				P	PG	PG	PGH	PGH	GH	GH	GH	H
Eggplant				P	PG	PG	PG	PGH	GH	GH	H	
Garlic	PGH	PGH	PGH	PGH	PGH	PGH	PGH	PGH	PGH	PGH	PGH	PGH
Kale	PGH	GH	GH	H					P	PGH	PGH	PGH
Kohlrabi	PGH	PGH	PGH	PGH	GH	GH		P	PG	PGH	PGH	PGH
Lettuce	PGH	PGH	PGH	GH	H			P	PGH	PGH	PGH	PGH
Okra				P	PG	PG	PGH	GH	GH	H		
Onions, bulbs		P	PG	PG	PGH	GH	GH	GH	H	H	H	
Onions, greens	PGH	PGH	PGH	PGH	PGH	PGH	PGH	PGH	PGH	PGH	PGH	PGH
Parsley	PGH	PGH	PGH	PGH	PGH	PGH	PGH	PGH	PGH	PGH	PGH	PGH
Peas	GH	GH	GH	H					PG	PG	PGH	GH
Peppers			P	PG	PG	PGH	PGH	GH	GH	GH	GH	H
Radish	PGH	PGH	PGH						P	PGH	PGH	PGH
Spinach	PGH	PGH	GH	H				P	PGH	PGH	PGH	PGH
Spinach, New Zealand	PGH	PGH	PGH	PGH	PGH	PGH	PGH	PGH	PGH	PGH	PGH	PGH

Crop	Months											
	J	F	M	A	M	J	J	A	S	O	N	D
Squash, summer		P	PG	PG	PGH	PGH	GH	GH	GH	H	H	
Squash, winter			P	PG	PG	PGH	GH	GH	GH	H	H	
Swiss chard	PGH	PGH	PGH	PGH	PGH	PGH	PGH	PGH	PGH	PGH	PGH	PGH
Tomatoes		P	PG	PGH	PGH	PGH	PGH	PGH	GH	GH	GH	H
Turnips	PGH	PGH	GH	H	H			P	PGH	PGH	PGH	PGH
Watermelon				P	PG	PG	GH	GH	GH	H	H	

Cool Greenhouse Vegetable Schedule

This chart applies to greenhouses that run winter night temperatures below 45° F (7° C) and to solar greenhouses that are in a climate that receives a winter monthly average of less than 45 percent of possible sunshine as listed by your closest National Weather Service office (see Average Percentage of Sunshine for Selected Locations appendix).

Crop	Months											
	J	F	M	A	M	J	J	A	S	O	N	D
Beans, bush		P	PG	PGH	PGH	PGH	PGH	PGH	PGH	GH		
Beans, fava	GH	GH	PGH	PGH	H	H			P	P	PG	GH
Beans, lima				P	PG	PG	GH	GH	GH	H		
Beans, pole				P	PG	PGH	PGH	GH	GH	H		
Beets	PGH	PGH	PGH	GH	H			P	PG	PGH	PGH	PGH
Broccoli	GH	GH	GH	H				P	PG	PG	GH	GH
Brussels sprouts	GH	GH	GH	H				P	PG	PG	PGH	GH
Cabbage	GH	GH	PGH	GH	H	H		P	PG	PGH	PGH	GH
Cantaloupe				P	PG	PG	GH	GH	GH	GH	H	
Carrots	GH	PGH	PGH	PGH	PGH	PGH	PGH	PGH	PGH	PGH	GH	GH
Cauliflower	GH	GH	H					P	PG	GH	H	
Celery	GH	PGH	GH	GH	H			P	PG	PG	GH	GH
Collards	GH	GH	PGH	GH	GH	H		P	PG	PGH	GH	GH
Cucumber		P	PG	PG	PGH	PGH	GH	GH	GH	H		
Eggplant				P	PG	PG	PGH	GH	GH	H		
Garlic	GH	PGH	PGH	PGH	PGH	PGH	PGH	PGH	PGH	PGH	GH	GH

Crop	J	F	M	A	M	J	J	A	S	O	N	D
						Months						
Kale	GH	PGH	PGH	GH	H			P	PG	PGH	PGH	GH
Kohlrabi	GH	GH	PGH	PGH	GH	H		P	PG	PGH	PGH	GH
Lettuce	GH	PGH	PGH	GH	H			P	PGH	PGH	PGH	GH
Okra				P	PG	PG	PGH	GH	GH	H		
Onions, bulbs		P	PG	G	GH	GH	GH	GH	H			
Onions, green	GH	PGH	PGH	PGH	PGH	PGH	PGH	PGH	PGH	PGH	PGH	GH
Parsley	GH	PGH	PGH	PGH	PGH	PGH	PGH	PGH	PGH	PGH	PGH	GH
Peas	GH	PGH	GH	GH	H			P	PGH	PGH	GH	GH
Peppers		P	PG	PGH	PGH	PGH	GH	GH	GH	H		
Radish	GH	PGH	PGH					P	PGH	PGH	PGH	GH
Spinach	GH	PGH	GH	GH	H			P	PGH	PGH	PGH	GH
Spinach, New Zealand	GH	PGH	PGH	PGH	PGH	PGH	PGH	PGH	PGH	PGH	PGH	GH
Squash, summer			P	PG	PGH	PGH	GH	GH	GH	H	H	
Squash, winter			P	PG	PG	PGH	GH	GH	GH	H	H	
Swiss chard	GH	PGH	PGH	PGH	PGH	PGH	PGH	PGH	PGH	PGH	PGH	GH
Tomatoes		P	PG	PGH	PGH	PGH	PGH	PGH	GH	GH	H	
Turnips	GH	PGH	GH	H	H			P	PGH	PGH	PGH	GH
Watermelon				P	PG	PG	GH	GH	GH	H		

Getting Started

Now that you have some schedules to refer to and an idea as to where your greenhouse or sunspace fits into the scheme of things (as to temperature), it is time to figure out a potential schedule. Make a list of what plants you wish to grow, and then refer to the schedules to see where they fit in. It might also be helpful to read about each particular crop that you plan to grow in Chapter 8, A Closer Look at the Plants. There they are discussed in depth, which could help you fine-tune scheduling as well as provide you with other tricks of growing them.

A
Closer Look
at the Plants
8

A Closer Look at the Plants

How to Use Chapter 8

Now that we've covered how to arrange the interior of your greenhouse, select varieties, propagate plants and schedule the growing of your crops, we need to look at the specific horticulture of each type of plant. This section is based primarily on my experience; it should be noted that there are always alternate methods to get good results. That's why gardening is still considered as much of an art as it is a science. There is never one proper way to grow any one plant. Gardeners are individualistic and often like to try things their own way. By doing so, they discover new and different ways to get plants to grow well.

This chapter is an encyclopedia of selected plants. It includes ornamental flowering crops, fruits and vegetables and herbs for the greenhouse or sunspace. It is not intended to be read straight through. Rather, it is to be used as a reference. I try to point out the common pitfalls of growing each particular plant and troubleshoot problems that may arise.

Some of the discussions about each plant are more lengthy than others. This is because some plants require more attention, while others are just plain easier to grow. The following recommendations are not hard and fast rules. In fact, I encourage you to break them occasionally. I ask only that if you do try something different, keep some records so you will learn from what you have done. It is all too easy to forget what you did many months ago. Record-keeping shortens the learning curve and the level of frustration. See the Record-Keeping appendix for some samples of forms you may wish to use.

ORNAMENTAL FLOWERING CROPS

ORNAMENTAL FLOWERING CROPS

I have avoided some of the more difficult ornamental plants in the following list, instead selecting those that are easy to grow or that produce spectacular results. A plant may be listed here because of its interesting bloom or foliage or solely because it smells good. Scent has a high priority when I grow plants. While the following list of ornamentals is extensive, it is not by any means a complete list of what can be grown in a greenhouse. To cover every potential ornamental plant for the greenhouse or sunspace would fill many books. Besides, I had to leave some exploring up to you. With a little effort, you too can find some new incredible plants not listed here. That's the fun of being a horticultural pioneer.

The ornamental plants in this chapter are listed in alphabetical order, with their common name first, followed by the scientific (or Latin) name in parentheses. Exceptions occur when the plants' scientific names are commonly used; then I may have listed them first. Hard-core botanists will hate this, but rest assured that you can find both common names and scientific names in the index, in alphabetical order. Of course, nothing identifies a plant more accurately than a Latin or scientific name. Still, it can be confusing to beginning gardeners. Try to spend some time learning the scientific name. Why? It will help you accurately tell the difference between the five plants known as black-eyed susan. Besides, when you learn the scientific name, it will spice up your vocabulary while impressing people in conversation. The main thing is to have fun and not take yourself, the greenhouse or the plants too seriously.

Ageratum
(Ageratum houstonianum)

Ageratum is sometimes known as **floss flower**. While it is known for its dense, fluffy cluster of small blue flowers, it also comes in **pink** and **white varieties**. I still prefer the **blue-flowered varieties**. It tends to look best when the greenhouse runs to moderate temperatures in fall, spring and early summer. If your greenhouse gets too hot, ageratum may suffer. If well established in August, it often can hold its own as temperatures get cool. It is an annual, and when it starts to look spent, it is usually best to just toss it out.

Ageratum is a common outside bedding plant and can be started in the greenhouse around late March for later transplanting to the outside garden. It is best planted in clusters. Most varieties grow only to about 10 inches (25 cm) high, but some varieties can get up to 20 inches (51 cm) in height. Most varieties of ageratum are not suitable as cut flowers, unless you are growing the taller types. It is best grown as a border plant along greenhouse paths (set out at 6 inches, 15 cm apart) or plant three or more in pots 6 inches (15 cm) or larger. Ageratum is best propagated from seed.

Aloe Vera
(Aloe vera)

Many people know of the succulent aloe vera plant as the burn plant, because its sap is often used medicinally as treatment for minor skin burns. While it is not exceptionally ornamental, it is something many people like to have on hand. Aloe vera occasionally blooms, but the

Aloe vera

flowers are not very striking. Propagation is commonly done by dividing a mature plant that has developed smaller "pups" growing in a cluster. Try to separate the cluster so that you can get some attached root, and set it in potting soil that has been mixed one to one with sand. If the plant is getting a purplish hue to the leaves, it is telling you that you are giving it too much light. Only water it after the top of the soil has completely dried out. It benefits from occasional fertilization.

There are many cousins to the aloe vera that are not used for burns but are grown for their ornamental foliage and flowers. Some put out blooming stalks in spring that are real showstoppers. If you have an interest in growing succulents (see Succulents, p. 284), be sure to see what is available in aloe species in a good greenhouse or cactus speciality catalog (see the Mail-Order Plants appendix). Diverse aloe species may also be available in a local retail greenhouses.

Alstromeria
(*Alstromeria* spp.)

This plant is grown primarily for its cut flowers and is a relative to the amaryllis. It is also known as the **Peruvian lily**. The plant can grow up to 4 feet (1.2 m) in height and has showy flowers in shades of orange, yellow, pink, red and white. Most are streaked or spotted in the throat of the flower. The cut flower keeps for many days.

Alstromeria plants are started at the end of summer for blooming the following spring. They are usually propagated from obtained rhizomes but can also be started from seed. Growing from seed can be tricky, however, as some may take many months to germinate. For best establishment, grow the plant around 65° F (18° C). Alstromeria

like to grow on the moist side with full sun and can be grown in either 1-gallon (3.8-liter) pots or ground beds. The best blooming is often best triggered by a 2-week cool period of around 40° F (5° C). The cool period is especially important if you are growing for red or orange blooms. The plants may need staking as they get taller.

Each plant will produce a fleshy, thickened potatolike rhizome. After blooming, the plant will go dormant but will often come back to life, sprouting from the rhizome again in a few months. The plant can live for many years but should be divided every 2 years.

Alstromeria are heavy feeders, so periodic feeding can be beneficial. Fortunately, they have few pest problems.

Alstromeria

Alyssum in hanging basket

Alyssum
(Lobularia maritima)

Alyssum, also known as **sweet alyssum**, is another common annual plant seen in the outside garden but it does great in a greenhouse too. Avoid the perennial alyssum, which is not suited to a greenhouse. Alyssum is a low-growing ground cover with dainty masses of flowers clustered like thimbles. Varieties are available with flowers in the colors of **white**, **pink** and **purple**. The flowers have a slightly sweet scent.

In the greenhouse, I use alyssum along walk paths as a colorful ground cover or trailing over the sides of hanging baskets. The plant does fine in the greenhouse year-round but suffers some in hot weather. They can get slightly aggressive because they readily reseed themselves. If you overwater, you will often find that alyssum provides a favorite habitat for slugs (p. 418). The slugs usually don't damage the alyssum, but they retreat to it during daytime to plan out nighttime attacks.

Alyssum is easily started from seed. Don't plant seed too deep; just barely cover them. If it grows much past 12 months, it may need to be ripped out and started over or kept regularly well pruned.

Amaryllis
(Hippeastrum spp.)

I remember when I was a child and I grew my first mammoth sunflower. As it topped out at 8 feet (2.4 m), I felt like I was Jack with his bean stalk. The plant seemed to touch the sky and made me feel like a masterful gardener. I remember a similar feeling when, as a teenager, I bought my first amaryllis bulb. When it flowered a month after I set it in a window, it was by far the largest flower I had ever seen.

The holidays are the season when you find amaryllis bulbs

commonly for sale, but they may be found in the nonholiday season in many catalogs. The amaryllis is a native to Peru and is one of the easiest flowering plants to grow. Because of the huge 8- to 10-inch (20- to 25-centimeter) flower it creates, it will take your brown thumb and instantly propel you into the green thumb category.

Like the flowers it produces, the amaryllis bulb is large, measuring up to 5 inches (13 cm) across. When you bring the bulb home, you'll need to grow it in a pot 2 inches (5 cm) larger than the bulb, usually a 6-inch (15-centimeter) pot. Set the bulb in any commercial potting soil so the top half is exposed. If it comes prepotted, it is often planted in pure peat moss, which is a cheap substitute for a good potting mix. I usually find it's best to repot preplanted bulbs into new store-bought potting soil.

The amaryllis likes to be on the wet side. It usually takes 6 to 8 weeks after planting before you see it flower. If the bulb seems to be taking longer to sprout, with no signs of growth, try setting it in a very warm place (like on top of the hot-water heater) for 3 days to trigger growth. Once it starts growing, it greatly benefits from applications of a liquid or water-soluble fertilizer once every 3 weeks.

When you do get blooms, the top can get so big that you might want to consider using some small stakes to prevent it from tipping over. Because an amaryllis may bend toward the sun, it is helpful to give the pot a one-quarter turn every few days to keep the plant growing evenly.

Horticulturists have a raging debate on the proper care after it flowers. For years the common belief was to give the plant a dormant or rest period. Now, many amaryllis enthusiasts claim that you can get the plant to rebloom bigger and better without the dormant period. I am on the "no rest" side of the fence, mainly because it is easier. All you have to do after flowering is continue growing it as you would any houseplant. After the blooms all fade, just trim off the flower stalk, and then it will grow long, gangly straplike leaves. It will do this until it decides to bloom again, usually in late winter. You can grow amaryllis in the same pot for 2 to 3 years before repotting it. Just wash away and replace the top inch of soil every summer.

Amaryllis are available in colors that range from bright scarlet through salmon, pink and white. There are also some beautiful bicolored varieties. If you want to have many months of bloom, try buying four or five bulbs and pot one up every few weeks from October through December.

Unlike many showy flowering plants, the amaryllis requires no special conditions or treatment, but you will easily get incredible results. When people see the 9-inch (23-centimeter) blooms you have produced, they'll think you are a greenhouse gardening genius.

Anemone
(Anemone coronaria)

Anemone, sometimes known as **windflowers**, are a handsome, poppylike flower (some may look more like daisies) that come in the colors of white, red, pink and purple and are 2 to 3 inches (5 to 8 cm) across on 8-inch (20-centimeter) stems. The variety **Mona Lisa** is a good choice for large, showy flowers, and the flowers have a wider color range. There are other varieties besides the *coronaria* species, but *coronaria* is the best suited to growing under glass. They are usually started from small tubers, which are best planted in late summer in the greenhouse. Set the tubers a couple of inches deep, and 2 to 3 inches (5 to 8 cm) apart in well-drained soil (soil that doesn't drain well can cause the

tubers to rot). They may occasionally be plagued by rot (p. 470). If so, be sure to go easy on the watering. Because they often bloom all at once and then stop blooming at the same time, you might want to stagger the planting over a month to spread out the period of bloom over a longer time.

Anemone

Anemone can also be started from seeds, germinating in 10 to 14 days. It is crucial when germinating anemone seeds to keep the temperatures below 60° F (15° C) because higher temperatures reduce the percentage of seeds that germinate. Seedlings are ready to transplant in about 10 weeks. When you transplant seedlings into larger pots or into beds, be sure not to set the plant any deeper into the new soil than it was before. If the crown gets buried, it may cause stem rot.

Anemones are best grown through the cooler months in the greenhouse because they just love cool temperatures (50° to 60° F, 10° to 15° C). Warmer temperatures can cause problems with setting of blooms. Place the flowers in a spot that receives full sun. Wait a day or two after the blooms have opened before you cut them for bouquets. Cut anemones last 5 to 6 days. When the plant's flowers are finished blooming, you can dig up the bulbs and store them in a cool, dry spot. Next August or early September is the time to pot them up again for another winter's show. There is something about anemone blooms that can really brighten up a winter day.

Angel's-trumpet
(*Datura-Brugmansia* spp.)

Angel's-trumpet is a name for many plants that are in the nightshade or Solanaceae family. They are found in both annual and the subtropical shrubby perennial flowering forms. Both the annual and the perennial plants are known for their large fragrant trumpet-shaped blooms. Flowers are found in the colors of **salmon**, **red**, **white**, **yellow** and **purple**. All these species are also known for being toxic if ingested, so take precautions with small children.

Angel's-trumpet

The shrub types, often sold under the name *Brugmansia,* are very showy greenhouse plants. Their flowers are real eye-catchers, sometimes reaching up to 1 foot (.3 m). Around evening the flowers start pumping out an exotic scent, adding to their charm. Angel's-trumpet can flower year-round with noticeable ebbs and surges in the number of blooms.

The **shrub angel's-trumpet** is an easy-to-grow plant that can reach heights of 12 feet (3.6 m) or more. Be sure you have room for this plant, or be ready to control its fast growth with some pruning shears. It needs to grow in full sunlight and may need watering every day when temperatures get warm.

Brugmansia versicolor has flowers that turn color in the first day or two. They start out creamy white and after a day or so, they turn a beautiful salmon color, having a delightful fragrance, especially in the evening. There is also a **double-flowered variety** found in some catalogs (with double the number of petals in a flower) that is quite showy. ***Brugmansia suaveolens*** is a heavily scented white variety that is bushy and compact.

Brugmansias can be grown directly in ground beds or in large tubs. They can be easily propagated from seed or cuttings; plants are also available from specialty greenhouse plant catalogs. Because the *Brugmansia* is a subtropical perennial, it is long-lived in the greenhouse and may need occasional shaping to groom back leggy portions.

The **annual angel's-trumpet** (often known as **datura** or **moon lily**) has similar flowers compared with its shrubby cousin, but the plant grows much shorter (around 10 to 18 inches, 25 to 46 cm) and has smaller flowers. I have seen some of the datura grow some ornamental fruit, but like all other parts of the plant, it is quite poisonous. The annual angel's-trumpet is easy to start from seed. Because it is an annual, it can begin to look

ragged after a couple of years and should be tossed out.

Aster
(Aster spp.*)*

Most annual and some perennial asters can be grown in a greenhouse. **Annual asters (*Callistephus chinensis*)**, sometimes known as **China aster**, are a colorful flower that is well suited to the greenhouse at certain times of the year. They make a great cut flower or a nice flowering potted plant. Because the flowering is triggered by the length of the night, the aster is genetically set to bloom in either early May or in August and usually continues for a month

Aster

or so. Commercial greenhouse operators have figured out ways to grow plants with special schedules and plant covers to simulate nights in order to trick them into blooming at anytime of the year. This is a lot of work for the home greenhouse. It is much easier to just grow them during their natural time period, planting seeds around April or May for bloom in late summer. You can also get good results with a July sowing for December flowering.

There are many options to select from when you are growing annual asters. They can be found in almost any color and come in heights from short (6 to 12 inches, 15 to 30 cm) to tall (18 to 30 inches, 46 to 76 cm). The taller varieties may need staking in the greenhouse. The shape of the flower varies from daisylike to pompon, similar to mums. Annual asters also have many interesting petal shapes to choose from. The flowers do not rebloom after the initial bud set, so after the plant is finished flowering, it is best to discard the plant.

Annual asters are subject to many fungal diseases that are sometimes hard to deal with (see Diseases, p. 460). You can often select varieties listed in catalogs that exhibit varying levels of disease resistance. It also helps to use new potting soil if you are growing

them in pots; or when growing them in beds, rotate plantings around to new spots year to year. Annual asters are best propagated from seed.

I have found one **perennial aster** that blooms well in a greenhouse botanically known as *aster* x *frikartii*. It has masses of blue daisylike flowers on a plant that gets around 2 feet (.6 m) high. It is a fine plant, except that I've found that white flies like to make it their home—so keep a close eye on the underside of the leaf. Frikartii asters are usually purchased as a plant. You can propagate frikartii from cuttings in spring or by dividing thickly growing plants.

Azalea
(Rhododendron simsii)

Most people end up with an azalea as a gift plant around the holiday season. Unable to toss it out after it quits blooming, people look to their greenhouse or sunspace for azalea salvation and another bloom period. In the greenhouse it is best grown in a pot.

Azaleas prefer growing in a cool, brightly lit spot. They suffer when the temperature hovers toward 70° to 80° F (21° to 27° C). They also like to stay uniformly moist, but not dripping wet. Azaleas can be propagated from cuttings taken in the spring.

After your azalea is finished flowering, remove faded flowers. If your greenhouse is too hot in the summer, you might consider moving the plant outside to a lightly shaded, cool spot until fall, when it should be brought back inside. Buds seem to set best after a cool period, when temperatures are above 65° F (18° C) and below 75° F (24° C), ideally in late summer or early fall.

If you see your azalea getting shriveled, it is an indication of underwatering, too much heat or too much sun. If newer leaves turn yellow, it lacks the acidic soil that it prefers. I have good luck getting the soil more acid by using an acidifying houseplant fertilizer (check a good garden center) or by monthly watering with a mixture of 1/2 a teaspoon of vinegar to a quart (.9 l) of water. Keep an eye out for spider mites (p. 416) on the underside of the leaves as indi-

cated by webbing and stippling of small yellow spots on the leaves.

Begonia
(Begonia spp.*)*

The **fibrous begonia (*Begonia semperflorens*)** is so named because of its fibrous root system and is often known as the wax begonia. It is a common bedding plant used outside in shady locations. It can also make a nice greenhouse plant. It is a low-growing annual (3 to 5 inches high, 8 to 13 cm high) that has either green or bronze leaves with small pink, red or white flowers. It is easy to care for and is best used in large hanging baskets and along walk paths. Fibrous begonia naturally gets bushy over time. It is easily started from both seeds or cuttings. It can tolerate some cool temperatures well. It suffers from too much moisture, so be sure to let it dry out between waterings.

Tuberous-rooted begonias (*Begonia* x *tuberhybrida*) are grown mainly for their large showy double flowers 3 to 5 inches (8 to 13 cm) across. It is a real sight once its colorful petals start blooming. These begonias are propagated from large tubers set out in mid- to late winter and are best grown when eventually set into 8- to 10-

Azalea

inch (20- to 25-centimeter) pots. It is best to work your way up to such a big pot, starting with smaller pots and up-potting as the flowers need more room. Tuberous begonias need more warmth than the fibrous types, doing best between 55° F (13° C) and 75° F (24° C). They like bright spots but not necessarily direct sun and prefer the soil on the dry side. After flowering, the plants are often discarded. If you hate to throw them out, cut them back after flowering and grow on the cool and dry side. They can be propagated from cuttings.

Another favorite begonia is the ***Begonia rex***, which has some of the most interesting multicolored leaves I have ever seen. Each leaf looks like an incredible colorful painting. *Begonia rex* will surely

Begonia

hypnotize you with their fascinating colors and dozens of named varieties to choose from. *Rex* needs to dry out between waterings; overwatering will cause it to fade fast. They suffer when temperatures drop below 55° F (13° C). I have seen them occasionally lose their leaves as if they were dead. Fortunately, they sometimes are just playing possum and going through a dormant period. If you suspect this, be sure to cut way back on the water and give it some warmth, and you may coax it to grow those beautifully painted leaves again.

Cane-stemmed begonias, sometimes known as **angel wing begonia**, are also common, but not quite as showy. They grow tall and usually have pink or reddish flowers that hang down in an interesting fashion. Some of the cane-stemmed begonias have whitish spots on the leaves.

Begonia feastii, usually known as **pancake** or **beefsteak begonia**, has interesting flowers and leaves. The leaf has a roundish flat shape that is incredibly shiny. Rising straight above the leaves are beautiful dainty pink flowers on pink stems.

All begonias benefit from similar conditions of indirect bright light and the need to dry out a bit between waterings. All can be started from stem and leaf cuttings in spring or summer. The tuberous and fibrous begonia can be started from seed in early to late winter. Some of the begonias are not known for being long-lived, so if they start looking scraggly, think about propagating some new plants.

Bird-of-Paradise
(Strelitzia reginae)

Photo by Jim Weis

Bird-of-paradise

The bird-of-paradise, native to South America, is one of the more exotic flowers you can grow in a greenhouse. Like its name, the flower looks as if it is a bird head or beak. It has the ability to make you feel your greenhouse or sunspace truly is a tropical paradise. Even the paddle-shaped leaves, which look a bit like a banana plant, create an exotic effect. The plant reaches heights of 3 to 5 feet (.9 to 1.5 m). Being tropical, it prefers temperatures above 45° F (7° C). I've had good luck growing the bird-of-paradise both in ground beds and in large pots (15- to 20-gallon, 57- to 76-liter size).

The most common question is how to make the bird-of-paradise bloom. Fertilize it with chicken feed? Nope. The main trick to get the bird-of-paradise to bloom is a large dose of patience. Flowering is mainly a matter of maturity. A new plant or even a good-sized transplant can take as long as 3 to 4 years to get into a good profusion of blooms. After that it seems to be a regular bloomer. If you're lucky, you may see an occasional bloom here and there in the first few years. Blooms can occur at most anytime of the year, but I tend to see the most in the fall.

The flower head can make an exotic cut flower for incredible arrangements. They are, for the most part, trouble-free, but they can get an occasional infestation of mealybugs, especially if you don't look them over once in a while. With some difficulty the bird-of-paradise can be propagated from seed, which is readily available from greenhouse plant catalogs. The best way to propagate the bird-of-paradise is to divide a larger clump with a sharp shovel, taking care to get a good amount of roots.

Bougainvillea
(Bougainvillea spp.*)*

The bougainvillea is one of my favorite greenhouse plants. The perennial vines require little work or attention but put on terrific displays of color at times when color is needed in winter and spring. Some even bloom well throughout summer and fall.

The colored flowers are really not flowers but bracts, which are a paperlike leaf that is positioned below an inconspicuous flower. The colors of the bougainvillea are bright and wonderfully diverse: **white**, **pink**, **scarlet**, **orange**, **yellow**, **salmon** and **lavender**. The bracts (which I'll just call flowers to simplify things) are also available in varieties that have double the traditional number of "petals" per flower.

Bougainvilleas are woody vines that can rapidly cruise through a greenhouse if given free rein. Vines can easily reach up to 15 feet (4.6 m) and may need tieing up or trellis support. But they take well to shaping. Prune the vines (if needed) only after they've finished a flush of flowering. The vines sometimes, but not always, have thorns, which can sneak up on you if you're not careful when working around them. When grown in a pot, they perform well but may need some tip pinching to keep the plant bushy.

A **dwarf variety** of bougainvillea called **pink pixie** keeps a compact shape, and **variegated types** have interesting patterns of white-and-green-colored foliage.

Double-flowered plants are available and have some different characteristics. They tend to have longer blooming seasons and are more compact growers. This makes them great for hanging baskets. The double-flowered varieties also differ from the single types in that they don't drop the flower petals. This is good in terms of being cleaner, but it means that you must occasionally cut the flowers off as they age and fade.

Aphids (p. 413) and mealybugs (p. 415) may make occasional visits to the bougainvillea vine, but if the vines are healthy, they seem to stay more pest-free. Occasionally you might see some new growth yellowing, which indicates a micronutrient deficiency. Refer to Chapter 9, Getting to the Roots, for help if this occurs. For best results, grow the bougainvillea on the dry side, letting the top of the soil dry out between waterings.

The bougainvillea bloom best for me in the greenhouse anytime from fall through spring. Because the petals drop readily, they are not the best choice for bouquets, unless you don't mind a little cleanup under the vase each day. I have heard from dried-flower enthusiasts that the bougainvillea can be successfully dried for arrangements. For general bright color, the plant is a real treat for any greenhouse or sunspace and a good choice for the moderately cool greenhouse. Bougainvillea prefer temperatures above 50° F (10° C) and can tolerate temperatures down to freezing.

I have had good luck propagating bougainvilleas from cuttings taken in late spring. They can also be purchased from greenhouse plant catalogs listed in the Mail-Order Plants appendix.

Bromeliads
(Bromelia)

There are thousands of species of bromeliads. The most familiar bromeliad is the pineapple. Many bromeliads (not all) share a quality with many orchids, that of being epiphytes. An epiphyte is a plant that in its native habitat grows lodged in the crotch of a tree or bush but is not parasitic and derives no nutrition from the host plant. Some people call epiphytes air plants.

The interesting thing about most bromeliads is that their structure is designed to get water not just from the roots but also from "cups" found at the base of the leaves. The leaves are often very tough, with some sharp serrated edges.

Bromeliads are slow-growing plants, but many have some of the most interesting flowers and leaves found in nature and interesting leaf variegations. Being epiphytic, they can be mounted in the crotches of trees, mounted on wood or bark, or grown in clay pots. When you mount them, you need to provide a bit of sphagnum moss in a little indentation where it can anchor itself. You may have to temporarily tie it with some wire or string until it gets established. If grown in clay pots, bromeliads need very well-drained soil containing a high percentage of sand

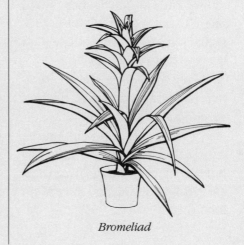

Bromeliad

or a mixture of bark chips and peat moss. **Tillandsia** is a common smaller bromeliad that can be placed in many small nooks and crannies. Tillandsia are often sold in seashells with a magnet glued onto the shell to be stuck upon the refrigerator. They look so much better in a greenhouse. I like to mount them in crotches of my fig tree.

Bromeliads are not difficult to grow, and many people develop a fascination for the many ornamental varieties. Some varieties require exacting care, but most are easy to grow. The general recommendation for growing bromeliads is to apply the water directly into the vaselike cups formed where the leaves attach to the main plant, allowing only a little to reach the soil. A few varieties do not have the cups that can hold water; for these types keep the soil on the moist side, but not muddy wet. I often just dunk the tillandsia bromeliads under water for a second every couple of weeks.

They can survive cool temperatures but do best in warmer greenhouses. Over time, they often produce offshoot plants at the base of the mother plant, known as pups by many people. These pups are easily split off and potted on their own.

Browallia

Browallia
(Browallia speciosa)

Browallia is a winter favorite of mine. I like to grow it in hanging baskets. It has star-shaped flowers borne above glossy dark green foliage. The flowers are about 1 1/2 inches (3.8 cm) across. Browallia can be found with either **blue** or **white flowers**. The particular shade of the blue flower is a welcome color in the greenhouse and is a perfect plant to complement red or warm-colored flowers. At maturity the plant can bush out to about 1 foot (.3 m) high and wide. If you grow it for more than a year, it can get bigger and more leggy and may be a good candidate for the compost. It benefits from some slight tip pruning to maintain the shape. The varieties *speciosa* *major*, the **bell series** and the **troll series** are compact strains that branch out naturally and need little pinching.

Although browallia is a perennial, I have found that it provides the best show in its first year or so. After that, plan to start new plants from seed or cuttings. If you start it from seed, cover the seed and keep it moist.

While cold temperatures will slow its growth considerably, it can tolerate the brisk air well and continue to flower. Beware because whiteflies (p. 420) have a good appetite for browallia, but fortunately, whiteflies slow down more than the browallia does in winter. Even so, keep an eye to the underside of the leaf for any impending attacks.

Cactus
(Cactaceae)

Many people turn to cacti thinking that they must be a good choice for anyone who has a hard time with plants, and usually they are forgiving plants when it comes to abuse. With a little special care, however, cacti can become some of your more treasured, exotic and interesting plants. They can also delight you with some of the beautiful flowers they grow.

In general terms, cacti can be split into two groups: **desert cacti** and **forest cacti**. Knowing which kind you are growing makes a big difference in how you care for your cactus.

Desert cacti are native to the sunny, arid climates and are usually characterized by having thick fleshy shapes, no leaves and sharp spines or hairlike filaments. Desert cacti need water only once a month between mid-October and late March. Then increase watering to at least once every two weeks or more in spring and summer. Be sure to place desert cacti in a sunny, warm location. Cacti like to be pot-bound, so don't give them too much room.

Because desert cacti don't need as much water as other plants, many people assume that they don't need fertilizer either. Not true. During the summer about once a month, give the plants a diluted water-soluble fertilizer. Most any houseplant food will do. With a little feeding, you'll see amazing amounts of new growth. New growth often means you'll get a good shot at getting your cactus to flower. Flowering usually occurs in spring and early summer.

Contrary to popular belief, desert cacti usually don't do well in pure sand. Give them a one-to-one mix of sand and potting soil.

Christmas cactus

Forest cacti, if treated like desert cacti will suffer unnecessarily. That's why it is important to know the difference. Forest cacti are native to the tropics and grow as epiphytes on trees (for more information on epiphytes, see Bromeliads, p. 209). They prefer darker, wetter conditions than the desert cactus.

Forest cacti tend to have trailing growth, and many have flattened leaves. The most identifiable forest cactus is the **Christmas cactus**, which likes bright conditions but not direct sun. It needs a watering about once every three weeks in midwinter and an increase in the frequency of water in the spring through the summer. If it is in budding or in bloom, give the cactus a little extra water.

To bloom, many of the forest cacti need cool nights as close to 50° F (10° C) as possible. That makes most greenhouses ideal spots for the forest cactus because often a cool enough spot in our centrally heated homes is hard to find. A few forest cacti are also triggered by the length of the night, as long as they are in a place that gets uninterrupted periods of darkness. If you turn on lights in your greenhouse, it might cause them some confusion, but if you regularly have cool nights, then the length of the night is a secondary concern. Some bloom seasonally with no concern for light or temperature. Treat most forest cacti like a houseplant, with regular waterings. After bloom, treat it more like a desert cactus, with more infrequent watering until summer, when you go back to treating it like a houseplant.

There is a lot of confusion surrounding the holiday cacti: Christmas cactus, **Thanksgiving cactus** and **Easter cactus** (also known as **crab cacti** because of its crablike leaves). The easiest way to tell the difference is by looking closely at the leaves. Christmas cactus leaves have smooth, scalloped edges. The Thanksgiving cactus has more-pointed teeth along the edges of the leaves. The Easter cactus has a thicker, slightly more upright leaf and often has a purple or maroon color along the leaf edge. Easter cactus also have bristlelike hairs, often called cat whiskers, at the stem joints.

These sound like hard and fast rules, but unfortunately there are a lot of cross-hybrids that can make it hard to distinguish between many of the new hybrids. Similar-looking to the holiday cacti is the **orchid cactus**, which also has very showy blooms.

Another favorite type of forest cactus is the **night-blooming cereus**. These produce huge, imposing blooms (up to 9 inches, 23 cm across) on large thornless succulent plants. The plants themselves can grow up to 8 feet (2.4 m) long or more. There are many varieties of the night-blooming cereus. Most bloom only at night, but some varieties are rebellious and disregard their name by blooming through the day. Blooms may be fragrant or odorless. I know of people who set up chairs around the cactus and invite their neighbors over when it gets dark, just to watch the grand opening of a night-blooming cereus. What a show!

Many people think that cactus are just slow-growing, boring plants with spines. With a closer look, that attitude usually changes. Given all the cacti varieties and all the unusual shapes, types and blooms that they have, it is easy to see how people can develop a real love for these plants.

Both forest and desert cacti can be propagated easily from cuttings. Take the cuttings in late winter and let them sit out overnight for the cut portion to dry out a bit. Insert the cut portion into a cactus potting mix. There is no need to place cactus cuttings in a humid or misty environment. If you get interested in making cactus a hobby, get ahold of a good cactus plant catalog and a book on cactus—you'll be an expert in no time.

Caladium
(Caladium bicolor)

The caladium is a plant grown for its unique colored leaf rather than a flower. The foot-long heart-shaped leaf has a display of color that is as beautiful as any flower. Usually the color runs along the veins of the plant, creating stunning combinations of red, pink, green and white. Caladiums need temperatures above 65° F (18° C). The temperature should never get below 60° F (15° C), so these are not a good choice for the cool greenhouse.

Caladiums also need a rest period. Usually around September, the foliage begins to look a little ragged and often begins to die back. This is a time to stop watering the plant and store the tubers in peat moss at around 50° F (10° C) until March. In March, replant the tubers and grow on the moist side. Give them a humid, well-lit place with little direct sun. A good place for caladiums is under a table or bench. They grow well in pots or beds. If grown in pots, put only one bulb in an 8-inch (20-centimeter) pot.

Caladiums are generally acquired as tubers. Sometimes you will find small bulblets attached to the mother tuber that can be separated and potted individually as a way to get new plants.

Calendula
(Calendula officinalis)

Calendula, sometimes known as **pot marigold** (no relation to the marigold), is a short-lived annual with apricot, orange, cream and yellow leaves. The 4-inch (10-centimeter) flower bears resemblance to the zinnia or daisy, de-

Calendula

pending upon the variety. Varieties can reach up to 36 inches (91 cm), but most reach 12 to 18 inches (30 to 46 cm). Some varieties have contrasting centers. There is one variety that even looks like a cactus dahlia known as **radio extra selected**, available from the Thompson & Morgan catalog (see Mail-Order Seeds appendix for address).

Calendulas grow well year-round, except when the greenhouse is at its hottest. When temperatures start running warm, calendulas can go downhill and not flower very well. Even in cool temperatures, the plant may look good only for 2 to 4 months, but they are fast to come into flower and are well worth the effort. As with many annuals, they benefit from the removal of spent blossoms. Grow calendulas in a sunny spot, either in pots or in beds spaced 8 to 10 inches (20 to 25 cm) apart. The stems are short, but with the right vase and a little creativity, they can make a fine cut flower. When the plant quits blooming, it is best to toss it out and start over. Calendulas are easily propagated from seed and start blooming in about 6 to 9 weeks.

Calla Lily
(*Zantedeschia*)

I always think of how the actress Katharine Hepburn rolled the words "calla lily" off her tongue in an old movie. If there ever was an art deco flower, this is the one. The flower has a perfect artistic swirl on a strong stalk.

The calla lily grows from a bulbous rhizome. Flowers are borne on stout stalks above shiny arrow-shaped leaves. The unique blooms are most commonly found as a pure **white** color, but there are varieties of **red**, **orange** and **yellow**. Some varieties have white spots on the leaf. The plant itself usually grows from 1 to 3 feet (.3 to .9 m) in height.

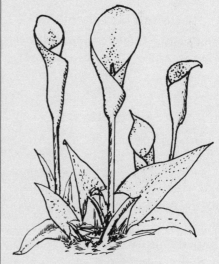

Calla lily

Calla lilies are native to bogs. They like their feet wet most of the time, but especially when the temperatures are warm. They can tolerate some shade, but bloom best when they get full sun. While they generally don't flower much in the winter greenhouse, you can leave them growing in a bed without much care and they'll surprise you in late winter or early spring with new blooms. Callas can also be grown in 1-gallon (3.8-liter) pots with good success. They bloom in flushes from late winter through fall. During the hottest part of summer, they may go dormant for a while.

If the leaf or flower tips turn brown, it is an indication of too much fertilizer or not enough water. Either can be remedied by the addition of water.

Callas can be started from either seed or bulbs. Large, older plants can be divided with good success.

Camellia
(Camellia spp.*)*

People who live in the South often brag of their beautiful camellias. Now that you have a greenhouse, you can join in on the fun. Depending on the variety, they can bloom anytime between late fall and early spring. Camellia is an

Camellia

evergreen shrub that is related to the tea family of plants and is native to China and Japan.

Camellias have roselike flowers that vary in color from white to pink and red. They are found on shrubby plants with dark glossy leaves and are famous for their use as corsages and in bouquets.

Camellias thrive in cool greenhouses in winter and not only tolerate but also prefer temperatures that regularly get down to the 40s (between 5° and 9° C). Camellias can tolerate hot summer temperatures well. I find that they are best grown in large pots or tubs, but they can be grown in a bed. Place them in bright or filtered light.

Camellias can not stand to have wet feet. Therefore, add extra sand or perlite to the potting soil mix. Take care not to let the roots dry out while not over- or underwatering.

They also like an acidic soil and may benefit from fertilizing with an acidic plant food if your soil is alkaline. Camellias are famous for dropping unopened blossoms, which can drive gardeners crazy. Some drop is normal, but when it seems to be getting out of hand, consider checking possibilities that may be causing the plant some amount of stress, such as the amount of water, heat or light.

The most common greenhouse camellia is the *Camellia japonica*, which can grow up to 20 feet (6 m) tall. Japonica varieties bloom best in cooler temperatures and are a good choice for corsages.

A camellia known as **fragrant pink** gives off a nice spicy aroma and grows to 3 or 4 feet (.9 to 1.2 m). *C. sasanqua* is a smaller camellia, good for greenhouse pot culture in the greenhouses that get real cold.

Camellias are best propagated from cuttings and are readily available in greenhouse plant catalogs.

Campanula
(Campanula spp.*)*

Campanula is generally considered as a hardy outside perennial or biennial used as a flowering ground cover or a tall showy plant. Some varieties, such as cup and saucer bells, can get taller. It is not often thought of as a greenhouse plant, but certain varieties can be grown much like an annual.

Campanula isophylla (**stella** or **stella blue**) can be grown much like an annual in a pot in the greenhouse. It has a spray of 1-inch (2.5-centimeter) star-shaped blue flowers on a smallish plant. Stella is well suited to a hanging basket.

Campanula carpatica (**bellissimo**) is a new hybrid offered by Thompson & Morgan with great potential as a greenhouse hanging-basket plant. It has 2-inch (5-centimeter) flowers that come in **blue** and **white**. It should be started in January for an early summer bloom but can be started anytime throughout spring.

Campanula won't tolerate real hot greenhouse temperatures, so blooms may slow or stop altogether in the middle of summer. Regular feeding with a high-phosphorus plant food can prolong flowering. They are best started from seed, or thick clumps can easily be divided. Cuttings can also be successfully propagated into new plants. Campanulas grow best in a potting mix that is well drained.

Canna
(Canna x generalis)

Cannas are generally thought of as a dramatic outside landscape plant, with tall stalks and broad tropical-looking leaves topped with colorful flowers. Outside, the canna must be treated like a dahlia in most zones. The rhizome must be dug up and stored inside through the winter. In the greenhouse, I like to have at least one canna growing because the tall shape (up to 3 feet, .9 m) is complementary to other plants. They seem to do best in ground beds but would do fine in a pot that is at least 5 gallons (19 l) in size. The colors of canna are generally **red** to **yellow** and **orange**.

Canna

There are a few varieties in which the leaves themselves have a bronzelike coloring, but most varieties have green leaves. Though cannas have handsome flowers, they are generally grown for the effect of their bold upright shape rather than for masses of color.

Many people who like to grow cannas as an outside bedding plant find that digging them up and replanting them in the greenhouse is a good way to store the canna rhizome and get a greenhouse plant for the winter. It is not a good bloomer when temperatures get below 50° F (10° C) but does well if given warm temperatures and full sun.

Cannas are best propagated from division of the rhizome taken in spring.

Carnation
(Dianthus caryophyllus)

The carnation is an old traditional greenhouse cut flower. The blooms are known for their long-keeping ability in bouquets. They come in colors of **yellow**, **white**, **pink** and **red**. If you want any other color, grow white carnations and set the cut flower in a glass of water with a concentrated solution of food coloring (try any color or mix of colors). Over the next 24 hours, you can watch the flower take up the color of the solution.

There are many carnation varieties sold for outside growing that tend to bloom best in the warmer months. Most varieties sold in catalogs are the more **dwarf types**, which need no staking and are easy to grow. Some common varieties include the **knight hybrids**, which reach 1 foot (.3 meter) high and the **lilipot series**, which are only 10 inches (25 cm) tall. Both can be grown in beds or in pots. Plants seem to go downhill after a year and should be tossed at that point.

Commercial greenhouses grow much taller types of carnations, up to 3 feet (.9 m), with large flowers borne on the long stems. These are not readily available to home greenhouse growers.

If you want to try these taller plants, you'll have to find a local commercial greenhouse that grows carnations as a cut flower and see if they will sell you a few plants or cuttings. If you grow the commercial types, you must set up a hori-

Carnation

zontal trellis system (see Chapter 3, Plant Layout, for more information) or they will be flopping around on the ground with poor blooms. The horizontal trellis may require at least three tiers, about 1 foot (.3 m) apart. The commercial-type carnations make great cut flowers, but you'll have to prune the smaller buds that develop to the side of the main bud, which forms at the tip of the stalk.

Burpee offers a **super giant carnation**, which reaches 18 inches (46 cm) tall and is easily started from seed. These taller types will also need some staking or trellising.

Carnations need to grow in full sun with a potting soil that drains well. Space three plants to 1 square foot (.09 sq. m). They are slow growers, so you must be patient because it can take up to half a year before you get many blooms. Some varieties are quite fragrant with a spicy clove scent, so look for fragrant varieties if that is a priority. Carnations seem to do best in cool temperatures, and blooming seems to slow when the temperatures start reaching for the upper 80s and 90s (27° to 37° C). Carnations are generally started from seed or cuttings.

Centaurea
(Centaurea cyanus)

Centaurea is also known as **bachelor button** or **cornflower**. It is a common reseeding annual often found in wildflower seed mixes. Centaurea is not usually thought of as a greenhouse plant, but I have had some good results growing it.

Centaurea has 1 1/2-inch (3.8-centimeter) flowers in the colors of **pink**, **white**, **blue**, **purple** and **dark maroon** on long stems. The thin leaves are gray-green. I like to grow it for cut flower purposes, especially the blue variety because it is hard to find blue hues in many other greenhouse cut flower plants. When grown in the greenhouse, it is not nearly as sturdy of a plant as when grown outside and tends to flop over unless provided some type of support, such as a stake or small cage. Most varieties reach up to 2 feet (.6 m) or more, but there are some dwarf varieties growing only 1 foot (.3 m) or so that are less likely to need much staking.

In the greenhouse, grow centaurea in a sunny spot in very well-drained soil. It prefers to be grown on the dry side; if conditions are too wet, it is susceptible to disease. If you don't harvest the flowers, be sure to clean up faded flowers as soon as they appear. They can get almost weedy because of their ability to reseed themselves. As an annual, it will begin to look ragged after a major flush of blooms. After that, it is time to pull the plant and start over. It tends to bloom best in warmer temperatures but does suffer a bit if the temperatures start to get real hot.

Another type of centaurea, which has an interesting flower with sharp pointed tips, is known as ***Centaurea moschata***. It is also fragrant and will need staking like the other centaurea but usually doesn't bloom quite as prolifically.

Centaurea is easily propagated from seed but must be carefully transplanted. It can be grown in 1-gallon (3.8-liter) pots; one or two plants per pot. You can also grow it directly in a bed with two to three plants per square foot.

Chenille Plant
(Acalypha hispida)

The chenille plant is grown for the unusual fuzzy red catkinlike flowers that dangle downward from where the leaf attaches. There are also varieties with pink or cream flowers. This plant is best grown as an interesting potted plant and is not suitable as a cut flower. It tends to bloom in the fall and winter and does best in warm greenhouses. Chenille plant prefers to grow in a spot with filtered light to full sun and needs a moderate amount of moisture. Chenille is a perennial and can live for many years, getting as big as 4 to 5 feet (1.2 to 1.5 m) tall unless pruned. It can be propagated from cuttings taken in fall.

Chrysanthemum
(Chrysanthemum spp.)

Chrysanthemums, or mums, are a rewarding plant for greenhouse growing, but they require a specific schedule because they are genetically programmed to set buds only when the days are short and the nights are at least 11 hours long (the night period must not be interrupted with artificial light). Commercial growers do this by simulating day with artificial lights and covering plants with a black sheet to simulate a longer night. That is a lot of trouble for home greenhouse gardeners. Instead, you can just plant to grow the mums when they will naturally bloom without extra work of night simulations. If you time the chrysanthemum to bloom in fall or winter, the flowering will work out naturally. By starting plants anytime from February through July, you should be doing fine.

Chrysanthemum

Chrysanthemums come in most every color except blue. The flowers are also available in much diversity. Besides the traditional-shaped flowers, there are also the more exotic incurve type of bloom, with glove-shaped petals that curve inward, and the spider type of flower, with many long tubular narrow blooms. Once you start looking, you will find many other interesting flower types.

There are mums available for outside planting and those that have been bred for greenhouse culture. Both can be grown in a greenhouse. Of the greenhouse types, some have been developed specifically for growing in pots, while others grow quite tall, up to 3 feet (.9 m), and are mainly for cut flower arrangements. These greenhouse varieties are hard to come by in most retail catalogs and are best obtained from your local commercial greenhouse that commonly grows them. If you want to grow the greenhouse types, you'll probably have to talk a grower into allowing you to purchase some special mum cuttings or small plants.

While you can use any chrysanthemum as a cut flower, the mums used for cut flowers by commercial growers tend to grow taller and need to be trellised with a horizontal trellising as described in Chapter 3, Plant Layout. You could also tie the plants to a series of bamboo stakes for support.

For mums grown in pots, it is helpful to grow a bushy plant. This can be done by regularly pinching off the tips of the plant as it is growing, promoting a fuller plant. If you are after bigger blooms, you may want to pinch the smaller flower buds that appear to the side of the terminal shoot and leave the big bud to develop at the top.

Many potted types of chrysanthemums benefit from a drastic pruning after they have flowered. They may also need to be repotted and regularly fertilized to bring on new healthy growth.

Mums can be grown in both ground beds or pots in full sun. Different varieties need different spacing, so refer to the source where you acquired the plants for help in proper spacing. Chrysanthemums are best propagated by cuttings taken from the tips (without flower buds) of healthy growth.

Cineraria
(*Senecio* spp.)

The cineraria is one of the more beautiful blooming plants for the greenhouse. It produces colorful daisylike flowers in almost every color. They are cool-loving plants that thrive when the night temperature drops to 50° F (10° C) and can even tolerate lower temperatures if need be. They do not like to grow in hot temperatures much above 75° F (24° C). For this reason they are best for the winter greenhouse.

Cinerarias are started from seed (just barely covered!) and when they are of decent size, they should be transplanted into a 6- to 10-inch (15- to 25-centimeter) pot, depending on the variety. Be sure to regularly up-pot them as needed because they wilt easily if root-bound. They are not a good choice for growing directly in beds. Grow them in full sun to partial sun.

For winter flowers, seed can be started in June, July and early August. After flowering, the plants decline rapidly and should be discarded.

As long as the temperature is not too hot, cinerarias are happy. The biggest problem with cinerarias is the love that aphids (p. 413) have for them. This means that you must keep a sharp eye out for these invaders by regularly checking under the leaves and washing or spraying off the aphids.

Cleome
(Cleome hasslerana)

Cleome is also known as **spiderflower** because it gets long spiderlike seed pods. It is commonly grown as an outside bedding plant and used as a tall background flower but can also provide some interest for the greenhouse. Cleome reach up to 6 feet (1.8 m) tall and have flowers in the colors of **pink**, **red**, **purple** and **white**. The flowers look best if grown in a clump of three or more plants together, placed at least 1 foot (.3 m) apart. Because of their size and rapid growth, they are best planted in a ground bed with some headroom and are not suitable in a pot unless it is a large tub. The flowers can be cut for large arrangements, but I like how they look among other plants in the greenhouse better.

The stems get small thorns as they mature, so be careful working around them. Cleome prefer moderate to warm temperatures and do best in full sun. They are easily started from seed.

Clivia, or Kaffir Lily
(Clivia miniata)

The clivia lily is similar to the amaryllis. It is not quite as showy but blooms longer. A bulbous plant with dark green straplike leaves and orange trumpet-shaped flowers, it should be grown in pots and seems to do best when left undisturbed for as long as possible. For this reason, it is fine to let it get pot-bound for some time. When you do up-pot the plant, try to not disturb the fleshy roots. Place clivia in full to partial sun. Unlike many bulb plants, clivia should never been given a rest period. Clivias bloom during the cooler periods of fall and winter. During budding and flowering, keep them on the moist side. The rest of the year, try to let the soil dry out between waterings. Clivia are propagated by division of the many bulbs that develop in a pot over time.

Coleus
(Coleus blumei)

Coleus is a common houseplant grown for the colorful leaves. The combinations of red, orange, yellow, purple and green are every bit as showy as any flower. Coleus can be grown in full sun but are a good choice for the darker areas of a greenhouse, where it is harder to grow colorful plants. Notice the square stems of the coleus, indicating that it is a cousin to the many herbs in the mint family, which all are identified by their square stems.

Coleus is one of the easiest plants to propagate from a cutting and readily roots-up in water. Most people acquire them as slips from friends. They are also easy to grow from seed. The seed is small, so just barely cover it. Growing from seed allows you more freedom to try some of the more interesting varieties. They have an amazing diversity of leaf colors and shapes.

Coleus tend to give the best show in the warm greenhouse but will survive cooler conditions in a state of suspended animation. They grow fine in moist pots and ground beds. The flowers are almost unsightly and should be pinched off when they appear. Coleuses are prone to mealybugs (p. 415), so look for the little cottony masses that might appear where the leaf attaches to the stem, and take action quick.

Coral Bells
(Heuchera sanguinea)

The coral bell is a common outdoor perennial grown for its wispy scarlet sprays of small bell-shaped flowers. The leaves stay low to the ground. As an experiment, I tried it in the greenhouse and have had great success. It flowers for most of the year, except for a few months around January and February. In the greenhouse, it tends to do best in full sun. The dainty flowers are perfect for small bouquets. It can be started from seed or easily divided from a mother plant. If you have an older coral bell growing in your outside perennial bed, try dividing off a part of it for the greenhouse garden.

Crocus
(*Crocus* spp.)

See Forcing Spring Bulbs for Winter Bloom (p. 229).

Croton
(*Codiaeum variegatum*)

Croton is another plant grown for the colorful leaves rather than any flowers. It has color combinations that run along the veins of the waxy leaf. Colors tend to be yellow and reddish-orange. This plant is suited only for the warm greenhouse that never gets below 60° F (15° C). It also prefers full sun; without it the leaves can lose some of their color. Most of the year it prefers to stay constantly moist, except for winter, when you can cut back on watering some. It can be propagated from stem cuttings.

Cyclamen
(*Cyclamen persicum*)

Cyclamen is a common gift plant usually found in stores during the winter. People instantly fall in love with the interesting windswept, butterflylike flowers borne above heart-shaped, compact patterned leaves. The flowers are available in **red**, **white** and **rose**. People often toss the plant out after it has

bloomed, but with a little care, it can be kept for many years. In the home, it is difficult to get it to flower again after the first bloom. In the greenhouse, however, you'll probably have an easier time of it because it needs cool nights of 50° to 55° F (10° to 13° C) to trigger flower buds. Cyclamens are best grown in a pot because they also need to be somewhat root-bound before they even will think about setting flower buds.

Cyclamen need constant moisture and are best if watered from below by filling the saucer. If you must water from the top, try to keep the water off the leaves. After blooming, cut back on the water for a couple of months, and the plants may loose a few leaves. Then start watering them again and fertilize regularly, and you will be on your way to more blooms as

Cyclamen

long as you maintain cool nights. If your greenhouse consistently runs hot, cyclamens may suffer and get burned or yellow leaves, so try to find a cool spot for them. In the greenhouse, cyclamens will do best in full to partial sunlight but can tolerate shade as long as it is not too dark an area. Sometimes under a bench in the summer can be a good spot for them.

Cyclamen can be purchased as small round dormant tubers, or you can start them from seed. If grown from seed, it may take up to a year before you see bulbs. Cover the seed with about 1/16 inch (1.6 mm) of soil, and try to keep the temperature around 60° F (15° C). They rarely all come up at the same time, so be patient and wait a while before you give up on all the seed you have sown.

greenhouse is similar to growing outside. The larger varieties are usually started from tubers in March and will not begin to flower until early to mid-July. The dwarf varieties can easily be started from seed in February through April and will bloom from 7 weeks old through fall. There is much diversity in flower types to choose from.

Plan on dahlias as a summer and fall flowering plant. The larger blossoms can be used in large bouquets. The dwarf varieties can be best grown in 6-inch (15-centimeter) pots or in beds along walkways. For some reason, dahlias can get floppy when grown in the greenhouse, especially the larger varieties. Try to gently tie them up to some slender stakes such as bamboo or grow them in tomato cages to contain them.

Dahlia
(*Dahlia pinnata* hybrid)

Dahlias are another plant commonly saved for the outside garden that can also be grown in the greenhouse with good success. You can grow both the **large-flowered** specimens and the **dwarf varieties**. The advantage of growing dahlias in the greenhouse is that you can benefit from a longer bloom period. Growing in the

Dianthus
(*Dianthus chinensis*)

These carnation relatives are also known as **pinks**. They have single-petal flowers in **white**, **red**, **pink** and **combinations** of all three. They are often highly scented. Dianthus tend to stay compact, growing only 6 to 12 inches (15 to 30 cm). Growing them is similar to growing carnations, only they need no staking. To promote

Dianthus

longer bloom periods, be sure to make an effort to keep the spent blooms well picked. They are a long-lasting cut flower but are on short stems. They tend to bloom best in the moderate temperatures of fall and spring. They are easily propagated from seed, but can also be started from cuttings.

Easter Lily
(Lilium longiflorum)

The Easter lily is a fun plant for the greenhouse. People commonly end up with one as a gift plant and wonder what to do with it after it is done blooming. The most common approach is to plant it in the outside garden, where it will often thrive and bloom in the summer every year. If you want to continue growing your Easter lily in the greenhouse, you will need to follow a specific schedule. After flowering, cut back on watering. The leaves will begin to turn yellow and die back. Water the plant when the top of the soil dries out. In late September repot the plant into a 6-inch (15-centimeter) pot with new soil. Move the plant to a very dark, cool spot, preferably at a temperature that runs 32° to 45° F (0° to 7° C). Leave it there until 180 days before Easter. Then move the plant into a well-lit area with the temperature around 60° F (15° C). Keep the plant moist and fertilize every 2 weeks.

Another way to grow Easter lilies is to purchase precooled bulbs. This is how the commercial greenhouses do it. The trouble is, it is hard to find precooled Easter lilies for sale anywhere because they are usually purchased only in large amounts on a wholesale basis. Perhaps you could talk your local commercial greenhouse into selling you some. With precooled bulbs, you need to store the bulbs in a cool spot only until 120 days before Easter.

Easter lily

With Easter coming at a different time every year, it is a task for even commercial growers to get the scheduling right. It is even more difficult to get the blooms right at Easter for the home greenhouse gardener because the climate control is often much less exacting. What I'm getting at is, don't be surprised if your timing is a bit off. Hopefully, you will still enjoy the large white trumpet blooms even if they miss Easter.

Felicia
(Felicia amelloides)

Felicia is grown for its profusion of 1-inch (2.5-centimeter) sky blue daisies with yellow centers. It is also known as the **kingfisher daisy** and the **blue marguerite daisy**. It grows only about 1 foot (.3 m) high and has rough-textured leaves that feel almost succulent. It blooms best when the nights are around 50° F (10° C). Felicia can be propagated from seed. By starting it in spring you will have bloom in the coming winter. It can be grown for many years before you will need to think about propagating replacements.

It can also be easily propagated from cuttings. The first felicia I ever grew was from one I saw outside an airport in California in winter. I plucked a 5-inch (13-centimeter) piece of stem, put it in my pocket and smuggled it home to Wyoming, where the next day I placed it in my propagation flat. Within 6 months I had a beautiful blooming twin sister to the felicia growing back in California.

Forcing Spring Bulbs for Winter Bloom

Many bulbs that normally bloom outside in early spring can be made to bloom in winter while the snow is still flying outside. Horticulturists use the term "forcing" when referring to getting plants to do things out of season. The word "forcing" makes it sound as if it's violent plant slavery, but the plants seem happy enough when forced, so don't feel bad.

The most common bulbs to force include **crocuses**, **hyacinths**, **irises**, **narcissus** and **tulips**, which all work well for winter forcing. To prepare bulbs for forcing, you must pot them up in the fall (preferably early fall) and give them a cold treatment to simulate winter. This is done by storing them in a cold, dark place for 9 to 12 weeks. Then bring them out of the dark and into the warmth of your greenhouse or sunspace. The bulbs think it's spring, and this "forces" them into bloom. You can even time the bloom to occur for special events or parties.

If you are able to hand pick the bulbs out of a box at a garden center or store, always try to select the largest ones, which give the better show when forced. In bulb catalogs the larger bulbs are often called exhibition or premium size.

Some varieties of bulbs work better than others. Here are some of the easiest and most reliable. If you can't find these specific varieties, go ahead and use whatever varieties of spring bulbs that you can find.

Narcissus

Easy Varieties of Spring Bulbs

Crocus: Remembrance, purple; Blue Ribbon, blue; Giant Yellow, yellow; Jeanne d'Arc, white.

Hyacinth: Pink Pearl, Queen of the Pinks, pink; White Pearl, L'Innocence, white; Blue Jacket, Delft Blue, Blue Giant, blue.

Hyacinths can be forced to bloom in winter.

Iris: One of the best iris to force is not the common bearded iris but rather the early-blooming dwarf *Iris reticulata,* which comes from a small crocuslike bulb. All types of *reticulata* work well and bloom in purple, blue and yellow.

Narcissus or Daffodil: Most all work well. Paperwhite narcissus do not need cooling treatment.

Tulip: Tulips are among the hardest to force and need a longer cold treatment (13 weeks minimum). Usually it is best to force varieties listed as the early flowering tulips, including: Brilliant Star, Couleur Cardinal, red; Christmas Marvel, pink; Diana, white.

The Process of Forcing

After you have purchased the bulbs, you will need to pot them up. Don't mix different bulbs in one pot, because the timing may be different for the varieties or types. You can use either plastic or clay pots, but they must have holes in the bottom for drainage. Smaller bulbs such as crocus and iris work well in 4- to 6-inch (10- to 15-centimeter) pots. For the larger bulbs, you can use pots that are anywhere from 6 to 10 inches (15 to 25 cm), depending upon how many bulbs you place in the pot.

While some people often use small pebbles as the growing medium, I prefer to plant the bulbs in potting soil. Store-bought works fine. Fill the pots with soil so that when the bulbs are placed in the soil, it will be slightly below the rim of the pot. I put enough bulbs in each pot to be close but not touching each other. Be sure to put the bulbs in the pot right side up. This can be tricky. Look for indications of old roots at the bottom. Usually the flatter side goes down, and the pointed part of the bulb goes up.

Fill the soil in over and around the bulbs. It's okay to leave the top 1/3 of the bulb exposed, except for crocus and iris, which should be covered with about a 1/2 inch (1.3 cm) of soil. It helps to tag each pot so that you can later know what is in each. The final step is to water each pot thoroughly and allow them to drain.

Next you must fool the plants into thinking that they have gone through a winter. They need a cool treatment (without going much below freezing) for at least 12 weeks. This can be the trickiest part, and finding a cool spot is one of the drawbacks to central heating. Some of you may have an old root cellar or a very cool place in a basement. If so, great! If you don't have a cool spot, don't despair. You can use the outdoors. Dig a trench in the garden or use a window well. If you use the trench method, you need to dig it about 2 feet (.6 m) deep and wide enough to hold all the pots. Place the well-watered pots in the trench or window well and cover with sawdust or straw (available at most feed stores). Once it gets cold outside, mark your calendar for 12 weeks (leaving them in longer is usually okay). Tulips can use 13 or more weeks. If it has been a very dry winter, then you should pull back the straw and water the pots once a month or so. The soil in the pots should never dry out completely.

After 12 weeks or more of cold treatment, you can bring the bulbs inside. Be careful of the delicate shoots emerging from the pots because they can break off easily. I like to give the bulbs a few days of transition by placing them in a cooler, dimly lit room in the house, where it is around 60° F (15° C) or cooler. Then move them right into the greenhouse or sunspace. They will be growing amazingly fast and the stalks turning green right before your eyes. You may have to support the flower stalks with small stakes if they look like they might flop over. I often place a few stakes around the outside edge and tie some green dental floss around the outside for support.

The blooming or almost blooming plants make great gifts and will bloom prolifically for a week or more, often giving off an incredible fragrance. These bulbs can't be forced to bloom again next year, but you can plant them outside in spring, and if all goes well, they'll bloom in 2 years—if you have the space and the patience. Many people just toss them out when the blooming has finished.

You'll be surprised at how these plants will affect your mood and remind you that, yes, there is a spring coming one day soon. In the meantime, you have a little private spring going on in your greenhouse.

Foxglove
(Digitalis gloxiniiflora)

Foxglove is a biennial commonly grown in the outside garden. When it finally blooms in the second year, it really makes a statement. Foxglove has 2-inch (5-centimeter) bell-shaped flowers in pastel colors with distinctive off-colored spots in the throat of the bloom. The flowers are borne on long spikes that can get 3 feet (.9 m) or more tall.

Biennials are usually difficult to grow in a greenhouse because most need a good cold period that is hard to provide in a warm sunspace. Luckily, a few years back there was the introduction of the variety foxy. **Foxy foxglove** has the unique ability to bloom in the first year of growth. If you grow foxglove for greenhouse flowers, it should be the foxy variety. Sow it from seed and it will bloom in around 5 to 6 months. Be careful to not disturb the roots when it is transplanted. Set the foxglove out in clumps of three or more plants, placed in full sun. In the greenhouse, they are best grown in beds or in pots at least 1 gallon (3.8 l) in size with a well-drained soil. It is only worth growing for the first bloom unless you have the space to nurse the plant for 12 more months. At best, you should toss the plant after the second set of blooms.

Freesia
(Freesia refracta)

I am convinced that heaven has the scent of freesias. Their scent is not known for being powerfully strong, but the scent it does have is my absolute favorite. Freesias have become more and more popular as a gift plant and in bouquets. Freesia blooms are found in most every color. The **white varieties** tend to be the most fragrant. There are also **double-blos-**

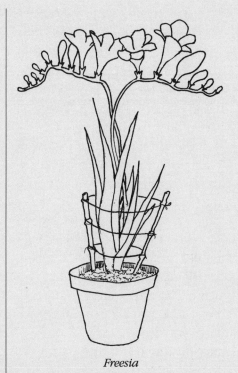

Freesia

somed varieties. Freesia has 2-inch (5-centimeter) trumpetlike flowers and leaves that resemble thick bladed grass. The plant itself reaches 8 to 12 inches (20 to 30 cm) high.

Freesias are best suited for the cool winter greenhouse, propagated from bulbs (corms) planted in late summer to early winter. A little cool treatment seems to make for healthier plants. I have the best luck if I refrigerate the bulbs for 3 to 4 weeks before planting. They grow well in both pots and beds. Place the bulb in the soil, pointed end upward, 2 inches (5 cm) deep and about 4 to 6 inches (10 to 15 cm) apart. As freesias grow, they can get a little floppy. Support them with a small bamboo stake, and gently tie the leaves to it with a thin piece of soft cloth. They will bloom in 3 to 4 months.

After blooming, let the plant continue growing for at least another month. Then you'll notice the foliage begin to decline. At that point, remove the bulb and store it in peat moss in a cool, dark spot until it is time to plant it again, usually late summer or fall. Freesias can also be started from seed, but it adds an extra 6 months to the time you'll ever see a bloom. I can never wait that long, so I always stock up on bulbs. I can't imagine a winter greenhouse without a crop of freesias to brighten up the winter's gloomy days.

Fuchsia
(Fuchsia spp.*)*

Fuchsia is grown for its beautiful flowers, which hang like ornaments off the plant, often with a splash of two-toned color. The flowers can be found in many color combinations, including **red**, **pink**, **purple** and **white**. The flower size varies from a thimble to as big as a billiard ball. The unique flower consists of showy colorful sepals, which are the part of the flower that flares back. Unfortunately, the flower has no fragrance, but it is so colorful that if you leave the door to your greenhouse open, don't be surprised to see a hummingbird working on the fuchsia flower. There are hundreds of named varieties to choose from.

Fuchsia needs a moderately cool environment to grow and

Fuchsia

flower. They can be gown in the greenhouse year-round, but when summer comes, you might try moving it to a cool spot to persuade it to continue the flower display. While fuchsias like cool temperatures, they don't flower much if the temperature runs below 48° F (9° C). They need to grow on the moist side but also need a well-drained soil. Fertilize with a houseplant food every 3 weeks during blooming for good growth. If the plant isn't bushy enough to your liking, pinch the tips for good side-shoot development. Occasional pruning for shaping the plant is helpful, especially during winter.

Fuchsia is easily propagated from cuttings taken from the tip. Be sure the cutting is at least 3 inches (8 cm) long. The biggest problem with fuchsias is their magnetism toward the whitefly (p. 420). Keep a keen eye on the underside of the leaf.

Gardenia

Gardenia
(Gardenia jasminoides)

The gardenia flower has perhaps one of the most hypnotizing scents in the plant kingdom. It has beautiful white to yellow blossoms on glossy dark green leaves. Some varieties can get large, up to 10 feet (3 m) tall. The smaller types are better suited for greenhouse potted plant culture, and these are the types most greenhouse plant catalogs offer for sale.

Before you get excited about growing a gardenia, I should warn you that it is famous for being temperamental to grow. It requires exacting requirements to set flower buds. The gardenia needs a night temperature of 60° to 65° F (15° to 18° C) and day temperatures only a bit warmer. It also needs ample water and should never dry out. It is prone to iron deficiency and may need an acidifying plant food. If the temperature is not right or there is any stress on the plant, it may drop its buds or never form them. It is also a favorite of many greenhouse insects. If this all sounds discouraging, you may want to wait until you get some more growing experience before you grow gardenias. Don't despair—there are other ways to get a similar intoxicating fragrance. Instead try jasmines, which are much easier and have a fragrance akin to the gardenia's. You may also find the Chilean jasmine a suitable substitute, mentioned under Mandevilla (p. 249).

Geranium
(Pelargonium)

Geraniums are one of the easiest, most trouble-free of all greenhouse flowering plants. They are perennial in the greenhouse and many types provide year-round blooms and interest.

Most geraniums can be easily started from stem cuttings taken from the tip. Be sure to pinch off any flowers or flower buds from the slips that you are taking, in order to speed up the rooting. All geraniums benefit from a well-lit location and can tolerate some drying between waterings.

There are four main types of geraniums you should know about. Let's look at each one.

GARDEN OR ZONAL GERANIUMS
(Pelargonium hortorum)

The **garden geranium** is the most common. It is the one that you first think of when you envision geraniums. The leaves are usually velvety and soft with a unique geranium scent. Some of the garden geranium leaves are totally green, while many others have what are called "zones." **Zoned geraniums**, or zonals, as they are often called, exhibit a zone of deeper color across the leaf. This color can be **purple**, **brown**, **orange**, **white** or **red**. Some varieties have interesting, colorful leaves. There are hundreds of types of garden geraniums. A good portion of them are great bloomers. The flowers are usually single or double and are found in a solid color (although spotted ones are gaining in popularity). **Garden geraniums** are commonly found with flower colors of **white**, **red**, **pink**, **orange** and **violet**. With proper care and feeding, they can bloom nonstop for many years even in a relatively cool greenhouse.

They are shrubby plants and can reach heights of up to 4 feet (1.2 m) if given a chance, but they look best if kept bushy and well shaped. They benefit from regular pinching to promote bushiness. They also need to have spent flowers regularly picked to promote more flowering.

Unfortunately, geraniums don't make a very good cut flower, because most drop their petals quickly after being cut. There are a few exceptions. I have had luck with many of the **cactus-flowered types**, such as the variety **Star of Persia**. I have also been able to make good cut flower arrangements with the variety **Apple Blossom** and many of the **double-rosebud varieties**.

Garden geraniums, like most other geraniums, are easily propagated from cuttings. Unlike the other geraniums, the garden geraniums can also be easily propagated from seed. Don't set the small seedling in too large of a pot until it has a well-developed root system.

By far the easiest way to bring color into any greenhouse is to grow a good selection of the many brightly flowered garden geraniums.

IVY GERANIUMS
(Pelargonium peltatum)
Like the name implies, the **ivy geranium** is known for its ivylike leaves, which are thick and almost succulent. While it doesn't bloom

as freely as the garden geranium, it is almost as trouble-free. The ivy geraniums are best suited for hanging pots because the leaves need to trail off of the side of the pot. For the pot to look thick, try to place at least three plants per pot. They seem to bloom best in the summer months, but the foliage is attractive year-round. They bloom less than the garden geraniums but more consistently than the Martha Washington geraniums. There are a few varieties with some interesting variegated leaves that are even more attractive during the nonbloom periods. Some varieties are **double flowered**. The **single-flowered** types (sometimes known as **cascade-ivy geraniums**) are more heat-tolerant. Don't let the soil dry out or it will cause some leaf burning.

Most geraniums are not prone to major bug infestations, but the ivy geraniums seem more predisposed to mealybugs (p. 415) than the other geraniums. Keep an eye on the bases of the leaves for cottony-looking critters.

MARTHA WASHINGTON GERANIUMS
(Pelargonium domesticum)
The **Washington geraniums** (also known as **regal geraniums**) have the most impressive flowers

of all. They are larger than any other geranium flower, growing 2 inches (5 cm) or more across. The flower often has other interesting darker markings in its throat. The leaves may or may not be scented, and the blossom is rarely scented. Unfortunately, people see the blooms and fall in love, only to find that the bloom period of the Washington geranium is often short-lived, especially when compared to the garden geranium. Blooming is prolonged as long as the night temperature remains below 60° F (15° C). They bloom most commonly only in spring and early summer.

SCENTED GERANIUMS

Many species of geraniums have the most interesting scented leaves. A few of these also have showy blooms and some have unusual-shaped leaves, but most are grown solely for their scent. The scent is not very volatile, which means that you must rub the leaf to get the air filled with their aroma. The most interesting thing about the **scented geraniums** is that they are incredible mimics. You can find scents that you would swear are almost identical to that of **strawberries**, **mint**, **rose**, **lemon**, **lime**, **apple** and even **chocolate mint**. You won't be-

lieve me until you grow some yourself. If you can't find some scented geraniums at your local greenhouse, check the Mail-Order Plants appendix for greenhouse plant catalogs. There are even one or two catalogs listed that specialize only in geraniums. Place the scented geraniums near walk paths where they can be easily touched or brushed against.

Gerbera Daisy
(Gerbera jamesonii)

The gerbera daisy, also known as **transvaal daisy**, are low-growing plants with striking flowers borne on thick stems. The flowers can be found in most warm colors. The plant reaches only to a height of 5 inches (13 cm), with sturdy flowering stalks reaching up to 1 foot (.3 m). The gerbera daisy is

Gerbera

not too particular about temperature but does require the sunniest spot possible. The hardest part about growing gerbera is getting the seeds to germinate. When you check your catalogs, you'll find that the seed is quite expensive in comparison with many other ornamental seeds, so it is important to get your investment to germinate. One trick that I have found in germinating gerberas is to place each seed vertically with half of the seed above ground and the other half below ground. They are small but not too small to do this, although you might find tweezers helpful. When you transplant them, take care not to bury the plants any deeper than they were originally. If the crown gets buried, the plant may have some problems.

Gerberas do fine in both ground beds and 6-inch (15-centimeter) pots. I have found that the plants can easily get deficient in iron, exhibited by yellowing between the veins in the leaf. Treat with a plant food containing iron.

You'll find that you get occasional blooms year-round, but you often get a good flush of blooms in spring and fall. If you are growing them for cut flowers, let the bloom fully open before cutting. They make a long-lived cut flower in arrangements. Keep an eye on the underside of the leaf because whiteflies (p. 420) like to hang around gerberas.

Globe Amaranth
(*Gomphrena globosa*)

Globe amaranth, also commonly known by its scientific name, ***Gomphrena***, is a so-called everlasting flower. It has papery thimble-shaped flowers that resemble a clover flower. Flower colors include **white**, **orange**, **purple**, **red** and **rose**. For years it was a good plant for cooler greenhouses, but the flower always had a short stem. A place called Woodcreek Nursery has bred a wonderful selection known as **strawberry fields**, also sold under the name of **woodcreek red** (found in Stokes Seeds and Park Seed catalogs; see Mail-Order Seeds appendix). The woodcreek red has a much longer stem than the other varieties, and the plants reach up to 20 inches (51 cm) in the greenhouse. While there are other colors of woodcreek gomphrenas, the red is by far the best of all. The woodcreek red is great for bouquets and ground beds. When in bloom, these are very showy plants. If started in late summer, they can provide many blooms throughout the winter. Gomphrenas look best if planted in large pots or beds in collections of five plants or more, spaced at around 6 inches (15 cm) apart. They prefer to be grown in full sun and on the dry side.

Gomphrenas are known for having an erratic germination habit. It is common to get only around 50 percent of the seeds to germinate, so plant them thickly. Barely cover the seed, and try to keep the soil temperature around 70° F (21° C). Also when germinating and growing, go easier on the watering. Overwatering will cause poor germination and growth.

Gloxinia
(Sinningia speciosa)

The gloxinia has long been a popular blooming houseplant. It has dark, fuzzy oblong leaves that sit under the 4-inch (10-centimeter) bell-shaped flowers, available in shades of **white**, **red**, **pink**, **purple** and **blue**, depending upon the variety. Some flowers have showy speckles in the throat while others have bands of contrasting colors toward the edge of the flower. They usually flower in the spring or summer.

Gloxinias are generally started from tubers, but with a lot of patience they can be started from seed. Grow them in 6- to 8-inch (15- to 20-centimeter) pots. The gloxinia grow best in the warm greenhouse where the temperature never gets below 60° F (15° C). They like bright spots but not direct sunlight. Keep the plant moist at all times but not dripping wet, using lukewarm water. Try to keep water off the leaves.

Many people give gloxinias a rest period after flowering by stopping any watering and setting the tuber in a dark, dry spot for a few months. There are many other growers who never give the plant a rest period with good success.

Most problems with gloxinias arise from growing too cool or overwatering. They also must have good humidity and be placed away from cool drafts. Getting the plant to survive for many years is not particularly easy, but it is always worth the challenge to see the beautiful display of flowers come again.

Golden-Trumpet Vine
(Allamanda cathartica)

As you can guess from the name, this plant is a vine with bright trumpet-shaped golden flowers. It is best suited to larger greenhouses with enough room to roam because its vines can reach 15 feet (4.6 m) in length. Because of its

Golden-trumpet vine

Hibiscus
(Hibiscus spp.)

Why not grow the state flower of Hawaii in your greenhouse? This is a plant for any sunny greenhouse that can tolerate both high and low temperatures. It is notorious for its large hollyhocklike blooms, which can be up to 10 inches (25 cm) across with some varieties. Their colors include **pink**, **red**, **yellow**, **orange**, **white** and **multiple variations** in one flower. They can be grown successfully in ground beds or large pots. If allowed to have their own way, they can reach 10 feet (3 m) tall or more. In their native habitat, they are a tropical evergreen shrub. You'll have more blooms and a healthier plant if you occasionally prune it, which stimulates new growth. New growth is where you'll find most of the new flowering buds appearing. Some hibiscus can bloom year-round, while others tend to bloom

size, it is best planted directly in a ground bed with a clear plan of where the vines are going to climb. Golden-trumpet vine blooms from spring to fall. The flowers are slightly scented. Plants can be obtained from greenhouse plant catalogs. It is best propagated from cuttings.

Logee's Greenhouses catalog (see Mail-Order Plants appendix) has a **smaller variety** of *Allamanda* that is easier to grow in smaller quarters or even a pot.

Hibiscus

mostly in late winter through spring.

Hibiscus is an easy plant to grow, especially if you can give it plenty of sun and maintain constant moisture. Feed with a general houseplant food once or twice a month. Plants can be obtained through plant catalogs or your local commercial greenhouse. Logee's Greenhouses catalog offers a wonderful variety sold as **The Path**, which has a sunset-colored flower that ranges from yellow on the edge to reddish orange, complemented with pink center. It gets more comments than any other hibiscus in my greenhouse. Hibiscus can be started from 6-inch (15-centimeter) stem cuttings taken from the tip.

Hibiscus may be bothered occasionally by whiteflies (p. 420) and mites (p. 416).

Impatiens

Hyacinth
(*Hyacinthus* spp.)

See Forcing Spring Bulbs for Winter Bloom (p. 229).

Impatiens
(*Impatiens* spp.)

The **common garden-variety** annual impatiens provides a good way to brighten up shady areas in the greenhouse that are bright but don't receive full sunlight. Given medium temperatures that don't run below 45° F (7° C), they can provide almost continuous bloom in the greenhouse. Because they grow only low to the ground with flowers on short stems, they won't make do as a cut flower. However, they are great in ground beds and hanging baskets. Impatiens are available in most any color except blue. Because they can live for so long in the greenhouse environment, they will need occasional tip pruning to keep the plant bushy. I have great luck planting them under garden benches and in corners. For the most part, impatiens are trouble-free.

Impatiens are easy to start from both seed and cuttings. When starting seed, just barely cover because they need to see a bit of light to trigger germination. Maintain a high humidity by misting the soil surface regularly and keep the temperature around 70° F (21° C).

New Guinea impatiens are a type with variegated leaves along with an impatienslike flower. The New Guineas are more difficult to grow compared to the garden impatiens, needing more water and more stable, warm temperatures. Still, they are interesting plants for the greenhouse.

Iris
(*Iris* spp.)

See Forcing Spring Bulbs for Winter Bloom (p. 229).

Jasmine
(*Jasminum* spp.,
Trachelospermum jasminoides)

This is the plant for fragrance. Most, but not all, jasmine have an incredible fragrance coming from **white** or **yellow** flowers. Many yellow species are not fragrant. A single blooming plant can set the mood in a greenhouse or sunspace.

Some are shrubby plants while most have a vine-type of growth. There are many species of jasmine worth growing. ***Trachelospermum***, commonly called the **star jasmine**, is not in the true jasmine family but has a jasminelike fragrance.

Jasminum nitidum is a good container plant, with bushy green leaves and star-shaped flowers. It can bloom in cooler months and in summer and can tolerate very cool temperatures.

Jasmine

Jasminum polyanthum has finely divided leaves that like to vine around other nearby plants or structures. It is a prolific winter bloomer and may continue into summer. It doesn't tolerate cool temperatures very well.

Jasminum sambac is commercially used in making both tea and perfume and is important in some Buddhist ceremonies. It has a bushy habit that adapts well to potted culture. *Sambac* prefers warmer temperatures and bright sunlight.

Jasminum humile is a yellow-flowered plant that, unlike many yellow-flowered varieties, has a nice fragrance.

Jasminum stephanense is good for summer blooms. It has fragrant whitish pink blooms and likes to vine up adjacent plants and objects.

Jasminum tortuosum is a good choice for a year-round bloomer. It grows as a shrubby vine.

Trachelospermum jasminoides, not a true jasmine, is available in both **white-** and **yellow-flowering** varieties. Both have a rich fragrance. While they can tolerate cool greenhouse temperatures, they tend to hold off blooming until things begin to warm up in spring.

Most jasmines are best suited to growing in pots. They usually have an open growth habit, which requires some pinching back and shaping. Over time, the plants can start to look a bit ragged and unkempt, especially if the foliage gets thick. Even though the plant may be healthy, sometimes certain leaves and stems may die back for no reason, lending to a untidy look if not groomed. People let the plants vine up a wall or trellis, and if they are eventually up-potted, the plants can reach 10 feet (3 m). They need moderate moisture and light levels. Jasmines are generally propagated from cuttings taken from the more mature stems a few months after a flush of blooms.

Kalanchoe
(Kalanchoe spp.*)*

Kalanchoe is a large family of succulent plants that varies greatly in leaf types and flowers. Some have incredible blooms and/or unusual leaves. Others are known for their peculiar ways of easily propagating themselves with little plantlets that form on the leaves themselves. It would be hard to tell you about every kalanchoe that can be found, but I must pass on some of my favorites. With a little looking, you will find even more interesting kalanchoes.

Kalanchoe

The first kalanchoe is probably the most common because it is often sold in stores as a blooming potted plant. It is known commonly as kalanchoe and scientifically as **Kalanchoe blossfeldiana**. It is also known as **Flaming Katie**. It has wide, thick waxy leaves and sprouts a profusion of **red**, **rose**, **orange** and **yellow** flowers. It holds the blooms on for many weeks. After blooming, pinch back the flowers and grow on until it blooms again. I have been able to get them to bloom two and sometimes three times a year with average care.

Some other kalanchoes that have caught my eye over the years include **Kalanchoe mortagei**, or more commonly, mother of hundreds. It is easy to see why it gets the name when you see that it produces hundreds of little plantlets along the leaf edge, which drop off onto the soil and almost immediately start to grow. The leaves of the *mortagei* also are interesting. The plant itself gets to 1 foot (.3 m) or more in height. Some similar plants that also produce an abundance of plantlets include **K. pinnata** and **K. diagremontiana**. These are fun plants for kids to have and experiment with and provide a good lesson in plant propagation.

Kalanchoe pumila is commonly called flour-dust plant because the silver-gray leaves look as if they were recently dusted. In the winter it produces an abundance of beautiful pink flowers. It makes a real show in a hanging basket and, like all kalanchoes, is easy to grow.

Another silver-leaved plant is **K. tomentosa**, which is commonly sold as panda plant because of its furry leaves.

One of the best sources for dozens of varieties of kalanchoe is the mail-order catalog Glasshouse Works out of Ohio (see Mail-Order Plants appendix for address), which has an incredible selection that could keep you busy experimenting with unusual-leaved and unusual-flowered kalanchoes for many years to come.

The general care for kalanchoes is to provide a very bright spot and let the soil dry out between waterings (see Succulents, p. 284). They do fine in most store-bought potting soils. Kalanchoes tolerate both cool and warm temperatures quite admirably. However, prolonged high temperatures may cause a lack of buds and blooms. Kalanchoes are easy to start from cuttings of the leaf or stem. They root-up rapidly and grow quickly. They seem to do best in pots rather than in ground beds.

Flowering Kale

Kale and Cabbage, Flowering
(*Brassica oleracea*)

Flowering kale and cabbage produces one of the most ornamental blossomlike shows that you will ever see—beautiful rosettes of pink, rose, red or white against a mottled green background. They need just one thing to bring on the color: cool temperatures. Therefore, they are a great plant for starting in the late summer or fall and then enjoying from mid-winter into spring.

Eventually, when the warm temperatures of late spring arrive, they will try to flower or just begin to look ragged. Neither is a pretty sight compared to the colorful show when they are at their peak. When this happens, it is time to toss them out.

Flowering kale has a more frilly leaf, while the flowering cabbage has flatter leaves. I have found that the hybrid flowering kale and cabbage colors up earlier with warmer temperatures than do the non-hybrids. There are dwarf varieties and a variety called peacock, which has finely cut leaves.

Flowering cabbage and kale are best propagated from seed. They can be grown in pots, which need to be at least 1 gallon (3.8 l) in size unless you are growing the smaller varieties. I like to grow them in ground beds, spaced about 10 inches (25 cm), along walk paths where they can easily be seen. Be sure to grow them in a cool, bright spot or they will never get the showy colorful leaves. On occasion, aphids (p. 413) may be a problem.

If you are wondering if flowering kale or cabbage are edible, the answer is yes. Not always tasty, but edible. Cooler weather produces the best-flavored flowering kale and cabbage. Still, I prefer regular cabbage or kale when it comes solely to taste.

King's Crown
(*Jacobinia carnea*)

The common name, king's crown, is apt when you see the

regal blooms that this plant produces. The tubular pink blooms resemble the most stately crown, made up of a cluster of flowers that is 5 to 7 inches (13 to 18 cm) in diameter. Usually, a few weeks after the main flower has faded you may be provided with some equally showy but smaller blooms.

I have the best luck growing it in a 1- to 5-gallon (3.8- to 19-liter) pot. King's crown benefits from regular feeding in the summer. When not in bloom, it still has handsome leaves. After the flower show is over, pruning the spent blossom is a good idea.

There are some other species of *Jacobinia* worth trying that may be more apt to bloom in the winter. Also some **yellow-** and **red-flowering** species are available.

Larkspur
(Consolida ambigua)

Larkspur is a tall-growing blooming annual that can grow anywhere from 1 to 3 feet (.3 to .9 m) in height, depending upon the variety. Larkspur has flowers borne on spikes in colors of **white**, **red**, **lavender**, **blue**, **purple** and **pink**. The blooms are not particularly fragrant, but they make up for it in their colorful show and are a fine cut flower. Take care keeping the plant away from toddlers as it is toxic if ingested.

In the greenhouse, larkspur does better if timed to bloom in winter through early summer. If not, warm weather may put them under much stress and may cause bloom failure. They are best in the cooler greenhouse, where the nights are around 45° to 50° F (7° to 10° C). Even so, I have been

Larkspur

experimenting around with sowing the seeds most any month with decent results.

The seeds should be buried at least 1/8 inch (.3 cm) because they prefer to germinate in a dark spot. It may take up to 25 days for germination, so be patient. Use your best technique when you transplant larkspur out of seed trays into pots or beds because it doesn't like its roots disturbed. Larkspur can be grown in 6- to 8-inch (15- to 20-centimeter) pots or directly planted in the ground with a spacing of 8 to 10 inches (20 to 25 cm). They like a well-drained soil with good fertility and often benefit from regular supplemental feeding. If you grow them in pots, don't let the soil run dry for any length of time, but be equally cautious of overwatering. A well-drained soil helps you create a good growing environment.

The taller varieties often need to be staked to prevent them from flopping over. Because they are annuals, larkspurs should be tossed in the compost pile after blooming has finished.

Lobelia
(Lobelia tenuior)

Lobelia is a low-growing annual flower that is best used along walks or spilling out the sides of hanging baskets. They have dainty little blooms that provide a mass of color: **blue**, **white**, **purple** and **reddish**. They are easily started from seed and prefer to grow in a slightly moist spot. In pots, never let the soil dry out. A favorite variety of mine is **crystal palace**, which has a bronze foliage. The darker foliage sets off the purple blooms, making them appear to glow. Unfortunately, I have found that in a greenhouse the foliage doesn't get nearly as bronze as it does outside. Still, it is a good-looker. All lobelias can benefit from an occasional haircut to help stimulate another flush of blooms.

Keep lobelia out of reach of young toddlers, as the foliage is reputed to be poisonous if ingested.

Malope
(Malvaceae trifida)

I discovered malope by chance when I saw it mentioned in a Thompson & Morgan seed catalog. To my surprise, it ended up producing a grand display of blooms in my greenhouse. It has large rich reddish purple blooms on a shrubby plant that reaches around 3 feet (.9 m) high and wide. Each bloom is about 3 inches (8 cm) across. The flowers have no

Malope

real fragrance, but it is worth growing and works well in bouquets.

After my first success in growing malope, I had many failures. One of my problems turned out to be poor timing. It needs to be started (from seed) in late summer or early fall. Any other time of year when I started malope, the plant either grew poorly or succumbed to stress and disease. So, in the greenhouse, timing seems to be everything. Now that I have returned to fall sowing, things are back on track. With that kind of schedule, you can usually expect to see your first blooms in March or April, running as long as early June, and it is well worth the wait. Still, I should caution you that it is not the easiest plant to grow, because it is susceptible to disease and moisture stress.

The plants get leggy, so before they get big, place a tomato cage over them for support. To promote bushiness and a fuller plant, pinch the tips of the stems while the plant is around 1 foot (.3 m) high. Be sure to place malope in a spot that receives full sun and regular moisture. As the plant gets larger, it wilts more easily and may need daily watering. After the bloom show, you'll sadly have to toss the plants because they go downhill rapidly. If they were big, be ready to put something new in the big empty space that they occupied.

— purchased) spring '04 of i.

Mandevilla
(Mandevilla spp.)

Mandevilla is not a commonly known plant, but it should be. It produces a wealth of flowers, blooming mostly fall through spring, which hold on the vine for many weeks. They look like a cross between the morning-glory and the petunia, usually having 3-inch-wide (8-centimeter-wide) blooms. The more common species is ***M. x amabilis***, which grows in a vinelike fashion, with glossy dark green leaves and pink flowers that often turn red as they open. It needs to be staked or set near some trellising as it vines. It can grow up to 10 feet (3 m) tall and can be grown in either a pot or a ground bed. I have had the best luck in pots. It can tolerate cooler temperatures well but seems to prefer more-moderate temperatures. Logee's Greenhouses catalog (see Mail-Order Plants appendix) offers a variety known as **red riding hood**, *M. sanderi*, a particularly beautiful plant with masses of striking lipstick-colored blooms, which has easily lived up to its billing. It also needs trellising.

Another mandevilla, known as **Chilean jasmine (*M. laxa* or *M. suaveolens*)**, unlike *M.* x *amabilis* and *sanderi*, produces fragrant white flowers that are around 2 inches (5 cm) across and tend to bloom more in the summer months.

Mandevillas are best propagated from cuttings. Grow them in rich, well-drained soil. They can look sickly when the soil is poorly drained—by mixing a little sand or perlite in the potting mix, you can prevent this. They like constant moisture in the summer but need to run a little dry between watering during the winter months. Yellowing of the new leaves might indicate a need for micronutrient fertilizing (see Chapter 9, Getting to the Roots).

Maple, Flowering
(Abutilon megapotamicum)

These plants are also known as parlor maples. They are aptly named because of the resemblance the leaves have to those of maple trees, but they are not related. They are a nice plant for greenhouse culture and are easy to grow. What makes them interesting are their bell-shaped, lanternlike flowers, which hang down as if casting a light below. The blooms are not fragrant but are showy and have the advantage of blooming year-round in the greenhouse. The flowers can be found in **pink**, **red**, **white**, **gold** and **yellow**. Some of the varieties have interesting mottled foliage with white or orange variegation that complements the flowers. Plants can grow up to 3 feet (.9 m) high but look best if kept pruned to a more compact shape. There are also dwarf varieties of flowering maples.

Flowering maples are easily propagated from cuttings. They can tolerate some light shade and cooler temperatures. They like to be on the moist side in warmer months and prefer to dry out between waterings in the winter. They seem to have some susceptibility to mealybugs (p. 416), so look for the cottony critters hanging around the undersides of leaves and branching nodes.

Marguerite daisy

Marguerite Daisy
(Chrysanthemum frutescens)

The marguerite daisy can produce white or yellow daisylike flowers year-round in the greenhouse. The plants can grow up to 2 feet (.6 m) tall but look better if kept pruned to a bushier shape. The leaves have a finely cut fernlike look and the flowers last well in bouquets. They can tolerate a wide range of temperatures. Unfortunately, the yellow variety is especially attractive to the whitefly (p. 420) and both the white and yellow are susceptible to aphid infestations (p. 413). In the greenhouse, the marguerite is a perennial but needs to be replaced every few years. Propagate new plants by taking stem cuttings. Marguerites like full sun and can tolerate most any soil. They do well in either pots or beds and need to have the soil dry out between waterings.

Marigold
(Tagetes spp.*)*

This common outdoor annual can provide some easy greenhouse color, especially in summer. Marigolds are divided into two main groupings, but there are also many odd hybrids, which can confuse the lines of classification.

African marigolds are the ones that tend to grow tall. They have large double blooms in either **yellow** or **gold**. There are some shorter types that reach only 1 foot (.3 m), while others can easily grow 3 feet (.9 m) or more. There are also some rarer colored varieties. Give the African marigolds at least 1 foot (.3 m) spacing. Avoid getting water on the flowers or they will quickly brown. Be sure to pluck faded flowers for continued bloom and a tidy look. The taller marigolds make long-lasting cut flowers.

Marigold

French marigolds are the smaller types, usually growing only 1 foot (.3 m) high or less. The flowers have either double or single petals, many of which are bicolored, with bands of brown or red on **yellow** or **gold** petals. The French marigolds are notorious for their ability to reseed.

Marigolds can be grown year-round in the greenhouse, but they tend to be at their best in the spring or fall.

Marigolds are not demanding in culture. They do have roots close to the soil surface, so take care when cultivating. They prefer full sun and moderate warmth and are readily propagated from seed. Being annuals, they reach a point where they begin to look unkempt and should be pulled. If you see a stippling of yellow on the leaves, get out a hand lens or magnifying glass and look under the leaves for spider mites (p. 416), which love to hang around marigolds. See Chapter 10, When Things Go Wrong, for help.

Marmalade Plant
(*Streptosolen jamesonii*)

Also known as **orange browallia**, this marmalade plant is so named for its floppy reddish-orange flowers that occur on the tips of the plant. If you are looking for a dependable winter and spring bloomer, try the marmalade plant. The blooms are not fragrant, but being so floriferous makes it a worthwhile choice. It is a floppy grower and therefore does best in a hanging basket. I have also had good results with tying it to some stakes. The marmalade plant does best in regular potting soil kept on the moist side. It can tolerate temperatures down to the 40s (5° to 9° C). Occasionally check the underside of the leaves for aphid gatherings (p. 413).

Mimulus
(Mimulus x hybridus)

Mimulus is also known as **monkey flower** because some people can see a monkey's face in the flower. They are a delicate plant, usually growing not more than 1 foot (.3 m) tall, although some rare varieties can reach up to 3 feet (.9 m) or more. The flowers somewhat resemble a large snapdragon, with interesting blotches of different colors, including mixtures of **red**, **orange**, **yellow** and **off-white**. They are a good choice for the winter greenhouse and semishady spots in the summer. Mimulus can be grown in ground beds, but I prefer them in hanging baskets so I can have the blooms at eye level in order to enjoy the interesting blotches of color in the flower. Occasional pruning can be helpful as it tends to get leggy. Mimulus is not particular about soil or moisture levels. It is easily propagated from seed (barely cover the seed) and can also be propagated from cuttings.

Calypso mimulus is a popular dwarf hybrid that is 6 to 8 inches (15 to 20 cm) tall and is quick to flower. **Mystic hybrid** is similar to calypso. Taller varieties are harder to find but can make a good cut flower with some staking. Mimulus can suffer if you run real hot temperatures, but you can always sow it in late summer for good production of winter blooms.

Mimulus

Mina
(Mina lobata)

The mina is also known as **quamoclit vine** and produces clusters of unique 1-inch (2.5-centimeter) flowers. The interesting thing about the plant is that each flower begins red and changes colors as it matures, going through a progression of red to orange, yellow and white. All colors can be seen simultaneously in a cluster of flowers. Mina starts to bloom in the first 3 to 4 months and can be grown for up to a year. It is an easy plant to start from seed. The seed, however, is hard to find in most catalogs but is available at this writing from Thompson & Morgan seed company (see Mail-Order Seeds appendix). Mina needs full to part sun. Provide the plant a trellis to grow upon, as it can reach heights of up to 6 feet (1.8 m). Space one plant every foot (.3 m) along the trellis.

Morning-glory
(Ipomea)

Morning-glory is a nice addition for the greenhouse with room for a good-sized vertical trellis. If you don't have room, try a variety that doesn't climb. There are more than one species of morning-glory to consider, each with special attributes for the greenhouse or sunroom.

Moonflower, *Ipomea alba* is a fragrant type that can vine to 12 feet (3.6 m) or more. Be ready with your trellis because they are fast-growing. If you like to sit in your greenhouse in the evening, the pure white flowers add a special touch of fragrance and will shine in the moonlight. Come morning, the 6-inch (15-centimeter) flower will neatly fold up. On occasions when the days are dark and cloudy, the flowers will remain open.

What most of us commonly think of as the morning-glory is one of the annual species *Ipomea tricolor*, *I. nil* or *I. purpurea*, which have the heart-shaped leaves with blue, lavender, red and pink flowers. After about 6 months of growth it may come time to pull it up if it looks ragged. A few selections of *tricolor* do not vine and remain a low-growing bushy plant.

Ipomea quamoclit has an interesting fernlike leaf with small tubular flowers flaring into a star at the end. The flowers are usually red. *Quamoclit* is a perennial in the tropics and can live for a few years in the greenhouse if you have the room.

The general care for the morning-glory is to be sure to grow them in well-drained soil with a good amount of sand or perlite in the mix. They also like to grow in full sun. Morning-glories can easily be grown in pots and still put on a good bloom. If you are growing them in pots, you may have to prune them regularly. They also do fine in ground beds as long as they get a lot of light. Morning-glories are started from seed, and for quicker germination, try soaking the seed overnight before sowing. Contrary to many books, morning-glories can be transplanted, but use your best technique, taking care to minimize root disturbance.

Mullein

Mullein
(Verbascum bombyciferum)

This particular mullein is commonly known as both **arctic summer** or **silver lining**, depending upon the catalog source. It is not often thought of as a greenhouse ornamental and can be seen in more and more outside gardens. Having loved its unusually large fuzzy silver leaves, I thought I'd give it a try in the greenhouse. It is a biennial outside, but when grown in the greenhouse, it gets a bit confused and may live for up to 3 years. The first year the silver lining grows large basal leaves up to 10 inches (25 cm) across and 1 foot

(.3 m) or more long. The silver color and the incredible fuzziness of the leaves always brings on a flurry of comments from visitors. The leaves have more fuzz than the most furry lamb's ear you've ever seen. If only they could make tissues this soft!

After about a year of growing the fat, fuzzy leaves, the silver lining then sends up fuzzy 1-inch-thick (2.5-centimeter-thick) stalks that reach up to 6 feet (1.8 m) in height. Sometimes the stalks go straight up, but they occasionally take creative bends as they reach upward. Along the stalks are many 1-inch (2.5-centimeter) yellow blooms. Several people have remarked on how the flowered stalk looks like popcorn. The plant may continue growing these flower stalks for a couple of years in the greenhouse before it finally begins to go downhill as all biennials must, even though in the greenhouse you might call it a triennial or more. The flower stalks will add much drama to any bouquet and keep for a long time in a vase.

Silver lining mullein is easily started from seed. Thompson & Morgan seed catalog sells it listed as **Verbascum**. I have the best luck starting it in spring to trigger a good number of the early low-growing large leaves. It does best in full sun and doesn't seem fussy about soil or watering. You don't need more than one or two plants growing in a small greenhouse at a time, because they can cover up to 5 square feet (.46 sq. m) of space, and one plant provides enough of a show. Silver lining is best grown in a ground bed or a pot that is at least 10 to 12 inches (25 to 30 cm) across. In spring grow a few extra plants for planting outside.

Narcissus/Daffodil
(*Narcissus* spp.)

See Forcing Spring Bulbs for Winter Bloom (p. 229).

Nasturtium
(*Tropaeolum majus*)

Nasturtium has recently become more popular as the trend of eating flowers has grown. Nasturtium is always at the top of the culinary list. The flowers have a sweet, peppery flavor, and the leaves are also edible but are too hot for my liking. I especially like to eat the tails that form at the back of the flower because of their high level of sweetness. Unfortunately, there is one common variety with no tail, known as the **whirlybird**. Nasturtium has handsome rounded leaves that almost resemble little

Nasturtium

water lily pads. Its 1- to 2-inch (2.5- to 5-centimeter) flowers can be found in shades of warmer colors and cream. Some flowers have splotches of two colors.

There are two main types of nasturtium, the **trailers** and the **dwarf varieties**. The trailers can climb like a vine if given ample nearby plants or poles to coil up upon, or they will just rapidly spread out over a hanging basket or along the ground, extending up to 8 feet (2.4 m). The dwarf varieties stay bushy and grow up to 2 feet (.6 m), depending upon the age of the plant. There are many varieties in between the trailers and dwarf types. A favorite variety of mine is called **Alaska**. Alaska nasturtium has variegated leaves with marbled white blotches on the green. It looks handsome even without flowers. I like to

Alaska nasturtium has an interesting varigated leaf.

grow nasturtiums in hanging pots, but they do equally fine in beds. They do seem to prefer soils that are well drained and not too rich. Nasturtium is generally a trouble-free plant and tolerates cool temperatures as well as warm. As a result, it can be a good plant to have growing most any time of the year in the greenhouse or sunspace. Besides using the sweet, peppery leaves to color up salads, you can use the flowers in arrangements, but they will last only for around 5 days. Nasturtium is easily propagated from seed. Plants that are in the ground for more than 9 months may benefit from some pruning. They occasionally self-sow if they are grown for more than a year.

There are some wilder cousins to nasturtium. One is known as canary creeper or canary bird flower, which of course has open yellow flowers, shaped almost like open hands or bird wings.

There are some other interesting cousins in the genus of *Tropaeolum* native to South America that have tuberous roots and exotic flowers. These plants are reputed to do very well in cooler greenhouses, but, unfortunately, the seeds and plants are difficult to acquire. I have yet to locate a source. If you find some of these plants, give them a try.

Nemesia
(Nemesia strumosa)

Nemesia is another good choice for the winter greenhouse, as it likes a cool environment. Flowers are usually less than 1 inch (2.5 cm) in size and come in most any color imaginable, in a shape reminiscent of snapdragons. The plant is also small, usually around 1 foot (.3 m) high. It can get lanky and benefits from some tip pruning as it grows to promote bushiness. It likes a moist, rich soil and can tolerate some light shade. For greenhouse color, sow the plants in late summer or early fall for winter and spring blooms. When the heat of summer comes, it is usually time to toss the plants in the compost pile.

With small flowers borne on short stems, it is not a good choice for cut bouquets. However, it is a good plant for growing along walks, in beds or in pots and hanging baskets. In my experience, the plants often may go downhill after only 4 to 6 months, but they are still a nice plant for brightening up the winter.

Nicotiana
(Nicotiana spp.)

Nicotiana is also known as **flowering tobacco**. This relative to petunia and tobacco produces masses of trumpetlike, star-shaped flowers about 1 inch (2.5 cm) across. The more common varieties are the **nicki series**, which reach up to 18 inches (46 cm) in height, and the **domino series**, which is a dwarf, only 1 foot (.3 m) high. The flowers are available in **red**, **pink**, **white** and **lime green**. I have never had an interest in growing a green flower, but it is out there for someone.

I first grew nicotiana because so many books talked about how fragrant the plants were. I never smelled a thing and later found that only some of the older varieties have a decent aroma. The older varieties are not hard to find with a little investigation. Some varieties of the more fragrant types include **fragrant cloud**, **sensation** and **sylvestris**. These tend to get much taller, growing up to 6 feet (1.8 m). They are not as colorful as the more common nicotianas but are good for their evening fragrance.

Nicotianas need full sun and moderate temperatures. If it gets hot, you may see the flowers closing during the day. The dwarf varieties are good in pots and the taller types in either large pots or ground beds.

Nicotianas are easily started from seed but can also come from cuttings. I prefer seed. I have found that they are somewhat susceptible to both aphids and whiteflies and tend to get more buggy in extreme cool and hot temperatures. For that reason, I usually plan to have them bloom during the moderate temperatures of spring and summer. This requires sowing them in the middle of summer or winter. Nicotianas can grow for many seasons but will need pruning and possibly some attention to the inevitable bugs. It is easier to enjoy them for only a couple of seasons or until they become trouble and then plan to start over again at an appropriate time.

Oleander
(Nerium oleander)

Oleander is an evergreen shrub that can be easily grown in a greenhouse but will need much pruning to keep it from reaching its natural height of more than 20 feet (6 m). It is best grown in a tub if you have the room. If you do grow it in the greenhouse, please take care as the leaves are poisonous if ingested. It is not a good plant if you have curious toddlers on the move. It has 6-inch-long (15-centimeter-long), leathery,

lance-shaped leaves. The flowers tend to bloom in the warmer part of the year. Oleander produces clusters of **pink**, **white** or **red** flowers at the tips of branches.

Oleander

If you see suckers forming just below the buds of future flowering blossoms, then pinch them out. These suckers can sometimes inhibit the flowers from forming.

The oleander plant prefers to grow in full light for best flowering. Pruning is best done in late winter to control the rapid growth. It needs a soil mix that is well drained; be sure there are good-sized holes in the bottom of your tub. It can tolerate temperatures down to 40° F (5° C). During blooming, the plant needs a constant supply of water, but cut back on water during the winter. Most oleanders have a nice fragrance when in flower. They are easily propagated from cuttings.

Orchids
(Orchidaceae)

I can't pretend to tell you everything you need to know about growing orchids. Rather I would like to encourage you to not shy away from them. While some are more difficult to grow, many are easier to grow and require less care than most houseplants. Why grow orchids anyway? First, they have incredible flowers with much color and diversity. Many species will hold one bloom open for more than a month, so you really get some mileage out of a flower. Another good reason to grow orchids is to impress people with your gardening skills. Hey, just grow a few of the easiest orchids, and people will think you are an accomplished gardener. Who knows, you might find it so easy that you'll venture into the exciting world of growing more of the unusual and select varieties. It won't be long until you truly are an accomplished orchid grower. After all, the most important person you need to impress with your ability to grow things is yourself.

Classifying orchids can become quite complex, so I would like to point out two major differences you should know. Most orchids are classified under one of the two major types: **epiphytes** and **terrestrials**. Epiphytes means that they grow up in the air, living in crotches or nooks of trees or shrubs. It should be understood that epiphytes are not parasitic. They derive their nutrition from the moisture and organic matter that collects around them. Thus, many orchids will not grow in potting soil. Often you will see epiphytic orchids sending roots straight up in the air because they sometimes don't take to pots. When they are successfully grown in a pot, they must have a very open growing medium often containing a mix of bark chips, cork or rocks. I prefer to use redwood bark chips. Epiphytic orchids will not survive long in wet potting soil. They are able to store water for long periods and are easily killed by overwatering. The epiphytes do need some nutrition, which is generally done by mixing in a water-soluble fertilizer at half (or less than half) the recommended rate found on the label, every second or third watering.

Terrestrial orchids are able to live in earth or soil mixes. There are also some orchids that fall between the terrestrial and the epiphytic and many other classifications of orchids that I will let you delve into on your own if you get growing orchids in your blood. For now, let's look at a few of the easier orchids that would be good to start out with for your greenhouse or sunspace.

***Brassavola nodosa*, Lady of the Night**, is an epiphytic orchid that gives off a wonderful evening fragrance. It produces 3-inch (8-centimeter) flowers that are usually white with some small colored spots. It can bloom most anytime of the year and doesn't need a rest period. This *Brassavola* needs full sunlight and is well suited to the greenhouse environment as long as temperatures remain above 50° F (10° C).

Cattleya labiata are among the easier orchids to grow. They are epiphytic and need to thor-

Orchid

oughly dry out between waterings (usually a week or two between watering). After they flower, they need a 2-month rest period in which you let them run even drier. Water no more than once every 2 to 3 weeks during this time. Many other *Cattleya* and *Cattleya* hybrids are worth trying in a greenhouse, as it is one of the more rewarding types of orchids to grow.

***Cymbidium* miniatures** are semiterrestrial, meaning they need a very well-drained soil. I usually mix 1 part bark chips to 1 part sand to 2 parts commercial potting soil. They need to be moist most of the time if possible, except during the rest period. The *Cymbidiums* have long narrow leaves. The miniature hybrids are not that small, reaching 1 to 2 feet (.3 to .6 m) tall, but they are more manageable than the 3-foot (.9-meter) nonminiatures. They flower on tall spikes anytime between December and June and need a drier rest period between October and January. As with many orchids, to induce flowering it is helpful to have a 10° (6° C) drop in temperature at night. You can find miniature *Cymbidiums* with varying colors of blooms, depending upon the variety.

Oncidium is a large collection of many diverse species. Most are epiphytic, but it also includes a few

Cymbidium orchid

rare terrestrials. The size and shape can vary, and most are on the easy side to grow. They benefit from full sun to bright shade and are well suited to the greenhouse. You can get anywhere from 10 to 100 blooms per stem. They can tolerate and even prefer cooler temperatures. Follow the care described for epiphytic orchids.

Phalaenopsis or moth orchids are mostly epiphytes, but there are a few that are terrestrial. These are often recommended for beginners because they are easier to get to flower, with many differ-

ent varieties available. They tend to prefer warmer temperatures and need to be watered at least once or twice a week. They need shadier spots of your greenhouse, so try to avoid setting them in full sun. Many of the *Phalaenopsis* varieties are among the most free-flowering orchids. The flowers are born on long spikes, with up to 40 blooms on one spike, and can easily stay in bloom for 3 months or more.

Many orchids last well as a cut flower. Be sure the flowers are fully open before you cut them to get the maximum life in a vase. Some orchids have a fragrance, but what fragrance there is often diminishes after the flower is cut for a bouquet or corsage.

If you are starting out with orchids, it is helpful to not invest too much money in the more expensive plants until you have had some experience in growing them. In many metropolitan areas you will often find orchid societies that meet regularly. The people in these societies love to help newcomers out with the hobby of growing orchids. They also often have regular orchid plant sales where you can pick up some real bargains. Check with your closest public botanic garden for more information on orchid clubs or societies near you.

There are many more orchids worthy of mention and much more to say about growing orchids, but there isn't room here. Find a good book on the subject to help you along, and give an orchid or two a try in your greenhouse. You'll find that, yes, they are different to grow, but they are not necessarily difficult.

Oxalis
(Oxalis spp.*)*

These plants are also known as the tropical shamrocks or lucky clover, because they look like a shamrock but are not a true shamrock. Many of these cloverlike plants can be grown in a greenhouse. Many fold up their leaves at night and many are tuberous. They have varying colors of flowers, including white, red, pink and yellow. Generally they are small plants that do fine in a 6-inch (15-centimeter) pot.

The care for oxalis is relatively simple. Let the soil dry out between waterings. The can survive well in light shade to full sun. If the plant becomes ragged or buggy, try cutting all the leaves down to the soil level and reduce watering. They will emerge again in a healthy manner. They are easily propagated from division. Just split the mature plant into two or three parts and repot.

Oxalis

Palms
(Palmae)

Palms provide a real feeling of having a tropical paradise within your greenhouse. There is a great variety of palms to choose from with varying forms of growth habits. Here are some of my favorite palms.

The **sago palm** (*Cycas revoluta*) has stiff leaves on a short, round trunk. The leaves can reach 2 feet (.6 m) or more and have sharp points. It is one of the oldest known plants on earth, and archaeologists regularly find it as a fossil in rock formations. The sago is very slow-growing but also very distinctive. It can tolerate more moisture than many palms and cool temperatures.

Fan palms (*Chamaerops humilis* or *Livistona chinensis*) have broad, pointed fanlike leaves that can reach up to 2 feet (.6 m) across. If you had enough leaves, you could roof a tropical house with them. The fan palm needs regular moisture but not soggy conditions. It also needs warmer temperatures or the leaves may yellow.

The ***Roebelenii* date palm** is the dwarf or pygmy version of the taller date palm (***Phoenix***). It has very fine leaflets and grows only to about 4 feet (1.2 m) in height. I have yet to get mine to produce any edible dates, but I still have high hopes. The pygmy date palm can tolerate cooler temperatures and more shade than others. It also likes to grow on the dry side.

The **lady palm** (***Rhapis excelsa***) produces fan-shaped leaves although not as perfect as the fan palm's. The plant is more sweeping and does best in light shade. It prefers to dry out between waterings. The lady palm prefers temperatures not higher than 65° F (18° C).

There are many more palms to choose from. Usually plants must be acquired from large greenhouses or catalogs, and, unfortunately, they are often expensive.

The general care for palms is to avoid letting the roots sit in stagnant water. They do not like to have their roots disturbed; repot only when absolutely necessary. Most palms can be propagated with much difficulty from seed, so try to find plants to get a start with palms. While palms can be grown in greenhouse beds, they are much easier to care for if you grow them in large pots or tubs, depending upon the size of the plant.

Pansy
(Viola x *Wittrockiana)*

The pansy is a great choice for cool winter greenhouses that have trouble growing any other colorful flower. It is also a good plant for most any greenhouse or sunspace in the winter. The unique flower can be found in most every color and many have the blotched markings in the center of the flower that many people say is the face. Pansies are best started from seed in August or September for winter and spring blooms. If you want to use them in bouquets, try the Swiss giant variety, which has larger blooms and longer stems. Unfortunately, the larger-bloom varieties are often less heat tolerant.

I like to grow pansies along walkways for entertaining color as people walk through. They can also be grown equally well in pots. Try the Thompson & Morgan's seed catalog. **Padparadja pansy** can be mixed with some blue-colored pansies for a great spring effect. I find they are not picky about care, but will begin to go downhill when summer temperatures return. Pansies will benefit from occasional tip pruning and dead heading. Also lift the leaves up and clean out any dead leaves that may promote underneath rotting of the plants (see Diseases, p. 460).

Pansies can get occasional attacks of aphids (p. 413), so get down close and look under the leaf to check for the little pear-shaped critters. If you see occasional holes in the leaf or flower, then you probably have slugs (p. 418). Clean dead leaf debris and cut back on watering a bit.

Pansy

Passionflower
(Passiflora spp.*)*

The passionflower is grown for its intricate and beautiful flower, which, depending upon the variety, is 2 to 3 inches (5 to 8 cm) across. The flower is often made of two or three colors that vary in **blue**, **white**, **yellow**, **lavender** and **red**. Some varieties (***Passiflora actinia***, ***Passiflora "incense"*** and ***Passiflora x alatocaerulea***) are incredibly fragrant. One variety, ***Passiflora edulis***, produces edible, egglike fruits that are purple or yellow. The passionflower grows as a very vigorous vine, which may be both a blessing and a curse in the greenhouse. If you do not regularly prune the plant, it will quickly take over any area where it grows. On occasion, I have used this quality to an advantage, making arched arbors out of the plant. If it does get out of hand, it can become very difficult to do a good pruning job.

The passionflower plant loves a cool winter environment and can tolerate temperatures down to freezing. It can be grown in a pot or bed, but the more space the roots have, the quicker it will try to rule the greenhouse. It prefers a bright spot, humid air and moderate moisture. Passionflower is easily propagated from cuttings.

Passionflower

Petunia
(Petunia x *hybrida)*

The petunia is a common outdoor bedding plant that does equally well in the greenhouse or sunspace. It does not flower as abundantly in winter as it does in summer. Still, it flowers enough to be desirable. Petunias can be found in most every color except orange and true blue. The yellow varieties are very disappointing and should be avoided. The two-tone and dark-veined flowers are interesting. It is also available in doubles. I have

Petunia

had good luck growing the variety series known as **madness petunias**, which come in many colors.

Petunias are easy to care for in the greenhouse and look good in hanging pots and in beds. They may benefit from occasional pruning to keep them from getting leggy. Petunias do best in bright spots, and the soil needs to dry out between watering. They are usually started from seed (just barely cover) but can also be propagated from cuttings. The plants should be discarded after a year of growth.

Pineapple Sage
(Salvia elegans)

This herb in the mint family has the distinct fragrance of pineapple. You must rub the leaf to release the aroma. It is listed here in the ornamental plant section because of its striking scarlet

blooms. The flowers are thin and tubular and about 1 inch (2.5 cm) long. The blooms are not a good choice for bouquets, because they tend to drop, or shatter, as horticulturists say, when picked. Still, the flowers are quite showy in the greenhouse and can bloom for many months in winter through spring.

The plant can reach up to 2 feet (.6 m) tall. You may see some of the leaves tipped with white edges. I have had good results growing it in pots or planted directly in beds. It does best in full sun and when allowed to dry between watering. Unlike many plants in the mint family, it is not aggressive. Whiteflies (p. 420) find this plant attractive in the summer, so it may need some special care and attention to keep them at bay. The leaves can be used in teas and potpourris.

Plumbago
(Plumbago auriculata)

Plumbago is a perennial subtropical known for producing phloxlike powder blue flowers. The blooms hold well in bouquets. It will wind up a trellis, if one is provided. Without a trellis, it grows shrubby. The light green leaves and spent flowers like to stick to clothes, and I find them all over me after working around them. The plants, if given time, can vine 10 feet (3 m) or more in length, especially if there is a trellis adjacent to the plant. If you want to control the shape and growth, prune plumbago regularly. The unsightly old blossoms should be regularly removed.

Plumbago prefers bright light and drier soil conditions. It can tolerate moist soil as long as it is sand or well drained. It is easily propagated from cuttings and is readily available in plant catalogs. Alba, a variety that has white blooms, generally is pest-free and easy to grow.

Pocketbook Plant
(Calceolaria crenatiflora)

The pocketbook plant produces one of the more interesting flowers you will ever see. The flowers have a rounded, pouchlike shape. If the odd shape doesn't fascinate you, the contrasting blotches or spots on the flower surely will. The plant's flowers tend to be two contrasting warm colors with broad leaves.

There are outdoor perennial varieties that are not as suited to the greenhouse environment as the annual types. Look for the anytime hybrids, which produce a 9-inch (23-centimeter) plant in a 6-inch (15-centimeter) pot.

The pocketbook plant takes some planning to grow to maturity from seed. Because it likes to flower in the cooler temperatures of winter, the best timing is to plant seed in June for a good winter flowering plant. For bloom around the Easter season, sow the seed in early August. Just barely cover the seed and when it has grown four or five leaves, transplant it into a 6-inch (15-centimeter) pot, using regular potting soil. It can tolerate cooler temperatures but prefers constant temperatures of 50° to 60° F (10° to 15° C), especially in its last 4 months of growth. It needs a bright spot to grow with sun for only a short time each day. It benefits from regular light feeding, especially when you see the flower buds appear. The pocketbook plant needs constant moisture. Try watering it from below by always keeping the saucer filled with water.

It is best grown as a potted plant, and like many annuals it is best donated to the compost pile after the blooms have faded. Maintain a steady eye out for aphids (p. 413), first appearing on the underside of the leaf and on stems and tips.

Poinsettia
(Euphorbia pulcherrima)

The poinsettia has become the Christmas plant of choice. Everyone will want to give you their leftover plants when they find out you have a greenhouse or a sunspace. To avoid growing only poinsettias in the greenhouse, I eventually have to tell my friends, "Thanks, but two plants are enough, and I don't need any more." But no matter what, most greenhouse owners will eventually end up with at least one poinsettia. What to do? General care for poinsettias is to provide a bright, cool spot and let the soil dry out between watering.

After blooming, or about late April, you may want to consider pruning it back to create a more bushy plant, if desired. They can get to be tall, lanky shrubs if left to

Poinsettia

their own devices. Spring is also a good time to repot poinsettia if it is root-bound or if you believe it is in some bad soil. Continue watering it as before and occasionally give it some plant food. Because poinsettia likes a cooler environment, many people move the plant to a semishady spot outside in summer to avoid the hot greenhouse. This is a good idea if your greenhouse runs hot.

When late September arrives, you will need to control the light that the poinsettia receives because the length of the night triggers the formation of the color. It needs 14 hours of uninterrupted darkness daily from late September for a period of 8 weeks (don't get lazy and skip a day!). Many people move the plant to a dark closet or slip it into a sealed black bag (it takes three black trash bags to give you total darkness). After the light-control period, continue growing it as before. You need to be dedicated to this and never miss a day, which is admittedly a lot of work. If it sounds like too much for you, there are two alternatives: (1) Toss the plant out and buy a new one next Christmas like everyone else, or (2) just continue growing it without the light-control treatment and see what happens. Sometimes, I get a poinsettia to do okay by placing it where no one turns on the electric light at night, such as a bright basement window. It is helpful if it does receive some natural light through a window. With this method, I have had some good results.

You can easily propagate poinsettia from tip cuttings at least 4 to 5 inches (10 to 13 cm) long. The poinsettia can be plagued by both whiteflies (p. 420) and mealybugs (p. 415), and gift plants should be checked for unwanted "guests."

Polka-dot Plant
(Hypoestes sanguinolenta)

This plant is also known as freckle-face. As its names imply, it has unmistakable spots on the leaves, which make the plant interesting and even colorful. The leaves are its main attraction, as the flower is insignificant. The plant usually grows to 1 or 2 feet (.3 or .6 m) in height and has spots that are pink, red or white against green leaves. Lately, there are varieties that have even more of the spots, to the point where the green seems to be spotted against pink, red or white.

This is an easy plant to grow, although I usually find myself tossing it out after about a year of growth because it becomes lanky and too preoccupied with flowering and tends to go downhill. Don't be surprised if, after flowering, it

Polka-dot plant

reseeds itself as baby polka-dot plants coming up everywhere.

The polka-dot plant seems tolerant of most any greenhouse condition and is relatively pest-free. It is easily grown both in pots and in beds, usually propagated from seed. You can also get good results from cuttings. I prefer starting it from seed because it is easy to germinate and grows fast. It does seem to prefer brighter locations for the best leaf-color development.

Poppy

(Papaveraceae spp.*)*

Poppies are not often considered as a greenhouse plant, but I have had wonderful color shows from them. I haven't tried all the many species, but many are good for the greenhouse. I have had good luck with both **shirley** *(P. rhoeas)* and **iceland poppy** *(P. nudicaule)*. I have also enjoyed the blue foliage and unusual flowers of *P. somniferum*, which includes a **double-flowered variety** that looks like a peony. I have found that the **perennial oriental poppy** *(P. orientale)* is not a good choice for the greenhouse, because the period of bloom is so short and the plant has a difficult time in the greenhouse environment.

Poppies seem to do best in the greenhouse when planted in late summer or fall for a spring bloom. Don't get too carried away, because it may take the plants most of winter before they get ready to flower. But still a few plants are always good to have blooming.

Because poppy seed is so small, it is often sown too thick and will probably need to be thinned. Contrary to what many will say, the poppy can be transplanted, as long as you do it while the seedling is small and take care to limit the disturbance of the roots. They need bright sun and may need staking if you have prolonged cloudy weather. I find that they do best if they can be planted in beds or larger pots of at least 8 inches (20 cm). The soil needs to dry out between waterings. Poppies should have the spent blossoms and seed pods that have developed picked off as soon as possible for continued bloom.

For bouquets, cut the stem as soon as the buds become upright and are just beginning to show some color. You should sear the base of the cut flower over a flame for the bloom to last in a vase.

Primrose
(*Primula* spp.)

Primrose, also known as **Primula**, is a lover of cool weather in the greenhouse. They are low-growing plants that bear clusters of flowers in most any color. They like cool, moist conditions to bloom and tend to suffer when the temperatures get warm. They also prefer only a few hours of bright sun, so pick your primrose location well. To best schedule your plants, start the seeds in February or March and just barely cover the seed, unless you are growing *P. sinensis*, which should be buried a bit deeper as it needs dark to germinate. When plants are large enough, transplant them into 5-inch (13-centimeter) pots. Try to grow them in a cool spot.

The species *P. obconica* is a good plant for the greenhouse, but you should know that the leaf can cause dermatitis in some people, so use gloves when handling this species. The **fairy primrose** *P. malacoides* is known for its large flowers.

While many people toss out the plants after the show of bloom, you can sometimes coax them into another year of bloom in the greenhouse. The main thing to remember when growing primrose is to think cool and moist, cold and sopping wet, or hot and dry. Plants also benefit from regular feeding in the summer months. Also, keep an eye out for mites (p. 416).

Ranunculus
(*Ranunculus asiaticus*)

Ranunculus is also known as **buttercup**. It is usually started from small, hard tubers. The tubers look like a miniature petrified jellyfish the size of a penny. The flowers are delicate and found in most colors except for the blue shades. The flower shape can be varied from a double that forms a small globe to a poppylike single-petaled blossom. A single tuber can produce a large number of blooms during a season. Each bloom can be 2 to 5 inches (5 to 13 cm) across. They are best sown in the fall through winter, for late winter through spring bloom.

Before planting the tubers, try soaking them in water for a couple of hours. Don't forget them, because longer soaking may cause damage. Plant the tubers with the points down, about 1 inch (2.5 cm) or so deep in well-drained potting soil. Adding a bit of sand to the potting soil is helpful in giving them the good drainage that they need. Let the soil dry slightly between watering. Don't plant all of your tubers at the same time. Vary the planting through the fall and early winter to provide a longer period of enjoyment of these beautiful flowers. The plants do equally well in pots or in beds. Give yourself around 5 square inches (32 sq. cm) of pot per tuber. In beds, space the tubers about 4 inches (10 cm) apart. There are other species besides *R. asiaticus* worth experimenting with in the greenhouse.

Ranunculus is a great winter and spring bloomer. The flowers are useful in bouquets but also look great blooming in beds and pots. After bloom, most people discard the plants, but you can let the plant continue to grow until the leaves yellow. Set them in a cool spot with semimoist garden dirt (not potting soil) until it is time to plant them again. You should know that the tubers are not easy to store with great success, so buy a few new tubers next season just in case. On occasion, when growing ranunculus in beds, I have forgotten about the plants after they die back. The next season they often come up as a surprise.

Rose
(Rosa spp.*)*

No flowering greenhouse would be complete without a rose. You can grow most any type of rose in a greenhouse, including

Rose

the **teas**, **floribundas**, **miniatures**, **climbers** and **shrubs**. I have found that the most rewarding rose for both visual and cut-flower enjoyment are the floribundas. They seem to put on more blooms than any other type and give you year-round flowers, often with incredible vigor, even in cool greenhouses. I have enjoyed the different characteristics of the large-flowered tea roses and the many offerings in miniature roses, but nothing seems to beat the profusion of blooms of the floribundas. Yes, the stems aren't as long as the teas, but I like quantity, and no one has complained about the rose's shorter stems when I give a bloom to someone. In small greenhouses, the miniature roses are always a good fit in a few small pots and are easy to grow.

Unfortunately, plant breeders have developed a plethora of beautiful roses that have no fragrance. What a waste! These roses are only half as good as a rose that not only looks good but also smells good. No matter what rose you grow, always think about fragrance. Read the variety descriptions well, and look for those that say "strong fragrance" or "spicy scent." Whenever possible, go for a variety that has smell. There should be a law banning all roses that lack a

Rose

decent fragrance. A fragrant rose can fill the greenhouse or sunspace with its wonderful aroma even better than it can in the outside air, and it is such a treat!

Roses are very tolerant of varying temperatures; from hot to cold, they usually do fine. They need to grow in a bright full-sun location in well-drained soil. They can easily be overwatered, so be sure to let the soil dry out between waterings.

As with outside blooms, if you want to cut some blossoms for a bouquet, wait until the flower is about 1/3 to 1/2 open. Be sure to cut just above a bud and down low enough so that you have at least five leaflets on the stem just below where you have cut.

Roses tend to benefit from occasional pruning, which will soon stimulate bushier and often healthier growth, especially if the plant is starting to get leggy.

Roses can be grown in pots as well as in beds. With the floribundas, I have the best luck planting either in large tubs or directly in beds. Roses are subject to many problems in the greenhouse as they are outside. Mites (p. 416), whiteflies (p. 420) and mealybugs (p. 415) all love to hang out on roses. If the blossoms are opening with some burned edges, you may have thrips (p. 419). Like mites, thrips are also almost microscopic and can cause havoc with blossoms. Get out the hand lens and you may see little cigar-shaped critters running around the buds. Try to spray the buds before they open with something like insecticidal soap (p. 429). Cut back on the dosage if the soap causes burning. If soap doesn't do the job, you may have to go to something stronger. Also, roses are subject to powdery mildew (p. 471). I have had good luck controlling the mildew by spraying an antitranspirant (p. 471). See Chapter 10, When Things Go Wrong, for more information. Overwatering often results in splotchy yellowing of the leaves. Try cutting back on watering and see if it helps if you have these symptoms.

Salpiglossis
(Salpiglossis sinuata)

Salpiglossis may also be known as **painted tongue**, and has one of the most beautiful blooms you'll ever see. It produces a 2- to 3-inch (5- to 8-centimeter) flower on 2-foot (.6-meter) plants. Inside the bloom are some incredible markings that often remind me of an extraordinary sunset. The flowers are available in **purple**, **yellow**, **red**, **gold**, **blue** or **pink**, and each has a deeper color of patterned venation, often turning to a lighter gold background in the throat of the flower. You have to see it to believe it! The blooms work well in bouquets. The leaves have a sticky feel, and I often see bugs getting stuck to the foliage as if on fly paper. As good-looking as the flowers are, I think that the leaves are equally ugly, so be patient until you see it bloom.

Salpiglossis is related to the petunia but is a bit more tricky to grow. It does not tolerate very hot or very cold temperatures. Additionally, it is an annual and often not long-lived. Usually I start the seed in late January or February to take advantage of the moderate spring temperatures as it is blooming. You can also start it in late July or August for a late fall bloom before the cooler temperatures of winter. When cold or hot weather sets in or when the plants stop blooming, I find it easiest to toss them in the compost and plan to grow more next season. Salpiglossis does fine in pots and in ground beds. Occasionally you may need to stake it up. Be sure to grow it in a well-lit, sunny location. It prefers drier soils and doesn't tolerate overwatering.

Some good selections for the salpiglossis include **bolero** and **casino**, which each have short, bushy tendencies. There is also a taller variety known as **splash**. Grow just a few salpiglossis, and you will always get a sigh from visitors when they first see them.

Salvia
(Salvia farinacea)

This type of salvia is not the common red-flowered variety most people are used to. The *farinacea* species has blue or white flowers. The leaves and bloom look very different, but it is a good plant for the greenhouse. The flowering stalk is less than 1/2 inch (1.3 cm) wide but grows straight up 8 to 10 inches (20 to 25 cm) above the 15- to 20-inch-tall (38- to 51-centimeter-tall) plant. One plant will produce many vertical flowering stalks. When you set many plants together spaced 6 to 8 inches (15 to 20 cm) apart, you get a beautiful effect. The **blue variety**, known as **Victoria**, is striking against other flowers in a bed or a bouquet. It is reminiscent of a lavender plant, with a more vertical nature to the blooms. A **white variety**, called **white bedder**, grows 2 feet (.6 m) or more in height. I tend to grow the Victoria because of the intense blue color, which is sometimes hard to find in a flower.

Salvia farinacea is best grown in sunny spots. It prefers warmer temperatures, though it can survive the cooler winter greenhouse climate. In cool temperatures, I find the stress often brings on the bugs. In the greenhouse it can live for many years but usually looks best for only 1 year or less. You may find the plant looks better when you remove the older flowering spikes as they finish blooming. Salvia farinacea is easily propagated from seed, taking a little more than 2 weeks to germinate, given the proper conditions.

Schizanthus
(Schizanthus x wisetonensis)

Schizanthus is also called the **butterfly flower** or the **poor man's orchid**, and when you see the bloom, you'll understand why. This is one of the shorter-lived plants for the greenhouse but has one of the most unusual and colorful blooms of any plant. The flowers come in most every color except blue. Each flower is only 1 inch (2.5 cm) or less across and is borne in profusion on a 12- to 24-inch (30- to 61-centimeter) plant, depending upon the variety. Like the salpiglossis, the schizanthus often has incredible markings in the throat. Sometimes they are set against a yellow center with another color around the outside of the flower. It is the unique markings that make people compare it to an orchid. The petals are irregularly shaped in a snapdragon manner, which reminds many people of butterflies. The beautiful blooms atop short branching stems are not fragrant. With a little creativity, schizanthus can be used as cut flowers for small vases.

Schizanthus will live at most only for a couple of seasons, blooming for a month or two before the foliage begins to die back, often with the flowers still in full bloom. Before flowering, it likes to be fed regularly. The plants may become lopsided, but a little tip pinching while it is 6 to 10 inches (15 to 25 cm) in height can make the plant much better shaped. It is not very tolerant of hot temperatures and grows slowly in cool temperatures. For these reasons I tend to grow them through the fall, winter and spring. Schizanthus can be grown in either pots or beds, but I have seen the best plants when grown in pots. It can tolerate varying soil moisture conditions.

The taller varieties of schizanthus may need some small stakes for support as they come into bloom. Schizanthus are best propagated from seed. Because they are so short-lived, if you want some schizanthus to be continually blooming in your greenhouse, you may want to sow a few seeds every 2 to 3 weeks, so as they die back new ones take their place.

Sensitive Plant
(Mimosa pudica)

The sensitive plant is revered for its sensitivity rather than its bloom. It has delicate, ferny leaves that fold up when lightly brushed or touched, almost as if it has a muscular response to your finger. If brushed a bit harder, the small branches may even fold downward. It is a novelty plant that delights children as well as adults. Its response to a light touch is almost magical. I have seen the

Sensitive plant

sensitive plant create a lifelong fascination with plants among some people (myself included). Occasionally, you may see it put out a small pink flower that looks like a powder puff.

The sensitive plant likes warmth of at least 50° F (10° C) and constant moisture most of the year. In winter, you can let it run a little drier between waterings. It needs to grow in a bright spot but not necessarily in full sun. It is best grown in a pot and is generally started from seed.

Shrimp Plant
(Beloperone guttata)

The shrimp plant is a long-lived shrubby plant that can bloom year-round. As its name implies, it has 3-inch (8-centimeter) salmon-colored prawnlike flowers at the end of arcing stems. It is a good choice for the greenhouse because of the long bloom period and its ability to tolerate diverse temperature and soil conditions. Though the blooming stems may not be of great length, flowers can be used in bouquets and are long-lasting.

Shrimp plants are best grown in pots. The bigger the pot, the more shrubby the plant will become. Occasional pruning can prevent the plant from becoming leggy

Shrimp plant

and will help you to maintain a more bushy plant. They have few pest problems and are easily propagated from cuttings. You may also like a solid yellow flowering variety.

Snapdragon
(Antirrhinum majus)

Snapdragon is tops on my list for a winter greenhouse cut flower. They are dependable and easy to grow, and they can provide you with long colorful spikes of flowers for many months. But before you go out and dig up the outdoor snaps, you should know that you need to grow special snapdragon varieties developed to bloom in the short days of winter. Ordinary outdoor snaps bloom poorly in the winter and pale in comparison to the greenhouse types. The greenhouse varieties (sometimes known as forcing snaps) produce beautiful blooms reaching up to 3 feet (.9 m), topped by the longest flower spikes you have ever seen. They come in all the traditional snapdragon colors. I have found the greenhouse varieties have a stronger spicy scent compared to the outdoor types. Obtaining these special varieties for the greenhouse is not easy unless you can talk a commercial greenhouse operator into selling you some seed. At this writing, I have found only one retail seed catalog selling greenhouse snaps: Stokes Seeds (see Mail-Order Seeds appendix for address), which has the variety "hybrid greenhouse mixture."

Timing is important in growing greenhouse snaps, and they are best sown September through December for winter through spring bloom. When you are growing greenhouse snaps, you will need to construct a simple horizontal trellis (see Chapter 3, Plant Layout) or they will never give you nice, straight flowering stalks. The

Snapdragon

trellis needs to be at least three tiers high, reaching a level of at least 3 feet (.9 m).

Snapdragons can easily tolerate most temperatures, including the very cold greenhouse, but will have more problems, including smaller flower spikes and wilting as the temperature starts to consistently reach above 80° F (27° C) during the day. They are a great winter plant because of their cold tolerance. They do best when grown in bright greenhouse areas.

Propagate your snapdragon seed by just barely covering it with soil. Snaps like to grow in full light, and I prefer to grow them in beds because of the horizontal trellis system, which is easier to set up in beds. If you want to try growing them in pots, you can place three or four pots in a 5-gallon (19-liter) pot (with drainage holes!) and put a standard tomato cage over the top of the plants when they reach 8 inches (20 cm) in height. The first bloom spikes are always the best in terms of length. Each succeeding bloom will be smaller but still well worth growing. When you pick bloom spikes for a bouquet, always cut the stem at least 8 inches (20 cm) below the first bloom on the spike to give you sturdy future flowering spikes. Try to maintain a good level of moisture in the soil, but not dripping wet mud. Wilting can set your blooms back and should be avoided, although with hot temperatures that can become difficult. I usually rip the crop out when the plant is putting on bloom spikes only around 5 inches (13 cm) long. For prolonged winter bloom, try staggering your planting. Start a few different beds (or pots) of greenhouse-type snaps a month or so apart.

Occasionally, you may see aphids (p. 413) hanging around. Get suspicious if you see some sticky substance on the leaves, and keep an eye on the underside of the leaves.

Staghorn Fern
(Platycerium bifurcatum)

The staghorn fern is a true fern, not a flowering plant, but an interesting plant to have in any greenhouse. It gets its name from the way it resembles mounted horns. It is best grown mounted on a slab of bark 8 by 10 inches (20 by 25 cm) or larger. Dig out a little pocket in the middle of the bark and fill with some peat moss or compost. Place the plant there and secure with thumbtacks and twine, and

Staghorn fern

over time it will get a good hold on the bark. Lower fronds begin to grow around the bark and turn brown, which provides a good anchor. About every 2 weeks, water the pocket; mist every 3 days if the humidity is low. Occasionally mist with a plant food (the type that is dissolved in water). It prefers the lower lighted areas of the greenhouse, and once it gets growing, it is relatively free of pests or problems. New plants must be obtained from commercial greenhouses or through the mail. You can propagate new plants from little "pups" that occasionally appear to the side of the mother plant. It is great to have some antlers hanging in the greenhouse that are alive and breathing without ever having to go hunting. The staghorn fern is always a good catch!

Statice
(Linmonium sinuatum)

Statice, also known as **sea lavender**, is often grown as an outdoor everlasting because the cut flower can last for many years in dried-flower arrangements. I have had good luck growing *L. sinuatum*, the annual type, in the greenhouse, giving new meaning to the term "everlasting." You can even transplant outdoor statice into

Statice

the greenhouse before frost, but you must get a lot of root to be successful; dig deep because they have a taproot. Good results can also come from sowing your own in mid-winter that will bloom from summer through Christmas or longer. While statice tolerates cool temperatures well, it grows very slowly in the winter. If the flower stalks fall over, try staking them. There are many varieties to choose from in *L. sinuatum* statice, and it is available in most colors. It can grow to a height of 2 feet (.6 m) or more. I prefer to grow **dwarf vari-**

eties, which only reach 10 to 12 inches (25 to 30 cm), because they bloom faster and need less staking. I also like the mixed selections with a range of colors, rather than growing just one color.

Sinuatum likes to dry out between waterings and does best in well-lit areas. It does well in both beds and pots. When grown in pots, use a 1-gallon (3.8-liter) size to accommodate the long roots.

When the plant is in flower, you can use the blooms as you would any flower in a water vase. If you want to dry the flower stalks, hang them upside down in a dark, dry room for 3 to 4 weeks. Then you can use them in dried-flower arrangements. You may have some grasses, dried wildflowers or other everlastings to mix into the bouquets, but don't put any water in the vase of your dried-flower arrangement or it will quickly rot.

Stock
(Matthiola incana)

Stock is one of the most fragrant plants in the greenhouse, especially in the evening. The spicy aroma can easily fill any space beginning about sundown. It can also be used as a cut flower but may drop some petals within a few days of being cut. Stock produces

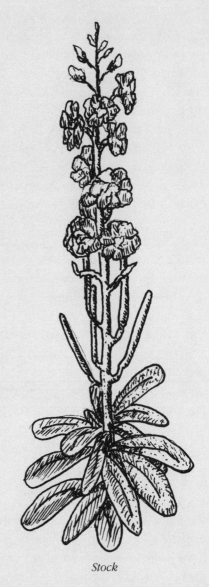

Stock

pink, red, apricot, purple, coral and white blooms.

Plants can be found in both **double-** and **single-flowered types**. Whenever possible, try to grow varieties that have a high number of double flowers because they are much more showy than the single-flowered plants. In any seed packet, there will always be a few single-flowered plants showing up. You can identify the doubles from the singles when the plants are still seedlings. The doubles tend to be the seedlings that are the yellowish, pale green plants. The less desirable seedlings will be a darker green and can be tossed before you transplant into any larger pots or beds. This leaf-color method of identification works best when the seedlings are grown at temperatures around 55° to 60° F (13° to 15° C). In warmer temperatures it is less accurate but still worth trying. Another indication, which is not quite as reliable with all varieties, is to look at the very first leaves that emerge (known as cotyledon leaves). If you see that one of the leaves has a little notch in it, that sometimes indicates a double-flowered plant. Because you may be throwing some of the nondouble seedlings out, sow more than you think you'll need to end up with the amount you want.

Varieties of stock vary in height from 8 to 30 inches (20 to 76 cm). The smaller varieties are best for potted production, while the taller types are best in beds. However, with a large pot and a few stakes, you can grow the larger varieties in a pot.

Stock is mostly a winter-blooming plant and can be nonproductive in the hot greenhouse, so timing is very important. It should be sown only between late July and early March. If not and they go through hot weather when they normally would be flowering, your stocks will just grow a lot of leaves with no sign of flowering, at least not until winter or spring. Once their clock gets wrenched by hot weather, you never know when your greenhouse stocks will flower.

After flowering, you can often get secondary blooms on new stalks, but you must make a concerted effort to prune off the old blossoms or any seed pods.

Another species of stock, commonly known as **evening scented stock—(***M. longipetala***)**, is not nearly as showy as *M. incana* but has a great smell. If fragrance is more of a primary concern than looks, you should try it. Stock does best in full sun and must dry somewhat between waterings. It is easily propagated from seed.

Streptocarpus
(Streptocarpus x *hybridus)*

Streptocarpus, also known as **cape primrose**, is a second cousin to the African violet. In the green-house it is easier to grow and has less exacting requirements. It does, however, prefer cooler nights, which makes it a better choice for the greenhouse than for the house. Streptocarpus is much larger than your average African violet, with some varieties having leaves up to 1 1/2 feet (.45 m) long. It has a showy tubular, trumpet-shaped blossom that can be up to 2 inches (5 cm) wide. Often there are intersting markings in the throat of the flower. Flowers are found in **red, purple, blue, white** and **pink.** It is always a good choice for a long-blooming potted plant.

Streptocarpus can tolerate higher light levels than the African violet, but still it would prefer the shadier areas of the greenhouse or sunspace. It have had the best luck with the streptocarpus when grown in pots. Let the top of the soil dry out between waterings, and try to avoid getting water on the leaves by watering the plant from below or between the leaves. Be sure to remove faded flowers for pro-longed bloom. While it can toler-ate cool temperatures, try not to let it grow in areas much below 45° F (7° C).

Streptocarpus can be easily propagated from divisions of large plants or from leaf cuttings. It is occasionally bothered by mealy-bugs (p. 415), so look for the cottony critters hanging around.

Succulents

Succulents are prized for their often unusual plump shapes. Like cactus, they are incredible at water conservation. There are many spe-cies of succulents worth growing in a sunroom or greenhouse, and you will always appreciate how easy they are to grow. Besides having interesting thick leaves, some have amazing flowers. The general care for most succulents is to let the soil run quite dry be-tween waterings. During winter, they can go many weeks without watering because many are dor-mant then. They need well-drained soil and will easily rot in wet soil conditions. Succulents prefer plenty of bright light but can tolerate some shady conditions.

I could fill pages with varieties of succulents to grow but because their care is so easy, I'll let you decide what to try. If you provide them with their basic care, it is hard to go wrong with these plants. Walk into any commercial retail greenhouse or garden center and you will likely find some interest-ing succulents that you can't live without. You should also check the plant catalogs that carry succulents for a great selection.

See **aloe vera** (p. 197) and **kalanchoe** (p. 244). Also look for **living stones**, **burro's tail**, **string of beads**, **pencil plants** and one scientifically known as *Cotyledon undulata*. Check out the many **Euphorbias**, which is a large family of succulents with diverse shapes. It would take up too much space to list all the interesting succulents, but once you start to see what is out there, you are sure to get hooked.

Swan River Daisy
(Brachycome iberidifolia)

The Swan River daisy has 1-inch (2.5-centimeter) **blue**, **purple** or **white** daisies borne on lacy foliage. One plant can bear a profusion of flowers. The plants themselves are only 7 to 10 inches (18 to 25 cm) in height. I prefer to grow them in hanging pots. The Swan River daisy prefers warm temperatures and is best grown as a summer plant. I usually start it in April for all summer bloom. The soil needs to dry slightly between waterings and the plant must grow in full sun for the best flowering response. When cool weather returns to the greenhouse, it tends to go downhill, so bid it farewell until next spring. Swan River daisy is easily propagated from seed.

Sweet Pea
(Lathyrus odoratus)

Sweet peas are a must for the winter and spring greenhouse, getting an A-plus rating in color, cut flowers and fragrance. No smell and no flower puts even the worst winter at bay so decisively as does the sweet pea. When you walk into your greenhouse, they will instantly

Sweet pea

brighten up even the toughest day you had at the office.

Because they like the cool weather to grow best, you should schedule the seeding in September or October. You can grow most any variety, but I have found some selections offered in the Stokes Seeds catalog (see Mail-Order Seeds appendix) that outperform all the others in the greenhouse. Look for the **cuthbertson floribunda** mixture, which produces a wide array of colors on long stems. The cuthbertson is also very heat tolerant and is at its best in the spring, as long as it has been sown in the fall. Be ready for this variety, however, because it grows tall, to 7 feet (2 m) or more in height. I have been able to prune the tips with limited good results to control the height. There are many other varieties of sweet pea that can be grown in the greenhouse, but be sure to select for varieties listed as heat tolerant for best results. For fall and early winter blooming, you might want to grow the **early spencers** or **early multifloras**.

With most every variety (except for the dwarf, which are not suited to the greenhouse), you will need some type of vertical trellising because they are fast climbers. It is best to build the trellis before you plant. Peas do best when di-

rectly sown into the location where you will be growing them. I have been able to transplant them with some luck and extreme care, but I didn't seem to gain anything in the effort when compared to those directly sown at a later date.

To prolong the bloom, it is important that you keep the vines well picked and prevent any flowers from forming seed. The peas formed on the sweet pea vine are not edible, so take precautions with toddlers.

You can harvest the flowers with a good pair of scissors. Another way to pick the flowers that a friend once showed me is to bend the flower stem back toward the main stem of the growing plant while gently pulling upward. It will often make a clean break, and I can pick a full bouquet without scissors or knife. However you harvest your sweet peas, be sure to not damage the plant by bending the main stem, ripping the flowers off at the expense of ripping stem tissue.

Sweet peas like full sun but can tolerate partial shading during the day. They grow best in ground beds, but with some creativity you could grow some in 5-gallon (19-liter) or larger pots, as long as you can provide some type of trellising or string that is possibly suspended from the roof. They like soil that is more on the moist side, but not muddy wet. Sweet peas can become susceptible to both aphids (p. 413) and mites (p.416).

Thunbergia, or Black-eyed Susan
(*Thunbergia alata*)

Of the many plants with the name black-eyed Susan, the thunbergia wins my support for the official dedication. The flowers are usually less than 1 inch (2.5 cm) in size and commonly have orange-colored petals with a very dark purple center, which in some light looks black. You may also find varieties with yellow o white petals. Thunbergia is a vine that can be grown in eithr pots or ground beds. They will often vine up the wires of a hanging basket or up a small trellis for a nice effect. They are slow growers, but over time they can reach 5 feet (1.5 m) or more if given an opportunity and trellising. Thunbergia does equally well in cool or warm greenhouses and can bloom year-round. I have had plants live for many years. they tolerate varying moisture, temperature and light levels as long as it is not dark shade. The only problem thunbergia seems to have is an occasional mite infestation (p. 416), as indicated by a yellow stippling of the leaves. They may also succumb to occasional visits from the whitefly (p. 420).

Tulip
(*Tulipa* spp.)

See Forcing Spring Bulbs for Winter Bloom (p. 229).

Venus's-Flytrap
(*Dionaea muscipula*)

There is always a fascination with any plant that has the ability to move on its own accord. When you combine that with a carnivorous habit, you really have a winner of a plant. The Venus's-flytrap is especially entertaining to children and worth growing for that reason alone. At the end of the leaves is a twin-lobed blade edged with long hairs. When these bristly hairs are touched by an insect, the lobes close together in the blink of an eye, trapping the bug. The trapped insect is then dissolved by a fluid contained in the lobes, which turns the insect into a nutritious meal for the flytrap. Plants are obtained through catalog sources. Mature flytraps can sometimes be divided into two plants. They can also be started from seed.

The Venus's-flytrap needs a constantly moist growing medium made up of mostly peat and sphagnum moss along with a small amount of rich soil. Never let them dry out. They also need a bright location and consistently high humidity. I find that regular misting is helpful. The flytrap does best in a greenhouse with the winter night low temperature on the cool side. Above all, the Venus's-flytrap does best with a steady diet of living flies. That is where most gardeners come up short, especially in winter. Dead flies don't seem to work. However, injured living flies dropped into the open lobes work great, if you have the constitution for this kind of care. I have had limited success with dropping cut pieces of fresh worm into the jaws of the plant, but that is only a short-term substitute for flies. For this reason, I have always had problems keeping the flytrap alive for more than a year or so. While they are alive, they are very entertaining.

Don't expect a Venus's-flytrap to be much help in bug control for greenhouse pests. Unfortunately, I have never seen one eat common greenhouse pests such as aphid or whitefly. They do best with the common black housefly.

Zinnia
(*Zinnia* spp.)

Zinnia is a common outdoor annual that can also be grown in the greenhouse with good results. It is a warm-loving plant that provides good cut flowers. Zinnias have colorful rounded flower heads that vary from being pomponlike to being daisylike. They range in height from 8 inches to 3 feet (20 cm to .9 m). Flowers come in most every color except blue shades. In the greenhouse they can be grown in either pots or ground beds. Because they like warmth, they are best grown in the warmer months of the year. You will probably have to discard this annual after a season of blooms. In the meantime, zinnias are nice as a colorful greenhouse plant and as a cut flower.

The most common problem in the greenhouse is the disease powdery mildew (p. 471), which turns the leaves powdery white. To avoid this mildew, try not to get water on the leaves, by watering below the leaf canopy. You may also have to take other measures.

A Quick Look at Selected Characteristics of Ornamentals

Ornamentals That Vine

Bougainvillea
Golden-trumpet vine
Jasminum polyanthum
Jasminum stephanense
Mandevilla
Mina lobata

Nasturtium (not all varieties)
Morning-glory
Passionflower
Plumbago
Sweet pea
Thunbergia

Ornamentals for Bouquets and Cut Flowers

Alstromeria
Anemone
Aster
Bird-of-paradise
Calendula
Camellia
Carnation
Centaurea
Chrysanthemum
Cleome
Coral bells
Dahlia
Dianthus
Gerbera
Gomphrena
Larkspur

Malope
Marguerite daisy
Marigold
Mullein
Orchid
Pansy
Ranunculus
Rose
Salpiglossis
Salvia
Schizanthus
Shrimp plant
Snapdragon
Statice
Stock
Sweet pea
Zinnia

Ornamentals for Fragrance

Alyssum

Angel's-trumpet

Carnation

Dianthus

Freesia

Gardenia

Geranium, scented

Hyacinth

Jasmine

Morning-glory *(Ipomea alba)*

Narcissus (not all varieties)

Nicotiana (not all varieties)

Oleander

Passionflower (not all varieties)

Pineapple sage

Rose (not all varieties)

Snapdragon

Stock

Sweet pea

Ornamentals for
Unusual or Colorful Leaves

Begonia rex

Bromeliads

Cabbage, ornamental

Cacti and succulents

Coleus

Croton

Geranium (not all varieties)

Kale, ornamental

Polka-dot plant

Sago palm

Sensitive plant

Staghorn fern

Venus's-flytrap

Ornamentals for the Greenhouse that Runs Cool In Winter

Anemone
Bougainvillea
Cactus
Calendula
Camellia
Carnation
Cineraria
Cyclamen
Date palm
Felicia
Freesia
Geranium
Globe amaranth
Hyacinth
Jasminum nitidum
Kalanchoe
Kale and cabbage, flowering
Maple, flowering
Narcissus

Nasturtium
Nemesia
Orchids (not all varieties)
Pansy
Passionflower
Pocketbook plant
Primrose
Ranunculus
Rose
Sago palm
Schizanthus
Snapdragon
Statice
Streptocarpus
Succulents
Sweet pea
Thunbergia
Tulip

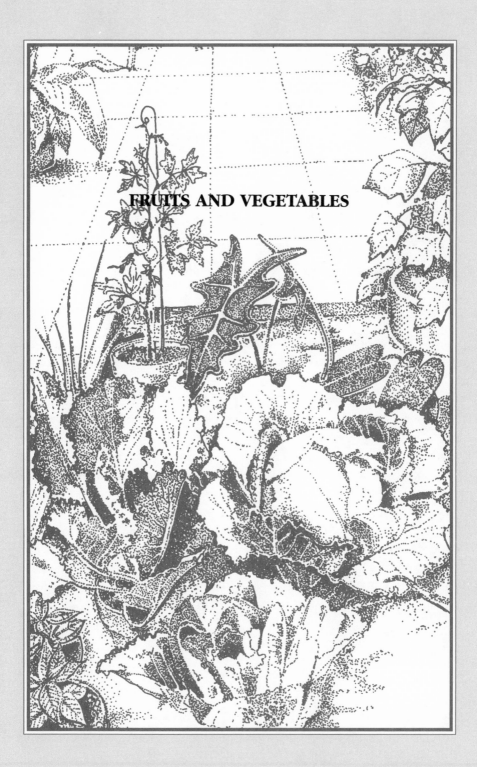

FRUITS AND VEGETABLES

FRUITS AND VEGETABLES

Besides using your greenhouse or sunspace for flowers, why not also mix in some fruit and vegetables? Nothing is more luxurious than eating a winter meal that includes some homegrown fresh food. With the price of winter fruit and vegetables always on the rise, it can also help save you on your food bill. For the best use of a greenhouse or sunspace, I prefer to grow those food crops that are more expensive in the grocery store. Greenhouses can become incredible food producers, although some crops are not as space efficient in terms of the amount of food they produce, and space is always at a premium when you are growing under glass. By following the recommendations in Chapter 7, Scheduling, you can maximize the productivity.

I will occasionally mention specific varieties and their catalog source. Unfortunately, many companies often drop varieties as new, improved varieties come along. They may also drop a favorite variety if they perceive a low demand for a particular choice. If you can't find a variety, you will have to see if you can locate it in another catalog or find a suitable substitute based on some of the important characteristics. You might also contact the catalog for help in locating a variety that has been dropped.

As in Ornamental Flowering Crops, these are not hard and fast rules, but they will help you avoid some mistakes in greenhouse food crop growing.

Artichoke

Artichoke

The globe artichoke resembles a large thistle, but unlike the thistle, this plant is not a weed. The artichoke is easily started from seed. You can also propagate it from small plants and roots, which are commonly available through seed and nursery catalogs. Artichoke plants grow about 4 feet (1.2 m) high and up to 5 feet (1.5 m) wide. They do fine in a ground bed but may also be planted in a 5-gallon (19-liter) container. After about 6 to 8 months of growth, they will start to produce the globular buds. They tend to produce the majority of them in the spring and fall but can give you a globe most anytime. Artichokes will not ever win any awards for being heavy green-house producers for the amount of area that they need, but green-house-grown artichokes are the sweetest that you'll ever eat.

Be sure to harvest the globes while the bud still looks tight. If you wait too long, it will produce a large blue or purple flower with a blue or purple center. Artichokes benefit from regular feeding of fertilizer. You may see the plant die back to the ground, but it usually comes up again from a new side shoot. It can be susceptible to both aphids (p. 413), which are usually found on the underside of the leaves, and mites (p. 416).

If you want a unique cut flower, go ahead and let your artichoke bud flower. Its incredible purplish blue flower sits in the middle of the lotuslike artichoke. It is truly dazzling.

Try using your greenhouse or sunspace to produce an outdoor garden artichoke. Those that live even in short-season areas can get a few good globes from an artichoke that had a head start in the greenhouse and then was transplanted to the outside. Try starting your plants around mid-January, and transplant out when you would normally set out tomatoes. They do best in rich soil in a spot with good sun penetration.

Avocado

Before you get too excited about homegrown guacamole fresh from your greenhouse, I need to tell you that avocados are difficult to get to produce fruit in a greenhouse. The plant itself is not hard to grow, as long as the soil is well drained. The avocado needs to dry out between waterings. Growing any old seed you find in a store-bought fruit is not a good idea if you want production. Normally avocados reach 30 feet (9 m) in height. The tree size can be maintained to fit into a greenhouse by keeping the plant well pruned or by growing smaller semidwarf varieties.

One thing that makes avocados difficult to produce is their tricky pollination requirements. While one plant may produce both female and male plant parts, they often are not self-fruitful, meaning one plant can't pollinate itself. To make things more difficult, the flower may release viable pollen (the male part) only in the morning or afternoon, but not at both times. The female part of the flower may also be receptive only in the morning or afternoon, but not at both times. What to do? First, for best compatibility, you need to grow two varieties of trees. Not just any two trees. Contact your mail-order source that sells avocado plants and ask which two they recommend. A mail-order source that I work with recommends growing the **haas** and the **bacon varieties** for good pollination. They are both full-sized trees, and in smaller greenhouses, they will need to be pruned as they grow toward maturity. Gardeners who are adept at grafting can eliminate the need for two trees by grafting one variety onto the other to save precious greenhouse space.

It can take between 3 and 5 years before the plants will come into flower. Most varieties flower in the spring. During flowering, get a small artist's paintbrush and dab it gently into the flower to pick up some of the pollen. Move this way from flower to flower, leaving any pollen that may collect on the bristles as you go. Pollinate both in the morning and in the afternoon. Do not clean the pollen off of your bristles between morning and afternoon of the same day. Keep at it, and with a little luck you will have fruit set. Then you'll just need to be patient because it can take as long as 10 to 12 months before the fruits are ripe. Now you can see why many people would rather buy their avocados in the store. But with a good-sized greenhouse and a fair amount of luck and patience, you just might find your-self in green guacamole heaven.

Banana

Bananas are worth growing solely for the tropical look they bring to a sunspace, and you can also get a harvest from your ba-nana. They prefer temperatures above 50° F (10° C) or they will suffer. Bananas tend to grow very slowly in the winter, even with relatively warmer temperatures. When the warm temperatures of spring begin, watch out! The ba-nana starts to grow incredibly fast. How fast? I have seen a plant grow one 5-foot (1.5-meter) leaf every

Banana plant

10 days.

There are many varieties to choose from if you decide to grow a banana plant in your green-house. Much of the decision will ride on the size of your green-house. Most home greenhouses have a roof at about 10 to 12 feet (3 to 3.6 m). That usually dictates that you grow the **dwarf variet-ies**, unless you want to cut a hole in the roof for a vertical room extension. The dwarf varieties reach around 10 feet (3 m) in height. If you are one of the rare people with a 30-foot-tall (9-meter-tall) green-house ceiling, then you'll be glad to find many varieties that will fill your roof.

Bananas are easy to care for. They like soil that has constant moisture and benefit from regular feedings. Even though the banana likes constant moisture, it is impor-tant that its soil is well drained, as it suffers in a stagnant situation. Plants are usually sold as corms, which leaf out soon after they are planted. Check the catalog com-pany The Banana Tree, in the Mail-Order Plants appendix. It special-izes in banana plants. Pay special attention to the height of different varieties. If you purchase a banana corm in the mail, be sure to plant it so the top sticks slightly above the soil. In the first few months, let the top 2 to 3 inches (5 to 8 cm) of the soil dry before watering to avoid rotting of the new corm. Bananas need regular feeding to accommodate their growth spurts.

Every year or two, your banana will produce a cluster of fruit at the top of the plant. The plant requires no pollination in order to set fruit. As the fruit ripen, they begin to curl upward. After the fruit have good size, a definite upward curl and a slight yellowing on the tip of the fruit, you can cut the fruit for ripening. Ripening is rarely done on the tree, as the fruits crack and rot if left on the plant. Instead, place the harvested cluster of fruit in a bag with three or four ripe apples. The apples will give off a naturally occurring gas that triggers ripening.

After the fruit is harvested, cut the main stalk down to the ground and allow for smaller side shoots to take its place. Generally I choose the tallest side shoot and prune all of the others to the ground too.

Beans

Do you have a solar greenhouse? How about fresh beans in early May? Yes, you can have a crop that early if you plant in March. If you have a conventionally heated greenhouse, you can

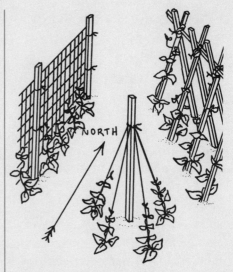

Pole beans can be supported in a variety of fashions.

grow them any time of the year. There are two major types of beans: **vines** (such as **pole beans**) and **bush** or **dwarf types**. The pole beans utilize the vertical space well when trellised and can grow to 10 feet (3 m) or more if conditions are right. The problem is finding a tall enough basketball player to pick them. Pole beans yield over a longer period than bush beans but take 10 to 20 days longer to reach maturity. The bush beans need no trellising, as they reach only 1 foot (.3 m) high. You will get more total yield and use greenhouse space more efficiently with pole beans, but the bush types grow better in containers. As long as the nights are above 45° to

50° F (7° to 10° C), you can always grow beans in some sunny spot.

Pole beans provide good shade when grown outside the south glass in the summer. This is a natural way to keep the greenhouse cooler, although it also cuts down on available light for plants growing in the greenhouse in summer. Inside the solar greenhouse, pole beans can be grown over the front of your thermal mass, such as water barrels, to help keep them from absorbing summer solar heat, thus keeping your whole greenhouse cooler in the warm months. Whenever you grow pole beans, make a trellis for the plants to climb up that is at least 6 feet (1.8 m) in height. Plant one seed every 4 inches (10 cm) along the trellis. To prevent shading problems among plants, think about where your summer shadows fall before you plant the pole beans. Running a trellis along a north-south axis will minimize problem shadows.

Most of the common beans can be grown with ease in a greenhouse, including **yellow wax**, **french filet bush beans**, **purple podded beans** and even **limas**. For greenhouses in the north country, you can even grow beans that are hard to produce in short-season areas, such as **garbanzo beans**. Garbanzos like sandy, drier soils, and their leaves look like locust tree leaves. For a novelty, you may want to try the **asparagus bean**, which can vine up to 15 feet (4.6 m) or more. It will set on beans pods that are more than 1 foot (.3 m) long and do well in greenhouses, if you have the room.

Bean seeds need a soil temperature of at least 60° F (15° C) for best germination. Lower temperatures often cause the seed to rot in the soil. A crusty soil surface can cause problems to emerging seedlings, so you may need to amend this type of soil with some compost to prevent crusting before planting. Legume inoculants, which are available in many seed catalogs, applied to the soil will help provide the beans with nitrogen from the air and make for healthier plants. Most bean flowers will set pods without

Pole beans

needing to be pollinated. There are a few rare exceptions, including the scarlet runner bean. These should be avoided in the greenhouse.

Beans are susceptible to a number of diseases that can be minimized if you follow these precautions: (1) Use disease-free seed from a reputable seed company; (2) don't work among your bean plants if the leaves are wet; and (3) rotate beans with other crops season to season when grown in beds (see Diseases, p. 460).

If a disease occurs, consult your county agricultural extension agent to assist you in discovering what the problem is. Then look through the seed catalog for a bean variety with some resistance to that disease.

In the greenhouse, be sure to not let your temperatures get much above 95° F (35° C). Such high temperatures will cause beans to have lower yields because the plant may drop flower blossoms. Blossom drop will also occur when you over or underwater the plants. When there are no blossoms, there are no beans.

With the right temperatures and varied planting dates, you can have non-stop bean production. This is especially helpful with bush beans, which tend to provide you with one large flush of harvest and then begin to die.

Keep an eye out for both whiteflies (p. 420) and mites (p. 416); they have a fondness for beans.

Beets

Each beet seed has up to five seeds inside what looks like just one seed. This can cause a problem for people who are lax about thinning, as they commonly end up with overcrowding and little to no yield. Plan on thinning and stick to your plan! Because both the leaves and the roots are edible, beets can be a good food producer. Try **golden beets**; they're very sweet. Beets like a slightly alkaline soil, so if your soil is on the acidic side, you may want to add a small amount of wood ash or lime to correct the soil. Be sure you have family members who like beets before you plant, or you'll end up with a wasted harvest. Beets resist many pest attacks. They do best in the cooler times of the year but can be grown almost any time in either pots or beds. Sow beets directly into the area where they will be growing, as they don't take to transplanting well.

Broccoli

Broccoli matures in 60 to 80 days in the greenhouse and is much more suited to the cooler periods of the year. When grown in the warmer months, it can have a problem with small heads. Some varieties produce more side sprouts than others. Side sprouts are small heads produced after the main head is cut. None of the side sprouts are as big as the first main head. Still, they are nice if you need a few small heads for stir-fry for dinner. Be sure to keep an eye on the crop, and plan to harvest the heads before they start to loosen up and go to flower. If a few heads get away from you and are flowering, prune them off and you'll encourage side

Broccoli can develop small heads due to hot temperatures.

sprouts to form (if it is a side-sprouting variety). Some favorite varieties include **goliath**, **premium crop**, **green valiant**, **packman** and **de cicco**, all of which have good side-shoot development. They are tolerant of varying soil conditions and need to be spaced 1 1/2 to 2 feet (.45 to .6 m) apart. Broccoli transplants well about 2 weeks after germinating. After you have harvested a number of side sprouts and when warmer temperatures of spring and summer return, you'll need to plan to pull up the broccoli and replant with a more warm-loving crop.

Brussels Sprouts

Brussels sprouts are slow growers, often taking more than 130 days to reach maturity. It is best to start them in early fall or late summer. If they mature in a warm environment, such as late spring, the taste may be bitter and the sprouts may form loose heads. This crop is best suited for those living in a cool, cloudy area. Space the plants 2 feet (.6 m) apart. Plan on their growing up to 3 feet (.9 m) high, and be careful of shading. Brussels sprouts are easily transplanted while in the seedling stage.

When the sprouts (small cabbagelike buds) are just beginning to form, pinch out the top center of the plant, the growing point. This encourages the upper sprouts to form. Remove lower leaves and leaf stems as the plants mature to further encourage the development of sprouts. They take up a lot of space and for this reason are not necessarily an efficient food producer. But if you have a passion for brussels sprouts, you can still be eating fresh sprouts while others are just dreaming about planting them.

Cabbage

Cabbage falls into three main categories: **early season**, **mid-season** and **late season**. These categories relate to how long it takes until harvest. The earlier varieties are smaller but produce faster. Usually the early and mid-season types provide better total yields in the greenhouse or sunspace. There are also choices as to the coloring of the leaf—**red**, **yellow** and **green** cabbage. All seem to do fine in the greenhouse. Also relating to leaf type is the savoy. The savoy is a handsome bubbly leaved variety, but it tends to harbor aphids and should be avoided.

Cabbage transplants best in the seedling stage 3 to 4 weeks after germination. Don't cultivate too deeply, because cabbage are shallow-rooted. If your greenhouse gets extremely cold (below freezing), cabbage may go to seed. Because cabbage is a biennial, the cold has fooled it into thinking it is 2 years old, and it is prematurely celebrating its birthday. Happy (last) birthday. Pull it up; it won't produce a head now.

Cabbage needs a rich soil and sun. It can grow in shadier areas, but growth will be slower. It does best in cooler weather but can tolerate growing in the summer as long as your greenhouse is not a real hot environment. Because you can eat all aboveground portions, it is considered to be an efficient food producer.

Rotate areas where cabbage is planted if you grow in ground beds to prevent diseases. Cabbage can be grown in containers if they are at least 1 gallon (3.8 l) in size.

Cantaloupe and Muskmelon

Those who live in northern areas with short garden seasons will go wild over the new experience of abundant homegrown cantaloupes in the greenhouse. I have even seen cantaloupe and muskmelon production as the primary reason for building a greenhouse!

Cantaloupe can be trellised, using nylon stockings for support.

fruit set (see Chapter 6, Pollination, for more information). Remember: no pollination, no fruit.

When the fruits begin to develop on the vines, they will need support. The fruits can get so heavy they will rip the whole vine off the trellis. When a fruit is about the size of a tennis ball, slip it into a nylon stocking and tie it securely to the trellis. (What a great way to recycle stockings with runs!) If you can't come

Cantaloupes like a rich soil full of decomposed organic matter and need ample moisture. Growing cantaloupe or muskmelon in a greenhouse is best done vertically, up a trellis to conserve on space. Make the trellis at least 5 feet (1.5 m) high and however long you wish. Set one plant every 3 feet (.9 m) along the trellis. You can plant a few seeds in each spot and later thin to one hardy plant. To minimize shading problems, run the trellis north-south.

When the flowers begin to appear, you will need to hand pollinate each flower to ensure

up with a stocking, you can also use cheesecloth. Take care not to tie any knots around the stem itself, which will damage the plant and fruit. If you are growing cantaloupe, it will tell you when to pick, as the stem easily slips away when the fruit is slightly twisted.

Both muskmelon and cantaloupe are quite susceptible to the fungus disease powdery mildew (p. 471). It is indicated by a white powdery substance forming on the leaves. Search catalogs thoroughly for varieties with some resistance to this disease to minimize the problem. I have had good luck

Cantaloupe

with a variety known as **Israeli cantaloupe (PMR)**, available from the Porter and Son Seedsmen catalog (see Mail-Order Seed appendix).

Expect to be halfway to heaven when you eat your greenhouse-grown cantaloupe or muskmelon. Be sure to invite me over to help you evaluate the quality of the fruit.

Carrots

When I think of carrots, I think of when I worked in a large community solar greenhouse project. I was giving a tour to a class of four-year-old Head Start students. They were all smiles, awed by the plants growing in the middle of the Wyoming winter. They were full of questions. As the tour progressed, the kids tended to become attached to me. I had two kids on my shoulders, a few on each arm and even one sitting on my foot. I managed to drag myself and the children over to the carrot bed and hollered above the questions and giggles, "Does anybody know what this plant is?" "Onions!" one little girl shouted. "Dandelion," another said. A shy one, shaking her head no, quietly mumbled, "I don't know." "Everyone watch carefully," I said, as I shook a few kids off,

Carrots

moving toward a carrot top. "Iiiiiits aaaaaa ..." They were all eyes as I exposed the orange root out from the dirt. "CARROT!!" they all screamed in unison. It was as if I were a magician ... presto: a carrot. I wondered how long it would have been before they learned where carrots came from if they had never seen my greenhouse carrots.

A year-round supply of homegrown carrots will add a spark to food that nothing else can provide. There is just no comparison between homegrown and store-bought carrots.

Carrots will fit into any empty place in your growing beds and can be planted anytime of the year in a greenhouse. However, unusually hot weather can sometimes cause a strange flavor and fibrous texture. High amounts of manure in the soil have an odd effect on the shape of the carrots, creating weirdly shaped roots that are perfect for modern sculpture lovers. Winter carrots in the greenhouse will take longer to produce than outside carrots, but the harvest is well worth the wait. Some winter carrots may go to seed if you grow a winter-planted carrot into the summer, especially in cool winter greenhouses.

Most gardening books will tell you that you should never transplant a carrot and that they should always be directly seeded. However, thanks to some proof provided by Cheyenne Botanic Gardens volunteer Jim Allread, they take to transplanting just fine. When you do sow the seeds, try not to drop too many seeds or you'll have a big thinning job ahead of you. Barely cover the seed and maintain moisture in the soil until you see them germinate. Each carrot needs about 2 square inches (13 sq. cm) of space to grow, so use that as a guide when you thin or transplant.

Carrots do best in well-drained soil. In heavy clay, you may have better luck with the shorter-rooted varieties. I've had good yields with the standard long varieties. I have also found some varieties developed specifically for greenhouse culture. These are good choices if you can get ahold of them. They include: **Flamant** from Thompson & Morgan; **Coreless Amsterdam** and **Touchon** from Stokes Seeds; and **Parmex**, **Kinko** and **Clarion** from Johnny's Selected Seeds. The addresses for these seed catalogs are listed in the Mail-Order Seeds appendix.

Carrots can be grown even in pots, as long as they are at least 8 inches (20 cm) or more in depth. The biggest problem most garden-

Cauliflower

ers have is failing to thin out thickly sown seeds. Put on your "ruthless gardener" hat; get out there and thin!

Cauliflower

Cauliflower grows much the same as cabbage and broccoli. It takes 70 to 90 days to mature and is best grown in the winter months from a late summer or fall sowing. If grown in prolonged warm weather, your plants may have very small heads and are not worth the space that they take up.

Cauliflower is easily transplanted in the seedling stage. As the plant begins to form the white curd, tie up the leaves around the head to prevent browning of the curd.

Because cauliflower does not produce side sprouts, you should toss out the plant after it produces the head. Overall, it is not an efficient user of greenhouse space for the amount of food that it produces. But for those who have a passion for cauliflower, it is easy to grow as a winter crop.

Celery

Celery is best grown where winters are long and icy, as it likes a long, cool growing period. If grown in warm greenhouses, the celery can become stringy and will flower prematurely with low yields. It is best started in late summer or early fall. Try growing just a few plants before you devote large areas to see if it is suited to your environment.

Celery likes a moist, rich soil. Due to its exacting requirements and slow growth, it is not an easy or efficient crop for greenhouses.

Chard, Swiss Chard

Chard is a close relative of beets and is a long-lived and productive spinach substitute for the greenhouse or sunspace. Everyone should have at least a couple plants growing at all times for some continued availability of fresh greens for the salad bowl. Swiss chard is very tolerant of both warm and low temperatures and can tolerate sun or shady spots well and grow rapidly.

Swiss chard comes in three colors to match any decor: **red-veined**, **white-veined** and **green-veined**. White-veined seems to be the most productive in the greenhouse, but the others also do quite well. As with beets, many seeds are contained within each seed, so be sure to thin when they come up thickly. Space plants about 6 to 8 inches (15 to 20 cm) apart. Harvest by breaking off the outer leaves when they are 8 to 10 inches (20 to 25 cm) in length. Don't leave the leaf stem (petiole) attached to the plant after harvesting, as it may rot on the plant and harbor disease. The leaf stem is edible too and may be cooked like asparagus. Chard can be eaten raw in salads or cooked like spinach. It's good both ways. If family mem-

Three-year-old chard plant

bers like spinach but are uneasy about substitutes, grow the green-veined variety, often sold as perpetual spinach, and just tell them that it is spinach. They'll never know the difference. The green chard is a little harder to locate, but keep looking through your catalog and you'll eventually come across it.

Because Swiss chard will go to flower only when triggered by extreme cold, in the greenhouse it can grow for many years before flowering. I have had some plants live for 5 years. After a few years they get to look like a 3-foot (.9-meter) palm tree and just keep getting taller and taller.

The red-veined chard, also known as **rhubarb chard**, is a handsome plant with brightly colored red veins in a dark green leaf. It looks like it is decked out in a Christmas motif. All parts of the leaf and stem are edible. Please understand that rhubarb chard is totally unrelated to rhubarb, which has poisonous leaves. Be sure that your children understand the difference.

Cherimoya

This subtropical South American native produces a tasty fruit. The tree grows to around 20 feet (6 m) but can be pruned to shorter, more manageable sizes. Because of its height, it is best suited to larger greenhouses. The tree may lose its leaves in winter and produce new leaves in spring.

The fruit is interesting in both appearance and flavor. It is about the size of an artichoke globe and even has a bit of resemblance to an artichoke. It almost appears to be an artichoke made out of Play-Doh™.

The cherimoya takes up to 5 years to flower and have a chance at producing fruit. Flowers tend to form on new wood, so on older trees you may have to prune to trigger new growth and fruiting wood. Pollination must be done by hand on a daily basis. You will find that each flower has both the male and female parts. The female is reputed to be receptive before the pollen falls. To be sure you have pollinated the flower, you'll have to keep at it daily with a small paintbrush, moving beelike (make a buzzing sound to get you in the mood) from flower to flower, including the flowers that have just started to open. If all goes well, you'll soon see fruit forming.

The flavor of the cherimoya is hard to describe, but it is sweet (although some varieties are said to be more bland) and commonly compared to a cross between the banana and the pineapple. The flesh is creamy with black seeds. The fruit is ripe when it turns yellowish green. Let the fruit sit until it just begins to turn brown for best eating qualities. Serve chilled. There are many varieties to choose from. Some easier-to-pollinate types include **booth**, **Spain**, **pierce** and **white**.

Chinese Cabbage

Chinese cabbage is a producer, especially for cool winter greenhouses. It is best grown while the temperatures are cool, as it quickly goes to seed with warm temperatures, and can be sown from late summer through mid-winter. If you have a warm winter greenhouse, look in catalogs for bolt resistant varieties, which are slower to go to seed.

Chinese cabbage transplants well in the seedling stage and can mature anywhere from 50 to 60 days. The biggest problem I have seen with Chinese cabbage is slugs. It amazes me how slugs come out of the woodwork to munch on the leaves, even in beds where there are no apparent slugs. I honestly believe that a slug would walk (or slime) a mile to get an opportunity to eat some Chinese cabbage. If slugs become a real problem, you'll have to set up a barrier for them or try other types of slug control (see Slugs, Snails, p. 418).

Chives

Chives are one of my favorite crops. Whenever there are some leaves to harvest, I always use chives rather than onions because I prefer their unique flavor. Because you harvest only the green tops, the root system is never disturbed and the plant grows new leaves rapidly after each harvest. Chives can be started from seed or divided from other existing plants. The common garden chives often grow very slowly in the winter. There are, however, a few varieties that are better suited to winter production. Nichols Garden Nursery carries through their catalog **grolau chives**, and Thompson & Morgan seed catalog carries what they call **fruhlau chives**. From what I can tell, they are about the same thing, but both can be counted on for better winter production. Chives can also be grown in 1-gallon (3.8-liter) pots. Simply provide a rich, well-drained soil and occasionally feed them. Let the soil surface dry between waterings. The pink flowers of chives are also edible when they first open and are great for soups and salads for those interested in a sweeter but also quite stronger onion flavor. Every greenhouse should have at least one clump of chives in production.

There is also what is known as garlic chives (not the same as garlic), which have broader flat leaves compared to regular chives and have a garlic flavor. They are perennial producers like regular chives. I prefer the flavor of the regular chives to the garlic chives, but you may want to give the garlic type a try. You can find garlic chives with either green leaves or white-striped leaves, which are often grown just for their ornamental value.

Citrus

Citrus is a great greenhouse plant, if only for the wonderful fragrance of the flowers when you walk in. Most any citrus plant can be grown in the greenhouse. You will be tempted to start them from seeds found in supermarket fruit, but these will usually produce sour, poor-tasting fruit. Instead, purchase good-flavored plants from nurseries or by mail order.

With some simple care, you can produce high-quality citrus in your greenhouse or sunspace. Most citrus do best if grown above 45° F (7° C). They need to be grown in a rich soil. Citrus like soil that dries out occasionally between waterings in the cooler months. In summer, they need more constant moisture. Citrus can be grown in ground beds or in tubs that are 5 gallons (19 l) or more in size. When selecting varieties, you might want to look for citrus that is available in **dwarf sizes**. These may work better in your greenhouse or sunspace, especially if you are short on room.

Citrus benefit from well-drained soil and regular feeding. If the new leaves turn yellow, try a fertilizer that contains iron or zinc (follow the application directions and don't add too much). It may take a few years before your citrus plant comes into flower, so be patient. Most all citrus are self-fruitful, meaning that they are easy to pollinate. Just take a small paintbrush and paint the pollen (the yellow powdery stuff) onto the female part (the short, sticky little stem protruding in the center of the flower). The fruit will start to grow noticeably in a few weeks.

I have found **lemons** and **limes** to be among the easiest and most rewarding to grow. If you are short on space, you might want to stick to these. The **ponderosa lemon** is a proven greenhouse plant and produces impressive large fruits. If you have the interest and the room to spare, move on to other types of citrus, including the many types of **oranges**.

The main pests of citrus are the whitefly (p. 420) and the mealybug (p. 415). You may have to keep a close eye out for these pests, and be ready to take quick action if they are spotted.

Coffee

Yes, you can even grow coffee shrubs in your greenhouse or sunspace! They are more suited to greenhouses that run moderate temperatures in the winter and don't do well when the temperature regularly drops below 45° F (7° C). They do best if grown in an area with some shade during the day. In their native habitat, they are an understory plant in the tropics, growing in the shade of other taller plants.

Coffee can be grown in tubs or planted directly in ground beds. It seems to do slightly better in pots, as long as it doesn't become root-bound. Grow in well-drained soil. After the plant is a few years old, you will see it make small fragrant white flowers (the best fragrance is at night). Soon it will set a few small berries that are green turning to red. Inside each berry are two coffee beans. When the plant is 5

to 8 years old, it can produce up to 2 pounds (.9 kg) of beans. Notice that only the horizontal branches produce flowers and eventually beans. After the plant has grown 3 years or so, occasionally pinch the top to encourage more horizontal branches.

The average plant is not a very prolific producer of beans. For this reason, don't plan on growing enough beans to be drinking home-grown every day. But growing enough for an occasional cup is not difficult.

Here's how to get from berry to cup of java. When the berries are fully red or, better yet, when the berries begin to shrivel, you'll know the two beans inside the fruit are ripe. Separate the beans from the skin and let them dry in a warm spot. There are a number of ways to proceed in processing the bean, but for simplicity, just roast in the oven at a temperature of around 200° F (93° C). Turn the beans occasionally and don't let them burn. Then get ready for the freshest cup of coffee you've ever had!

Collards

Collards, for those of you who may be culturally deprived, are like a nonheading cabbage. They are generally eaten as a cooked

Collards

green much like spinach. Grow collards as you would cabbage, but be ready for it to grow a bit taller. Like many cabbage relatives, collards prefer cooler temperatures and are a good choice for the greenhouse that has cool winter temperatures. Start the seeds in late summer through fall. Avoid growing it in the warmer months of spring and summer. In cool greenhouses, it can reach up to 3 feet (.9 m) or more. In warmer greenhouses, it usually will flower before it reaches over 2 feet (.6 m) in height. It can be harvested over many weeks, if not months. Remove the lower leaves when you harvest, letting the new growth on top continue to produce for you. When it starts to flower, the flavor tends to go downhill and you need to think about a replacement for collards.

Cucumber

Cucumbers are one of the most productive summer crops you can grow. For best greenhouse production, grow what is known as the **European seedless** or **forcing cucumbers**. Their fruit resembles the burpless cucumber, with each fruit growing up to a whopping 20 inches (51 cm) long. They are thin-skinned, seedless and very sweet. Best of all, the European greenhouse cucumbers are high yielding and need no pollinating. Avoid the common garden types of cucumbers, unless you want to be diligent about pollinating on a daily basis; it is not easy, but it can be done (see Chapter 6, Pollination).

The European cucumber is for fresh eating only and won't pickle very well because of the thin skin. There are a few American seed catalogs that carry the European cucumber seeds. Stokes Seeds carries one of the best retail selections for greenhouse hobbyists (see Mail-Order Seeds appendix). The price of the seed is much higher than most any seed you have ever purchased, but given their high yield, the price is worth it. Besides, can you imagine how hard it must be to wrench a seed from a plant that produces a seedless fruit? It's a

European cucumbers

dirty job, but some rocket-scientist horticulturist somewhere has figured out how to do it, and it's probably a big corporate secret.

If you want to develop a backdoor approach to getting more European cucumbers without having to pay for the seed, refer to Chapter 5, Plant Propagation, and try making new plants from cuttings.

It is not a good idea to try growing both regular outside garden variety and European cucumbers in the same greenhouse at the same time. If a stray bee were to infiltrate the greenhouse and do some cross-pollinating, you could find your cucumbers producing misshapen, bitter-tasting fruit.

When selecting a European cucumber variety, read about the characteristics of each, and try to grow the one best suited to your particular environment. Some will tolerate higher temperatures better, while others have more tolerance to lower night temperatures (a good characteristic for growing into the fall). I always like to grow those that have some resistance to powdery mildew.

Most European cucumber varieties have only female flowers, but a few may have an occasional male flower. Male flowers don't produce fruit, and pollination only causes poor-quality fruit. You may want to prune off the male flowers if they appear. The males are identified by their lack of small immature fruit below the petals, which you will find on all females.

Because the seed is so costly, don't waste even one. Try planting one seed into a peat pot filled with regular virgin potting soil at a depth of about 1/4 inch (.6 cm). Maintain a soil temperature of around 70° F (21° C) and keep the pots in a well-lit location. Make sure the pots are moist at all times, but not soggy. Never allow them to get dry.

When the seedling has four to five leaves, it can be transplanted. Poke a hole in the bottom of the peat pot to ensure quick root development. Transplant into moist soil. Cucumbers do best when they have at least 2 feet (.6 m) of soil depth and do best in ground beds with a spacing 3 feet (.9 m) apart. One plant could be grown in a 5-gallon (19-liter) pot or larger if you have no ground beds. Cucumbers are very heavy feeders and need regular fertilization, but if the leaf edges turn brown, you are overdoing it. If this occurs, leach the excess fertilizer salts out of the pot with a few heavy applications of water.

Cucumbers love warm temperatures and are best in the spring and summer. Wide temperature fluctuations can adversely affect flavor, and they won't tolerate much cool weather. High temperatures may also cause misshapen fruit. Cucumbers like high levels of light, so growing in shade is not worth trying. If your greenhouse is running cool, try watering the cucumbers with some slightly lukewarm water. As with most crops, morning watering is best. Avoid getting the plant leaves wet when watering to prevent disease. Also, try ventilating to remove excess humidity, which can also contribute to cucumber diseases (see Diseases, p. 460).

The European cucumber can be grown upon a fixed trellis with ease. However, another way to grow them is on suspended string or twine that hangs from the ceiling to the ground. You can anchor the twine to the soil, but do not make the string taut. Leave a lot of slack, as it will eventually be taken up as the plant wraps itself around the string. You may occasionally need to wind the main stem around the twine to help it climb up. Avoid any bending or pinching of the stems. If needed, you can loosely tie the cucumber stem to the twine with soft strips of cloth, but don't tie too tightly and strangle the stem.

As the plant grows up the trellis or twine, you will notice that

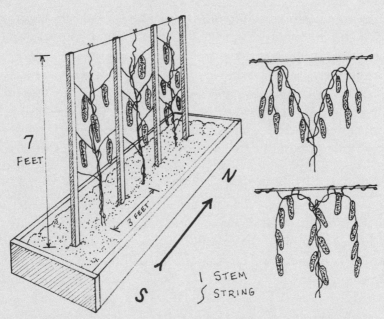

7 FEET

3 FEET

N

S

| STEM
5 STRING

Trellising options for European forcing greenhouse cucumbers.

there are suckers coming off the main stem. For best production, it is a good idea to do some pruning of these suckers. There are a number of ways to train a greenhouse European cucumber. One is to cut off any suckers (side-shoots) that form at the first four leaf axils. The next 8 to 10 shoots should allow new suckers to grow one leaf on each new shoot, allowing one to two fruits to form here. The remainder of the shoots should be trimmed to two leaves each. When the plant reaches 7 feet (2 m) or so, select two shoots at the top and allow these to head downward, back toward the ground. If you don't do any training, they will form one massive vining bush and will quickly get out of hand.

The European cucumber is such an eager beaver to produce fruit that it will often start setting cucumbers at just 1 or 2 feet (.3 or .6 m) tall. The plant should not be allowed to produce these first small fruits. If you see it flowering too early, prune off the flowers and/or small fruits until it reaches a healthy size, at least 4 feet (1.2 m) tall, to support the fruit production.

Cucumbers will slow fruit production if they have a few fruit on the vine. New fruits forming will often shrivel if they sense that there is an ample amount of other fruits on the vine. For this reason, it is very important to keep the vine well picked. The more you pick, the more you get. Keep an eye out for whiteflies (p. 420) and mites (p. 416), as both have a good appetite for the cucumber. You may also need to take some measures against powdery mildew (p. 471) if it appears to be a problem.

After harvest, the European cucumbers do not keep well unless they are stored in plastic bags in the refrigerator. This prevents them from going limp and allows you to store them over a longer period. The European forcing cucumbers are so sweet, it's no wonder that they are the most popular cucumber in Europe.

Edible Chrysanthemum

I know it doesn't sound very tasty, but the leaves of the edible chrysanthemum have a sweet, mild nutlike flavor. They are great when added fresh to salads along with other greens and can also be mixed into stir-fry or cooked with spinach or chard. The edible chrysanthemum goes by a few different aliases, including **garland chrysanthemum**, **chop-suey greens** and **shungiku**. All of the leaves are edible. It is a good winter producer and is best sown in late summer for

harvest from winter through spring. Come warmer temperatures, it tends to get more buggy, especially on the tips of the plant. If it gets bad enough, it may be time to pull it out. The plant grows to a height of about 3 feet (.9 m). Each plant needs about 2 feet (.6 m) of space when mature. After it reaches 6 to 10 inches (15 to 25 cm), you can harvest the older, lower leaves on the plant. In early spring, this chrysanthemum provides you with a beautiful crop of yellow daisylike flowers that are a nice addition to a flower arrangement, a true dual-purpose plant.

Eggplant

Eggplant is another lover of warm greenhouses. It does best from March through October, unless your greenhouse or sunspace maintains good warmth in winter. Each plant needs about 1 1/2 square feet (.1 sq. m) of growing space. They can be grown in both pots—minimum 1 gallon (3.8 l) in size—and ground beds. Eggplants like a rich soil, with a high level of moisture. To ensure good fruit formation, you will need to pollinate the plants every few days or so (see Chapter 6, Pollination). Some varieties need more hand pollination than others. At the very least, you

Eggplant

Greenhouse Tomato Disorders, p. 345). Because of this, they aren't a good rotation plant for the same bed. Grow one plant for every two people you are feeding.

Fava Bean, Broad Bean

These are the ultimate cold-hardy bean and probably the only one that will grow in a cool winter greenhouse. Start them in late summer or early fall. You'll quickly notice that they look different from the common garden bean. They grow upright and have bluish green leaves that reach 3 feet (.9 m) or more, depending upon the variety. They will benefit from some staking, as they may start to lean or fall over as they get taller. They are valuable because they are one of the best protein plants for the winter greenhouse. Because they are so cold-blooded, growing them in the warmer or summer greenhouse usually produces poor plants. The beans are borne in fat pods. Inside the pods the beans look much like soybeans. They have a lower oil content than soybeans but are similar in protein levels. To induce earlier and larger crops, you can pinch off the tops when the plants bloom. Some but not all varieties give off a wonderful evening scent that rivals any ornamental flower's fragrance.

should gently tap the flowers with a stick every other morning.

When it comes to harvest, try to do it before they lose their glossy shine. I have had better luck growing the earlier, more slender varieties. The eggplant is a relative of tobacco and is also susceptible to tobacco mosaic virus (p. 348). If you are a user of tobacco, wash your hands before handling the plants in any way. There are some resistant varieties to this disease that may be of interest.

Eggplants are also close relatives to tomatoes and peppers and are susceptible to many of the diseases they get (see Common

Fava bean

However, fava beans should be eaten with caution. Some people are genetically unable to properly digest favas. Within 24 hours of eating, symptoms including vomiting, diarrhea and dizziness may occur. Fortunately, fatalities are rare and recovery is usually quick. The genetic groups most susceptible to this problem with favas include people (and their descendants) of Mediterranean countries, Egypt, Iraq and Iran. More rarely, it can occur among people of Chinese and African descent. Check with an allergist for more information. Most people can enjoy fava beans to their heart's content. Check recipes that originate in Australia for the best ways to prepare fava beans, as they are a favorite down under.

Feijoa

The feijoa, also known as **pineapple guava**, is a small tree or shrub that produces beautiful red and white flowers and tasty roundish fruit. The plant grows to 15 feet (4.6 m) or more and has thick leaves, which it keeps year-round. It is a perfect plant for the greenhouse because it likes cooler winters and warm summers. Some varieties are not self-fruitful, meaning you need to grow more than one variety. Fortunately, there are also varieties that readily set fruit solo. Some self-fruitful varieties of feijoa include **apollo**, **collidge** and **nazemetz**. When the feijoa flowers in spring, take a small paintbrush and dab the yellow pollen onto the female element in the center. The fruits begin to mature mid-summer into late summer and are about 2 to 3 inches (5 to 8 cm) across. They are easy to tell when to pick because they fall to the

Feijoa flowers have edible petals.

years before the plant is mature enough to produce fruit, but after that it can be productive for many years. The plant is drought tolerant and needs to dry out between waterings. It takes well to pruning if you need to control the growth or height. You will probably have to purchase your first plant from a catalog that specializes in subtropical plants. Once you have a plant, it is easy to propagate new ones from stem cuttings of new growth.

Fig

If you live in the north where winters are cold, you may have never had the opportunity to experience the pleasure of eating a fresh fig. Figs are an easy plant to grow in the greenhouse or sunspace. They can be grown either in large tubs or planted directly in the ground. In their native habitat, figs are trees reaching 15 to 30 feet (4.6 to 9 m) tall. When grown in tubs, they tend to stay a more manageable size, as the limited root space causes natural dwarfing.

When it comes to soil, all they need is something that drains well, and if they are in a pot, there must be some sizeable drainage holes. If they sit in constantly wet soil, the stems may rot and die. Figs need to

ground when they are at their perfect state of ripeness (don't let them sit on the ground too long). The skin of the fruit is tough and not edible. Cut the fruit in half and scoop out the inner sweet meat. The small seeds inside are quite edible too. The taste is akin to pineapple but hard to relate to anything else. I think it tastes delicious. For adventuresome eaters, you may want to try the flower petals of the feijoa, which are entirely edible. They are succulent and slightly sweet with no bitter aftertaste.

Feijoa does fine in a tub of at least 10 gallons (38 l), as well as in ground beds. It may take a few

Fig tree with developing fruit

grow in a sunny location with occasional feedings. They are fast growers, especially if they are growing in ground beds with more root room. If the branches start to cause too much shading, they take to pruning quite well. You'll notice that when you prune the stems, leaves or branches, they will bleed white sap. This soon stops, and the plant will usually forgive you for the pruning (and bleeding).

.Most of us call the fig itself a fruit, but what we actually eat is an assemblage of many inside-out flowers with all of the flower parts located inside the so-called fruit. The structure looks like a fruit, but when you cut it open, you can see what I mean: It is a collection of flowers (without petals), all facing inward. The edible crunchy seeds are not viable unless pollinated, which is done only by a specialized small wasp found only in certain geographical regions. For simplicity sake, I will just refer to this unusual flower structure as a fruit.

After the plants are 2 years old or so, they will start bearing fruit. Some varieties of fig must have the special wasp for pollination for the fruits to mature to an edible size. Fortunately, many other varieties of fig will develop edible fruits without the need for pollination. Most of the varieties sold for home growing do not need pollination. Just in case, check with your nursery or catalog source to be sure that you are getting the proper variety.

Most fig varieties bear fruit throughout the summer. It usually comes in two flushes. The first crop of fruit starts around June, and a larger second crop occurs around August into the fall. As the fig fruit approaches maturity, the outer skin becomes soft and darkens a bit, and the figs become easier to remove from the branch. They might even drop from the plant when mature. With a few taste tests, you'll figure out the best time to pick them.

When the dead of winter comes around, you'll notice that many of the fig leaves begin to turn brown and yellow. After a while, most of the leaves will drop. Don't fret. This is a normal dormant period that they must go through. When spring arrives, so will a new crop of healthy green leaves.

If you have a choice of fig varieties, besides being sure that the variety you choose needs no pollination, try to avoid the so-called hardy varieties. There seems to be less production of fruit on the hardy varieties in a greenhouse because they require more of a winter cooling period for good fruit production. In a greenhouse, you really can't provide a winter cooling treatment. That's why the less hardy types are a better choice. Some varieties to look for include **kadota**, **celleste** and **brown turkey**. There are probably many more good choices out there. If you are good at grafting, you can try grafting more than one variety onto one tree.

If you have an established plant, you can easily propagate more plants from cuttings taken from stem tips in spring. Use cuttings that are around 8 to 10 inches (20 to 25 cm) long.

Kale

The cultivation of kale is similar to collards, and like collards, kale is a member of the cabbage family. But it should be noted that kale is not nearly as heat tolerant as collards and many other members of the cabbage family. The flavor of kale improves as the weather gets colder, and it tastes best after going though a few frosts. Because frost in the greenhouse is usually rare, it is hard to get good quality. The only time to ever consider growing kale is through the cool months of winter. It would be a good choice for greenhouses that run quite cold. Better yet, it would do best in a cold frame during the winter if started in August.

Kale is very nutritious, and the older leaves should be harvested first, as with many other leafy crops. If it begins to go to seed on you as indicated by the formation of flowers, then the flavor may become bitter. Ornamental kale is a colorful plant that does great in most winter greenhouses, as long as the temperatures aren't too hot. It can be eaten as you would any other kale, but the flavor may easily become hot and bitter. It is better used as an ornamental plant or as a garnish to the dinner plate. Read more about ornamental kale in Kale and Cabbage, Flowering (p. 246).

Kohlrabi

Kohlrabi is often described as an aboveground turnip. I think that it tastes better than a turnip. It grows relatively fast in the greenhouse and may be planted as close as 6 inches (15 cm) apart. There are both **purple** and **green varieties**. A hybrid variety known as **grand duke** is quicker maturing and more

Kohlrabi

tolerant of the adverse warm and cold temperatures that can occur in solar greenhouses. Occasionally, alternating hot and cold temperatures can cause the bulb of the kohlrabi to crack, but it is still edible. When it is a bit smaller than a baseball, it is ready for harvest. Peel the fibrous outer skin off, and then you can prepare it any number of ways, including eating it fresh (great with dips) or cooking it as you would a turnip or carrot.

Lettuce

Lettuce, one of the oldest known greenhouse food crops, is also one of the most popular. It is the king (or queen—nobody knows for sure) of the salad greens and is very productive in the greenhouse. Lettuce is best grown from fall through spring, as it prefers cooler temperatures and can tolerate cloudy weather well. Warm temperatures and longer daylight hours of late spring and summer cause lettuce to prematurely go to seed and become bitter.

Lettuce prefers a rich, well-drained soil. When planting seeds, don't bury them too deep; they need to see a little light shining through the soil to trigger germination. Keep the soil moist until the seedlings emerge. Lettuce also transplants well. The root system is shallow, so be careful if you are cultivating near them. Space the plants about 5 to 6 inches (13 to 15 cm) apart when they are growing toward maturity. When you water, try not to splash soil up on the leaves to avoid sandy salads. You can grow lettuce with good results in 4- to 5-inch (10- to 13-centimeter) pots, but I prefer to grow many square feet of lettuce in a ground bed. It can resemble a winter edible lawn and looks great when there are nearby winter flowers in bloom for contrast.

The key to good greenhouse lettuce production is not only understanding its growing requirements but also knowing the differences in types and varieties of lettuce. There are four basic types to choose from: **leaf lettuce**, **head** or **iceberg**, **Boston** or **butterhead** (forming a loose head) and **cos** or **romaine**. The leaf and loose-headed varieties are the earliest maturing varieties and the best choice for the greenhouse or sunspace. For example, if you are growing a leaf lettuce, you can expect a crop in 50 to 80 days. Head lettuce will take up to 150 days before you can harvest, a big difference if you are waiting to eat a fresh salad!

Even within one single lettuce type, there is a great difference in growing characteristics. These include the time it takes before the plant goes to seed (called bolting), resistance to an assortment of diseases, the likelihood of the tips burning and even the color of the leaf (**dark green**, **light green**, **yellowish**, **red**). Many of these characteristics are listed in seed catalogs. It is these characteristics that greenhouse growers consider to get maximum lettuce production. Some varieties, usually leaf and bib types, may have even been developed for growing in a greenhouse. One important characteristic to select for the greenhouse is heat tolerance, often indicated in catalogs as "slow to bolt." This is because it takes only a few good sunny days in winter to make a greenhouse heat up tremendously and trigger the plant to go to seed and become bitter. When that happens, the plant ends its period of productivity as far as harvesting the leaf goes.

My absolute favorite type of lettuce, if you haven't guessed yet, is the leafy type of lettuce. Of the

Oak leaf lettuce in hanging basket

leaf lettuce varieties, I have found that a Burpee variety known as **green ice** is very productive. Another favorite can be found in the Stokes Seeds catalog—**royal green M.I.** Both of these varieties have a darker green leaf. I have found that the lettuce varieties with dark green leaves are less susceptible to both aphid (p. 413) and whitefly (p. 420) attacks. (These pests are attracted to the lighter green varieties.) Also, both of these varieties are heat tolerant and slow to bolt. A good red loose leaf variety also carried by Stokes, known as **super prize**, is good, especially if you are looking for a little color in your salad. One of the most heat-tolerant varieties available is **oak leaf**, which has oak-shaped leaves. Unfortunately, it is not as crispy as the other varieties listed.

The butterhead types are more popular in European greenhouses than in the United States. They form a loose head and have softer, thicker leaves than other types of lettuce. They are also more perishable. You can grow common butterhead varieties in the greenhouse with limited success, but there are many butterheads developed in Europe specifically for greenhouse culture. Stokes Seeds catalog offers a few varieties of greenhouse bib lettuce. One variety, known as **sitonia**, has been bred to do best in fall or winter, while another variety, **titania**, has been developed for spring and summer production and is very heat tolerant. Johnny's Selected Seeds catalog offers a few good greenhouse butterheads known as **buttercrunch**, **salina** and **morgana**. Johnny's also offers what is known as **french crisp lettuce**. It has a loose head, much like a butterhead or bib lettuce, but is crispy, like leaf or head lettuce. The french crisp types are often heat tolerant and good for the greenhouse.

If you have your heart set on growing romaine (cos) lettuce, you can try **Erthel**, offered by the Thompson & Morgan seed catalog, as it is one of the few romaines that is slower to go to seed and is well suited for the greenhouse. It also resists bottom rotting, which is a common problem when growing romaine.

Iceberg or head lettuce can be grown in the winter greenhouse or sunspace, but it will be the slowest producer and the lowest in nutritional value. That is because most of the leaves never turn green and are mostly water. Other types of lettuce have up to five times the vitamins that the iceberg has. If you still insist upon growing it, be sure to plan around 1 foot (.3 m) of space for each plant. It is also hard to find varieties that are well suited to the greenhouse environment. Instead, grow the crispy leaf lettuces, such as green ice or royal green as mentioned earlier, or try some of the bibb types bred for greenhouse culture. Like your mother told you, "it's good for you," and (like oatmeal) it is the right thing to do.

Harvesting lettuce can be done in one cut (harvesting the whole plant). Better yet, you can get three or more cuttings off the plant before it goes to seed. To do this, be sure to cut only the larger, older leaves. Leave the center young leaves to continue growing. Clean off old, dead or broken leaves from the soil surface. If you don't, they'll begin to rot, which may spread to the underside of the healthy lettuce plant. This bottom rot can become very destructive.

In the wintertime, you can keep lettuce disease to a minimum by providing good ventilation. On a sunny day, if the greenhouse or sunspace is warm enough, open a vent to the outside a few minutes for a breather. Use a small fan to prevent air stagnation during the day. Lettuce is a heavy feeder and tolerates a high amount of fertilization. That can cause a fast growth rate but can also increase diseases. If the air temperature is cool, the leaves may accumulate increased levels of nitrates, which may not be good for the health (see discussion in Chapter 9, Getting to the Roots). For this reason, go easy on the fertilizer if the air temperature is on the cool side. To ensure continuous production during the winter greenhouse season, it's a good idea to always have a few lettuce seedlings started for later transplanting to fill in empty areas after harvesting other crops.

Lettuce is very productive, and no wintertime greenhouse should be without it. Start studying the seed catalogs now. Those fresh-picked winter salads alone are a good reason for having a greenhouse or sunspace—what an incredible luxury!

Luffa Squash

Luffa squash is also known as vegetable sponge. That is because when you harvest mature squash and let the fruit dry, you can peel the skin to find a spongelike interior that can be used as a bath sponge and scrubber. It is a heat-loving plant that has long vines. Because it vines so much, it is best grown only in larger greenhouses with some surplus space. It grows best in ground beds and will use space more efficiently if you trellis it up a vertical support. Luffa is best started in early spring and needs around 100 warm days to reach maturity. It will need to be hand pollinated for fruit set. For the most part, you treat it like you would any other vining squash. According to the USDA, the immature squash is edible but not very tasty.

New Zealand Spinach

This thick-leaf spinach alternative has one great advantage over spinach: It's a perennial that doesn't die after it flowers. One plant can produce for many years. Also, the leaves still taste fine during flowering and in hot conditions. As it grows, it spreads out over a bed, and it grows slightly slower than traditional spinach, especially in cool temperatures.

You can make efficient use of space by tying it to a north-south trellis. The vines are very delicate and break easily, so tie it up gently.

New Zealand spinach

By growing it vertically, you will gain much more yield per square foot. It can also be trained to hang off the edge of a raised bed, thereby making aisle space productive. I have also had good luck growing two or three plants in a 6-inch (15-centimeter) hanging basket for an ornamental foliagelike look that is quite edible. It likes a rich soil, and the large seeds germinate easily. Don't be surprised if you see new seedlings popping up under a mature plant, as it has a tendency to self-sow. New Zealand spinach can be easily transplanted when young. I have made efficient use of space by transplanting it under taller plants for two-tiered production.

Okra

Growing okra in a greenhouse is a real treat for southerners who have found themselves transplanted to the okra-scarce north. Okra can be grown in a greenhouse when the temperatures are on the warmer side. It loves heat, so try it from spring through fall.

Okra varieties differ considerably. Height can vary from 5 to 10 feet (1.5 to 3 m) tall. Pod size varies in length and width. Varieties also differ in color, leaf shape and the look of the flower. For quicker maturity, I have grown mostly the shorter types. The flower of the okra is extremely ornamental and rightly so because it is a close cousin to the hibiscus. It seems to do best in soils containing lower amounts of nitrogen, so go easy on the fertilizer. Heavy amounts of nitrogen may cause excess leaf production at the expense of the edible pods. It likes soil on the dry side and sunny locations. Seed germination is hastened if the seeds are soaked overnight prior to planting. Space plants 12 to 15 inches (30 to 38 cm) apart. Small plants can be started in small pots for later transplanting into beds.

The pods develop soon after the plants flower. Okra needs no pollination in order to produce. The production can occur over a long period, as long as it is warm. If cooler temperatures of late fall be-

Okra

gin, production will drop off, and if your greenhouse tends to run cool in winter, it may signal a good time to pull the okra up and switch to more cool-loving plants. I have found okra to do best in ground beds or in small tubs that are well drained to prevent overwatering.

Onions

Onions are almost as old as civilization, originating in ancient Egypt. Onions can be grown for bunching (onion greens) or for their bulbs. For bulb production, they need slightly cooler temperatures and longer days (shorter nights). This often limits onions for bulb production to the summer months. You may find you get better-quality bulbs by growing them outside. Use your greenhouse as a nursery for starting your own plants by sowing the seed on March 1 and transplanting out around a week or two before the last average frost date.

Growing onion greens is practical all year long and easy to do in the greenhouse or sunspace. They are easy to start from either commercially available onion sets or by starting your own seeds. When growing onions for greens, space the plants much closer than you would onion bulbs. A spacing of 2 to 3 inches (5 to 8 cm) works fine. The planting will soon resemble an onion lawn if sown in a block in a ground bed. The greens can also be easily grown in pots and greens can be cut as needed or pulled up and consumed. Many varieties of onions have been developed for green onions, often called bunching onions. Check out some catalogs, especially Stokes, and you'll come across several excellent choices.

Another type of onion, called the multiplier or top-set, is very tolerant of cool temperatures and is quite productive in the greenhouse. During mid-summer, the multiplier produces bulblets at the top of the flowering stalk. These

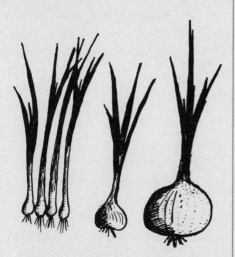

Onions can be grown to varying stages of maturity depending on the type, time of year and spacing.

can be planted like onion sets for more plants or even eaten as small pearl onions.

Because any type of green onion takes up relatively little space and can add so much flavor to winter food, I highly recommend them for your greenhouse. Another choice for onion flavor is chives.

Peas

Whenever I've tried to get people to record greenhouse food yields by weight, I've noticed that it's rare to get any record of a pea harvest, even though peas are growing healthily, producing an abundance of pods. After a little closer investigation, I discovered the problem. The peas never make it to the scales! The peas usually get eaten on the way. Maybe I should weigh people before and after they work around the peas.

Peas are one of the best wintertime treats a greenhouse can provide. They make good use of vertical space as they grow up trellises and are also a good source of protein. Pretty good for a vegetable that is as sweet as candy! In the summer when the temperatures are warmer, they are harder to grow, as they long for a cool environment. I have the best luck when I plant them directly in ground beds in September. You can also grow them in tubs, using tiered tomato cages wired on top of each other, depending on the height of the variety you plan to grow.

Using a bacterial inoculant powder (available in many catalogs for peas and beans) to coat the seeds before planting will help them capture nitrogen from the air. It is not generally needed in soils that peas have been grown in before.

There is a great choice of pea varieties, and I urge you to experiment with a few different ones each year. Pea varieties have been bred for many characteristics, including vining or bushiness, disease resistance, edible pods, earliness and heat tolerance.

For the most efficient use of space, especially if you have the luxury of ground beds in the greenhouse, try to grow the pea varieties that vine as opposed to the bush types. The bush types do have a place; they are good choices for

Peas

growing peas in pots. Disease resistance is also important, especially against powdery mildew, a common problem, so keep an eye out for any varieties listed with resistance to this. For people who live in sunny winter climates, heat tolerance is also an important characteristic to consider when perusing a catalog. Temperatures above 80° F (27° C) greatly slow the flower production and subsequent pod development. I have had good luck growing the pea varieties **maestro**, **wando** and **green arrow**. **Snowflake** is a good choice for a snow pea, and I always grow some of the delicious **sugarsnap variety**, which allows you to eat both the pod and pea at the usual "shelling" time, when the peas are full size.

If you are growing a tall type in a bed, run the trellis north-south to minimize shading. Chicken wire or other woven wire works fine when strung up on some stakes. Even a short trellis, 3 feet (.9 m) long, can give you a good amount of peas to eat. In tubs, 5 gallons (19 l) or more in size, you can grow peas with a tepee trellis. Pea vines are very fragile and frequently get damaged during harvesting. To prevent this, pick the peas with two hands instead of ripping them off with one hand. Keep the vines well picked to prolong harvest. Give peas a chance.

Peppers

Peppers are in the same family as eggplants, tomatoes and tobacco. Like its cousins, the pepper also prefers warm temperatures and is best grown from spring through fall. It likes a moderately rich, well-drained soil. Each plant needs approximately 4 square feet (.37 sq. m) unless the variety you have is a smaller dwarf type. Being a relative of the tomato, the pepper is susceptible to many of the same diseases (see Common Greenhouse Tomato Disorders, p. 345). A common problem is tobacco mosaic virus (p. 348), which is easily transmitted by users of tobacco. If you use tobacco, wash your hands well before handling or working around pepper plants. The tobacco mosaic virus is indicated by angular yellow splotches and lower yields. There are some varieties known as "TMV resistant" or "TMV tolerant" that may be good choices for smokers.

Peppers can grow as high as 4 feet (1.2 m) and may need a small stake to keep them from toppling over. As with staking any plant, use a piece of soft cloth loosely tied up to the plant to prevent stem damage.

Pepper seeds are notorious for erratic and slow germination. They can take as long as 8 weeks to germinate. For best germination, use fresh seed and place the germinating seeds in a warm, sunny spot at least 65° F (18° C). Hot summer temperatures over 97° F (36° C) that occur when the plants are flowering can damage the pollen and reduce the fruit set. Temperatures below 60° F (15° C) will slow fruit production. High levels of nitrogen in the soil can cause luxuriant leaf growth at the expense of fruit production, so be alert if you suspect this problem and try to water heavily a few times to leach out excess nitrogen. Peppers benefit from high soil moisture levels until the fruits begin to mature. This doesn't, however, give you permission to overwater them.

There is an incredible variety of peppers to choose from, including **bell peppers** for sweet fruits; **cayennes** for hot, slender fruits; **chilies**, which are banana shaped and range in hotness; and, of course, the **jalapeño**, which is a good choice if you can stand a red-hot tongue. Many varieties are worth trying, including the many "yuppie"-colored bell peppers, which are sweet and turn beautiful shades of **red** and **yellow** at maturity.

Pineapple

Pineapples can easily be grown in a sunspace or greenhouse, but they are not known for being highly productive in that environment. You can start pineapples by using one from the store that you plan to eat. Select a pineapple with the greenest, healthiest-looking leaves. Twist off the top of the pineapple (you can still eat the fruit) and let the top dry in a shady place for about 1 week. This is to let the exposed tissue dry so that it will not rot. Then brush a small amount of rooting hormone on the bottom of the tissue, and place it in a 6-inch (15-centimeter) clay pot that is filled with a mix of half potting soil and half sand. Keep it slightly moist (overwatering will cause bottom rot) in a warm place with filtered light. Soon the plant will root and begin to grow.

Pineapples are bromeliads and like to be watered from the top where water can sit in the leaves for a few hours before evaporating or being absorbed. After about a

Pineapple

year, if the plant has been steadily growing many new leaves, you can trigger a fruit to set. The triggering is done with a treatment of a naturally occurring gas given off by many fruits, known as ethylene. Ethylene is commonly given off by ripe bananas, apples and tomatoes. For our purposes a banana is less messy. To trigger fruit set, place a freshly peeled banana skin on the soil next to the pineapple, and cover both the banana skin and the pineapple with a clear plastic bag. Keep it out of direct sun. Leave it over the plant for about a week. With some luck, you'll soon see a fruit forming out of the top of the plant after 4 weeks or more. If triggering doesn't work, the plant needs to keep growing;

try again in another 3 months or more.

You may need to stake the plant as it begins to set fruit. Before you start your greenhouse pineapple farm, you should know that the pineapple is a slow grower compared to many other food plants you can grow in the greenhouse. Start out with one or two and get a little experience first. When one does fruit, it is a beautiful plant and a real conversation piece.

Potato

The only reason I list potatoes here is to encourage you not to waste the precious space of a greenhouse or sunspace on growing them unless you really have your heart set on it. Why? Because they can be purchased so very cheaply in the store. Why tie up precious space on this crop when you could be growing a more valuable plant in your greenhouse or sunspace? Besides, potatoes can be grown in most any climate and keep quite well. If you still want to try it, plant them in February and grow as you would outside, giving them full sun and well-drained soil. If you don't have luck growing potatoes outside, don't try it inside. Wait until you have perfected the tech-

nique outdoors a few seasons. Also, when planting tuber seed, be sure it is USDA certified free of disease. Potatoes do best in ground beds or large tubs.

Potato, Sweet

These potatoes are the orange-fleshed, sweet types. They grow in a vine fashion and need both full sun and a 3 foot (.9 m) trellis. Run the trellis on a north-south axis to minimize shading. They also like rich soil. While sometimes you can get away with it, you should avoid starting sweet potatoes from store-bought potatoes, because many are treated with a hormone that will not allow the plants to sprout or will slow the growth of sprouts. Rather, purchase plants from a catalog or garden center. I have had luck starting plants anytime from February through July in the greenhouse.

Fresh sweet potatoes are a luxury in northern climates, where the season is too cold and short for them. It will take them 4 months or more to reach maturity. Keep an eye out for the whitefly (p. 420), which loves to hang around them and cause problems.

Radish

As with growing radishes outside, in the greenhouse or sunspace they are fast producers, given the right environment. They like cool temperatures and moist, friable soil. Most varieties do best when sown in the fall and do well throughout the winter season, as long as your greenhouse is not too hot at night. A common problem with radishes is when they produce all tops and no edible radish. This is generally caused by prolonged warm temperatures. The optimum night temperature is between 45° and 50° F (7° and 10° C). Be sure to thin the seedlings to at least 2 inches (5 cm) apart. The application of excess manure or nitrogen may also cause too much top growth. Radishes are a great crop to interplant under or among other garden plants in ground beds. They can also be easily grown in pots. Be sure the radishes are growing in a bright spot. Because the seed germinates quickly, it is always best to seed them directly into the bed or pot rather than transplanting seedlings.

If all goes well, you will have radishes to complement your salad in 4 to 5 weeks. The closer they're grown to the winter solstice, the longer they will take to mature because of the shorter days. **Win-**

Radish

ter radishes are different from the common **garden radish** and will take 8 to 12 weeks or even longer. In contrast with the common garden radish, they are much larger and longer keeping. The winter radish is also more pungent.

Sorrel

Sorrel, also known as **French sorrel**, is a real favorite of mine. It is a perennial green that almost always has some leaves to harvest. No matter what time of year it is, or whether your greenhouse runs hot or cool, you'll find that sorrel is dependable. The flavor of the leaf is lemony-pungent and is a great addition to other fresh greens and vegetables in a salad. I have also had good luck cooking it up with spinach. Because of its acidic flavor, you won't want a salad made solely with sorrel. But as a complement to lettuce, chard or spinach, it will taste as if you have put a bit of vinegar or squeezed some lemon in your dish. Every greenhouse should be growing at least one sorrel plant.

Sorrel is an almost effortless plant to grow. You may find that it occasionally produces seed stalks, which should be immediately pruned to conserve its energy for producing leaves. It does well in full sun or light shade and is not picky about soil or moisture. Harvest only the outside leaves, leaving the new ones to form in the center. Sorrel benefits from dividing every 3 or 4 years. If you don't need any more plants, you may have some friends who could use some. Sorrel has very few pests.

Spinach

Spinach has one of the lowest tolerances to high temperature of any edible plant. When it experiences warm temperatures for a number of days, it quickly goes to seed and no longer produces edible leaves. For that reason, don't even attempt to grow it between late March and August. If you run your winter greenhouse on the warmer side, you may want to avoid spinach in favor of a good alternative such as chard. For greenhouses that run cold in winter and for people in cool, cloudy winter climates, spinach is a great choice.

For the longest productivity, you must put off the plant's urge to go to seed on you. This is best done by selecting varieties that are slow to go to seed or, as commonly called in catalogs, slow to bolt. Some good varieties include **tyee**, **America**, **bloomsdale longstanding**, **olympia** and **Indian summer**. If you have particular disease problems occurring on spinach (see Diseases, p. 460), try switching to the variety **melody**, which has tolerance to many common diseases.

Spinach transplants fine in the seedling stage and likes a light soil that is somewhat on the moist side. Space plants 6 inches (15 cm) apart. It can be grown in pots as well as in beds. The best harvest and quality can be obtained when grown in temperatures below 70° F (21° C). When the climate isn't suitable for spinach, the best choice as an alternative is chard, as it will outlive and greatly outyield any spinach variety.

Squash, Summer

Summer squash includes the **zucchini**, **patty pan**, **gold** and **yellow** squash. It is known as summer squash because the fruits are harvested at an immature stage (before the seeds mature within) in the summertime. When grown outside, it must also be eaten in the summer, as it will not keep. Winter squash, on the other hand, is allowed to mature and can be stored and eaten in the winter.

Most available summer squashes are **bush varieties**. There is a wide range of varieties; some grow more compact, some are more open. I have found the **straight-neck** and **crook-neck yellow squash** very prolific producers. Most every summer squash yields abundantly (as it does in the outside garden) but only if the temperature remains warm, with night temperatures above 50° F (10° C). When the temperatures drop below this, so do the yields. For this reason, summer squash is best grown from late February through October in most greenhouses, unless yours runs warm in the winter. Seed may be started in small pots and can be transplanted (with care) into beds or large tubs, 5 to 10 gallons (19 to 38 l) in size. If you are growing in tubs, put only one plant in each tub. They germinate quickly, and seeds can be directly sown into the bed or pot.

Squash likes a rich soil with a lot of well-decomposed organic matter. Each plant will need at least 9 square feet (.8 sq. m) by the time it's ready to produce. While the plant is small, you can often sneak a few radishes into the area the mature squash will occupy. Always grow squash in a warm, sunny spot in the greenhouse or sunspace. After it starts producing fruits, you can help things along with an application of plant food in the form of fish emulsion or another type of fertilizer that is watered into the soil.

After it grows five or more large leaves, the plant will start to flower. See Chapter 6, Pollination, for instructions on how to get the flower to produce fruit. There is a new variety of zucchini that can potentially save you time and trouble because it has the reputed ability to set fruit without pollination. It is sold under the most boring name in squash varieties, **type 1406**, and is available only from The Cook's Garden catalog (see Mail-Order Seeds appendix for the address). Early tests seem a bit disappointing, but the jury is still out. I do encourage you to try it. You'll find some other interesting squash, as well as other plants, while perusing the Cooks Garden catalog (try the **vining trombocino squash** if you have a lot of room). At present, the type 1406 zucchini is the only variety on the market that needs no pollination, but perhaps there will be more available in the near future, so keep a lookout.

On some varieties, you may see small angular spots forming. This is characteristic of some summer squashes. If, however, you see more of a white powderlike material forming on the leaf surface, you may have the fungal

A bushy summer squash can be trained to grow vertically up a string, allowing area underneath to be planted with another crop.

disease powdery mildew (p. 471). If this becomes a problem, find catalogs that carry some varieties tolerant or resistant to powdery mildew. Stokes Seeds catalog offers two good tolerant varieties of zucchini known as select and super select. I have grown both with good results.

Harvest most summer squash when they are relatively small, 8 inches (20 cm) long for zucchini. Anyone can grow a large summer squash fruit, but large ones are not nearly as tasty and sweet. The large ones become fibrous and seedy. Also, the more you pick, the more the plant will go on to produce.

After a plant has yielded fruits for 2 to 3 months, it may begin to slow in its production. At this time, it may also be a large gangly plant, taking up a lot of space. This is usually a good time to be thinking about starting more new plants and pulling out the old ones.

Though most summer squash are classified as a bushy plant, I've had luck making them grow up a thick string suspended from above. After the stem is 2 feet (.6 m) long, I carefully lift the tip of the plant so the whole stem is vertical. Then I wind the string, with a little slack, down through the squash and loosely tie it to the base of the plant or to a ground anchor, such as a wooden stake. As the plant grows, wind it around the string, and you have created a vertical bushy-growing squash. This process must be done with extreme care as it is easy to crack the stem and cause permanent damage to the plant. Unfortunately, you may have to sacrifice a couple of plants to get good at this technique. You may be wondering, why grow squash vertically up a string? With the plant growing vertically, you free up space to grow more plants. With this vertical-growing technique, I have even had two-tiered production, with the squash growing vertically and, under the leaf canopy, other leafy crops such as chard or lettuce. This affords you some really productive square footage.

Squash, Winter

Winter squash includes many of the well-known storage squashes, such as **butter**, **buttercup**, **hubbard**, **pumpkin**, **acorn** and **spaghetti** squash. The fruits are considered mature when thumbnail pressure doesn't mark the skin. If stored properly, around 50° F (10° C), they will keep for many months. These squashes usually grow **vinelike**, but there are a few good **bushy varieties** available. All nonbush varieties will need a trellis and can really sprawl. They may take up so much space that they're not a good choice for a small greenhouse or for gardeners not wanting to give up so much space to squash. In contrast, the bush varieties of winter squash are more restrained in their growth and may even be grown in a 5-gallon (19-liter) container. If you are looking for a bush winter squash, you are limited mostly to the acorn and a few bush pumpkin varieties, but I think in the near future there will be more types available.

Winter squash is slower to produce edible fruits than summer squash, so if you are looking for speed and efficiency, you may want to stick to summer squash. For the most part, growing winter squash is identical to the cultural needs of summer squash, including the feeding and pollination.

Northern gardeners with short seasons may want to use the greenhouse to get a head start on growing the winter squash inside for later transplanting. Whenever transplanting any squash, use your best transplanting technique, taking care to minimize the disturbance of the roots. See Luffa Squash on page 326.

Tea

Tea is a relative of the camellia and is grown with much the same culture. It is a dense shrub with leathery dark green leaves. It has fragrant white flowers that are around 1 inch (2.5 cm) across. Tea plants are usually started from seed, but occasionally you may come across a nursery selling tea plants. Seeds are large and may take up to a year to germinate, so it will stretch even the best gardener's patience. For this reason, it is easiest to try to locate plants.

Tea likes to grow in damp soil (but not muddy wet) and likes a bright location. It can be grown in large tubs or planted directly in a bed. When the plant seems healthy and can spare some leaves, harvest some for a fresh cup. Here's how to process the leaves.

Black tea: Crush the leaves, place them in a sealed plastic bag for about 10 days, then bake the tea at 190° F (88° C) until the leaves are dry.

Oolong tea: Crush the leaves, place them in a sealed plastic bag for only 3 days, and then bake at 190° F (88° C) until dry.

Green tea: Crush the leaves and immediately bake at 190° F (88° C) until dry.

Tomatillo

Tomatillo is also known as the **husk tomato** and is often used in Mexican salsas. It is a relative of the tomato but has smaller leaves and fruits that are only slightly bigger than a cherry tomato. Each fruit is covered with a paperlike shell. The tomatillo needs warm temperatures and long days for best fruit production and is best grown from March through September. If your greenhouse runs warm, you may extend the period by a month or so on either side. The plant needs soil that is not too high in nitrogen, or it will favor leaf production over flowering and producing fruits. I have found that you can grow the tomatillo in a tomato cage or just let it sprawl on a bed. It can also be grown in a pot. Each plant needs 2 to 5 square feet (.2 to .46 sq. m) for good production. In smaller pots, the plants will be correspondingly smaller but will still produce. They need full sun and a warm spot to grow healthy. You can tell that the fruits are ripe when the husk just begins to yellow, but if you are impatient, you can harvest the little fruits at any stage you find something to pick. It is best, however, to let the fruit fill out the husk first. Blend the fruits with a bit of cilantro, chives or onions and some chilies (fresh or dried), and you'll have a great salsa for dipping.

Tomatoes

Tomatoes are one of the most popular greenhouse crops. They are also one of the more difficult plants to grow, primarily due to pests (see Chapter 10, When Things Go Wrong) and diseases (see Common Greenhouse Tomato Disorders, p. 345). But with some care and planning, you can minimize the effort toward having fresh greenhouse-grown tomatoes. This can be a great luxury, as much of the year the tomatoes found in the grocery store are low in quality, poor in taste and high in cost. While common outside garden tomato production techniques will sometimes work in the greenhouse, they can also lead to failure. Using varieties developed specifically for the greenhouse will give you even better yields, fewer problems with pests and diseases and, most importantly, better-quality tomatoes.

Like many fruiting crops, the tomato prefers to be grown at temperatures between 65° and 80°

F (18° and 27° C). Growth slows and fruits stop setting when temperatures are below 50° F (10° C) and above 95° F (35° C). Tomatoes will live when the temperature gets near the freezing mark, but the plant won't grow and its developing fruits may look sickly because of stress. Tomatoes grow best when the days are longer and when placed in full sunlight or the brightest spot available. Given these constraints, you may find that growing greenhouse tomatoes in the middle of winter may not be as productive as in the other three seasons. So, if you live in a cloudy winter climate and have a cooler greenhouse, you may want to save yourself the trouble and wasted space of a winter greenhouse tomato crop.

There is such a wide range of characteristics in the many tomato varieties that choosing the best ones can, at first glance, be confusing. Selecting the right variety is one of the most important decisions you can make, and you should avoid automatically growing your favorite outside variety, unless you test it against some other tomato varieties that have been selected with the greenhouse environment in mind. Let's look at what is out there. First, tomatoes are split into two major categories: **bush** and

vining types. The bush varieties are commonly known as **determinate** and the vining types **indeterminate**.

The indeterminate tomato has a growing tip that's capable of growing indefinitely. The determinate tomato, on the other hand, will eventually produce a flower cluster that tops off the growing point, producing a low, bushy habit. The determinate tomato was developed mainly for use on large acreages with mechanical harvesting and for home gardeners who have limited space and want more-manageable plants and early production. In the greenhouse, the bush tomato is best utilized for growing in pots or other containers that have a limited root space.

Vining indeterminate tomatoes are best for growing in beds, where the roots have plenty of room to roam, as the plants can get very large. When you grow the vining tomatoes, you can train them up strings or stakes and get them to grow in a vertical manner. This enables a high total yield when compared to bush tomatoes or vining tomatoes that must sprawl on the ground. You can grow the vining tomatoes in larger pots—5 gallons (19 l) on up. For smaller pots, stick to the bushy types. There are many vining indeterminate tomato varieties that have been specifically bred or selected for the greenhouse.

Besides being able to select tomatoes that are vining or bushy, you can also find varieties that have been bred for tolerance to varying temperatures, resistance to cracking, fruit size, earliness, coloring and disease tolerance.

Tomatoes do best in a well-drained soil with plenty of decomposed organic matter. It is important to keep phosphorus levels high, especially for fruit and flower formation. Try to use fertilizers that have a fair amount of phosphorus in comparison to the nitrogen content. Bonemeal is an excellent source of phosphorus, especially in acidic soils, but it is slow to

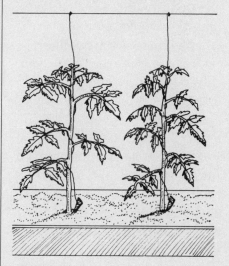

Vining tomatoes can be supported with string.

release its nutrients. Besides providing phosphorus, it also contains calcium, which helps prevent the tomato disorder called blossom-end rot (p. 345). Do a soil test to see what your soil needs before you go off and overfertilize your tomatoes (I assume overfertilization because I rarely see a greenhouse plant that is underfertilized). Tomatoes are sensitive to a buildup of soluble salts, which occurs when there is too much fertilizer in the soil. Try to avoid chemical fertilizers that contain chlorine, sodium or high amounts of manure.

Tomatoes will need to be pollinated. This is easily done by lightly tapping the yellow blossoms in the morning with a pencil or small dowel cut 2 or 3 feet (.6 or .9 m) long for easy reaching. If you can't do it every morning, every other morning will work fine.

Tomato seed is generally quite easy to germinate, and it comes up in only a matter of days, as long as the temperature is 70° to 75° F (21° to 24° C). Cooler temperatures will slow the speed of germination. Be sure to move them to full light as soon as they come up to prevent elongated seedlings. Don't sow any thicker than one seed every inch. As soon as they get their fourth or fifth leaf (including the cotyledon leaves), they are ready

for transplanting into larger containers or beds. If you are a user of tobacco, be sure to wash your hands well before handling tomato leaves, stems or seeds to prevent the spread of the tobacco mosaic leaf virus (p. 348).

Tomatoes like the soil to dry out somewhat between waterings but should not be so dry as to cause wilting. Water at regular intervals, as irregular watering will promote blossom-end rot (p. 345).

Space each tomato plant at least 2 feet (.6 m) apart, unless it is a very small-leaved plant such as the patio varieties. Tight spacing increases the incidence of disease. In areas of many cloudy days, it might help to space the plants even wider, to provide optimum light penetration. I've found that tomatoes receive the most light when rows are planted north-south.

Never prune bushy determinate varieties of tomatoes in a greenhouse. They are not good candidates for training or pruning and are best grown in traditional tomato cages if they start to sprawl. To best utilize greenhouse space, grow indeterminate vining varieties in a vertical fashion by pruning and training the plants. To properly prune, you need to locate the tomato plant's side-shoots (usually called suckers). They can be found growing immediately above where each leaf stem (petiole) is attached to the main stem. They grow at almost every crotch up and down the stem. If a sucker is not pruned early, it will quickly enlarge. Soon it will be hard to distinguish from the main stem. Begin pruning as soon as the first side-shoots appear, and do it at least every 5 days. After plants are 8 to 10 feet (2.4 to 3 m) tall, prune out the top 5 inches (13 cm) of the leader (the highest tip of the main stem) when it touches the ceiling or when it is getting too high to reach. Tip pruning will hasten the development of the existing fruits. If it seems that you have more than one leader, it is an indication that a sucker got away from you. As a result, it has become hard to determine which is the main stem. Many people prefer to grow tomatoes with two main stems per plant in a V-shape. To do this, follow the above procedure, but early on let one sucker survive pruning at about the 1-foot

PRUNE HERE
(Leafy stems *only*
—not flowers!)

Indeterminate tomato can be pruned and trained to grow up string or stakes.

(.3-meter) height. Let this sucker grow on to become the second main stem. Keep this second stem pruned as you did in the single-stem method. Space plants at about 3 feet (.9 m) apart using this two-stem system.

To prevent the spreading of disease, always prune any plants suspected of disease last. You don't want to spread it with your fingers or knife.

To support the vertical-growing trained and pruned plant, you will need to suspend a long twine (thicker twine works best) from the ceiling, directly above each plant. Use two lengths of twine if you are using the two-leader system. Tie the end of the twine to a well-anchored stake in the ground or to the base of the tomato. If you tie it to the tomato, don't use a slip knot as it may strangle the stem. Leave about 6 inches (15 cm) of slack on the twine. As the plant grows you will need to gently spiral the stem around the string. As it gets taller, it will eventually take up all of the slack. While it may sound like the plant doesn't have much to hold on to, this method holds the plant up very well.

You can also support the vining plants with a tall stake pounded firmly into the ground or tub, such as a sturdy straight furring strip. Don't use bamboo on tall plants; it is too apt to fall over. As the plant grows, tie the stem to the pole with a soft strip of cloth. Tying it too tight may strangle the plant, so keep it on the loose side.

Don't remove leaves covering the fruits. They prevent the sun from heating the fruit, which may cause cracking. Having good ventilation is important in preventing tomato diseases. Sometimes it helps to cut off some of the lower leaves of a tall tomato plant to get better air circulation under and through the plant. Except for suckers, never prune any leaves above the blossoms or forming fruit. I say this because it is easy to get carried away with pruning, and if you cut too much, you will be removing too many leaves, which are the food factory that nurtures fruit production.

I'm sure that you'll want to test the ability of your greenhouse or sunspace to produce winter tomatoes. If your greenhouse runs cold, it probably won't be that great, but if you want to give it a go, stick to varieties that are both early and cold tolerant. Often they are sparse-growing, low-yielding bush types. Some suggestions include **subarctic**, **gem state**, **scotia** and **Oregon spring**.

If you want to grow small or cherry tomatoes in small pots, try **toy boy**, **patio hybrid** and **whip-**

persnapper. For larger tomatoes in 2- to 5-gallon (7.6- to 19-liter) pots, try the above-mentioned cold-tolerant types or **starfire**, **basket vee**, **stakeless** and **valley girl**. For tall greenhouse types with good disease resistance, try **caruso**, **vendor**, **early cascade**, **boa**, **sierra**, **danny** and **buffalo**. For a tall vining greenhouse type of cherry tomato, try **sweet 100**.

As you read the description of available tomato varieties, you will notice many are listed with varying types of disease resistance or tolerance. In order to select a variety with resistance to a particular disease problem that you experience, you must first get a positive identification of the disease. You may need some help from a university that has a plant pathology department or your local county agricultural agent.

Tomatoes are also very susceptible to a few insect attacks. The most notable is the whitefly (p. 420). Keep an eye out, especially on the undersides of the leaves, for early indications of these critters to give you a head start in controlling them.

Because most people like to grow at least a few tomatoes in their sunspace or greenhouse, everyone is likely to experience at least one type of disease sooner or later (preferably later). For this reason, I have listed some common greenhouse tomato disorders to help you in trying to diagnose a particular problem. For more insight into disease problems, see Diseases (p. 460).

Common Greenhouse Tomato Disorders

Blossom-End Rot

Description: First, water-soaked spots appear at the blossom end (bottom) of the fruit. Later, the spots increase in size and become sunken, flat, brown and leathery round areas.

Cause: Environmental. Resulting from moisture stress, irregular watering or low calcium levels in the soil. Vertical training intensifies the symptoms.

Control: Water regularly, never allow the plants to wilt, but take care to not overwater. Try mulching the soil. Use bonemeal for extra calcium in the soil. Spray a 1 percent solution of calcium chloride on the leaves for immediate results. Some varieties have some resistance. Noninfectious.

Catfacing

Description: Indicated by deformed marks or lines on the fruit. Also may cause odd-shaped fruit.

Cause: Insect damage, growth disturbances and cold temperatures.

Control: Provide even-growing conditions. Prevent temperatures near freezing. Some varieties have some resistance. Noninfectious.

Early Blight *(Alternaria)*

Description: Tan-colored spots appear on the leaves and sometimes occur on the stems. Spots enlarge to a 1/2 inch (1.3 cm) or more. Close inspection shows concentric rings inside of the spots. Whole leaves may yellow and defoliate. The fruit may also show dark brown spots. This disease is among the more common in a greenhouse.

Cause: Fungus.

Control: Try to reduce humidity and avoid water on the leaves. Control insects, which may spread the problem. Use tolerant varieties, such as kotlas and early cascade hybrid.

Fruit Cracking

Description: Cracks in the skin of the tomato fruit.

Cause: Widely fluctuating temperatures.

Control :   Maintain foliage covering fruits to avoid direct sun on the fruit's skin. Moderate temperatures. Many varieties are resistant. Noninfectious.

Fusiarium *(Fusiarium)*

Description: Usually, at first, all leaves on one side of the stem become yellow and wilt. Later, all leaves wilt and die. There are two main races of the disease, fusiarium 1 and fusiarium 2.

Cause: Fungus.

Control: Best control is to plant resistant varieties and promote healthy soil with a good level of organic matter.

Gray Mold *(Botrytis)*

Description: Fruits rotting during and after harvest. Some forming on the stems.

Cause: Fungus.

Control: Promote good air circulation. Lower humidity, raise temperature slightly, remove all infected stems or fruits. Keep the area and soil surface around the base of the tomatoes free of debris.

Gray Wall

Description: Gray-brown streaks on fruit; blotchy ripening.

Cause: Low light intensities, low temperatures, high nitrogen levels, low potassium levels and high soil moisture levels. Sometimes caused by a mosaic virus.

Control: Keep soil potassium level high. Try to increase temperature above 60° F (15° C). Use resistant varieties. Usually noninfectious.

Leaf Mold *(Cladosporium)*

Description: Whitish spots on upper surface of older leaves. They may enlarge and turn yellow. The underside gets a velvet, olive-brown coating. Spores of this fungus are spread by air and water and more rarely may be carried on the seed.

Cause: Fungus.

| *Control:* | Improve air circulation. Lower humidity. Grow resistant varieties, including floradel, marion, marobe, globelle, vetamold, tuckcross. |

Tobacco Mosaic Virus *(Marmor tabaci)*

Description:	If plants are infected when young: Stunted, with light green and dark green angular mottled leaves forming a mosaic pattern. Few blossoms set. Yield is reduced. What few fruits do set are often of poor quality.
	If plants are infected during or after blooming: Leaves have light green and dark green mottled areas. Yellow netting appearance may occur. Uneven fruit ripening, sometimes having yellow streaks appearing on the fruit.
Cause:	Virus. Lives in leaves of plants of the Solanaceae family, such as tobacco, tomato, pepper, eggplant, petunia and salpiglossis.
Control:	Avoid use of tobacco in any form while handling tomato plants. Don't allow any smoking in your greenhouse. Don't let strangers touch your tomato plants. Wash your hands before handling tomato plants or seeds. Wash after touching infected plants. Pull up badly infected plants. Control insects. Prune infected plants last. Clean your pruning knife with disinfectant between cuts on suspected plants. Pour milk into soil of suspected infection area (try to use milk that would otherwise be discarded, if possible). If it becomes a common problem, grow only those varieties listed as having resistance or tolerance. The disease is often mentioned using its acronym TMV.

Verticillium *(Verticillium)*

Description:	Yellowing of older, lower leaves, which later turn brown and die. Wilting of the tips of plants during the day; may recover at night. Defoliation is common. Branches droop. Leaves are dull in appearance and fruits are small. Brownish, discolored look to the interior of the stem when cut in half.
Cause:	Fungus.
Control:	Best control is to plant resistant varieties and use healthy soil with a good level of organic matter.

Turnips

Turnips are an easy crop to grow in a greenhouse or sunspace. I have even seen them grown in a hanging basket. It wasn't the prettiest plant in a basket, but it did yield three large turnips in a 6-inch (15-centimeter) basket. They are also very easy to grow in the outside garden and keep nicely in a root cellar. Still, it is a treat to have a fresh turnip in the dead of winter. Being a root crop, it tends to grow best in the fall, winter and early spring in the greenhouse or sunspace. You can even eat the turnip greens, cooked as you would cabbage or spinach. There are varieties of turnips that have been bred to just produce greens.

Grow turnips like radishes, only give them more space. They need a minimum of 4 to 6 inches (10 to 15 cm) per plant, however I have seen them tolerate tighter spacing with good light intensity. Because the seed germinates fast, it is best to seed directly into the bed or pot rather than transplanting. Because both the tops and roots are edible and it is a fast-growing plant, the turnip is an efficient food producer in terms of time and space in the greenhouse or sunspace.

Watermelon

Growing watermelons in the greenhouse uses many of the same techniques described for cantaloupe. In comparison, cantaloupes yield more and are easier to grow by nature of their smaller size. Watermelons need a night temperature well above 50° F (10° C). The two required ingredients for growing watermelon are plenty of room and a warm greenhouse. Watermelons will sprawl fast if given the hot temperatures they prefer. Like cantaloupes, watermelons can be trellised and require hand pollination in order to get fruit development. With the weight and size of a watermelon, the large fruit can easily pull the vine off the trellis, unless you have engineered a sturdy trellis and sling to hold the developing fruit. One way to prevent the disaster posed by the development of a large fruit is to grow the smaller **icebox varieties**. Unfortunately, the vines of the icebox types still need a lot of room to roam.

If I haven't discouraged you from planting the watermelon, here are more specifics for getting a good crop. If you plan to transplant them, use a peat pot because they don't transplant very well.

Plan to provide each plant a minimum of 12 square feet (1 sq. m) or more. While plants are young, you can interplant with carrots, kohlrabi, lettuce or chard. But as soon as watermelons start vining, they will need all of their allotted space. Watermelons like a well-drained, sandy soil, high in decomposed organic matter. They also need to grow in full sun.

One of the hardest things about growing watermelons is knowing when they're ripe, especially if you are not used to growing them. You can read all the garden books, talk to the old experts, thump it, look for when the tendrils turn brown near the fruit, count the days and so forth, and still pick the watermelon too early or late. I've concluded that knowing when a watermelon is ripe is a God-given gift reserved for a chosen few. If you grow the smaller icebox watermelons, they will produce more fruits per vine, which gives the unblessed grower a better chance in the ripening lottery.

HERBS

HERBS

Though herbs are often considered exotic, don't be fooled. For the most part, herbs really are very easy to grow. Herbs can provide teas, medicines, tonics for natural health, home remedies and, best of all, fresh flavorings for cooking and salads. Herbs can be made into pest repellents and insecticides, and they have beneficial effects when interplanted with food crops. Most of us know that food tastes better when cooked with selected herbs. Growing herbs year-round is another luxury of having a greenhouse or sunspace. It will provide you with an opportunity to learn more about the many amazing properties of herbs.

Because so many fine books on herbs already exist, I won't go very deeply into every potential herb plant that you can grow. There are, however, some special considerations when growing herbs in a greenhouse. For instance, because winter temperatures are lacking in a greenhouse, certain perennial herbs never grow very well, because they need the cyclic cold treatment that winter provides. In greenhouses that run real cool in winter, there may be a problem growing some of the tender annual herbs, such as basil, that need consistent warm temperatures.

People, and especially children, are pleasantly impressed when you take them on a smell tour of your herb plants. I recently gave a tour to some six-year-olds. When they smelled the mint, they said it was like toothpaste; when they smelled the dill, they said it came from pickles; when we came to the fennel, they said it was from black licorice!

One of the best uses of your greenhouse-grown herbs is to pick fresh herbs for a special family dinner. You can even follow it with some fresh herbal tea.

Anise

Anise is an annual herb that has an aroma similar to that of licorice. Anise overwinters well in the greenhouse if started in spring. Avoid excess nitrogen fertilization, as it may inhibit or delay seed production. Each plant requires about 1 square foot (.09 sq. m) of space. It can also be grown in 6-inch (15-centimeter) pots and may need to be up-potted after 9 months or so. Outside, this plant needs a long season to mature; inside your greenhouse it will thrive and mature year-round.

Anise Hyssop

This plant is also in the mint family. Although it is not aggressive like many mints, it can easily reseed itself. It has sweet leaves with a wonderfully unique flavor. I love to add them to salads, and they are great when made into a tea. It is also known as **licorice mint** and scientifically known as ***Agastache foeniculum***. It grows best in sun and, when mature, produces a blue flower stalk that is edible and can be used in bouquets. The plant reaches 10 inches (25 cm) and needs a bright spot to grow. It is easily started from seed. Mites (p. 416) may frequent the plant, so keep an eye out for these invaders. I have yet to find someone who doesn't like the flavor of the raw leaf after they take that risky first bite. Give it a try!

Basil

This is one plant that is hard to overwinter in cooler winter greenhouses, especially if your winter temperatures fall below 45° F (7° C). But basil is still well worth planting for production from spring through fall. It likes a rich soil and needs to be grown in a bright spot. It will want to flower after it has grown a couple of months, but the flowers rob the plant of its ability to

Basil

produce the culinary leaves. When possible, keep the flowers pruned. Basil is easily propagated from seed. According to an old tradition, you should curse the seeds as you plant them. I've found it's best to do my planting and cursing after paying bills. It is great therapy.

There are many varieties to choose from. For culinary purposes, the **larger-leaved green basil varieties** are usually the best. If you want to experiment around, you can find some varieties that include a **lemon-fragrance basil**, **opal-colored basils** and even a basil with a **clove fragrance**.

Basil is great to throw into Italian dishes and is even good fresh in salads. Look in a recipe book for instructions on how to make pesto, which is great for a quick, tasty meal.

Bay Laurel

The bay leaf is a must for spaghetti sauces and soups. Having a fresh leaf is a real treat. It is an aromatic evergreen tree or shrub and is very slow-growing in the greenhouse. One plant will live many years. It can be easily grown in either pots or beds and requires

Real Salads for Real People

You will find that I list many herbs for eating fresh in salads. Since my love affair with greenhouse gardening began, my salads have never been the same. A common dinner salad found at a restaurant (or on many dinner tables) has got to be the most boring dish ever devised. To spice things up, we often douse the salad with dressing. Instead, try some fresh herb leaves and edible herb flowers cut into a salad. It makes the salad much more exciting, colorful, and tasty. Now we're talking a real dish! It will also be more nutritious. You will probably find that the salad needs little, if any, salad dressing. This is real salad ... with real flavor! All you have to do is have a greenhouse and a willingness to throw out any traditional concept that you have when you think of the word "salad." Granted, eating habits are very hard to change, but life is short and you really should not deprive your taste buds of a full-flavored experience (see p. 357).

Bay laurel

no special care as long as you don't overfertilize it. The bay can be occasionally plagued by scale (p. 417) or mealybugs (p. 415), so keep a close eye out for them. If after many years the plant gets too big, it takes to pruning very well and can even be shaped. Save your pruned leaves for future meals. Generally, it is acquired from catalogs but can easily be propagated from cuttings taken from the tips of the branches.

Borage

Borage grows larger than many herbs, so be sure to provide it with 2 to 3 square feet (.2 to .3 sq. m) of space per plant. It will also get up to 3 feet (.9 m) high, even in winter. If you grow it in a pot, make sure the pot is at least 1 gallon (3.8 l) in size. Borage can

tolerate some shading but grows best in well-lit areas. It has large rough, hairy leaves and dainty blue flowers that can fade to pink. Many people like to grow it solely for the look of the flowers, as an ornamental. It is easily started from seed.

Borage grows well in the greenhouse year-round and can occasionally reseed itself in an adjacent area. Its flowers have a sweet cucumber flavor and, when eaten, are said to make you happier with life. The leaves are often made into teas to give a cooling effect and are reputed to provide some relief from congestion and coughing.

Catnip

Catnip is also known as **catmint** or by its scientific name, ***nepeta***. It is in the mint family, as indicated by the square shape of the stems, and is a perennial. It can be propagated from divisions or cuttings or started from seed, and can be grown in either pots or beds with ease. Keep an eye out for mites (p. 416), which seem to like catnip as much as cats do.

Catnip gets its name because of the odd effect that it has on cats. Despite years of research in botany, neurophysiology and chemistry, scientists still don't understand why

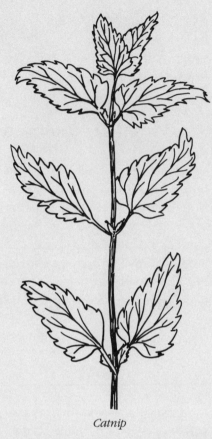

Catnip

cats are affected by catnip. Some speculate that chemicals in catnip cause cats to hallucinate, while others suspect that the chemicals in the plant mimic certain social odors to which cats respond. These odors, if this theory is true, would be triggering territorial or sexual behavior. Regardless of the deliberation by scientists as to why cats start licking, chewing and rolling around in catnip, the phenomena can pose a problem to greenhouse gardeners if they choose to grow catnip.

Catnip is not alone in its ability to induce such symptoms in your cat. Other nonrelated plants have been noted to cause the same symptoms, such as valerian, baby-blue-eyes and some species of viburnums.

There are also some species of catnip that don't seem to affect cats. If your cat is not affected by any type of catnip, then your kitty is part of the one-third of all domestic cats that don't react to catnip. Those pet owners who have a catnip-immune cat don't have to worry about a feline-made mess in the indoor herb garden. If you do have a catnip-sensitive feline, you may want to exclude catnip plants in your greenhouse. There are those humans who delight in watching a poor pussy have an out-of-body experience. Just don't get too cruel. Besides, your cat never spikes your breakfast cereal, so go easy. Most veterinarians I've talked to say that occasional exposure to catnip is not harmful to your cat. Just be sure to use a little moderation.

Catnip has been valued in history for its medicinal effects on humans. It is reputed to bring down fevers. Unlike its effect on cats, catnip tea is said to relax and decrease nervousness, unless you have a feline nature.

Chamomile

Chamomile is a low-growing plant that is treasured for the little yellow-centered, white-petaled daisylike flowers it produces. It forms a ground cover that reaches only 3 to 4 inches (8 to 10 cm) high. It is easy to start from seed and needs to grow in a sunny spot in well-drained soil. The seeds are tiny, so lightly cover them with peat moss to ensure germination. Transplant the seedlings when they are 1 inch (2.5 cm) tall. A mature plant takes up about 1 square foot (.09 sq. m) of space when it is mature. It can grow year-round in the greenhouse or sunspace.

To harvest, cut the flower heads and crush them for fresh tea, or dry them for later use. Watch out for aphids (p. 413); they love to camouflage themselves in the leaves. A cup of chamomile tea is said to help bring sound sleep and calm the stomach. Chamomile tea is tasty and worth drinking for absolutely no reason at all.

Chives

See under Fruits and Vegetables (p. 309).

Salad Herbs

Anise hyssop

Basil

Borage flowers

Chives (listed in Fruits and Vegetables)

Dill greens

Fennel

French sorrel (listed in the Fruits and Vegetables)

Lemon balm

Mint

Nasturtium flowers (listed in Ornamental Flowering Crops)

Orange mint

Oregano

Root beer plant

Sage flowers

Tarragon

Coriander/Cilantro

Coriander is also known as cilantro by many Hispanics. Coriander is the seed of the plant used as an herb, and cilantro is the leaf. Because I love Mexican food, my greenhouse is rarely without the plant. A good hot salsa must have some diced cilantro in it. Cilantro is also common in Chinese cooking. I have found that most people new to the flavor of cilantro do not like the smell of the leaves. One Hispanic friend told me that he never met an Anglo who liked the smell of cilantro the first time. But, please, don't pass judgment on it until you have tasted it in a dish or as a seasoning in salsa. Many a mind has been changed after tasting it.

Cilantro is easily grown from seed, but the plant is not productive for very long, especially in the summer, when it quickly goes to seed. If you are growing it for the leaf, you will notice that the young leaves are not finely divided in contrast to the leaves that the plant produces prior to flowering. Because it goes to seed rapidly unless there is cool weather,

you may want to plan to sow a few seeds every 5 or 6 weeks for a continual supply. Nichols Garden Nursery (see Mail-Order Plants appendix for address), a great catalog that specializes in herb plants and seeds, offers a slow-bolting coriander, which will give you a longer period of producing lush tasty leaves. The leaves of cilantro lose most of their flavor when dried. That is why it is so nice to have fresh-picked cilantro leaves on hand.

Dill

Dill is an annual that is ideal for the greenhouse or sunspace. It can

Dill

be productive through both high and low temperatures and does fine in partial shade. Dill plants may reach heights of up to 6 feet (1.8 m) tall, but a shorter variety called bouquet maintains a compact habit and would be a good choice for growing in pots.

Dill is easily started from seed, but beware if you ever let a plant go to seed in the greenhouse! Because it is a prolific reseeder, you could end up with dill coming up everywhere in a very short time. Harvest the seed heads before they turn brown to save you hours of weeding. Both the flowers and foliage are tasty and edible. I like to use fresh dill greens in salads, dips and soups.

Fennel

Except for its celerylike stalk, fennel greatly resembles dill. Upon close inspection you'll also notice that it is a greener color than dill, which has a bluish tint to the leaves. This plant tastes like licorice. It's a perennial and is easily started from seed. Fennel grows abundantly during all seasons in the greenhouse, and one plant can be productive for many years. It can tolerate partial shade and varying soil conditions. Because it can reach up to 6 feet (1.8 m) over time, it needs a large pot of at least

1 gallon (3.8 l), unless you wish to grow it in a bed. The bronze variety has coppery-colored foliage and looks interesting against other ornamental plants.

The common florence fennel produces a bulbous root that has a sweet flavor. Use it as you would use celery. The leaf of fennel is also edible and is good in salads or used as a

Fennel

garnish. My favorite part of the fennel plant is the small yellow flower, one of the tastiest edible flowers around. It has a sweet candylike licorice flavor and is great for munching fresh as you work in the greenhouse. It can also be used in salads, soups and many other dishes. If you let the fennel plant go on to produce seeds, they are great in Italian dishes. Every greenhouse or sunspace should have at least one fennel plant.

Garlic

Garlic can be grown year-round and can tolerate a wide range of temperatures. It can be started from

Garlic

store-bought divided bulbs. Plant them about 2 inches (5 cm) deep. It does not take up much space, so if you like garlic, you can look forward to fresh garlic in the winter. It's a good natural food for lowering blood pressure, not to mention its hundreds of other medicinal uses.

Lavender

There are two main types of lavender, **English lavender** and **French lavender**. English lavender is a perennial outside in temperate climates and has narrow 1-inch (2.5 cm) leaves. It has a problem growing in the greenhouse because it needs a winter cold treatment to feel comfortable. In the greenhouse it seldom thrives, but it does survive. I have found the French lavender to be a much better choice for greenhouse growing. You'll know you have the French lavender because the leaf edge is scalloped, unlike the smooth edge found on the English lavender. The French lavender always outdoes the English and generally looks healthier. It blooms year-round and can grow to 2 feet (.6 m) or more in height. It takes

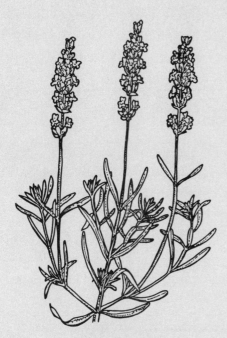

English lavendar

like mint, it is not aggressive and won't spread much. One plant will need about 1 square foot (.09 sq. m) of space. Use lemon balm in iced tea or add a few sprigs in a salad.

Mint

There are many varieties of mint. Some but not all of these perennial plants can become aggressive and appropriate large areas of ground if left to their own devices. For this reason, you should consider growing mint in a 1-gallon (3.8-liter) pot rather than in a bed. When potted, mint can easily get root-bound and may need some root pruning and new soil every couple of years. While mint can tolerate diverse soil, it seems to do best on the wet side, especially if you give it a well-drained soil. It can also tolerate diverse light and temperature conditions. It can be started from

Mint

well to pruning if it gets too large. French lavender can be grown in pots or beds with equal success. It is hard to find a seed source, but I have found plants sold in catalogs regularly, especially if the catalog specializes in herbs (check Nichols Garden Nursery in the Mail-Order Plants appendix).

Lemon Balm

This hardy perennial is a relative of the mint family and is also known as lemon mint. It has wonderful lemon-flavored leaves. It can be started from seeds, cuttings or division of a mature plant. Un-

seeds, cuttings and divisions from mature plants.

You will be amazed by all of the choices of different mints when you look in a catalog that carries a good selection. Let me list some of the choices: **curly mint**, with curly leaves; **chocolate mint**, reminiscent of the candy; **spearmint**, incredibly aromatic; **chewing-gum mint**, fragrance like bubble gum; and **apple mint**, a fuzzy leaf with a green apple flavor. There is a mint known as **corsican mint**, which is not aggressive and is a delicate low-growing plant. It forms a handsome carpet and thrives in moist, low-light conditions. The leaves look moss-like, very different from the traditional mint varieties.

Orange mint is also not overly aggressive. Like its name, it has an orange flavor, but sometimes it even reminds me of basil. It is easy to grow in the greenhouse and needs the same culture as lemon balm or mint. Try it in teas or put a few sprigs in a salad.

Now you can have fresh mint for year-round mint juleps. Bring on the Kentucky Derby!

Oregano

There are many types of oregano, but it is easy to end up growing a variety that is disappointing if you expect a good

Herb Processing

Herbs may be processed in a number of ways, including drying and freezing. Many of the books on herbs explain this in depth. If you decide to dry your herbs, avoid drying in the greenhouse, as the humidity levels are too high and may even cause the growth of dangerous molds on the leaves. So, after cutting, always dry herbs in a place with low humidity.

Using your herbs fresh is a real treat. Many people have never had this opportunity and are familiar only with dried herbs. When using fresh herbs—for cooking, making teas—bruise or crush them to bring out their full flavor. It takes 4 parts fresh herbs to equal 1 part dried herbs when cooking or making teas.

The following is a list of herbs that do well in a greenhouse or a sunspace, along with tips and comments on their cultivation. There are thousands of herbs, and I list only the common ones or those that are particularly interesting. With so much potential for pioneering with herbs in a greenhouse, look in some catalogs specializing in herbs and you'll be sure to make some discoveries.

pizza-flavoring spice. Many catalogs sell the less flavorful varieties of marjoram as oregano. To really get the good-flavored oregano, look for the scientific name ***Origanum heracleoticum*** or, as it is sometimes known, **Greek oregano**. This is the type that has the true oregano flavor most of us are used to. It can be started from seed and needs well-drained soil with a sunny location. Grown in 6- to 10-inch (15- to 25-centimeter) pots, as well as in beds, one plant can grow for many years and is relatively easy to care for. The leaf can be used fresh or dried with good results.

Oregano

Parsley

Parsley is frequently put on plates to sweeten your breath at the end of a meal, but people seldom touch this nutritious leaf and often let it sit all lonesome on the plate. What a sin! Try eating it. It tastes good, really! It's great in salads and is chock-full of vitamins, especially A, C and iron.

Parsley is a biennial and will often go to seed on you (ending its productive life) in spring. It is very productive, even in cooler greenhouses, during the winter if started before the end of September. Parsley can take up to 4 weeks to germinate. Soaking the seed overnight before planting will help it along. Warm soil temperatures in the middle of summer may slow the germination further. It does best in sunny locations but will tolerate a bit of shade. You can transplant parsley grown in the outside garden in fall, but you have to make a real effort to get the long carrotlike taproot.

There are two primary varieties of parsley: **curled-leaf** and **flat Italian parsley**. Both do fine in the greenhouse, but I've found it easier to get people to try eating the curled-leaf parsley. If older leaves turn yellow, the plant may need a feeding.

Many people, including me, have a slight allergic reaction if they consume parsley that is in the process of elongating and going to seed (instead of growing in a more traditional mound). When you see it going to seed, it is time to pull it up and donate it to the compost pile.

Parsley has a perfect globe shape after it gets a good collection of leaves and is quite ornamental among flowers and vegetables.

Parsley

Pineapple Sage

See under Ornamental Flowering Crops (p. 267).

Root Beer Plant

When I first grew this plant, I was surprised to find that it really does have the aroma of root beer. Scientifically, it is known as ***Tagetes lucida***, but it also goes by **sweet-scented marigold** and **winter tarragon**. Once you smell it, however, you will call it only the root beer plant. Children especially delight in a plant that smells

of root beer in the greenhouse. Like many herbs, the leaves must first be touched before the volatile aroma is released. The plant is often used as a substitute for tarragon, but I have decided the best use is to entertain children and adults alike, who love the fact that a plant really smells like root beer. It is not, however, actually used in flavoring root beer.

Root beer plant is also valuable for the nice orange flower it has in the winter. The plant is a cousin to the marigold, but you won't immediately recognize any resemblance. It is generally started from acquired plants and cuttings. Check Logee's and Nichols catalogs in the Mail-Order Plants appendix for plants, but be sure to look under the scientific name.

Rosemary

Rosemary is an evergreen perennial. It grows slowly, but after a few years you can have quite a specimen. I have often ended up with 6-foot-tall (1.8-meter-tall) rosemary "trees." They take well to pruning and can be easily poodled (made into a topiary) if you are interested in creating plant sculptures.

Rosemary can be started from seed or cuttings. Cuttings are most successful if taken in spring or summer. It does best if grown on the dry side and does equally well in pots or beds. Being perennial, one plant can live for years. Fresh leaves can be harvested anytime.

Rosemary

Try it with fish or potato dishes. Besides culinary uses, rosemary is also reported to have medicinal and cosmetic qualities. It is traditionally believed that in the house where rosemary thrives, the woman is dominant. Watch for results.

Sage

Sage is a hardy perennial that tolerates a wide variety of conditions. It is easily propagated from seed or cuttings and it will do best with full sun and well-drained soil. It can grow to 1 foot (.3 m) high or more. The flowers are a beautiful shade

Sage

of blue and often bloom throughout the year. The flowers, as well as the leaves, can be used for culinary purposes.

Tarragon

Tarragon is another plant that I love to graze on while working in the greenhouse. It survives the winter and tolerates the greenhouse, but I have found it to be a plant that prefers to have a real

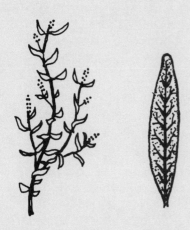

Tarragon

winter. For this reason, greenhouse-grown tarragon never seems to thrive as well as tarragon grown outside. The best tarragon is known as **French tarragon**, which has the best flavor and is propagated only vegetatively (through cuttings or division). If you see tarragon seed for sale, it's the wrong stuff.

For best results, give tarragon full sun in well-drained soil. I have had better luck growing it in clay pots, but it does reasonably well in beds too.

For years, I had childhood memories come rolling back every time I tasted tarragon. Finally, a friend of mine clued me in to my reaction. He said,"It tastes like candy cigarettes." Every kid growing up in the sixties ate an abundance of candy cigarettes, which explained my memories triggered

by tarragon. I'm not sure that tarragon is what the candy is flavored with, but my brain says it's close. If you eat too much fresh tarragon, your tongue may get tingly or numb. I call it the tarragon tingle. At the risk of getting the tingle, I love to munch on tarragon fresh. I also throw fresh sprigs into salads. Of course, there is always tarragon chicken and a plethora of other culinary uses for tarragon in a good recipe book.

Thyme

Thyme, a hardy perennial, is a handsome ground cover as well as an herb. There are a number of types of thyme, including **common thyme**, which grows about 1 foot (.3 m) tall; **golden lemon thyme**, with gold and green leaf variegation and a lemon scent; **lemon thyme**, which has a lemon scent with green leaves; **caraway thyme**, which has red stems and caraway-scented leaves; and more.

Many of the thymes have ornamental flowers blooming in spring and fall. Thyme can be grown in a pot, but I like it as a ground cover along walkways. It can tolerate some traffic and gives off a nice scent when stepped on. Most thymes can tolerate full to partial sun. It is helpful to occasionally divide plants and trim them back to keep them healthy. For harvesting, it is best to pick the leaves just prior to flowering. In years gone by, thyme plants were found in almost every garden and were thought to bring good spirits to the household.

Thyme

*Getting
to the Roots*

9

CHAPTER 9

Getting to the Roots

Underneath every healthy plant is a healthy root system. The root system provides nutrition for the plant as well as anchoring it into the ground. I could have titled this chapter Greenhouse Soils and Fertilization, but all we are trying to do is to make the roots happy. When the soil is well, the plant is well.

Whenever I think about roots, I remember an experience I had running the Cheyenne Botanic Gardens (see Epilogue, The Future). One primary purpose of the Botanic Gardens is to provide garden-oriented therapy to seniors, youth and the handicapped. At the Botanic Gardens, I was working with a fellow, aged 37, who was mentally handicapped. He functioned at the level of a six-year-old, and he loved plants. There was a problem, however; he was afraid of plant roots. He often said, "I think roots are scary, don't you?" He always avoided any physical contact with a plant root. I searched my memories of childhood and remembered when there were parts of plants that scared me too. I tried to reason with him to no avail. No logical explanation seemed to help.

One day, however, I had him adding some compost to the soil for an early spring planting. I left him to work by himself on a bed, preparing it for a new planting. Later, when I looked at the bed, I saw that he had done a great job except for leaving a curious-looking something in the corner of the bed. I pointed to the big many-branched root system sticking out of the soil. "What's that?" I asked. He said it was an upside-down tomato plant that he had fished out of the compost pile. He beamed with pride as I realized that he had actually handled a plant with, God forbid, ROOTS! I dug around the root sticking out of the ground, and sure enough, there was a whole tomato plant buried under the ground. "I just wanted to see how it would grow this way," he said. I thought about it for a few seconds and replied, "Why not?" For many months, when giving public tours, I had a hard time explaining the upside-down tomato plant, but it was worth it. His fear was totally gone from that day on. He had found his own solution to his root phobia. Also from that day, he seemed to fit in better with all of the other people around the Botanic Gardens. I have always been convinced that gardening is the best therapy, whether you are handicapped or not.

THE YEAR-ROUND SOIL

When you garden outside, your soil has all winter to recuperate and regenerate. In a greenhouse or sunspace, things are growing year-round. This means year-round depletion of your soil and its nutrients, leaving no time for soil to rest and regenerate. When greenhouse plant growth slows, as temperatures get cooler in the winter, the plant's use of soil nutrients also slows. Still, a substantial amount of nutrients may be taken up by the roots over time. That is why greenhouse soil requires special attention between crop plantings when growing in beds. In pots, it means you need to pay attention to the health of the plant and repot as

necessary. Plant nutrition and soil science are vastly complex. Numerous books can help you get a basic understanding of plant and soil nutrition, but they are some of the most boring books you'll ever read. So in this chapter, I will try to give you the basic information you'll need to know how to maintain soil and plant health. Hopefully, you will learn how to deal with problems and, better yet, how to prevent them from happening.

In general, I prefer using organic-biological sources of fertilizers. However, I am not against using chemical fertilizers in the greenhouse. They are especially handy when you are growing in pots or containers, where you lack the ability to maintain a well-rounded soil ecology.

Maintaining proper nutrition for your plants requires that you do some occasional testing for soil pH, salt content, organic matter and specific elements such as nitrogen, phosphorus and potassium. You'll need to be aware of symptoms indicating nutrient deficiencies or excesses.

When it comes to fertilizing, people generally overdo it. Keep this in mind when you are following a label or recommendation. People tend to love their plants to death—literally! If a little is good, people rationalize, then more must be better. When it comes to fertilizing, especially with chemicals, it is better to err on the side of discretion and frugality.

BASIC REQUIREMENTS FOR HEALTHY SOIL

Soil is an ecology (almost) unto itself. For it to be healthy, it requires a cast of characters all at a certain level of health. Let's look at the requirements for healthy soil.

Aeration

Roots need air as well as water; they'll suffocate from overwatering.

Sandy soils, or soils containing perlite (see p. 389) and some decomposed organic matter, will help aeration. Earthworms also greatly help aerate soil in greenhouse beds, but they are not usually present in the soil of smaller pots. Try adding some worms from your outside garden to an inside greenhouse growing bed (if you have one).

Organic Matter

Organic matter results from the composition of things that were once alive, including plants, food scraps, manures and leaves. It has multiple beneficial effects on soils.

Beneficial Effects of Organic Matter

1. Adds nutrients.
2. Increases water-holding ability.
3. Holds mineral nutrients available for root uptake (much like a sponge).
4. Promotes beneficial microbial life.
5. Helps aerate soil.
6. Keeps soil diseases and nematode (microscopic critters that eat on roots) infestations to a minimum.
7. Adds CO_2 to the air during decomposition, which increases plant growth (see Chapter 1, The Greenhouse Environment).
8. Buffers the soil pH, that is, helps to raise low pH and lowers high pH.

Moisture-Holding Ability

Soil needs to be able to retain water for the roots. Two substances primarily hold water in the soil: clay and decomposed organic matter. Organic matter is my preferred choice (see Organic Soil Amendments, p.384).

Drainage

Greenhouse soils should drain well, unless you are growing a special ornamental plant that prefers to have wet feet. A well-drained soil is your main remedy when you have overfertilized a bed or pot. It also helps prevent the accumulation of soil salts, which can be damaging to many plants. For a well drained soil that provides sufficient aeration, you need some larger particles in the soil mix, such as sand, small pebbles or a special growing medium known as perlite. Some soils are inherently well drained as they contain a fair amount of sand naturally. Other soils, however, may be high in clay and need the addition of amendments that can remedy the poor drainage (see bed construction details in Chapter 2, Interior Design).

Proper pH

This is not the name of a shampoo or an acne medication. The pH describes the acidity level of a substance, in this case, your soil. It is based on a scale that ranges from 1 to 14. The halfway mark, 7, is the neutral point.

Try to keep your soil very close to neutral. A professional soil test or home soil test kit available in many catalogs or garden stores will usually include a pH analysis. There are pH meters on the market

The pH Scale

14	
13	
12	
11	Alkalinity
10	
9	
8	
7	RANGE OF GOOD GROWTH
6	
5	
4	
3	Acidity
2	
1	

Plants grow better in a pH-neutral soil.

but you must purchase an expensive one (around $160) to get accurate results. The cheap ones that often run for $20 or less are usually not very accurate. You can also purchase what is known as pH litmus papers, which when moistened with wet soil or soil in solution, will turn colors that correspond to certain levels of pH. Still, I feel a professional soil test is the best one to trust if you suspect a real pH problem. Many county extension agents offer soil testing for a minimal fee.

When pH is below 6.5 or above 7.3, it is much harder for plant roots to use minerals and nutrients in the soil, even though they are present in adequate amounts. The result is a sick-looking plant. This is why a plant grown at a poor pH level resembles one with a nutrient deficiency. A high pH can be corrected by adding well-decomposed organic matter, such as compost (avoid manures), gypsum, sulfur or even commercially available acidifying plant foods. A low pH is generally corrected by adding wood ash or limestone. Read more about wood ash or limestone later in this chapter or see some general gardening books. They usually go into this problem extensively.

Healthy Soil Microbial Life

Microbes (microscopic organisms) that live in the soil, such as bacteria and fungus, are beneficial to plant growth. They decompose the organic matter into more basic compounds. Microbes are important in controlling diseases caused by "bad" bacteria and fungi. The "good" microbes may actually feed on or parasitize the "bad" microbes. This is not unlike a tick on a dog or a coyote eating a rabbit in the nonmicroscopic world. It's amazing what goes on in the dirt, isn't it? When microbes are in short supply, there seems to be an increased likelihood of more diseases or nutrient problems. For growing beds, the addition of decomposed organic matter will provide a healthy environment for microbial life. Occasionally repot a containerized plant to help maintain a good environment and good level of soil microbial life.

Low Salt Content

Salt is a broad term that doesn't refer just to table salt (sodium chloride) but describes the result of a chemical reaction occurring when acid compounds react with alkaline compounds. Certain fertilizers, both organic and inorganic, are noted for their potentially high salt content. Salt problems occur when high levels of fertilizers are used in soils that have poor drainage. It can also result from having a water source that contains a high level of salt compounds. Besides a plant's symptoms tipping you off, there is only one sure way to tell if you have a salt problem—with a soil test. It's almost impossible to escape some salt accumulation, but luckily, salts move with water. With heavy water applications, you can often leach the salts out to a level below the roots. This is why you hear the term "well-drained soil" so much. Salts tend to accumulate in the root zone of poorly drained soils, so there should

---

Symptoms of Salt Damage

1. Leaf tips or margins brown.
2. Leaves drop.
3. Soil surface gets a buildup of white powdery stuff (resembles ground table salt).
4. Slow growth.
5. Roots are damaged.

Salt damage causes browning of leaf tips and margins.

Preventing Salt Damage

1. Go easy on fertilizing. Follow recommended rates; more is not better!
2. Avoid raw manures.
3. Soak old clay pots in water for a day and clean with a wire brush before replanting in them.
4. Be sure the soil drains well. A relatively high sand content helps if you have recurring problems.
5. Leach salt-affected soil by applying two to three heavier-than-usual waterings, then resume normal watering rhythm.

always be drainage holes in the bottom of growing containers.

Salt concentration also rises as your soil becomes drier. If a lot of water has been evaporating from your soil, you may actually see white salt crystals on the soil surface.

NUTRIENTS FOR SOIL AND PLANT

When asked, "Do plants grow?" a youngster replied that he was sure they grew, but "they don't let you see it or hear it." When asked where plants get their food, he responded, "I think they eat the soil and the air, but I'm not sure how." The garden is a pretty good teacher of how our planet works.

Yes, plants do have to eat, and we have to help feed them. Feeding plants can become a complicated thing because it gets into the chemistry of the soil. Whenever you involve the word "chemistry," things tend to become confusing. But to keep it simple, the best thing to do when confused about feeding your plants is either to do nothing or to do less of what your natural urges tell you. This is because most of the problems with gardens and plants are not a result of underfeeding, but rather overfeeding ... killing with kindness.

But when the time comes that the plant is talking to you with its symptoms, saying, "Things are not right," and you have to do something, home-type soil tests or professional soil tests are a great help. Most people do not realize that when a plant is suffering from a particular nutrient problem, the problem actually started long before you could see the symptom. By the time you see that the plant has a problem, you can be sure it has been suffering from this malady for some time. In the case of growing fruits or vegetables, yields could have already been lost. The same holds true for flowering ornamentals. That is why prevention is better than cure when it comes to plant nutrient problems. Still, plants do tell us, with some specific symptoms, what may be bothering them.

Nutrients needed by plants are generally split into two groups: the major nutrients and the micronutrients. The major nutrients are those that are needed in larger quantities and are essential to growth, meaning that without them the plant will die. The micronutrients are needed by the plants just as much as the major nutrients, only they are needed in smaller quantities.

When people talk about fertilizing, they generally talk about

This plant shows evidence of iron deficiency. The veins of the leaves remain green, while the area between the veins yellow. This occurs on new growth and tips of plants.

three major nutrients: nitrogen, phosphorus and potassium. Nitrogen promotes leafy growth. It can be easily washed out of the soil because it moves with the water. It is also easy to overapply, which can trigger leaf burning and the reduction of flowers and fruit. Phosphorus is generally associated with root growth. It also promotes flowering and is important for establishing seedlings. Unlike nitrogen, it moves slowly in the soil and does not move with water. Therefore, it is important to maintain a good supply in the root zone of the plants. Potassium (also called potash) helps regulate water movement in the plant and contributes to its overall health.

The many micronutrients are equally important. But because they are needed in such small quantities, people often overapply them, causing big problems. Micronutrient problems often occur not because they are in short supply but because the pH of the soil makes it harder for the roots to use the existing elements in the soil. Usually, adequate amounts are contained in organic matter. Micronutrient deficiency may result from a pH being too high or low, or may result from a high level of soil salts or overapplication of another fertilizer nutrient.

The following is a listing of the many important nutrients that plants need. I have included some general symptoms of both deficiencies and excesses of the elements for plant troubleshooting. Keep in mind that plants don't read books like this and may not always follow the prescribed symptoms. Anyway, it may help.

Major Soil Nutrients
"The Big Three"

Nitrogen (N)

Function: Required for leaf growth. Important for protein and amino acid production.

Contained in: Manure, fish and ocean plants, compost and blood meal.

Excess: Luxuriant leafy growth, dark green leaves, few flowers or fruit. Look for salt damage. Leaf tip and margin may brown. Increase in aphids and other insects.

Deficiency: Light green to yellow older, lower leaves. Yellow leaves may fall off. Stunted growth.

Applying N: If severe, try a foliar spray of fish emulsion or houseplant food. Mix at half the recommended rate and repeat weekly until the symptoms disappear. For a long-term solution, add a slow-release fertilizer, such as compost (preferably a rich compost if available)or Osmocote.

Phosphorus (P)

Function: Seedling hardiness, fruit and root production, helps in disease resistance.

Contained in: Bonemeal, ground rock phosphate, fish emulsion, compost, super phosphate and triple super phosphate.

Excess:	Very rare. May cause micronutrient deficiencies.
Deficiency:	Red- to purple-colored leaves. Dwarfed plants, small leaves, few fruits, leaves dropping early.
Applying P:	For severe problems, water in a water-soluble houseplant food with a higher middle number (phosphorus) than first number (nitrogen) on the label. Fish emulsion may stimulate the roots to utilize the available phosphorus in the soil. Bonemeal takes many months to work, especially in alkaline soils, but is good for long-term soil health. Be sure to check for neutral soil pH for phosphorus to be taken up by plant properly.

Potassium (K)

Function:	Regulates water movement within plants. Helps with stress and cold/heat tolerance, starch and sugar production. Increases the efficient use of other nutrients.
Contained in:	Wood ash in small amounts (not good for alkaline soils), granite dust, compost, manure, kelp.
Excess:	May create magnesium deficiency.
Deficiency:	Lower leaves mottled, dead areas in leaf, yellowing begins at leaf edge and continues toward the center. Weak stems.
Applying K:	Add compost to soil, fertilize with water-soluble fertilizer containing potassium. Add a kelp-based fertilizer to soil.

Other Major Soil Nutrients

Calcium (Ca)

Function:	Cell-wall and enzyme production.
Contained in:	Bonemeal, eggshells, limestone, milk, gypsum, ground oyster shells.
Excess:	Not very common, may affect pH or deficiencies of potassium, magnesium, iron.

| *Deficiency:* | Yellow, hooked plant tip. Tips may die back, short roots. Blossom-end fruit rot on tomatoes. Centers of lettuce and celery may rot. |
| *Applying Ca:* | Gypsum applied at manufacturer's recommended rate; bonemeal or ground oyster shells lightly dusted on the soil and then dug into the top inch will help. |

Magnesium (Mg)

Function :	Chlorophyll production and respiration.
Contained in:	Organic matter, Epsom salts, liquid kelp, seaweed extract.
Excess:	Causes micronutrient imbalances.
Deficiency:	Yellow between veins or yellow spots on older, lower leaves, which may eventually turn brown. More common in acid soils, especially where much dolomitic limestone has been applied. Deficiency may trigger calcium deficiencies and higher levels of insect infestations.
Applying Mg:	Add compost to soil mix. Mix 1 tablespoon of Epsom salts to 1 gallon (3.8 l) of hot water; apply cooled mixture to plants once a week until symptoms disappear.

Sulfur (S)

Function:	Protein production. Helps in maintaining soil pH.
Contained in:	Ground sulfur, rain near coal-fired power plants, gypsum.
Excess:	Causes soil to become too acidic.
Deficiency:	Light yellow on new leaves including yellowing of the leaf veins.
Applying S:	Add compost to soil. Add 1/2 pound (.2 kg) ground sulfur to 100 square feet (9 sq. m) of soil. To use sulfur to lower an alkaline pH (common in western arid soils), add 1 pound (.45 kg) of ground sulfur to 100 square feet (9 sq. m) to lower pH by one

number (i.e., to change a pH of 8 to a pH of 7). Sulfur is slow to react in many soils, so the results may take several months. The finer ground sulfur will be quicker to work.

Micronutrients

Boron (B)

Function :   Cell-wall formation, carbohydrate transportation.
Contained in: Organic matter, seaweed.
Excess: Slight excess may kill plants. More common in acidic soils. Try to maintain a neutral soil to avoid excess.
Deficiency: Malformed leaf tips that may die back. Cabbage family plants develop hollow stems. Stunted heads of cauliflower and broccoli. Commonly found in soils low in organic matter.
Applying B: Correct soil pH, add organic matter (compost), foliar spray of liquid kelp or seaweed extract every 2 weeks.

Copper (Cu)

Function: Enzyme and photosynthesis regulation.
Contained in: Seaweed, kelp, manure, compost.
Excess: Rarely found. May cause iron deficiency.
Deficiency: Often the result of too much nitrogen. Leaves look bleached. Light-colored leaf veins and margins. Stunting.
Applying Cu: Apply compost to soil. Water in seaweed or kelp fertilizer every 2 weeks until symptoms disappear.

Iron (Fe)

Function: Chlorophyll formation.
Contained in: Organic matter, bonemeal, iron chelate, iron sulfate.
Excess: Darker green foliage; then turns into magnesium or zinc deficiency.
Deficiency: Yellowing between veins on newly developing

leaves. Old leaves remain green. Often due to a soil pH that is too high, poor drainage or cold soils.

Applying Fe: The quickest solution is to apply a foliar application of iron chelate (take precautions to not overapply). Blood meal or compost will provide longer-term solutions.

Manganese (Mn)

Function: Helps in photosynthesis and respiration.

Contained in: Manganese sulphate, organic matter.

Excess: Similar to deficiency: dark spots, crinkling and cupping of leaves.

Deficiency: Much like iron deficiency, but even the smallest veins remain green while all new growth turns yellow to white. Old growth remains green.

Applying Mn: Try correcting for an iron deficiency, using iron chelate; add organic matter to soil for long-term solution.

Molybdenum (Mo)

Function: Nitrogen fixation, nitrogen metabolism.

Contained in: Usually present in soil but often triggered by low pH or low organic-matter content.

Excess: Slight excess causes rapid death.

Deficiency: Stunting, similar to nitrogen deficiency, leaf may curl upward, some leaf-edge burn.

Applying Mo: Correct soil pH, common in acidic soils; add limestone or wood ash to correct deficiency.

Zinc (Zn)

Function: Chlorophyll formation, bud development.

Contained in: Zinc sulfate, organic matter.

Excess: May result in other micronutrient problems. Sometimes resembles an iron deficiency.

Deficiency: Top leaves remain very small; stunting, dwarfing. Mottled yellow leaves.

Applying Zn: Zinc deficiency is often caused by an alkaline pH. Try to correct the pH to a more normal level (near a pH of 7), and often the zinc deficiency will disappear. May also be corrected by the application of compost and zinc chelate.

FERTILIZERS

When a problem comes up, we usually reach for some type of fertilizer to help bring back health to the soil and plant. There are so many fertilizers on the market that trying to decide what type to use can be mind-boggling. All fertilizers can be classified as either synthetic or organic. There are also mixtures of the two. Let's look at some of the attributes of organic and synthetic fertilizers.

Organic fertilizers are more forgiving when you overapply because they are slower to release into the soil and are generally less concentrated. Organic fertilizers usually contain some of the micronutrients. As organic fertilizers decompose, carbon dioxide is often produced. Increased carbon dioxide levels in your enclosed winter greenhouse increase plant growth. Also, organic fertilizers promote a healthy microbial life in the soil, which helps keep many diseases in check.

The downside to organic fertilizers are few, but they do exist. First, if you need to purchase them, they can be more costly than the synthetics. If you make your own (compost) or have a cheap local source (leaf mold, composted manure), cost may not be a problem. It also takes more labor to get the organic fertilizers into your soil, often requiring that you dig it in. (Don't let this stop you. Exercise is good for you!) Organic fertilizers are also slower to work, which may be a disadvantage if you have a big problem that needs to be solved fast. In general, however, the slowness of the organic fertilizers is a good quality. All things considered, when time and ability permit, I prefer to use organic sources of fertilizers.

There are times, such as when I need a fast solution, that I find it is helpful to use a synthetic fertilizer. I particularly prefer using synthetic fertilizers with plantings in containers where the root area is limited by the constraints of a small

Fertilizers must display the percent of nitrogen, phosphorus and potassium (in that order) on the container label.

pot (i.e., growing bedding plants in small containers).

The Fertilizer Numbers Game

Whether in a bag or a box, organic or not, most all fertilizers have three analysis numbers listed somewhere on the package. It'll say something like 5-10-5 or 20-20-20. These are the percentages of nitrogen, phosphorus and potassium, in that order. It is often referred to as the NPK ratio. The letters N and P are logical, but why the letter K? It is used because K signifies potassium in the periodic table.

When you are shopping for fertilizer, read the numbers and compare. The lower the numbers, the lower the percent of the element contained in the bag. Also, the lower the number, the less you get per dollar. Generally it is a good idea to get the highest analysis for your money, as long as the analysis has a good balance. For instance, lawn food may be sold with a high percentage of nitrogen but contains very little phosphorus and potassium, not a good balance for greenhouse gardening.

Some plant foods are mixed for certain uses. Some try to encompass all uses, such as those known as general plant foods. A general plant food has all three numbers on the label either very close or identical in value, such as 20-20-20. A food chosen to promote leafy growth would have a higher percentage of nitrogen, the first number, compared to the middle and last numbers. A plant food chosen to promote flowers and fruit and help young plants get a good start would have the middle number, phosphorus, higher than the other two.

The standardization among state laws and fertilizer manufacturers requires only the listing of the three major nutrients. To find out if your fertilizer contains micronutrients or other important ingredients besides the three major ones, you will have to read the label closely. Sometimes they are mentioned, sometimes not. A call to the fertilizer company (especially if it is toll-free) could possibly tell you the exact contents.

ORGANIC SOIL AMENDMENTS

Peat Moss

Peat moss is the remains of dead plants that have partially decayed and may be hundreds of years old. Because it's often quite low in nutrients, it is not considered a fertilizer but is a great soil conditioner. It increases soil aeration and water absorption and helps the soil hold other nutrients in an available state for plant roots to use. Some peat moss may have fertilizer added to it. The label will tell you if that is the case. Peat moss is the major ingredient of most commercially available potting soils because it is lightweight (cheap to ship) and holds water well.

Most of the world's peat moss now comes from Canada. There is also what is called mountain peat, which usually comes from the mountainous bogs of the United States, and you may see some originating in other countries. Canadian peat tends to have a very acidic pH, which is good for alkaline soils. The mountain peat from the United States is closer to neutral pH and more soillike in consistency. Peat moss is sold in different grades, depending on its degree of decomposition and how fine the particles are.

Peat moss is a good soil amendment, particularly if your soil is low in organic matter. As much as 20 percent of your soil's total volume can be peat moss. Excess peat may cause an acidic reaction, and you will have to add wood ash or lime to bring the soil up to a neutral point. Excess peat or organic matter can also cause your soil to become waterlogged.

Dry peat moss is hard to moisten and may need to be premoistened with warm water prior to mixing it into the soil. Commercial potting mixes that contain peat moss often have an added wetting agent that makes the peat moss easier to moisten.

Peat moss is extracted much like a mineral is mined. It is a renewable resource. Some claim that the supplies of peat moss are being depleted. But the Canadian peat harvesters claim that more than 10 times as much peat moss forms each year than is harvested in their country. In some countries, peat is burned as a fuel for heat and cooking. Many researchers are testing alternatives to peat, including compost and decomposed wood fibers. Peat is somewhat more expensive than other organic soil conditioners.

Manure

Manure is both a soil conditioner and a fertilizer. Because of its high content of soluble salts, it can also cause plant burning. Manure should never be applied fresh. Always compost it for 1 year or more. Impatient? Check your local farm. Someone will have some well-aged manure.

Manures vary greatly in nutrient content. The age and the type of manure create many variables. This makes it almost impossible to know how strong it is. As a rule, the older the manure, the less nutrient value, but even old manure makes a good soil conditioner (for poor soils). Rabbit and poultry manure are about twice as rich as that of horses, cows and pigs. Sheep and goats sit somewhere between the two.

It's hard to give accurate recommendations for application, because even the same type of manure may vary a great deal. But I'll do it anyway.

Manure is not very suitable for pots and containers, as it is too easy to cause burning. Generally, I use manure only in soil beds. First, do a soil test to be sure that your soil needs fertilizing. In soil beds that are at least 18 inches (46 cm) deep, I add no more than 1 inch (2.5 cm) of well-composted manure (half that amount for chicken or rabbit manure). Blend it thoroughly into the existing soil to prevent hot spots. If the manure is made up of large clods, try to break it up prior to applying it. There's nothing like the smell of manure (or a fresh application of fish emulsion) in the greenhouse to make everyone else wonder if you have truly lost your mind over this greenhouse gardening stuff.

Manure is usually higher in nitrogen than phosphorus or potassium. Farm manure may also contain weed seeds. You may want to look into the addition of some other materials to compensate here if your soil test shows a need.

Manure Teas

Manure tea is made by simply infusing water with a source of manure. Prepare an old bucket to hold the manure. Take a nail and hammer, and poke hundreds of holes in the bottom and sides of the bucket. Set the "holy" bucket full of manure into another bucket of water for a few hours. Remove the manure bucket and your tea is ready. It is primarily a source of nitrogen and can be absorbed through the leaf as well as the root. Avoid getting it on the foliage of edible crops. As you might have guessed, it doesn't smell great. If it is flavor you want, try Lipton.

Sewage Sludge

Many cities sell their sludge in a dried and bagged form. One of the most famous is Milwaukee's Milorganite. Cities vary in their treatment and content of human waste. Some noncommercial sludge may need to be composted before using. Talk to your sewer plant operators about the contents of their sludge. In general, sewage sludge is not recommended for use on vegetables, although the country of China would never feed itself if this were its public policy. If you fear some may have mixed into your food-growing soil, I wouldn't worry too much. As should be a common practice with homegrown or store-bought fruits and veggies, you should always wash your produce before eating.

Sludges in some cities may contain toxic heavy metals. A common one is cadmium, which doesn't leach out of the soil and can be taken up by plants. It has been found that plants take up heavy metals easiest when the soil's pH is acidic (usually below 6.8 pH). That is another reason to maintain a soil pH around 7, or neutral.

Leaf Mold

Leaf mold is simply composted leaves. It is very high in micronutrients and is a great soil conditioner. It is not very high in the major fertilizer elements, such as nitrogen, phosphorus and potassium, but does contain enough to increase soil fertility. Use well-rotted leaves as you would peat moss. As with peat moss, an excess of leaf mold may cause a high level of acidity. I make leaf mold in a trench with a light sprinkling of manure and occasional watering to maintain moisture. You can also make it in a mound as you would a compost pile. Let it sit 12 months or more for it to properly age, like a good wine.

Fish Emulsion

Fish emulsion is high in nitrogen, with a nitrogen-phosphorus-potassium (NPK) ratio of 4-1-1. It is often treated with sulfur or phosphoric acid to inhibit bacterial growth. Fish emulsion has an incredibly strong smell. Many manufacturers claim that their fish emulsion is deodorized. This means that it smells only slightly better. Fortunately, the smell goes away after a day or two. Many plant researchers feel that there is more than just a nutrient value in fish emulsion when applied to plants. Recent research confirms that fish emulsion seems to have a positive effect on plant growth and increases the overall health of the plant, although no one can explain exactly why. Maybe it contains special enzymes, micronutrients or just plain old magic.

Fish emulsion can be absorbed through both the root and the leaf. Generally, it is applied at a rate of 4 tablespoons per gallon (3.8 l) and either sprayed onto the crop or watered into the soil. See the label for more specifics.

Bonemeal

Bonemeal contains mostly phosphorus, with some calcium and a trace of nitrogen. It slowly releases its nutrients in alkaline soils but is a good choice in acidic or neutral soils. It contains 10 to 12 percent phosphorus. Add 1 pound (.45 kg) per 10 square feet (.9 sq. m) of soil. Bonemeal is sold in either steamed or raw forms. The steamed form is faster acting.

Sawdust

Sawdust can work as a soil conditioner, but it ties up much of the soil nitrogen until it becomes a composted part of the soil. This is because to break down raw sawdust, soil organisms steal the soil's nitrogen that is used by plants. The organisms grab the nitrogen right out from under the poor plant's roots, often leaving plants with a nitrogen deficiency. To prevent this, add compost, manure, fish emulsion or some other additional source of nitrogen along with the sawdust. It would even be better to wait and add sawdust only after it has been composted along with some other nitrogen sources. Avoid using sawdust from cedar, redwood or walnut. They contain chemicals that inhibit the growth of other plants.

Wood Ash

Wood ash is added to soils to raise a low pH and to add small amounts of calcium, potassium, phosphorus, magnesium and sulfur. The exact amounts of these minerals is variable and hard to determine. Ash is used mainly to move an acid soil toward neutral because of its alkalizing effect. Wood ash is about two-thirds as effective as ground limestone in raising a low (acid) pH. If you live in arid areas where high pH soil (alkaline soil) is a common problem or have a soil pH above 7, you should avoid using ash altogether. If you have an acid soil below 7, then it might be worthwhile. Wood ash is commonly added at a rate of 1 pound (.45 kg) per 10 square feet (.9 sq. m) of soil. Try to avoid using wood ash to adjust the pH more than once every 3 years, as it can cause an excess potassium level in the soil, which can cause other imbalances.

Wood ash spread around the base of plants can also keep slugs at bay. Coal ash is not good for soil or plants and should never be added to soil.

Blood Meal

Blood meal is basically a nitrogen fertilizer but also contains some small amounts of phosphorus. The NPK ratio is generally 10-0-0. I have also seen blood meal help with iron deficiencies. It is on the expensive side when compared to other fertilizers. It is generally added at a rate of 1/2 pound (.2 kg) per 10 square feet (.9 sq. m) of soil, or follow label instructions.

Compost

Composting is a great way to deal with plant wastes. It can be an excellent soil conditioner because it is pure decomposed organic matter. There is enough written in most gardening books on com-

Finished compost provides an excellent soil conditioner.

posting procedures. More and more you can find commercially available compost, but nothing solves your home garbage problems like a home compost pile.

If you are having problems with diseases and use a lot of homemade compost, try to break any potential disease cycles that occur. Do this by using only greenhouse plant waste in the outside garden and outside plant wastes in the greenhouse. This may mean that you need two separate piles. Having parallel composting will help break up possible disease infestations.

Many people attempt to compost inside the greenhouse. I don't recommend this for the following reasons: If you don't know what you are doing, it may start to smell. It is a waste of precious greenhouse space. Greenhouses should be used either for growing things or for relaxation (often this is one and the same). You can compost outside.

Yes, as mentioned in previous chapters, compost creates carbon dioxide, which helps plants grow, but you can get the same results from using compost in your soil mix and as a mulch (see Chapter 1, The Greenhouse Environment, for more information).

The recommendations for using compost in greenhouse/sunroom growing beds is to add 1 inch (2.5 cm) of compost dug into the top 6 to 8 inches (15 to 20 cm). Renew the beds with additional compost when you are planting new crops or every 6 months or so. It can also be used as a mulch by laying a thin layer of compost on the soil surface.

INORGANIC SOIL AMENDMENTS

Sand

Sand is basically ground rock. It contains no real fertilizing ingredients, although it may help provide some minerals. Sand is usually added to the soil to help drainage and aeration and will greatly aid soils high in clay. Sands vary in pH depending upon the parent material. Ocean sand should be avoided because of its high salt content. Planting beds in greenhouses should always be on the sandy side to promote good drainage, which is needed for most crops.

Perlite

Perlite is used for the same reason as sand: to promote drainage and help provide aeration. Perlite is a very lightweight white particle that is often mixed into commercial potting mixes. It is mined as an ore, then heated until it expands like popcorn. Perlite has no nutrient value and has a neutral pH. It is a good material to root cuttings in.

Precautions should be taken when pouring pure perlite into a soil mix because it generates much dust, which can easily irritate the lungs. It helps to moisten the perlite before you mix it. Wearing a protective dust mask over your nose and mouth is a good idea.

When plants are heavily watered and are growing in a soil that contains perlite, you may see some of the small white particles floating up to the top of the pot.

Rock Phosphate

Rock phosphate is a ground mineral that is primarily calcium phosphate. It is roughly 30 percent phosphorus. It is a very slow-release material but is good for providing long-term phosphorus reserves in the soil. It is generally added at around 5 pounds (2 kg) per 100 square feet (9 sq. m) of soil.

Super Phosphate

This is basically rock phosphate that has been treated with an acid to speed its reaction in the soil. As a result, super phosphate is faster-acting on plants. There is some worry that initially super phosphate can have a very acidic reaction in the soil. It is recommended that super phosphate be mixed in evenly and thoroughly. Super phosphate is 20 percent phosphorus and should be added at the rate of 5 pounds (2 kg) per 100 square feet (9 sq. m) of soil.

Colloidal Phosphate

This is a clay product that is high in phosphorus. It contains about 2 percent phosphorus, so it is not very concentrated but is quicker in its availability to roots than rock phosphate or bonemeal. It is usually applied at 5 pounds (2 kg) per 100 square feet (9 sq. m) of soil. It also contains some small amounts of potassium and other minerals.

Vermiculite

This micatype mineral is similar to perlite. It, too, is mined, heated and expanded. Each silver-colored piece looks like a miniature accordion. Unlike perlite, vermiculite can hold water (up to 300 percent by weight). And much like organic matter, it has the ability to hold some nutrients in the soil for plant roots. It also helps the soil resist changes in pH, and, like sand, it improves drainage. It is a common ingredient in commercially available potting mixes.

Vermiculite contains potassium, magnesium and calcium, but they are in such small quantities that it is not considered a fertilizer. You should use only horticultural-grade vermiculite. It's available at greenhouse and garden supply stores and catalogs. Construction-grade vermiculite, used for roof insulation, should not be used in soils, because it is often coated with small amounts of oil that may be harmful to young roots.

Over time, vermiculite can wear out and collapse, losing many of its inherent benefits as a result.

Gypsum

Gypsum is used to lower a high pH and to improve drainage. It will help improve clay soils by loosening them. It also contains calcium and sulfur. Gypsum is usually applied at the rate of 4 pounds (1.8 kg) per 100 square feet (9 sq. m) of soil.

Epsom Salts

Epsom salts are good not just for soaking your feet. They can also be used as a fertilizer, supplying magnesium and sulfur, because Epsom salt is actually magnesium sulfate. The sulfur can help alkaline soils become more acidic. It is usually applied at the rate of 1 pound (.45 kg) per 100 square feet (9 sq. m) of soil. Do not just randomly apply Epsom salts, unless a soil test shows that you need to reduce the pH or your soil is low in magnesium. Overapplication can cause problems with other soil nutrients.

Limestone

Ground limestone is commonly used to raise a low soil pH. There are two main types of limestone used in soils: calcitic and dolomitic. Dolomitic limestone contains magnesium, which can be helpful if your soil test shows that you are low in magnesium.

The amount required to raise the pH one unit is approximately 1 pound (.45 kg) per 20 square feet (1.8 sq. m) of soil. Sandy, well-drained soils need less limestone to alter the pH. Clay soils may need more. It can take a few weeks before the reaction that changes the pH is fully complete, so wait at least 2 weeks and then recheck the pH. Take care not to overapply, because it can cause problems with other nutrients as well as increasing the pH too much. If you are using dolomitic limestone and overapply, you may end up with an excess of magnesium, which can cause poor calcium uptake and injure the structure of the soil. Talk to an agricultural extension agent about the particular characteristic of your local soil if you are adding limestone to correct native soil used in a growing bed.

OTHER SOIL AMENDMENTS

Chelated Micronutrients

Deficiencies of copper, iron, magnesium, manganese and zinc are sometimes not deficiencies at all, but just a problem of pH not allowing the element to be taken up. Chelation is a process that attaches these elements to other molecules, which allows the roots to take up the element, even in poor soil conditions. Chelated micronutrients can be absorbed directly through the foliage when the liquid is sprayed on the leaf. They can quickly correct a deficiency and will last longer in the plant than many other solutions. The most common use of a chelate is iron chelate. As with any fertil-

izer, overapplication can cause big problems. This is especially true for micronutrients, so follow the label closely.

Chelated micronutrients are not the easiest material to find but are sometimes available at garden centers and can also be found through garden and greenhouse supply catalogs. They are more expensive than other fertilizers, but when they work, they are well worth it.

An alternative to using chelated micronutrients is to try a liquid kelp spray for supplying a good balance of micronutrients to the plant.

Water-Absorbing Polymers

New to the arena of soil amendments are what are known as water-absorbing polymers. They are irregular-shaped plasticlike granules that swell many times their size and hold up to 500 times their own weight in water (talk about thirsty!). Besides water, they can also absorb soluble minerals and nutrients. Roots readily grow into these jellylike blobs and can easily extract water and nutrients from the polymers. Polymers last up to 5 years, and manufacturers claim they eventually break down into harmless water, carbon dioxide and traces of ammonia.

These polymers are chemically known as polyacrylamides and have the potential to replace the need for other water-absorbing materials in a soil mix, such as peat moss. These polymers have been rated nontoxic by the EPA. They are gaining popularity among commercial growers, who often add them to soil mixes or potted plants to help the plants survive dry periods better. They are available from many garden catalogs. Follow the label recommendation for application rates.

ROOT STIMULANTS AND MIRACLE PRODUCTS

For many years, there have been products claiming to reduce transplant shock. One of the most common is a product that contains a synthetic hormone called indolebutyric acid and vitamin B1. I have seen this product help, but it wasn't a great help. It would be advisable to use this material only when you are worried about the transplanting of a very valuable plant. As with anything you put in the soil, more is not better. Follow the directions exactly.

There are always new so-called miracle products on the market that make incredible claims about boosting plant growth or soil fertil-

ity. Please view all of these products with a healthy amount of skepticism. Only a few actually do any good. A good indication of a scam is when there is no listing of an active ingredient. The company that sells the so-called miracle product should also be able to supply you with a list of independently generated research data validating its claim. Always use any miracle product in limited areas so you can compare the result with a nontreated area.

FOLIAR FEEDING

As mentioned earlier, an advantage to using chemical fertilizers is that they are quick-acting. What many people don't know is that plants not only take fertilizer up through their roots but can also absorb nutrients through the leaf. Foliar feeding is incredibly fast, and it is not limited to synthetic fertilizers. You can also use manure teas or fish emulsion, both of which are organic fertilizers. With foliar feeding, it is just a matter of getting the liquefied material on the leaves with a watering can, fertilizer siphon (found in many garden and greenhouse supply catalogs) or sprayer. When using synthetic chemicals or fish-emulsion fertilizer as a foliar spray, cut the label's recommended rate for dilution in half, then apply with a watering can or fertilizer siphon.

Do not use manure teas on leafy vegetables. Because you can get a buildup of nitrates in an edible leaf that can be slightly toxic in cooler temperatures, it is a good idea to minimize the use of foliar feeding on all leafy vegetables (avoid it altogether in winter months). Thoroughly wash the leaves before consuming. All other plants are fair game for foliar feeding.

THE EFFECT OF SOIL TEMPERATURE ON FERTILIZER UPTAKE

Cool soil temperatures are common in winter greenhouses and sunrooms. Since this slows the uptake of nitrogen by plants, it can create a reservoir of nitrogen that might be released in excess amounts as the temperature warms up in spring. For this reason, it is important to not overapply nitrogen in the cooler months of winter. Always fertilize in moderation, but be especially careful in the winter.

As mentioned in Chapter 4, Selecting the Right Plants, leafy vegetables such as spinach, chard and lettuce grown in a cool winter greenhouse can accumulate high

levels of nitrate, which can be dangerous to infants and pose potential health problems to children and adults. The nitrate is taken up by the roots from the soil. When there is adequate light and heat, the nitrate is a beneficial fertilizer that is quickly converted into plant proteins. When there are low light levels in the greenhouse, accompanied by cool temperatures, the nitrate is not converted into protein and instead accumulates in the leaf. The nitrate accumulation increases when the soil is rich in nitrogen.

According to research done by the New Alchemy Institute, nitrate levels are highest in crops harvested near the winter solstice. Levels were much lower on crops harvested in the warmer, sunnier month of March. See Nitrate in the Cool Winter Greenhouse (p. 125) for guidelines on avoiding a buildup of nitrate in your leafy vegetables.

MAINTAINING SOIL FERTILITY IN BEDS

When you are growing plants in beds year-round, you will need to put something back to make up for what you harvest and for what the plant itself takes from the soil. When you are growing perennial plants that stay in the same location for many years, it is almost impossible to remove or replace any of the soil with compost, amendments or new, rich soil. What you can do is water in nutrients that may be needed as indicated by the plant. Better yet, using the information provided by a soil test, you can add a suitable fertilizer to the top of the soil to correct a possible problem. In greenhouses, this feeding is usually needed a minimum of twice a year, but many plants may be heavy feeders and need feeding every few weeks, depending upon the conditions.

Fertilizer for plants growing in beds may be applied in a liquid form that is watered in or a granular or composted material dug into the top few inches of the soil. As mentioned earlier, I prefer the regular addition of organic components because they release their fertilizer elements more slowly, over a longer period. They also have the added benefit of giving off carbon dioxide, which feeds the plants through the air.

It is very helpful to rework the soil prior to planting in the beds. Usually I apply 1 inch (2.5 cm) of compost to the soil surface and dig it into the first 6 inches (15 cm). (If the bed is full, I may have to remove some of the soil to make room for the compost.) At least yearly, I add a phosphorus fertilizer to the soil and regularly feed the plants with a foliar spray of fish emulsion. In the cold parts of winter, because of the slower growth and cooler greenhouse temperatures, it is best to stop using the fish emulsion or other nitrogen fertilizers to prevent a nitrate buildup, at least until your greenhouse warms up. In heated greenhouses, this is not as much of a concern.

MAINTAINING SOIL FERTILITY IN POTS

When plants are growing in containers, maintaining soil fertility can be a bit more tricky. Because of the nature of a container, there is less of a dynamic soil ecology occurring. For this reason, it is harder to keep the soil healthy. With potting soil, the health of the plant is directly tied to the health of the soil.

Sterile Soil

People often ask if they should sterilize all of their soil (as explained in Chapter 5, Plant Propagation) for both pots and beds in order to kill all potential disease and weed seeds in the dirt. Yes,

Enriching the soil between crops helps create a healthier growing environment.

you can sterilize your own potting soil, but it is much easier to just purchase a good commercial potting soil mix. Virgin store-bought soil mixes are usually sterilized. To sterilize all of your soil in a large growing bed is virtually impossible, unless you have a commercial greenhouse and the equipment.

Killing the diseases in the soil is usually needed most for growing seedlings. That is the only time to use sterile soil. After the seedling is up and going, it can usually tolerate the real world, complete with soil diseases. In beds, it is easy to keep soil diseases to a minimum.

Keep your soil healthy by regularly adding organic matter in the way of compost, peat moss and the like. The good microbes that break down the organic materials in the soil also prey upon the bad soil organisms that cause trouble to your plants. It is not foolproof in preventing soil diseases, but neither is sterilized soil.

MAKING POTTING SOIL

If you need only a small amount of potting soil for only a few pots, it is generally much easier and better to purchase a bag of commercial potting soil. Maybe add a little soil and compost to it if the plant will be growing in it for many years. If you are going to need large quantities, it is still hard to beat the economics of commercially available potting soil. But many will still wish to make their own.

Unless you need a specialty potting soil for specific types of plants such as cactus, orchids or the like, a good potting soil must be well drained while at the same time able to hold at least some water. Almost every commercial greenhouse has its own special recipe. Most potting soils include three equal parts: soil, an organic material to act like a sponge and a material to help promote drainage.

Recipe for Potting Soil

Instead of using only garden soil for your containers, you can make your own. A good potting soil must be well drained and at the same time able to hold at least some water. Almost every commercial greenhouse has its own special recipe. Most potting soils include three equal parts: soil, an organic material to act like a sponge and a material to help promote drainage. Here is a recipe:

1 Part Soil	1 Part Organic Material	1 Part Drainage Material
Rich top soil	Peat moss, leaf mold or screened compost	Sand, vermiculite or perlite

Mix well in a tub, soil bench or wheelbarrow. Do not use ocean beach sand, because it is high in salts and hard on plants. If you live in an area with acid soil and regularly have to add limestone to the soil, then you should add about 1 tablespoon of ground limestone per 1/2 gallon (1.9 l) of soil to adjust it toward a neutral pH. (A home or professional soil test will tell you the pH.) For more-tropical houseplants, you may want to add a bit more peat moss for more acidity and water-holding capacity. For cactus and succulents, add more sand for faster draining. Sterilize any homemade soil mix to be used for germinating seeds (see Chapter 5, Plant Propagation).

Customizing the Recipe

Over the years, I have played with this recipe and found that it is only as good as your base soil. If your soil is poor or has some troublesome idiosyncrasies, it can become a problem. I often end up tinkering with the recipe to compensate for a poor top soil. If this is the case, try adding a higher proportion of the organic and drainage components at the expense of the soil in the recipe. If the base soil is high in clay and tends to hold water excessively, try to increase the drainage component. In cases where only very acidic soils are available, try to lessen the soil component, avoid the use of peat moss and leaf mold altogether and increase the use of vermiculite, sand and compost. Where the soil is highly alkaline, try to increase the use of peat moss at the expense of both soil and the drainage component. If your top soil is chunky, you may want to screen it to get a better blend. You can make a cheap screen for screening compost and soil by stretching some hardware cloth across some two-by-twos.

As you have probably gathered, soil-mix recipes are not set in stone and require a bit of experimenting before you end up with the perfect mix for your soil and plants.

Soilless Potting Mixes

More and more commercial potting soils are what are known as soilless mixes and contain absolutely no soil whatsoever. They are primarily made up of peat moss, vermiculite and perlite. They also may contain some starter fertilizer to help the plants get established and a wetting agent that makes the mix absorb water better. These mixes are lightweight but hold water like a sponge. Soilless mixes have the advantage of being sterile, which makes them good for starting seedlings. When used for growing plants for many months, the soilless mixes usually perform well. After a year or more, they can begin to get more acidic and compacted. The plants may begin to show signs of stress.

For potted plants in trouble you might try repotting with some beefed-up soilless mix. Try adding

10 percent dark healthy top soil and 10 percent well-decomposed compost. This mix will help plants showing signs of stress and will usually put them in a better mood. Do not do this to store-bought potting mixes to be used for seed germination, because the mix is no longer sterile when you add unsterilized soil to it.

Just the name "soilless" sounds like gardener's blasphemy, but even without adding soil to these mixes, you can get good results. Wait and see what happens before you try any additions to store-bought soil for plants growing in pots.

FERTILIZING PLANTS IN CONTAINERS

It is hard to add compost to a large plant growing in a large container, but it can be done. It is far easier to deal with containerized plantings by adding liquid fertilizers as needed. Fertilizers such as fish emulsion, seaweed, or chemical houseplant foods that are mixed with water can help keep a potted plant happy. When using chemical houseplant foods, try to find one that contains some level of micronutrients if possible. Look for iron or zinc on the ingredient label. Peters, Rapid-gro and DynaGro

have fertilizer products that contain micronutrients. Follow the label on the product, and try to use a NPK ratio that is compatible with the plant you are growing. Some manufacturers make this easy by offering plant foods specifically for certain potted plants, such as African violet plant food and orchid plant food. Repotting a plant with fresh soil mix can also be a good way to maintain fertility for a potted plant.

Slow-Release Fertilizers for Pots

A common characteristic of chemical fertilizers is that they are usually fast-working and fast-disappearing. They often move with the water and, in the case of large farming and even commercial greenhouse operations, have been found responsible for polluting groundwater. This is not only a waste of good fertilizer but a preventable source of pollution. Over the years, the makers of synthetic fertilizers have tried to emulate the slow-release quality that is inherent with organic fertilizers. They have come up with many products that are better for the environment and the plants.

One common slow-release fertilizer for potted plants is called

REPOTTING SEQUENCE

Step One

Step Two

Step Three

Step Four

Step Five

When plants become rootbound or the soil seems to be causing problems, it is time to repot. Never repot into a container more than 4 inches larger than the original pot.

General Trends in Crop Needs

Different crops have different needs. Because most of you can't (or won't) do a test every few months to keep abreast of what is going on, sometimes it is helpful to get a handle on what certain plants need. Here are some generalizations.

1. Crops grown in summer will need more nutrients, especially more phosphorus.
2. Winter crops can get by with fewer total nutrients.
3. Squash, cucumber and melon crops are heavy feeders and need about 20 percent more nitrogen than most other crops.
4. Tomato crops respond well to slightly lower nitrogen and higher phosphorus applications.
5. Peas, beans and flowers respond to lower amounts of nitrogen and steady levels of phosphorus.
6. Plants in small containers will benefit from more-frequent but diluted feeding than plants grown in larger containers.
7. Avoid fertilizing germinating seedlings. Very young plants should have only very diluted fertilization (cut the label recommendation in half or more until the plant is more mature).

Osmocote Potting Mix Plant Food, or more simply Osmocote. One application can feed your plants for up to 9 months. The little BB-sized spheres containing fertilizer leak over time, through the process of osmosis, and the fertilizer doesn't seem to cause burning, a common problem in slow-release fertilizers.

There are other types of sticks, plant food stakes and tabs, which can be inserted into the pots of plants, but I have found that they can burn the plant's roots.

The slow-release fertilizers work well for a potted plant that is in healthy shape and is not in need of a "quick fix." Whatever you end up using, please don't overapply. (I know that I say that a lot in this chapter. That's because a lot of people routinely overapply fertilizers. People are plants' best friends and worst enemies.)

The slow-release fertilizers can also be used for plants growing in beds.

USING MULCHES IN A GREENHOUSE

All good outside gardeners know the incredible benefits of applying a mulch. It reduces weeds, conserves moisture and helps the overall health of the plant. In a greenhouse, you get all of the above benefits as well as one other. It helps increase the level of carbon dioxide in the winter air (when the greenhouse is more sealed to the outside).

After some extensive trials with mulches, I have found that there is only one problem, unfortunately, a big problem. Mulching in greenhouses greatly increases soil-dwelling pests. Problems with fungus gnats, slugs, sow bugs and pill bugs increase tremendously. These are all pests that are difficult to control and create a new set of problems (for more information on these pests, see Chapter 10, When Things Go Wrong). It can also cause you to overwater easier. So for these reasons, I would recommend that in greenhouse beds and even in large pots, tubs and containers, you go slow on using mulches.

WILL HYDROPONICS SAVE THE WORLD?

I always smile when people ask me about using hydroponics and mispronounce it as "hydrophonics." I'm not sure what hydrophonics is (water music?), but a lot of people are talking about it. Still, I know what people mean, and I give them my biased opinion of hydroponics, which I am about to give you. (Hydrophonics does sound like fun to me—grab the waterproof guitar!) You should also know that this is not the book to buy if you are absolutely interested in learning how to set up a hydroponic system. There are many complete books on the subject that would suit you better as well as numerous manufacturers who sell all of the stuff you will need (get your wallet ready) and who are helpful in the instruction of using hydroponics as a growing medium.

In hydroponics, plants are grown without soil, using water-soluble nutrient solutions. Usually the plant roots are grown in all kinds of (usually inert) material, such as sand, gravel, rock wool and even sawdust. The plants are watered with special fertilizer solutions, supplying all of their needs.

Hydroponics has a space-age, high-tech reputation, and as a result, many people assume that it creates phenomenal yields. This belief is further perpetuated by the many manufacturers that sell all of the things required to do hydroponics. While hydroponics can be set up in a simple manner, it lends itself to being what I call capital intensive.

Despite the widespread belief that hydroponics is a new, modern technique, it has actually been practiced for more than 80 years. Only in recent history has it become more popular, as labor prices increase and fertilizer prices decrease. The belief that hydroponics is a yield enhancer is based upon the premise that the limiting factor in yields is fertilizer. This is an incorrect assumption. In fact, fertilizer is rarely the limiting factor in controlling plant growth. Usually, it is light, temperature or carbon dioxide. Fertilization is way down the list. Most experts agree that yields will be much the same in a soil-based culture when compared with hydroponics. There are many advantages to hydroponics, but it probably won't solve the world's food problems or save us from ourselves.

Advantages of Hydroponic Gardening

So, why hydroponics? The absolute main advantage is that it can be easily automated, which saves labor. This is great if you are in the commercial greenhouse business, because labor is a major expense, if not the biggest expense. It takes a lot of money to set up a commercial system. However, in the long run, it may be a profitable way to go.

What are some of the other advantages to using a hydroponic system? Hydroponics enables more-creative potting designs. For example, using a vertical plastic pipe with a number of holes drilled into the length and filled with perlite enables growing lettuce plants in each hole up and down the pipe. The so-called aeroponics or aerohydroponics uses no pot or root medium. The nutrient solution is just misted onto the roots of the plants, which are anchored at the stem to a support. This is the kind of thing you see at Epcot or a NASA demonstration (see Epilogue). However, I believe that we will probably end up taking our old-fashioned soil with us when we take our farms to the stars because of the need to establish whole ecosystems that support life.

Hydroponics also has the advantage of eliminating most of the need to weed and cultivate. But I spend probably only a few minutes a month weeding in my soil-based greenhouse.

Disadvantages of Hydroponic Gardening

As long as I am giving you my biased view of the advantages, I might as well proceed to the disadvantages. First, hydroponics will make you inseparably tied to a fertilizer manufacturer or supplier because it is hard to manufacture hydroponic plant fertilizer at home. You'll always end up buying the stuff, which takes away the feeling of self-sufficiency (a feeling that I treasure). Soil is a very forgiving medium. If you overapply something, such as a fertilizer, soil has the ability to absorb it and buffer much of the abuse before you (or your plants) are affected. Hydroponics, on the other hand, is an exacting practice. If you overapply your fertilizer, you will be immediately affected. Hydroponics doesn't tolerate mistakes very well at all. A minor problem with hydroponics is that with a nonsoil medium, there is little if any generation of carbon dioxide, which is beneficial to the plants.

It is hard for hydroponics to adjust when you are growing a lot of different plants. I like to grow many different plants in a greenhouse, such as tropicals, cut flowers, salad crops, fruits, succulents, ornamentals and herbs. It is almost impossible for one type of fertilizer to supply the diverse needs of diverse plants. One plant needs higher nitrogen, while another needs more phosphorus. Hydroponics makes planting a diverse greenhouse that much more difficult.

One of the main problems that I have with hydroponics is that it requires so much equipment—at least that's what the manufacturers want you to believe. They'll claim you'll need pumps, timers, soilless mediums, special tubs, special enzymes, reflectors and, because there is no carbon dioxide generated (as in a soil system), a CO_2 generator. Of course, you must purchase some fertilizer too. This can really get expensive when you add it all up. But you don't have to have an exotic system, and you can make a relatively simple design, using what is known as the ebb-and-flow system, with a simple pump. This is where you have a reservoir (for fertilizer), a timer and an irrigation line with emitters feeding into growing containers. The timer will periodically trigger the pump to water the plants with the nutrient system, which sets below the plants. After the plants have been watered (with the solution), the fertilizer drains back down into the reservoir. You can eliminate the timer and the pump if you are willing to lift the reservoir filled with the solution to a height above the plants. This drains the solution into the pots or containers. The solution will need to fill the pots at least two to three times a day, and the nutrient solution should be changed once a week.

There are many variables in going about doing a hydroponic system. After you thoroughly understand what is involved—and that you really can't expect higher yields—I think that the less glamorous soil-based plant growing methods will begin to look appealing. If automation is what you are really after, then it can be done just as easily with a soil-based system, using automatic watering and venting. It is easy to set up a system that will allow you to leave your greenhouse unattended for a few days.

In conclusion, hydroponics is good for people who are curious about automation. It is especially suited for commercial growers with high labor costs. It works particularly well when you are growing only one crop on a commercial basis.

A WAY TO APPROACH WORKING WITH SOIL

Soil is forgiving, and I may make this all sound like such a science. The study of soils is a science, but working with soil is more akin to baking a cake or making a casserole. If you're like me, you rarely follow a recipe to a T. Besides, that is how all of the world's best dishes are made. When you approach working with the soil, don't be afraid to experiment. Get your hands dirty! You're not building a watch. Things just happen. Sometimes you should just let things happen. People get too serious about soil, and view it as a win/lose chemistry experiment. Because soil is forgiving, you rarely lose as long as you heed this final advice: When it comes to the soil, moderation is always the best course to follow.

When
Things Go
Wrong

10

CHAPTER 10

When Things Go Wrong

When your first plant dies or you discover your first bug infestation, you realize that plants and the ecology you have created won't always do as you wish.

Joan Loitz, a solar greenhouse pioneer who has written and taught extensively on greenhouse pest control, likes to say that all new greenhouses go through a honeymoon period. She is so right. It usually takes 2 to 8 months before the first pest or disease attacks occur. Just when you start to get cocky about how pest-free things are, watch out. From then on, it will be constant excitement, with a few new pests or diseases regularly finding a way to prevent boredom in your greenhouse. Some will be easy to deal with while others will be quite challenging.

Where do you start when things go wrong? You have three options. You can fight the problems with a warlike extermination attitude (which I have heard some people call the S.A.S. method: see and spray). You can let it all "go to hell in a hand basket," allowing the pests and diseases to run rampant. Or you can manage the problems that come up ecologically, trying to create new balances and micro-environments to produce the desired result ... namely food and flowers.

The first step when things go wrong is to learn to look at the plants growing in your greenhouse or sunroom. Yes, I know you think you are looking at your plants, but I mean really look! It is surprisingly easy to look and not see. Real looking is best done at a relaxing time, when you can look at the tone and texture of the green in the leaf or the shine of the plants. Look at the tips of the plants, look under the leaves, look at the soil, look in the nooks and crannies. We are talking about some intensive looking. To enable you to look even better, it is helpful to have a hand lens or magnifying glass. You can purchase a hand lens for very little money. They are commonly available at a power of 10x. I have found hand lenses in college bookstores (because they are often used in labs), scientific supply houses and even some office supply stores. If you like gizmos and have big pockets, there is a fat Swiss army knife that has a built-in hand lens among the knife blades. The knife is perfect for looking at leaves as well as for pruning plants. I highly recommend it; I feel naked when I'm without my knife.

While you are looking, don't just look at the plants near the aisle. Get back in there to those plants in back—that is where many problems begin. Make a point to look around your greenhouse or sunroom on a regular basis. I like to do it before my day gets going, walking around the greenhouse with my coffee cup in one hand and my hand lens in the other. Check out the Record-Keeping appendix for a record sheet that may be helpful in keeping track of pest populations.

Greenhouse problems are caused by an organism (disease, insect or human), the environment (heat, light, soil) or combinations of both. It can get mighty complex. It is my hope to simplify it for you. The true time to learn is when things go wrong. The plan is to minimize those experiences by learning about what to do when things go wrong so that for the most part, things will go right!

WHAT TO DO?

Who would read a chapter titled When Things Go Wrong until things actually go wrong? Writing about pests and diseases could be such a glum subject, and in some ways it is. But I actually have as much fun controlling the pests and diseases as I do growing the plants. Before you decide I'm off my rocker, let me tell you why. Ever since I discovered that you can use good bugs to control the bad bugs, along with occasional safe sprays, it has been more like growing a well-balanced ecology than just an extermination job. Yes, I have had some good failures in controlling bugs (that's one way to learn this stuff). But the successes are many and are as much an accomplishment as growing the most difficult plant.

I don't expect you to read this chapter from beginning to end (although you are welcome to). Rather, I assume that you will be referring to it as problems arise. Some sections should be read even before you have problems. It would be a good idea to get acquainted with our cast of the pests and learn about their modi operandi before you find yourself face to face with them. It is also a good idea to look at the common diseases that afflict plants. Take note of the idiosyncrasies in the environment that promote these pests and diseases. This can help prevent many future problems.

When problems do arise, you will be looking for solutions. This chapter has a lot of possible solutions. There may be many potential solutions to a given problem. I have made an effort to provide what I call "biologically sane" types of solutions to greenhouse pests and diseases.

How do you decide which solution to use? With controlling bugs, you must first decide if you want to take the route of extermination, using relatively low toxicity types of sprays (such as insecticidal soaps), or develop an ecology of good bugs working to control populations of bad bugs. The choices are simple after you decide.

When it comes to diseases, you will need to decide either to use preventative types of controls or to alter the environment, the plant, the timing or the location to gain control. In the case of diseases, you can mix both types of regimens. Unlike with insect problems, you can rarely spray a diseased plant back to health.

CAUSES AND EFFECTS

One thing you will learn as you garden in a greenhouse is that pests and diseases don't just happen. There are causes and effects. For instance, too much nitrogen in the soil causes soft, lush growth, which in turn attracts aphids, a common greenhouse pest. The aphid then can spread a leaf disease around as it feeds. When aphids feed, they exude what is known as honeydew, which lands on lower leaves. The honeydew on lower leaves is sweet and encourages a black fungus mold to grow on the leaf. All this because of too much nitrogen! I don't mean to scare you about nitrogen, but it makes a good example of how things can go wrong. Admittedly, this is an extreme but not an impossible chain of events. It is a domino effect that can occur between the environment and plants.

Another example is that a nutrient imbalance may mimic a disease by causing yellowing or leaf splotches. And some sprays used to control pests turn out to be toxic to the plants, causing more damage than the original pest. The cure may be worse than the disease. The point is that everything is connected to everything else, in your greenhouse and on your planet.

The health of the plant is an important factor in preventing pests and diseases. When a plant is under stress, it becomes more susceptible, just as when people are tired or run-down they are more apt to catch a cold. Stress on plants can be caused by age. The older a plant, the more likely it is to have problems.

Stress is caused by a number of environmental factors, including problems with temperature, light, nutrients and water. When these factors are not at their optimum, stress results. I once kept an eggplant bed alive long into the winter, even though my greenhouse temperature was far too cold for what an eggplant likes. The longer it lived into the cool winter, the more pests and diseases were hampering it. It really shouldn't have been growing then, at least that is what it was trying to tell me. Kohlrabi, a cabbage family crop that likes cool winter temperatures, was growing in my hot summer greenhouse one year. Soon it had bugs all over it, while the more heat-loving crops such as tomatoes and

cucumbers were pest-free. Somehow, the pests knew which plant was under stress.

Rather than trying to understand what is going on, many people just resort to poisons. Unfortunately, spraying poisons can adversely affect human health and create a pest resistance to the poisons, rendering them less effective. Poisons also can cost an arm and a leg.

The effects of chemicals on human health is constantly being questioned. Rarely a year goes by that another chemical isn't pulled off the shelves because of safety concerns. Home food and flower production may be our only form of independence from pesticides.

The more we spray, the more insects become resistant to the chemicals. Compared to 1965, twice as many insects (including many greenhouse pests) have developed resistance to sprays. Also, when massive spraying occurs, it kills many beneficial insects that often prevent harmful insect populations from developing. With no good bugs to eat or parasitize the bad bugs, bad bugs will have an even faster-growing population. The use of beneficial insects to control harmful ones is known as biological control, and I'll go into it later in this chapter.

Not every product you find in a spray bottle is totally harmful, nor should every chemical be considered evil. There are many new biologically safe materials that are being released to control insects. However, chemicals should be used only as a last resort. Selecting the proper chemical should be an informed decision, made with a biologically sane attitude.

GREENHOUSES NEED DIFFERENT APPROACHES

Because greenhouses and sunrooms are usually attached to the home, we must be especially careful how we go about controlling pests and diseases. Let's compare pest control effects for the inside and the outside garden.

Sprays in the Outside Garden

1.   Repellents work well; the pests move out of your garden.
2.   Pesticides rapidly break down because of the action of unfiltered sunlight.
3.   Pesticides wreak havoc if sprayed in the wind.
4.   The outside garden has a wealth of naturally occurring beneficial insects.
5.   Purchased beneficial insects often fly away with the first wind.

Sprays in the Attached Greenhouse or Sunroom

1.   Repellents don't work in an enclosed environment, because they can't repel insects anywhere but to your home.
2.   Sprays can easily get into the household air.
3.   Beneficial insects released into the greenhouse or sunspace will not escape and will stay in the environment.
4.   Spraying pesticides in a greenhouse leaves little fresh air for the person spraying. Thus, filter masks are recommended.
5.   The effect of a spray lasts longer.
6.   Greenhouse pests and diseases often differ from those in the outside environment because the environment is different.

A greenhouse or sunroom garden is probably the closest garden you'll ever live with. Because of the many health concerns associated with chemical pesticides, it's especially important to rethink traditional methods of pest control for the attached enclosed garden. For this reason, much of the pest and disease control strategies discussed in this chapter use what is known as integrated pest management, often known as IPM, because it provides for a safer environment while doing a good job of controlling pests.

IF YOU CANNOT IDENTIFY A PEST

It is important that you know what your problems are. While bugs have a tendency to give people the creeps, the bug you see may not be a bad bug but in fact a good guy out eating the bad ones. For this reason, always assume innocence unless you have identified the bug as bad or until you catch it in the act of damaging the plant.

Try to first read the following descriptions of common greenhouse pests. If nothing seems to fit the bill, then you need some help. Try to capture some and put them in a plastic bag, or tap some of these bugs into a small jar of alcohol (rubbing type, not drinking). Take it to your county agricultural agent (listed in the phone book) for positive identification. The agents may provide you with a positive identification as well as some spray recommendations. Take their spray suggestions with a grain of salt, as many extension agents may be unfamiliar with the lower toxicity types of controls listed in this chapter. Unfortunately, few extension agents are schooled in using beneficial insects to control the bad bugs, although more and more are learning about it as time goes on.

COMMON GREENHOUSE PESTS

The following is a list of the more common pests encountered in a greenhouse or sunspace with many types of controls recommended for each pest. To learn more about each type of control, look up a more detailed discussion of how to use each control in Pest Control Measures (p. 423). For quick reference, refer to the index, where each type of control will also be listed.

Aphids

Description: Pear-shaped and quite small, with long legs and antennae. They have a pair of small "exhaust pipe" structures on their rear ends. They vary greatly in color, ranging from black and gray to red, yellow and green, but by far the most common color is pale green. Adults may be winged or wingless. Females can give birth to live young without mating. Offspring can reproduce within 7 to 10 days. Fast, huh? Colonies are found on new buds, on plant tips and under leaves near veins. Especially check seedlings. Also, ants may carry aphids to your plants.

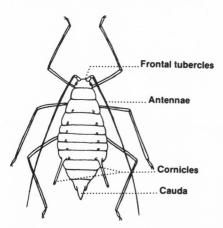

Aphids are between 1/32" and 1/16" in size.

Damage: Aphids are sucking insects that cause spotty marks, deformation and curling of leaves and flowers. In high populations they can greatly stunt growth or even kill plants. They also secrete a sticky substance called honeydew, which drips onto lower leaves. Sticky, shiny leaves are a good indication of aphids. A black mold often grows on the sticky honeydew. Commonly known as sooty mold, it is also damaging to fruits and leaves. Aphids may transmit plant diseases that result in yellowing tissue and plant death.

Control: Brachonid wasps, aphid predator midges, green lacewings, ladybugs; soap sprays, Enstar 5E, summer oils and pyrethrins. Control the ants sometimes associated with the aphids.

Cabbage Looper, Green Worm

Description: Green caterpillar up to 1/2 inch (1.3 cm) long. Moves with a looping gait. Adults are small gray moths.

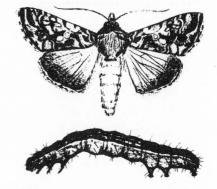

Cabbage looper/Green worm and adult moth

Damage: The caterpillar causes small holes in leaves. May defoliate plants. Usually found on cabbage and cabbage relatives but may found be on other plants such as peas, tomatoes and potatoes. Not common but may occasionally come into the greenhouse in mid- to late summer.

Control: Use microbial insecticide *Bacillus thuringiensis* (BT), safe for use around beneficial insects.

Cats and Dogs

Description: If unsure, refer to encyclopedia or look in every other backyard.

Damage: Crushed plants, uprooting of plants, leaves chewed on (common around catnip).

Control: Keep 'em out. Training. Positive and negative feedback. Squirt guns?

Fungus Gnat

Description: 1/8 inch (.3 cm) long, gray-black, with long legs. Found near soil surface, especially where there is decomposing organic matter. Often seen flying around your nose or collecting near windows. Larvae are white and wormlike; about 1/8 inch (.3 cm) or smaller.

Damage: Often more annoying to people than to plants. I have heard that they are attracted to the carbon dioxide in our breath. Larvae may sometimes feed on roots, which in turn may promote invasion of root-rot organisms. Populations of fungus gnats tend to increase with more use of peat moss and the heavy watering needed for seedling germination.

Control: Cultivate soil surface, reduce watering slightly as they can be a sign of overwatering, remove any dead plant debris from the soil surface. Use the microbial insecticide *Bacillus thuringiensis* (BT) *israeliensis*. It can provide great control. It is commercially sold as Gnatrol and Vectobac. Release beneficial nematodes (be sure to use the Hh strain, see p. 434). Enstar is also effective. You can also try dusting soil with tobacco from cigarettes. Pyrethrins may control adults.

Leaf Miners

Description: Very small flies—1/32 to 1/16 inch (.8 to 1.6 mm)—with black and yellow markings. Adults are seen flying when foliage is disturbed. Eggs are white and laid in clusters on the underside of leaves.

Damage: Damage is usually more visual than actual to vegetable crops. Severe disfigurement of the leaves can occur. Look for serpentine tunnels in leaves.

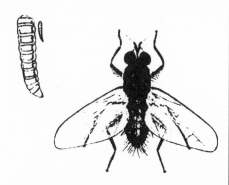

Leaf miner larvae (left); adult fly (right).

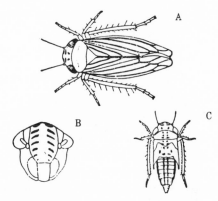

Leafhopper: A) Adult; B) Front view of head; C) Nymph.

Control: Control measures required only in extreme cases. Using a magnifying glass, rub off white eggs found on the underside of the leaf. On ornamentals, you can spray with Avermectin B (commercially known as Avid). Discard leaves with visible "mines."

Leafhopper

Description: Small light-colored (yellow or green) insect up to 1/4 inch (.6 cm) long. Look for them jumping and flying when foliage is disturbed. They are fast.

Damage: The leafhopper is not a common greenhouse pest, but it occurs here and there. They cause spotting on leaves and are known for transmitting diseases. They also produce sucking effects similar to aphid damage.

Control: General predators give slight control; spot spraying with insecticidal soap, botanicals, summer oils or Enstar 5E.

Mealybugs

Description: White to tan, oval shaped, 1/3 inch (.8 cm) or less. Produce a waxlike cottony substance. Found near buds, leaf bases, along leaf veins and even in the soil. When not covered in the cottony substance, they may have a pink coloring to them.

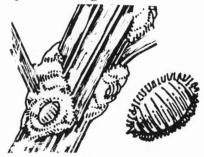

Mealybugs

Damage: They are sucking insects causing problems similar to aphids, including honeydew secretions. They damage crops by removing plant sap.

Control: Dab or spray a 50 percent rubbing alcohol solution on them, taking care to not get much on the plant itself; use botanical spray, insecticidal soap, refined summer oil sprays; ladybug, green lacewings, *Cryptolaemus* predator or *Leptomastix* parasite.

Millipedes

Description: Long, slender white to brown bodies with many legs. Up to 1 inch (2.5 cm) long. Found on soil surface, often under debris.

Millipedes

They run for cover fast when disturbed.

Damage: May occasionally feed on roots, causing stunting of plants. Not a common problem.

Control: Practice good sanitation. Keep debris off soil surface. Even when pest is present, need for spray is rare. Usually they are helping you out by consuming debris and turning it into organic matter.

Mites (Two-spotted Mite)

Description: Small—1/32 to 1/16 inch (.8 to 1.6 mm)—pale yellow to light brown to reddish. May have red spots. Mites are a type of Arachnid, more closely related to spiders than insects, therefore they have eight legs. Get a hand lens or a magnifying glass to see them. Adults may have two spots on either side of their body. This is the

Mite

two-spotted mite. Mites look like tiny dots associated with webs found on the underside of leaves and growing tips.

Damage: Injury causes leaves to look lighter colored, as if they are drying out or parched. Upper surface may look spotty or stippled. Also, look for webbing over foliage. High populations greatly reduce yield and may damage the appearance of plants or kill them.

Control: Predatory mites are excellent biological controls. When using predatory mites, discontinue all other types of sprays (including soap and botanical sprays) to avoid killing the good predatory mites. Insecticidal soap works well on mites when direct contact is made. Also, water (when sprayed onto the underside of the leaf) sometimes knocks them off the plant permanently. Sulfur-based dusts and sprays, pyrethrin and nicotine and summer oils are all effective on mites. Avermectin B (Avid) is particularly effective on mite populations when used on ornamentals.

Nematode feeding on plant

Nematodes

Description: Live in soil, not visible to the eye; root feeders. Not to be confused with beneficial nematodes mentioned earlier.

Damage: Leaves may be abnormal color; plants become prone to wilting; discolored roots; low productivity. Hard to positively identify this damage as being attributed to nema-

todes. You may need an expert. Not common in home greenhouses.

Control: Unless common in your area, nematode damage is hard to confirm. Interplant marigolds. Soils with good amounts of organic matter are rarely affected as there is a fungus that lives in organic matter that preys on nematodes.

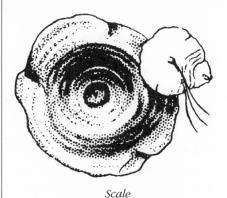

Scale

Scale, Soft Brown Scale, Armored Scale

Description: Looks like a flat, oval brown bump on the stem or leaf (mainly along the main leaf vein). They may have a small "nipple" in the center. Usually they are no more than 1/4 inch (.6 cm) in size. To distinguish from a normally occurring bump on the stem, try lifting it with a small knife or fingernail. If it comes off easily, it is probably scale.

Damage: Scale weakens the plant by sucking the juices from the stem. In high populations, it can cause plant death.

Control: In low populations, hand removal is the best control. Control may also be gained from repeated applications of refined summer oil sprays.

Slugs, Snails

Description: Slugs are slimy dark gray, soft-bodied creatures up to 1 inch (2.5 cm) long. They glide on the plants, leaving a wet-looking reflective trail. They are usually nocturnal feeders but may feed on cool, cloudy days. They are often found hiding under debris. Snails are similar in habit and appearance to slugs, except they have a roundish shell that varies in color and markings.

Damage: They eat holes in the leaf about 1/2 to 1 inch (1.3 to 2.5 cm) in diameter. Often they kill seedlings and make foliage so full of holes that it is unmarketable or unpalatable.

Control: Avoid mulching and keep top of soil clean. Slugs and snails can indicate overwatering; try cutting back on water if you feel this may be the case. Set out beer baits in shallow-sided containers. Set out small flat boards or potatoes cut in half on soil surface. In the morning, handpick pest from un-

derside and destroy. Barriers such as diatomaceous earth and ground red-hot peppers will protect young seedlings. Use metaldehyde baits only as a last resort. See Baits and Traps (p. 423) later in this chapter.

Sow Bugs, Pill Bugs

Sow bug

Description: Gray flattened, oval bodies—up to 1/3 inch (.8 cm)—with the scalelike plates. May roll into ball (pill bugs, A.K.A. Roly-Polys) or run away (sow bugs) if disturbed.

Damage: Usually they prefer to feed on dead litter laying on the soil or near the soil surface. However, they occasionally feed on roots, seedlings and stems.

Control: Cultivation; clean debris from soil surface; avoid use of a mulch. Release beneficial nematodes (be sure to use the Nc strain for best control). Trap under boards or on potatoes cut in half and placed on soil surface. Dispose of them in the morning.

Sweet Potato Whiteflies

Description: They look very similar to the regular whitefly. Here's how to tell the difference: The sweet potato whitefly adult is smaller than the regular whitefly. It tends to fly more rapidly. The sweet potato whitefly is best distinguished from the regular whitefly by looking for a yellow appearance of the body as opposed to the solid white appearance of the regular whitefly. The scale or crawler (usually found on the underside of the leaf) is also more yellow than the generic whitefly. They also have a translucent color with a slight indentation at the center of the body. A hand lens or magnifying glass will help greatly.

Damage: Same as regular whitefly.

Control: Insecticidal soap sprays, Enstar 5E, botanical sprays, summer oil sprays, whitefly egg predator (*Delphastus pusillus*), general predators.

Thrips

Description: Very small—1/50 to 1/32 inch (.5 to .8 mm)—yellow to brownish; cigar-shaped.

Damage: They suck on the leaves and flower buds, causing a stip-

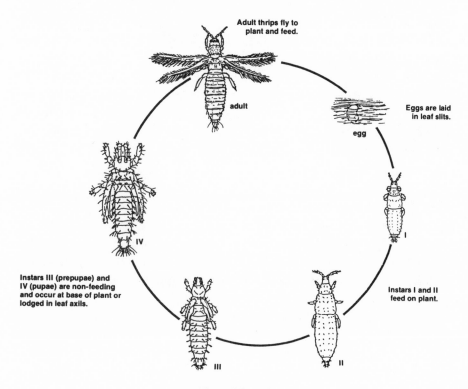

Adult thrips fly to plant and feed.

adult

Eggs are laid in leaf slits.

egg

Instars III (prepupae) and IV (pupae) are non-feeding and occur at base of plant or lodged in leaf axils.

IV

III

II

I

Instars I and II feed on plant.

Thrips life cycle

pling or small brownish areas on the leaf, and can transmit diseases. *Control*: Spray underside of leaf with insecticidal soap spray, garlic or hot-pepper solution, botanical sprays or summer oil spray. Release predator spider mite listed for thrips.

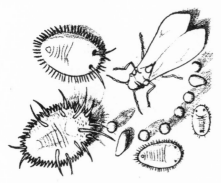

Various stages of whitefly development

Whiteflies

Description: Small—1/16 to 1/8 inch (1.6 mm to .3 cm)—white flying insects. Eggs, which usually go unseen, are very small black slender, flame-shaped specks; young are roundish, flat and white (known as the whitefly scale stage). All are found on underside of leaf. *Damage*: Similar to aphids. *Control*: *Encarsia formosa* is an excellent biological control. The whitefly egg predator, *Delphastus pusillus*, is hard to acquire and still experimental but has good reports. Make or purchase yellow sticky

traps and hang near infestation (not to be used with beneficial insects). Control also gained with pyrethrin and Neem, soap sprays, summer oil spray, Enstar 5E and general predators.

CONTROL STRATEGIES

Now that we know the enemy—the bad bugs—we need to go over the options for providing the best control without sacrificing a safe environment. There is only one control that can accomplish this, but it requires a commitment on your part as a gardener. This is not a pest control that you just spray and walk away from. Sprays that kill are best used in spot applications. They should be of low toxicity and work in tandem with other types of controls and preventative measures. In the end, you will have a greenhouse or sunspace that is easy to manage and that provides enjoyment without any worries associated with the old methods of using poisons.

I would like to encourage you to develop integrated pest management, often known as IPM.

Integrated Pest Management

1. Maintain pest populations at tolerable levels by using biological controls (beneficial insects and organisms). This means deciding to put up with a low level of bad bugs by having the good bugs keep them in check.

2. Use cultural controls whenever possible. This means hand-picking bad bugs, crop rotation, changing the environment and using resistant plant varieties to control your pest problem.

3. Use pesticides and sprays only as a last resort. Be sure the pesticide you use is well selected (to have a minimal long-term effect on the environment), properly timed and precisely and safely applied to work in harmony with the above pest-control regimens.

10 Steps to Minimize Pests

1. *Clean it up.* Keep dead leaves cleaned up and off the soil. Don't let plant parts rot on the soil surface. Eliminate places where pests can thrive, or at least keep them away from the windows or vents of the greenhouse or sunroom. This includes weeds, poorly managed compost piles and debris.

2. *Beware of gift plants.* This may be the best way to avoid having a new pest to romp in your indoor garden. Don't be a hospital for a friend's sick plant. If you must take on any new plant, including a store-bought one, inspect it closely. Take it outside and spray it before bringing it into its new home (see Sprays for Pest Control, p. 427).

3. *Pull up plants past their prime.* If a plant is starting to look sickly or infested, it quite possibly is past its prime. Unless it is a treasured plant, pull it up and toss it in the trash. Be very careful when removing a heavily bug-infested plant. If you are clumsy, you could easily sprinkle bugs all across many other plants,

triggering a massive epidemic. The best thing to do is to sneak up on the plant with a plastic bag. Quickly and gently slip the bag over the plant, covering the total aboveground portion of the plant. Gather the bag together at the base of the plant and pull it up, keeping the bag sealed at the base as you take it to the garbage.

4.   *Isolate plants in poor health*. If a plant is in poor health or under attack from a pest or disease yet you can't bear to part with it, set it away from other plants. It is best to move it to another room out of your greenhouse or sunspace, if you have a suitable location (with the right light and temperatures for the plant). By isolating an unhealthy plant, you prevent the spread of bugs or diseases to healthy plants. I often try to take an unhealthy potted plant outdoors to spray it, which protects the good bugs that help control other harmful insect infestations.

5.   *Before reusing pots, wash them*. Old pots can harbor diseases and insects. They also may have salt deposits that may cause soil problems later on for a new plant. Salt deposits are indicated by a white crystalline or powdery substance. Sometimes you'll need a wire bristle brush to clean a clay pot. When you wash any pot, use hot water, soap and a diluted bleach. Rinse well.

6.   *Keep the air moving*. Both diseases and insects love stagnant air. So even in winter, run a fan during the day (a small fan set on low works well). Moving air also helps increase the level of beneficial carbon dioxide adjacent to the leaf surface (see Chapter 1, The Greenhouse Environment). A fan exhausting warm greenhouse air into your home in winter is often enough air movement. It will also prevent air stratification, where the hot air stays at the ceiling and the floor remains cool.

7.   *Integrate your planting*. As described in Chapter 3, Plant Layout, planting beds with mixtures of crops (intercropping) rather than a single crop may help keep infestations of pests and diseases to a minimum. It confuses them. Also vary your potted plants by mixing in some pots containing other types of plants.

8. *Rotate your crops.* When growing in beds, try not to plant the same crop in the same place in consecutive years. Keep records to help you remember what you have done.

9. *Grow varieties resistant to potential problems.* As explained in Chapter 4, Selecting the Right Plants, some plant varieties may be resistant to insect or disease problems. Unfortunately, in real life the term "resistant," when listed in a catalog, may mean only more tolerant. The plant still may succumb to the problem. Still, it is worth trying those particular varieties. It is also helpful to keep your own records (see Record-Keeping appendix for help). You will soon find differences among varieties and their responses to pests and diseases. This is where record-keeping really pays off.

10. *Maintain plant health.* When your plant is infested, it may be telling you something. Are you growing it at the right time of year or in the right location? Does it have the proper light intensity, nutrition, water levels or temperature? Maybe a different plant would do better in that spot. Is the infested plant just getting too old? Give it some thought.

PEST CONTROL MEASURES

There are many options when it comes to controlling pests and diseases. In this section, you will find a listing of the more common choices. Safety, both for the environment and for you and your family, is discussed for each type of control. Later in this chapter, you will find a listing of the most common diseases and their controls. Always start with the safest and most ecological choices.

Baits and Traps

Not all pests can be controlled by baits or traps. But for certain pests, they work well. Some growers use a trap only as an indicator to notify them that a certain critter is on the loose and requires some attention. For instance, many growers use sticky yellow cards to attract the common greenhouse pest, the whitefly. Others set many sticky yellow traps to actually control the population. Let's look at some of the traps you can use.

Sticky Yellow Traps

The color yellow attracts many pests, including whiteflies and winged aphids. Yellow flypaper will help control some populations. You will find the sticky yellow traps sold in some garden catalogs, but I have found them to be quite expensive for what you get. One alternative is using yellow-painted boards and spreading a thin layer of axle grease on the boards. Reapply it every week or so or stir up the grease because it gets dusty and loses its ability to catch bugs. You can also purchase a can of Tanglefoot or Tangle Trap. These are commercially available sticky substances made for trapping insects, but they are messy to deal with and seem to get on everything. Somewhat less messy is a material that comes with a brush built into the lid. It is also available in a more expensive aerosol formula, which is cleaner to use. Some people have had luck with motor and cooking oil on yellow cardboard or wooden stakes.

When using sticky yellow traps, place them where they won't stick to you or your visitors. One accidental brushing against them can ruin a shirt. Avoid using sticky yellow traps when you are releasing the beneficial insect used to control whitefly, *Encarsia formosa*

(discussed later), because they too will stick to the yellow traps.

With a heavy whitefly infestation, I have found that I can reduce the numbers by making a hand-held yellow sticky trap. Just staple a card or the prepared yellow cardboard or painted board onto a handle such as a stake. On a good warm day, go into the heaviest infestation and shake the plants. Instantly you will find yourself in a snow of whitefly. Hold the yellow trap in a bright spot and move it around slowly. You will catch hundreds of adult whiteflies, which in a few more weeks would have translated into thousands.

Traps, Baits and Barriers for Slugs, Snails, Sow Bugs and Mice

Slugs and snails are attracted to beer, so they can be controlled with beer traps. The beer must be renewed every week, and there should be a trap in every 5 square feet (.46 sq. m) of infested area. Put the beer in something they can easily crawl into. Using beer as a control for slugs is somewhat labor intensive, and you may find something better to do with your beer. If so, you can substitute sugar water and baking yeast.

The most common bait for slugs is metaldehyde, found in pellets, paste form or mixed with sawdust. It is placed on the ground near plants, and when the slugs eat it, they tend to dry up. It readily breaks down in soil but still has the disadvantages of a pesticide. It is poisonous and should be kept off food. Also it can be absorbed through the skin, so wear gloves when applying. If used constantly, slugs and snails may become resistant to its effects. It is best if used sparingly as a last resort. Keep it locked up and out of the way of children and pets.

Slugs hate to crawl on sharp or very dry, dusty materials. Many gardeners have had good luck keeping slugs from roaming by using barriers of crushed eggshells, wood ash (go easy on this stuff), hydrated lime, ferrous ammonium sulfate, sawdust and diatomaceous earth (available in some specialty garden catalogs). There are also salt-impregnated vinyl barriers on the market, which a slug is unable to cross. Somehow, somebody discovered that slugs will not crawl across copper. As a result, there is copper foil material on the market for protecting crops from slugs. Another home remedy is to sprinkle cayenne or dried chiles around the

Traps for slugs can be made of plywood as on the left, or commercially purchased as in center.

affected plant as a repellent. The coarser ground pepper lasts longer than the fine powder. When the slugs get close, you can almost hear them screaming "aye-yi-yi-yi!" as they slide away in quick retreat.

There are commercial slug and snail traps available (one such trap is known as Slug Saloon) that may contain metaldehyde, or beerlike stuff, but it is easier to make your own. Small, thin boards, such as pieces of plywood, or potatoes cut in half placed on the soil surface make great traps for sow bugs, pill bugs, slugs and snails. All of these pests tend to be night feeders. Come morning, they retreat to dark, moist places, where they have parties, hopefully under your board or potato. You can spoil the fun and dispose of them. It's sort of like a homemade roach motel, where they check in but don't check out. As mentioned earlier in this chapter, slugs and snails can be controlled environmentally by reducing watering and removing debris from the soil surface.

Mice can be a real pest in the greenhouse, where they eat into your harvests. They can be eliminated by ... you guessed it, mousetraps. Of course, a household cat may also solve this problem.

Freeze Outs

A freeze out is a form of pest control that alters the environment to freeze out the pests. This is generally done in the dead of winter. All the doors and windows are left open and the whole place freezes up. This includes the plants too. If you don't plan it out well, it could mean your water system as well. Yes, people can get desperate when they have a bad bug problem. Is it effective? On occasion. But there are often survivors. I know it is hard to believe, but insects are amazing. Over in some protected corner, one or two survivors are ready to populate the whole place. The bugs think like Arnold Schwarzenegger, "I'll be back." And they will. They will come back sooner or later on a neighbor's clothing, a gift plant or a salad leaf from the kitchen. They'll fly or hitchhike, but you can count on their return. You end up where you began, except without the plants you froze. This is a method that only postpones the problem. There are better ways.

Vacuum the Pests out of Your Life

There is something magic about a vacuum that just sucks up the dirt in your life and takes it to a place where you will never see it again. On certain occasions, you can do the same with vacuuming up the pest problems. It will not single-handedly solve a major infestation, but it can reduce the numbers substantially. Vacuuming works best on whitefly adults (the whiteflies that are flying around). I have experimented with plug-in vacuums and Dust Busters. Both work at sucking up a substantial number of critters, but you must take care to not injure the leaf of the plant. Sometimes a suction too strong can actually suck the leaf right off the plant. It is best to sneak up on the whitefly and turn over a leaf to expose them all hiding on the underside, having their tea party (or whatever whiteflies do when they congregate). Then run the vacuum across the leaf, holding it just a fraction above the surface. Dispose of the vacuum bag or catcher carefully and far away from the greenhouse or sunroom. Happy cleaning!

Eat the Bugs?

I've eaten raw aphids (usually by mistake). They are tiny, sweet morsels. It takes a real infestation and a lot of time to get full. I don't suggest this as a real way to control bugs but it does give rise to some interesting thoughts. Bugs are probably more nutritious than what you last ate. Roasted grasshoppers have about 75 percent protein and 20 percent fat. They are high in niacin and riboflavin. The idea may seem repulsive to modern sophisticates who dine on delicacies such as snails, frog legs, chicken embryos (eggs) and rocky mountain oysters, not to mention BHA, BHT, sodium nitrate, artificial sweeteners and yellow dye number 5. No, don't eat your bugs. I just mentioned this because we should be equally repulsed by the poisoning of our food, air and water. The attitude that each and every bug is bad must change. In the meantime, I encourage you to grow some food crops in your greenhouse for some real wholesome food (with no additives). Maybe further research into eating bugs can help to solve the world food shortages. If you happen to accidentally consume an aphid or whitefly, don't worry—you'll live.

Sprays for Pest Control

Don't assume that I mean only synthetic chemical sprays. There are a number of things you can spray to help keep pests down.

They include homemade, botanical, microbial and synthetic sprays, as well as some new and old remedies that can't be classified into this listing. Let's look at the many options of materials for spraying.

HOMEMADE INSECTICIDES

Many garden books have recipes for homemade pesticides. They include such ingredients as garlic, nicotine, red peppers, onions, baking soda, potatoes, flour, oil, dead insects and soap. Many act only as repellents, which is not that helpful in a closed environment. Others can kill a bug or control a fungus as well as anything on the market. While you will find many people who swear by homemade formulations, you should realize that you are experimenting when it comes to these controls. Play around with dosages and notice the effects on the plants until you find something that works.

Some of the stronger formulations include nicotine and soap. Nicotine tea, a spray made from cigarettes, is very effective. It is so effective that it can be toxic and requires some precautions. Steep a cup of cigarettes (or butts) in water overnight until the water is dark-colored, and spray on plants the next morning. Don't let the liquid touch the skin, and don't inhale any vapors. They may be quite toxic.

Garlic has long been known to repel insects and also has some mild fungicide effects. Many gardeners have reported being able to keep fungus diseases down by regularly spraying homemade garlic preparations. Usually, people just crush or blend 4 to 10 cloves in a quart of water and boil for 25 minutes. Strain out the solids, and spray when the solution cools. It works best on leaf-surface diseases such as powdery mildew. While you're at it, eat some garlic—it will keep colds at bay and friends at bay (then you won't catch their colds), and it might even reduce your blood pressure.

Rubbing alcohol is an effective agent against mealybugs as well as may other insects. Use a mixture of 1 tablespoon per pint (.47 l) of water, but first do a leaf check. Spray on a small area of one leaf a couple of days prior to spraying a whole plant to be sure it doesn't burn the leaf. This is a good way to prevent burning a whole plant that might have a sensitivity to alcohol. You can also dab undiluted rubbing alcohol on individual mealybugs, using a Q-tip or swab, but avoid getting it on the plant tissue, because the pure alcohol will burn most leaves.

INSECTICIDAL SOAPS

Insecticidal soaps on the market work quite well on soft-bodied insects. I highly recommend using soaps on insects. They work well on aphids, scales, whiteflies, thrips, mealybugs and spider mites. In fact, one test at the University of California found that a soap spray was more effective on bush beans infested with whitefly than Malathion (a common synthetic chemical insecticide). You should know that soap can also kill the good bugs that you might be introducing and can derail a biological-control program. I once used soap after I had released the beneficial parasite *Encarsia formosa* (a small wasp that controls whitefly). The good news was that soap helped kill the whitefly, but it also killed all of my *Encarsia*. With soap as a control, I was locked into regular spraying to stay on top of the whitefly problem all summer and well into fall. The moral is: Soap is not good for bugs, both good and bad bugs.

No one seems to know exactly how soap works in killing bugs. But most researchers believe that the soap affects the insect with a dehydrating effect. The nice thing about soap is that it is relatively nontoxic, unless you can't stand to have clean hands. Soap has no residual effect, which is good for people entering a recently sprayed greenhouse (or even eating a recently sprayed plant). But no residual activity also means that if new bugs land on the plant after spraying, they won't be affected. So, repeated applications are very important, usually every 3 to 5 days for bad infestations, until the bugs seem to be under control.

Soap can cause problems to some plants by burning the leaves. The best way to use soap on a plant that has never been treated with it is to test a small portion of a leaf and wait at least 24 hours to see if there is any burning. If not, have at it. Do this test for any plant you intend to spray. Soap can be used on both ornamental and edible plants. Commercially available soaps are becoming more and more readily available. I even found some at the hardware store, which was unheard of a couple of years ago.

Instead of purchasing the expensive store-bought insecticidal soaps, why not make your own? You can, and they work very well. To make a homemade insecticidal soap, avoid detergents and soaps for automatic dishwashers. Instead, use mild dishwashing liquids, flakes or soaps, such as Ivory Liquid, Ivory Snow, Fels Naptha or Dr. Bronner's. Generally, you want a 1 to 2 percent solution, which is 3 to 6 tablespoons per gallon of water. But again, before spraying your homemade soap spray, *please* be sure to test it on small portions of the leaves and wait 24 hours to test for any potential leaf burning. Plants that often have serious burning are leaves with waxy or hairy coatings. Other plants may show only slight injury. The best is when the only injury that occurs is to the insects.

BOTANICALLY BASED INSECTICIDES

Derived from plants, they're commonly believed to be easier on our environment. These commercially available insecticides usually (but not always) have a low toxicity to humans compared to many synthetic insecticides. Botanicals tend to break down quickly into harmless substances. They also have a shorter effective life in your garden. For this reason you may have to spray more often.

When spraying commercially available botanical sprays, don't be any more lax than you would be with any other pesticide. Yes, botanicals are better on the environment in the long term, but the immediate hazards still require caution. You can get sick, headaches, dizzy and nauseated just as quickly with a botanical spray as

with a synthetic spray. Always read and follow the label instructions on botanically based sprays and reread the safety procedures that are outlined in this chapter.

You should understand that most commercially available botanically based pesticides also kill beneficial insects. They should not be used when you're using a biological control, or used only in spot applications. When an infested plant is in a pot and you have beneficial insects in your greenhouse, consider taking the plant out of the greenhouse for spraying.

Let's look at some of the commonly available botanically based insecticides.

1. **Pyrethrin**. Also known as pyrethrum, pyrethrin is derived from the flower heads of the pyrethrum chrysanthemum daisy. It is a contact insecticide, which means that the pyrethrum must physically touch the insect's body before it will kill it. The vapors have little effect. It is effective on most common greenhouse pests, including whiteflies, aphids, spider mites and mealybugs. Pyrethrin can be applied on edible plants up to 5 days before harvest. Commercial formulations are becoming more commonplace than they were even a

few years ago. Some are mixed with other active ingredients, such as insecticidal soap or other botanically based chemicals. Pyrethrin is more effective when sprayed at sundown, as the warmth and sunshine tend to lessen its ability to kill critters. Pyrethrin is not recommended for use when you have beneficial insects at work. It is toxic to fish, so take care to never let any get into a water supply.

Don't confuse pyrethrins with pyrethroids, which is a term for a whole class of synthetic pesticides based upon the chemical makeup of the natural pesticide pyrethrin. Many pyrethroids are not registered for use on food crops, while pyrethrin is.

2. **Rotenone**. An extract of tropical legume plants, rotenone is a contact insecticide and stomach poison that acts on most common greenhouse pests. Amazonian natives used rotenone extracts to kill fish for large harvests. Commercial rotenone is toxic to fish and birds, so take care not to allow any material to get into watersheds. Always be sure that you use standard protective equipment. Rotenone is available in a dust formulation that is just shaken onto plant leaves and a powder that is mixed with water and sprayed. Old rotenone can lose much of its punch, so purchase only what you will need in the immediate future.

3. **Rayania**. As with many botanicals, rayania is also derived from a tropical plant. In this case, it comes from the stem of a shrub. It is not a quick knockdown pesticide, but after a few days you'll notice the pest numbers have greatly dwindled. It is especially effective on aphids and thrips, as long as you can get a direct hit on them as you spray. It is available as both a spray and a dust, although the dust is more common.

4. **Sabidilla**. Derived from the seeds of a tropical plant resembling corn, sabidilla is a powerful stomach poison that kills many pests, with the exception of mites. It is generally sold as a dust and works as a broad-spectrum contact poison. Sabidilla has limited application in the greenhouse because it is hard to get dust on the underside of leaves (where many greenhouse pests like to hide). Rarely you may find it as a wettable powder that can then be sprayed. Take caution because there are some recorded instances of human poisonings with sabidilla. Keep the dust or spray off any skin and wear gloves, protective clothing and a chemical filter mask when applying.

5. **Neem**. One of the newer botanicals on the market, neem has been used for centuries in India, where the neem tree is native. Research is ongoing to determine its effectiveness as a botanical pesticide. It is well proven as a repellent, which doesn't help much in the closed environment of a greenhouse or sunroom. Currently, there are a few commercial sprays containing neem, such as Margosan and NEEMisis. At this writing, it is registered for use only on ornamentals and is prohibited on vegetables or other edibles. It is sold mainly through wholesale channels.

6. **Nicotine**. An age-old pesticide, nicotine has a high toxicity to both humans and insects. Even if you smoke cigarettes, you'll be surprised how sick you can get if you use this pesticide improperly. Its vapors are also quite toxic. Keep it off your skin, and always use great caution. It is very effective against most all greenhouse pests. While it is mainly a contact pesticide (requiring that the bugs come in direct contact with the spray), the vapors also seem to control insects in deeper hiding places. Nicotine is sold commercial as Blackleaf 40.

MICROBIAL/BIOLOGICAL INSECTICIDES

Like biological warfare, these microbes attack specific pests by causing a disease that kills them. Luckily, microbial insecticides won't affect humans or even most beneficial insects. They are famous for being incredibly safe and usually kill only the target population, leaving the people and other critters in the environment unaffected. Many microbial insecticides are safe enough that they can be used in conjunction with a biological pest-control program. This means that, generally, they don't harm the good bugs that help control the bad bugs. Here are a few examples.

Bacillus Thuringiensis. One of the most common microbial products for controlling bugs is a bacteria known as *Bacillus thuringiensis*. Because this bacteria's name is such a mouthful, many people refer to it as BT. It is sold under a variety of names and is available in both dust and liquid forms. Some of the commercial products include Dipel, Thuricide and Attack. These more common BT products work mainly on pests in the caterpillar family. While caterpillar infestations are relatively rare in the greenhouse or sunroom, they can occur and a little BT can easily control them. There are, however, a few strains of BT that have been isolated and provide control for some other pests. One such strain of interest to greenhouse gardeners is *Bacillus thuringiensis israeliensis*. It can help control fungus gnats, which are a common soil-borne pesky critter in the greenhouse. The most common products containing BT for controlling gnats are commercially known as Gnatrol and Vectobac. By the way, this same strain of BT, *israeliensis*, can also control mosquitoes in certain situations.

Unlike other pesticides, many BT products have a relatively short shelf life if stored in warm places. If a container is exposed to extreme heat, the product will lose its viability because it is a container full of microscopic creatures that suffer in extreme environments. The product is best kept in a dark, cool place (don't let it freeze). Also, when you mix up a spray from a concentrate or powder, the dilution will be viable for only a day or so. For this reason, never mix up more than you will need to use in a day. I prefer the dust formulations over sprays because they require no mixing or preparation. I just sprinkle a bit on the leaves after I have watered, when a caterpillar is sighted eating dinner regularly in my greenhouse.

Parasitic Nematodes—A Good Nematode. Nematodes are microscopic worms (not related to earthworms). In soils with a very low organic-matter level, some nematodes can become plant pests, feeding on roots. For years, if someone mentioned the word "nematode," growers would think only of the nematode that is a plant pest. Fortunately, there are species of nematodes that are helpful in controlling soil-borne pests—they are good guys. The way they control insects and other soil pests sounds like a scene from the horror movie *Aliens*. They seek out soil pests and insects and enter their natural body openings, such as the mouth. Once inside, the nematodes release a bacteria that kills the host. They then eat the dead insect or soil pest from the inside out.

They are one of the few safe biologically based controls for the sow bug and pill bug. In addition, these good nematodes feed on earwigs, onion maggots and many root weevils, which for years were some of the hardest critters to kill without turning to harsh chemicals. Now that we have these good nematodes, we have an incredibly safe alternative. The nematodes are usually sold in a live semi-dehydrated condition and have a 3-month shelf life at room temperature (a little longer if you can keep them cooler).

It is important that you understand that there are two types of nematodes on the market. They are known either by their scientific name or sometimes by the abbreviations of their scientific name. These are "Nc" and "Hh." The Nc, scientifically known as *Neoaplectana carpocapsae* (sometimes also known affectionately as *Steinernema carpocapsae*), is better in controlling pill bugs, sow bugs and maggots. The Hh strain, scientifically known as *Heterorhabditis heliothidis*, is best for controlling fungus gnats, among other critters. Be sure to choose the right type of nematode for your problem. There are a number of commercial beneficial nematode products on the market, including BioSafe and Seek. Read the label closely or contact the manufacturer to find out which species of beneficial nematode is the active ingredient.

There are other microbial agents that control pests of plants, but most of these are for outside crops. BT and the beneficial nematodes are the only commercially available products providing control for common greenhouse pests.

OTHER BIORATIONAL PEST SPRAYS

The term "biorational" refers to commercially available sprays that are derived from or work with nature. Usually they are lower in toxicity than synthetic chemicals. Some but not all biorational pest sprays are more specific in what they kill, meaning that some don't hurt the good bugs that control the bad ones. This doesn't mean that you should not exercise the same care when applying them that you would use when applying synthetic chemicals. They still can pose a hazard. For this reason, always read the precautions on the label and follow the proper spraying procedures outlined later in this chapter. Not all of these are registered for use on edible plants, even though they may be biologically more "sane" than many registered nerve poisons on the market. This could be because they are truly toxic when consumed, or it may be that the company can't afford the expensive process of registration with the EPA. To be on the safe side, when a spray is not registered for application on edible crops, don't spray it on an edible crop. Read the label or call the manufacturer for more information on a particular product.

Avermectin B. Utilizing a product derived from a bacterial soil organism known as *Streptomyces avermitilis*, researchers have discovered a naturally occurring toxin that affects many insects. If the word *Streptomyces* sounds familiar, it's because it is the same family of bacteria in antibiotics used to cure human ailments, including the antibiotic streptomycin. The toxin derived from this bacteria for use on insects is known as Avermectin B.

Avermectin B on some pests can be slow-acting, taking up to a month to kill, but usually it is quicker. Currently, Avermectin B is registered to control only spider mites and leaf miners (which it has a rapid effect upon). It is registered for use only on ornamental plants such as flowers and houseplants. Do not use it on ferns or poinsettias, as it will burn the leaves. Avermectin B is not currently registered for use on food crops, with one exception: In certain parts of the United States and in certain situations, it can be used on pears and strawberries. If you hope to use it on these food crops, please first talk directly to the manufacturer about this special use registration. Avermectin B has also been known to help control other pests, including whiteflies, fruit flies and cabbage loopers. However, it is not registered for use on these pests and may be very slow-acting on them. It will also negatively affect your good bugs, so limit any use with a biological control program. It is one of the few products that does a good job controlling spider mites and leaf miners and is lower in toxicity than many synthetic chemicals designed to control these same critters.

Commercially, Avermectin B is available only through wholesale outlets and is sold under the name of Avid. I have seen Avid sold in the Peaceful Valley Farm Supply catalog (see Mail-Order Supplies appendix). The first thing you will notice is its high price. One 8-ounce (.24-liter) bottle can cost well over $50. The reason it is so expensive is that it is recommended for commercial use and is available only in a highly concentrated form. For instance, 1 ounce (30 ml) of Avid can make 25 gallons (95 l) of spray for spider mite control. I put only four drops or so in a quart bottle. At that rate, one bottle will last for many years. When you figure out how much "control" one bottle contains, the price really isn't that out of line. Maybe you can go in on a small bottle of Avid with a few other gardeners to make it more affordable.

Kinoprene. Kinoprene is one of a new type of insecticides known as growth regulators. Basically they are hormones that interrupt the natural growth process of certain insects, resulting in death of the insect. In the case of kinoprene, it tends to affect those insects in the Homoptera order, which includes a number of favorite greenhouse enemies such as aphids, whiteflies and mealybugs. By killing only a specific family of bugs, it has little or no effect on other insects. It is one of the few commercial sprays that has a low toxicity to humans as well as to good bugs. I have tested it with great success in using biological controls such as the whitefly parasite *Encarsia formosa* discussed later in this chapter. Still, all the normal spraying precautions should be followed.

Commercially, kinoprene is sold as Enstar 5E or just Enstar. It is registered for use only on ornamental plants growing in greenhouses and is not registered for edible crops. A developer once told me that kinoprene could be registered for edible plants if the company could afford the high costs of registration. Unfortunately, the investment would not be worth it because kinoprene breaks down too rapidly in direct sun, eliminating all potential sales to outside farmers and gardeners. It is useful only when used under the protection of a glazing, where it does not break down as rapidly.

Enstar is available from wholesale suppliers that deal with commercial greenhouses. It is hard to come by for average greenhouse gardeners. You could talk to local greenhouse growers to see if they could order a bottle for you. If you do find a source, you'll be amazed at how expensive it is. A 1-pint (.47-liter) bottle runs close to $100 or more. It's sold in a glass bottle, so don't be fumble-fingered when handling. Fortunately, it is also very concentrated; 1 ounce (30 ml) of Enstar, at the normal rate, can make up to 20 gallons (76 l) of spray. At a few drops per spray bottle, one bottle could last for many years, or you could go in on a bottle with others. Perhaps there are other greenhouse gardeners you know who would be willing to share in a bottle to reduce the cost.

OILS FOR KILLING BUGS

Oils have long been used as a pest control, usually on outdoor plants such as trees and shrubs. Because many oils burn the leaves, they are used only while plants are dormant and leafless. More recently, insecticidal oils have been refined to minimize the burning that occurs on leaves. The advantage of using oils as an insecticide is that most oils have a low toxicity to humans in comparison with other pesticides. It is also difficult for insects to gain resistance to oils.

Some oils, when sprayed on a leaf, will expel insects from the plant altogether. I have had good luck spraying a product known as Sunspray Ultra-Fine Spray Oil on many edible and ornamental greenhouse crops. Another commercial product is known as Volk Supreme Oil (note different application rates on label for leafy plants that are not dormant).

If you use an oil, make sure that it is registered for use on leafy plants as opposed to only plants in a dormant stage. Sometimes manufacturers call an oil for leafy plants a summer oil. Avoid using any dormant oils, as they will cause massive burning of the leaves. Also, take precautions to test the spray on a portion of a leaf before going whole hog on many plants, to prevent any possible burning. Always mix according to directions. Oil can also be mixed with insecticidal soap to increase the efficiency of both the oil and the soap on insects.

Oil is especially effective on mealybugs, whiteflies, aphids, scales and spider mites. I have found a good selection of oils for controlling insects in the Peaceful Valley Farm Supply catalog (see Mail-Order Supplies appendix.)

COPPER- AND SULFUR-BASED MINERALS AS PESTICIDES

These minerals can be used successfully to control certain types of leaf-based fungus diseases and spider mites. When applied at the recommended rate, they are generally considered quite safe. Copper is available as both a dust and a liquid spray. It is rare that you can cure a plant with a mineral-based spray, but you can help slow the spread and even reduce or prevent further infection. Copper is usually sold mixed with some sulfur (copper sulfate).

For centuries, European gardeners and grape growers have used what is known as a Bordeaux spray, which is a mixture of copper sulfate and hydrated lime. It is usually available as a powder that can be dusted or mixed with water and applied as a spray.

All copper- and sulfur-based mineral sprays are safe for both humans and the environment, as long as they are applied at the recommended rates. They do, however, have a great potential for burning the leaves. To prevent leaf burn, test the spray on some small portions of a leaf a couple of days before spraying the whole plant. Also, it is better to apply these sprays in the morning hours after you have watered. The main thing is to apply these sprays as recommended on the label. Higher concentrations are famous for causing leaf burning.

Sometimes, after a sulfur-based spray is applied, it can trigger a spider mite population explosion a month or two later. This is because the sulfur will often kill both the bad spider mites, which feed on plants, and the good predator spider mites, which feed on the bad spider mites. When both are killed, the bad mite tends to return at a faster rate, causing a worse infestation. You may want to release predator mites a month after spraying to avoid problems. Look for more discussion on using sulfur-based sprays in Mineral Sprays (p. 467).

WATER AS A DETERRENT

Not only is water good to drink and important in plant nutrition, but sometimes you can use water as a pest deterrent. On occasion, I have been able to control some infestations of spider mites and aphids by just giving the infested plant a good bath, taking care to rinse both the top and the bottom of the leaf surface. Sometimes when

an insect pest is knocked off its roost, it may never get back up to feed again. The water may also permanently damage or kill the bug because many of them are quite fragile. Anyway, if you knock it off the plant and down the sink drain, it is a sure goner.

Using water to control pests is far from being a cure-all. It also has the drawback of causing overwatering stress on a plant. But on certain occasions, think about giving it a try.

SYNTHETIC INSECTICIDES

Synthetic insecticides should be considered a last resort after you have tried all of the others. These are totally human-made preparations, famous for a quick knockdown of the target pest, almost always taking along with them a knockdown of any beneficial pests that may be present. They tend to have longer-lasting activity, which is bothersome to the ecology of the greenhouse and possibly to you. Little is known about what these products break down into as they degrade in the environment over time, but some products of the breakdown of synthetic pesticides have been shown to be worse on the ecology than the original spray. Some of the synthetic pesticides that are on the market with lower toxicity rates include Malathion, Methiocarb, Resmethrin, Sevin and Sumithrin. The last two are not registered for edible crops.

SYSTEMIC INSECTICIDES

Systemic insecticides are also synthetic chemicals but have the ability to be taken up by the plant's vascular system. When a bug takes a bite of the plant it will also get a small amount of pesticide. If you use a little logic, you will quickly understand why you should never use a systemic pesticide on or near any edible food crop. If you do, you too will be ingesting the pesticide. Luckily, the label of all systemic insecticides states that they should not be used on food. This is good as long as people read the label. Please, be the kind of person who reads the label on any spray you plan to use.

A systemic insecticide is not a good choice for plants that are heavily infested. If systemic types of insecticides are used at all, it should be only on ornamentals as a bug preventative. I usually try to steer people away from these chemicals entirely, because the danger they pose is far greater than their effectiveness.

SPRAY ADJUVANTS AND ADDITIVES

These are matter that are added to the spray to enable it to work better, enhance the life of foliar-applied pesticides and/or increase their toxicity. Some good examples follow in spreader-stickers and what are known as PBOs.

Spreader-stickers. Have you ever noticed how a spray can bead up on some leaves after it is applied? This is especially true on plants with waxier leaves. A spreader-sticker enables the spray to flatten out and spread over the leaf to help the insecticide "reach out and touch" a bug (which is essential to enable most sprays to kill them). If it beads up too much, it is much less effective. Spreader-stickers are usually quite safe in terms of human and environmental effects. However, with so many brands of spreader-stickers on the market, you should thoroughly check it out for the intended use (i.e., food crops, ornamentals, etc.). Insecticidal soap, by its very nature, is good at sticking to waxy leaves compared with many other types of insecticides and can be mixed with other insecticides for better sticking ability.

Spreader-stickers are not readily available to home gardeners, but they are in grower catalogs and wholesale catalogs. One of the few catalogs that sells a number of spreader-sticker choices is Peaceful

Valley Farm Supply (see Mail-Order Supplies appendix). Follow the dilution rate closely, as too much spreader-sticker can burn leaves.

PBOs. PBO is an acronym for piperonyl butoxide. It is added to many sprays to enhance the toxicity. It is a synthetic substance, and there are many questions among experts as to its possible negative side effects on people and the environment. Unfortunately, you can often find botanical sprays mixed with PBO. It seems to me this takes away the advantage of using a lower toxicity spray in the first place. Make an effort to check the list of ingredients when purchasing pesticides. If you can buy the same product without PBOs, do so.

SPRAYING PROCEDURES

Before you go grabbing for that spray, be sure to confirm that what you think is a pest really is doing the damage. More than once I've come across greenhouse owners about to wipe out a bug that turned out to be a baby ladybug (it looks nothing like the adult, and the baby ladybugs are as important in controlling pests as the adults). Try your best to catch the suspect in the act of doing the damage. That may mean sneaking up on a

plant in the middle of the night with a flashlight. Look at the newer leaves of a plant, the ones toward the tip ... are they being damaged too? If not, the bug that did the damage may have stopped and is already under control. Get out your hand lens and check around the back beds to see what's going on. If you can't identify the bug, take a prisoner down to the local agricultural extension agent or plant (or bug) expert.

If you have a pest and want to spray (having decided against other listed options), pick out a safe pesticide and be sure it will be effective. The label should tell you what it will kill—and for what crops it is registered. By reading the fine print on a label or phoning your nearest extension agent or agricultural expert, you may find out more information about a pesticide, if you are curious. Get important questions answered, such as how many days before you can consume an edible plant that has been sprayed and what crops the spray will burn.

You can also find out the relative safety of a pesticide by finding out its LD-50 number. The EPA has set up a system that puts a measure of toxicity on a pesticide. The LD stands for lethal dose. The LD-50 is a way to measure how much pesticide it takes to kill 50 percent of test animals, usually mice (aren't you glad you're not a test mouse?). The amount is expressed in milligrams per kilogram. There are LD-50 tests for each pesticide that reflect the amount it took to kill the animals dermally and orally (those poor mice!). Generally, it takes more dermally applied pesticide to kill the animals, so the dermal LD-50 numbers are higher. The higher the LD-50 number, the more pesticide it took to kill the test animals. So, the higher LD-50 numbers indicate a safer pesticide, at least if you were a mouse. The LD-50 test does not reflect the pesticide's long-term effects and effects on the environment. Still, like mileage figures for cars, you can use them for comparison.

SPRAYING EQUIPMENT

You have a lot of options in spray equipment, everything from old window-cleaner pump sprayers all the way up to fancy expensive pressure sprayers. Because most home sunrooms and greenhouses are so small, you really don't need a big sprayer. A plastic squeeze bottle that holds just a quart or less will usually work fine. A favorite sprayer that I have settled on, after trying many brands, is what is sold as the Polyspray 2. It

runs about $16 to $18 in the catalogs and is well worth the price. It is a small pressure sprayer that you pump up a few times for an easy-to-control spray. It can give you a fine mist or a 30-foot (9-meter) stream (for reaching the tops of the banana tree). It is durable and English made. I have used other hand-held pressure sprayers, but none seem to have the quality of the Polyspray 2. (No, I don't own stock in the company. I just really like this little sprayer.) Still, the cheap pump sprayers or recycled sprayers also do the job adequately.

If you use more than one pesticide, you should strongly consider having a spray bottle for each type of pesticide you use. Spray bottles can also be used for applying foliar fertilizers. If you use the same container for spraying different types of pesticides, you risk contamination, even with good cleaning. Contamination can be a serious problem when two different pesticides mix, causing a pesticide that is usually harmless to beneficial insects to kill the good critters along with the bad. You may also find that you have some unexpected leaf burning. Never use a sprayer that has held an herbicide or dandelion killer with an insecticide. The latent herbicide may never wash out of the sprayer and cause big plant kills through-out the greenhouse.

I highly recommend purchasing a respirator mask for all pesticide spraying inside a greenhouse or sunspace. Masks are available through agriculture supply or feed stores and occasionally are found in some supply catalogs. Wear them over your nose and mouth when you are spraying, and be sure that they are sealed. You should never smell the stink of a pesticide through these masks. They run $30 to $40. A paint or dust mask is not enough. The greenhouse is an enclosed environment, and you need protection. This holds true even if you use a botanically based spray. The only exceptions are insecticidal soap or BT.

Plastic or rubber gloves should always be worn when spraying because many sprays can be easily and quickly absorbed directly through the skin.

Goggles are important equipment in preventing any spray from getting into your eyes. Your eyes can actually absorb some pesticides.

Also, have an old toothbrush around. Nozzles often get plugged and gummed up. An old toothbrush is the best way to clean them. After cleaning the nozzle, dispose of the toothbrush, and please don't reuse it on your teeth! Never clean nozzles with metal pins or the like. It will damage the nozzles permanently.

Safe Spraying Techniques

With the safe types of homemade pesticide sprays as well as the soap-based sprays, many of the following safety concerns are not needed. For instance, you won't need to wear a respirator mask for a spray of garlic or insecticidal soap. When in doubt, follow these precautions for over-the-counter pesticides.

1.　Read the label at least twice. It can tell you much about the material: how to store it, how to apply it, what it controls, what plants it should be used on, what plants it should not be used on and often how long before it is safe to consume food that has been sprayed with the material. Call a local county agent if you have any questions about the spray that are unanswered.

2. Seal off the greenhouse from the home until the spray has dissipated (not necessary with insecticidal soap or BT).

3. Wear protective clothing: gloves, goggles, respirator mask.

4. Use the recommended dosage listed on the label; more is not better.

5. Spray mostly the undersides of the leaves and tips of plants; that is where most pests hang out.

6. Spraying is usually best done in the afternoon or evening, with 70° F (21° C) being the temperature at which sprays are most effective.

7. Spot spray if possible. This means spray in only the infested plants or even just the portions of a plant that are infested. Just don't miss any infestations. If the plant is growing in a pot and you can take it outside or to a garage to do your spraying, do so.

8. Follow "days to harvest" guidelines on the label or from your county agricultural agent. Even with botanicals, it may be a few days before your food is safe to eat.

9. One spray application is rarely enough, especially for heavy infestations. This is because you never get every single pest. Even if you did a thorough job, the eggs (which are often resistant to insecticides) will soon hatch into a new problem. Mark your calendar for a repeat spray somewhere between 5 and 10 days. It is often a good idea to plan on a series of sprays to gain good control.

10. Clean out your sprayer with hot water and soap after using it. Don't forget to run some soapy water through the nozzle too.

11. Store the stuff as recommended on the label and in the

Proper equipment provides safety when spraying.

original container. Always store away from children and pets and far from where food is prepared.

12. Wash hands, shower and change clothes soon after spraying (not necessary with soap sprays or BT).

13. Don't open the doors to the greenhouse or return to the space until the sprays are dry.

Nonspraying Pest Controls

DUSTS

Many common insecticides of all types are available in dust formulations to be spread on and around plants. They have the problem of not getting coverage on the undersides of the leaves. There is also the problem of people's inhaling the dust when applying it. A respirator mask is helpful here. With some exceptions, sprays are generally superior to dusts in the enclosed greenhouse or sunspace.

DIATOMACEOUS EARTH

One material that is found only as a dust is diatomaceous earth. It is composed of fine silica remains of the skeletons of prehistoric one-celled organisms. To the untrained eye, it looks and feels like a fine baby powder. But when it comes into contact with an insect, it is a potent insecticide. It kills by cutting into soft-bodied insects' skin

and dehydrating the poor critters. It kills good and bad bugs alike, so avoid using it in a biological control program.

Diatomaceous earth is especially effective against slugs, pill bugs and sow bugs when spread around the base of the plant on the soil. It is a good idea to wear a respirator mask or dust mask when applying the stuff to avoid irritating your lungs.

Avoid pool filter diatomaceous earth, as it is not suitable for the garden and is hazardous if inhaled. Try to find only what is sold for controlling pests or diatomaceous earth products sold as "natural grade." Some manufacturers are mixing diatomaceous earth with the botanical insecticide pyrethrins to give it more punch.

Biological Control/ Integrated Pest Management

Integrated pest management (IPM) is, as the name implies, a strategy for the management of pests, not for their total annihilation. The end result is a tolerable level of pests in balance with the environment. IPM uses biological control, crop rotation, integrated planting, cultural controls and also (but only when absolutely necessary—and rarely) some spot pesticide spraying of isolated plants. In the greenhouse, this can be tricky.

Biological control is the management of pest populations by the use of natural enemies, known as beneficial insects. The beneficial insects are classified as either predators or parasites. A predator actually eats the bad bug. A parasite lives in or on the pest, at the expense of the pest. Predators usually feed on more than one pest. They are sometimes called general predators. Parasites tend to be specific, able to control only one target pest.

Biological control is the cornerstone of an IPM bug control setup. In using IPM, I deal with infestations by first releasing a predator or parasite. Supplementing this action, you can use the spraying of homemade pesticides, handpicking of the bugs, planting resistant varieties, maintaining a vibrant state of health in the plants and mixing up the plantings in a given area. Spray botanical or soap-type pesticides as a last resort because they usually adversely affect the beneficial insect. Try to avoid synthetic pesticides.

Biological control is not a new science. Mother Nature has been using it with good results since the beginning of time. It took a while for people to catch on to the idea of good bugs controlling the harmful ones. There was a flurry of researching and applying biological control techniques in the first half of the twentieth century. But with the advent of the pesticide DDT and other effective chemicals developed during World War II, the use of biological control measures came almost to a halt. However, there was a rediscovery of biological controls in the seventies—and for good reason. As the expense and environmental hazards of pesticides came to light, along with the fact that insects developed quick resistance to them, there was a renewed interest in poisonless pest controls.

In nature, biological control is a continuing action, constantly creating and maintaining a dynamic balance. Of approximately 1 million insects listed as plant feeders in the world, only about 1 percent are listed as actual pests of agriculture.

When using IPM and biological controls, you must ask yourself, "What level of a pest or disease is personally tolerable?" Unfortunately, people have little, if any, tolerance for even one bug (good or bad). If you can put up with a few bugs here and there, the rewards are great. This means establishing a balance of both good and bad bugs at levels that are not causing substantial damage to your plants. The reward is having a healthier environment, fewer overall costs and less labor. For instance, it takes an incredible amount of time and labor for me to spray once a week, taking care to get the undersides of the leaves of almost every plant in the greenhouse. It is much easier to plan and order a crop of good bugs, release them at the proper time and place, and then sit back and let them do all of the work. Of course monitoring their progress is a must in the management of a good control system.

When an infestation occurs, first identify the pest. Identification of the pest problem will lead you to the next decision: Which is the proper beneficial insect to use in controlling the pest? Read on for help in making this decision. Usually, the beneficial insects are purchased (mostly through mail order). Once you have released your good bugs, you must put a stop to most all spraying in the greenhouse. Most sprays are toxic to the good bugs as well as the bad, and you would not want to destroy your investment by killing the good guys. Even soap sprays can kill good bugs, but they are good to use for spot spraying because they release no toxic vapors. Spot spraying means spraying only a few leaves or just one plant, rather than entire areas. One spray that is relatively nontoxic to most good bugs (when used properly) is known generically as kinoprene or commercially as Enstar.

To acquire beneficial insects, you often order them through the mail (see Mail-Order Bugs appendix for sources). Sometimes, however, I have been able to import my own good bugs by collecting them from the great outdoors (see Braconid Wasp, p. 451). Acquiring beneficial bugs has gotten easier in recent years. When I first started using biological pest control back in the seventies, it was difficult to find much available on the market. I used to beg for beneficial insects from local university research programs. I even had a special permit to directly import them from Canada and Europe. Now a number of commercial outlets in the United States sell beneficial insects. Even many of the common seed companies sell beneficial insects.

Establishing a biological balance that keeps pest populations in check requires certain environmental conditions. First, you must create a pesticide-free environment. The best time to release the beneficial critters is *before* the infestation gets out of hand. This requires planning. If you already have a full-blown infestation, it is a good idea to apply a thorough spraying throughout the greenhouse or sunroom with soap or pyrethrin to knock the numbers down to a reasonable level. But wait at least 6 days before releasing any beneficial insects.

Next, remember that this type of control requires patience. It can take many weeks (sometimes even months) for the beneficial bugs to get established. You just have to put up with this out-of-control period but keep the faith by looking for slight increases in the good bug population and slight decreases in the harmful pests. If you don't see even slight improvements, then you need to think about why. Did

you accidently kill the good guys? Did you order enough? What about temperatures? If it is too hot or cold, beneficial bugs slow down. Usually the best temperatures for establishment are between 55° and 90° F (13° and 32° C). It takes a while for the population of the good bugs to get in gear. But once the balance is established, it is great, like a well-tuned piano that plays itself. If you are worried that things are not working, perhaps a call to your beneficial-bug supplier could shed some light on your situation.

When you order bugs through the mail or by phone, be sure to shop around. It is common to find a great discrepancy in prices. You may first find the prices to be a bit high, but if you are successful, it is always cheaper than spraying chemicals (not counting the expense to your health). The more bugs you buy at one time, the cheaper they are. This is because much of the price can be the shipping cost (usually overnight delivery). To get bargain-basement prices, think about going in on the purchase with other friends with greenhouses or sunrooms. When the order comes, you can split it up.

When you order the bugs, agree on a definite shipping and arrival day with the seller. That way, you can plan to spray to help bring down the infestation to manageable levels for the beneficial critters.

Once your good bugs arrive, get a few of them under a good light and look closely at them through a magnifying glass or hand lens. Make sure they are alive. If not, contact your supplier. Know them well, but don't hesitate in releasing them. Give them your best blessings. Follow the instructions that usually come with their packaging. You need to release them on the plants that have the highest populations of pests. Mark these plants or leaves with a tag so you can periodically check on their performance with your hand lens. Look on the underside of leaves, and always check adjacent plants for indications of the beneficial insects at work in new locations.

If you know you have a plant or area where your beneficial insect is in high numbers and well established, try plucking a few leaves and carefully relocate them to a heavier infested area of bad bugs. This is best done by hanging or perching the plucked leaves in upper portions of other infested plants needing more good guys. This is an important task in helping to spread around your good bugs and may help you reduce the num-

ber of beneficial insects you will need to order.

If you are ever pulling up or throwing out a plant while using biological control, be sure to check the leaves for any good bugs. If you discover a population of good bugs, consider leaving the plant for a while. If you must get rid of the plant, try to pluck some leaves containing good bugs and relocate where needed. I have seen hundreds of beneficial critters thrown out on one plant that, if saved, could have made a great difference in long-term establishment of biological controls.

When people are considering using biological control methods on an attached greenhouse or sunspace, there is a great worry about beneficial insects getting into the house and causing trouble. You can relax. A home is not their preferred environment. They want to be where the plants and bugs are. Besides, most are so small that you probably wouldn't even see them. It is my experience that this is a rare problem and one not to be concerned with.

A common question about biological control is: "What do the good bugs eat when they have eaten up all of the bad bugs?" This is a good question. The answer depends upon the type of predator or parasite that you introduce into your greenhouse. They usually do one of two things when they have devoured all the bad bugs. Their population drops drastically because their preferred food is gone. Sometimes the population drops so low that they become "extinct," at least in your greenhouse, and you will have to reintroduce them if the pest population rises again (this often happens with the predator spider mites). Other critters cope with the reality of having few bad bugs to feed on by feeding on nectar and pollen of the flowers. Good bugs rarely go "bad" when life gets rough on them. The ideal situation is one in which the population of the good and bad bugs is in an ongoing balance and there are always a few of each.

The beneficial critters are not limited just to insects. There are other greenhouse pest control friends. Some reptiles have excellent appetites for insects. I have a native salamander hiding in the corner of the greenhouse that I see only about once a year because he is nocturnal. At night, he takes a little feeding walk and then goes back into his hole. If you are daring, you can have snakes (nonpoisonous, of course), toads, chameleons and other lizards. They have excellent appetites for slugs,

flying pests and even a few (oops) beneficial insects, which all contribute to their balanced diet. They are also fun to watch. I had a small lizard that was the most patient character I have ever seen. He would perch on a stake and wait for the better part of a day for a fly or bug to come near. Some days he didn't catch anything, but others, he struck gold. It was great to be there once in a while when he would catch something. If the reptiles' food supply gets low, they may require supplemental food, usually available at pet stores. Many people have had good luck with birds in the greenhouse. I know some folks with zebra finches flying around the greenhouse, feeding all day long as well as adding to the ambience of the place.

If an infestation is limited to just one plant, consider taking the plant outside (if it is a potted plant) and spraying it there where it won't affect your good bugs. If you can't move it, pull it up and toss it. If it is not potted and is an incredibly special plant, try placing a bag over the plant or the immediate area and spraying with the safest material to try to gain a measure of control. Even spot spraying is chancy when you have beneficial insects in the greenhouse, because the good guys usually have even less of a resistance than the bad insects. Just a whiff of a pesticide can knock good bugs out.

The experience of having a self-contained ecosystem within your greenhouse or sunroom is a source of continual amazement. The fun of having a room that produces food and flowers is doubled when you're growing not only plants but also animals and insects in a dynamic balance. It will become a self-contained biological island (or at least a peninsula) to help bring your mind, body and spirit into a better dynamic balance of its own. At least it will help get you through a long winter in fine style.

Let's look at some of the most commonly used beneficial insects and critters.

The Greenhouse Friends

APHID PREDATOR MIDGE
(Aphidoletes aphidimyza)
Biotype: Predator.
Description: Adults are 1/16 inch (1.6 mm) in length and have long trailing legs and translucent wings that are larger than the body. The orange-colored larvae are slightly larger than the adults; they are wormlike and taper to the head. It is the larvae that feed on the aphids while the adults feed on flower nectar and pollen.

Controls: Aphids.
How to acquire: Mail order.
Comments: Eggs are laid near aphid infestations, and larvae hatch out and feed on the aphid for 3 to 6 days before burrowing into the soil to pupate into an adult. It kills the aphid by injecting a paralyzing toxin into the aphid and then sucking out their body fluids. During the winter months, when the days begin to shorten, the aphid predator midge will often hibernate in the soil. Also, at temperatures below 55° F (13° C), the midge is not effective in controlling aphids. For best control, release 3 to 5 midges per infested plant, or 250 to 500 for an average-sized home greenhouse. The drawback to this predator is that it is dormant in winter. Research is attempting to develop strains needing less hibernation. For now, though, it is good to complement this critter with the brachonid wasp for winter control.

AUSTRALIAN LADYBUG
(Cryptolaemus montrouzieri)
Biotype: Predator.
Description: Also called mealybug destroyer. A cousin to the ladybug, 1/6 inch (.4 cm) long, blackish hairy beetle with orange head and wing tips. The larvae have a white coating that makes them look similar to the mealybug. The larvae

and young feed on mealybugs.
Controls: Mealybugs.
How to acquire: Only through commercial supply houses. Sometimes the supply is limited.

The larval cryptolaemus (left) is also white and cottony like the mealybug (right).

Comments: This beetle has the distinction of having helped to save California's citrus industry in the early 1900s. It feeds mainly on mealybugs. The hardest thing about using the cryptolaemus against mealybugs is identifying it in the larva stage. Cryptolaemus is distinguished by having a longer body, longer legs and visible movements. Don't derail your control by accidently spraying the cryptolaemus larvae. Releases should be on the order of two to five per square foot (.09 sq. m). It does best in temperatures of 70° to 80° F (21° to 27° C). Recolonization is often necessary because these beetles depress mealybug populations to such low levels that they themselves starve.

BRACONID WASP
(*Aphidius matricariae* or *Aphidius ervi*)

Biotype: Parasite.
Description: Brownish or black small wasp from 1/16 to 3/8 inch (1.6 mm to 1 cm). Young larva stage is parasitic.
Controls: Aphids.
How to acquire: Until recently, commercial suppliers were unheard of. However, the *Aphidius matricariae* has now become more commonly available. In summer you may be able to collect them outside. Look for naturally occurring outside aphid infestations in a field or valley. Curled or deformed leaves may indicate an aphid party. Look for both aphids and bloated copper-colored aphids. These bloated ones will hatch out brachonid wasps. Bring these parasitized aphids into your greenhouse, where hopefully they will set up shop working on your greenhouse aphids. I've had great success with

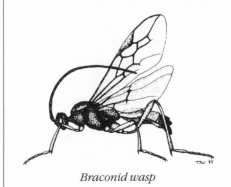

Braconid wasp

this method. They may occasionally move into your greenhouse from the outside garden naturally. Release at the rate of one per 20 to 80 square feet (1.8 to 7.4 sq. m).

Comments: Most good parasites are in the wasp family. This brachonid is among the better parasites. Look for copper-colored bloated aphids for indications of control. The adult chews an escape hatch out of the bloated (dead) aphid and then moves on to find new aphids to lay eggs in. It tends to provide the best control in fall through spring (the hot temperatures of summer seem to slow it down. That is the best time to use *Aphidoletes aphidimyza*). The *Aphidius* is attracted to the color yellow, so remove any sticky yellow bug traps that you may have set.

ENCARSIA FORMOSA
(*Whitefly parasite*)

Biotype: Parasite.

Description: Adult: Small and harmless (it never stings anything but whiteflies); about 1/16 inch (1.6 mm) in size (not easy to see unless you use a hand lens). The head is black and the abdomen light yellow. Eggs: Black and round, about 1/32 inch (.8 mm). Found on the undersides of leaves near and among whitefly populations.

Controls: Whiteflies. Much less effective against sweet potato whiteflies.

How to acquire: Usually through commercial suppliers. May be collected from other greenhouse growers who use the wasp for whitefly control.

Comments: When purchased, the *Encarsia* will arrive as black "eggs" on a leaf or card. Hang these leaves or cards on the lower part of a plant that has an infestation of whitefly scales (the white round wingless critters on the underside of the leaf). If slugs are a problem, put a control or repellent under the release area (such as dried chile pepper). Slugs love to climb up plants to eat *Encarsia*, derailing your control. The young wasps will hatch out of the scale and fly to the area where whitefly young are developing. The young whitefly scale is immobile. The *Encarsia* will lay eggs into the developing whiteflies by "stinging" each scale. The *Encarsia* young will begin to grow in the whitefly scale, feeding on and eventually killing this developing whitefly. The white scale will eventually turn black as the wasp grows within, becoming the "egg" for the new wasp. The wasp will hatch through a small slit it makes in the now blackened scale and fly off to lay more eggs in a similar fashion. As with all parasites, in completing their life cycle they control the whitefly. They parasitize only the whitefly and affect no other insect. Establishment of the *Encarsia formosa* is indicated by the blackening of many young developing whitefly scale 2 weeks after *Encarsia* have been introduced. If you have a good hand lens, you can look at the blackened scale under magnification to see if the *Encarsia* has hatched. Look for a slit or small hatch door, indicating that they have flown the coop. This is helpful in determining if the leaves (with the black scale) have some viable *Encarsia* yet to hatch. For good establishment, repeat releases two to three times, at 1- to 2-week intervals. After establishment, you can spread the *Encarsia* to other problem areas by plucking off a leaf full of the black dots (developing *Encarsia*) and hanging it in a new area of infestation. While establishing the wasp, do not prune the plants in the area of initial release until the wasp has begun some control of the whiteflies. Also, while using the *Encarsia* in your greenhouse, do not use any control methods for whiteflies involving yellow sticky traps or boards. I have found far too many *Encarsia* dead on these traps. The only

insecticide relatively safe to use around the *Encarsia* is Enstar, but use it only as per the label instructions. It is a good idea to reduce the population of heavy infestations of the whitefly a few weeks prior to the release of the *Encarsia* by using insecticidal soap, pyrethrin or Enstar. Essential to establishment of the *Encarsia* is warm temperatures averaging 65° to 80° F (18° to 27° C). Unfortunately, the whitefly can survive cooler temperatures better than the *Encarsia*, which may become sluggish during the short days of winter. During this time you may need to look at using supplementary controls, such as Enstar and/or general predators, such as green lacewing. Establishment of *Encarsia* may take up to a month, so plan ahead and be patient. To overwinter the *Encarsia* in a cool greenhouse, maintain some hardy poinsettias or geraniums with a healthy population of both whitefly and *Encarsia*. Grow them near the warmest part of the greenhouse. With a little luck, the *Encarsia* will spend the winter here. As the temperatures warm up and the whiteflies start doing damage, repeat the spreading of *Encarsia* eggs around the greenhouse, using leaves from the overwintered plant. You may still need to release newly purchased *Encarsia* if the whitefly seem to have the upper hand. Unfortunately, the *Encarsia* does not provide effective control against the sweet potato whitefly.

GREEN LACEWINGS
Biotype: Predator.
Description: Adult: up to 1 inch (2.5 cm) long; slender green body; large lacy wings; beautiful golden eyes; large antennae. Young: known as aphid lion, 1/16 to 1/8 inch (1.6 mm to .3 cm) long; large jaws; tapered body down to tail; looks like small centipede without all the legs. Eggs: 1/16 inch (1.6 mm) round, found on the end of a 3/4 inch (1.9 cm) long, thin hairlike stalk.
Controls: Only young are predaceous; adults feed only on nectar from flowers. The young feed on a wide variety of greenhouse pests, including mites, and do a good job on whitefly young, but their favorite dish is succulent aphid sushi.
How to acquire: Usually through the mail. They may fly in from the outside on their own, if your vents are not screened. They can also be collected from the outside if you know how to look for the young, which are borne on the thin stalks.
Comments: Green lacewings are usually very good predators but are subject to being eaten by other predators and each other. For this

reason, try not to release them all in one spot—spread them around. Don't release any other predator or parasite in adjacent areas. If eggs have hatched when they arrive, release them immediately, as the young will eat each other in close confines. To release, scatter on the leaves, in crotches of stems and as near to pest infestations as possible. Early-morning application is best. Even better, release them the moment they arrive in the mail.

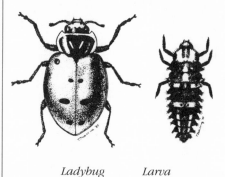

Ladybug   Larva

LADYBUG OR LADYBIRD BEETLE
Biotype: General predator.
Description: Adult: 3/16 inch (.5 cm) long, oval-shaped; red-orange outer wings with dark spots. Young: 1/16 inch (1.6 mm) long; flat-looking, tapering to the rear; dark gray with orange spots. Eggs: elongated football-shaped, 1/16 to 1/8 inch (1.6 mm to .3 cm) long; yellow; laid in bunches on the leaf.
Controls: Both adults and young

feed on many insects, including aphids, whiteflies (young), spider mites, mealybugs, scale. Usually, best with aphids.

How to acquire: Usually through the mail—may come into the greenhouse naturally, or you may hand carry them in. Purchase by the gallon, quart or pint. One gallon is approximately 75,000 ladybugs. A pint is plenty for a small greenhouse.

Comments: Generally ladybugs aren't all that they are stacked up to be for pest control in an enclosed greenhouse or sunspace. This is because of the higher temperatures and their on-and-off feeding habits. Sometimes they will do wonderful jobs on aphid populations. Then there are times when the aphids almost dance in front of the ladybugs' noses with reckless abandon; the ladybugs yawn (perhaps they're too preoccupied with mating, which they do a lot of). To sum it up, they are sometimes good and sometimes not. Ladybugs will store in the refrigerator for up to 3 months, but do not freeze them. Use as needed out of the refrigerator; release them only in the evening after a watering. The bugs are very thirsty when first released and must have some water droplets around immediately. Ladybugs may not be available during certain times in winter, so check with a supplier. Ladybugs will feed on flower nectar and pollen during times of few pests. They usually need to be periodically reintroduced into the greenhouse as their numbers dwindle over time. Be sure to learn what an immature ladybug looks like so you don't mistake it for a pest.

MEALYBUG PARASITE
(*Leptomastix dactylopii*)
Biotype: Parasite.
Description: Small wasp from 1/16 to 3/8 inch (1.6 mm to 1 cm).
Controls: Mealybugs.
Comments: This parasite works well when used in tandem with the *Cryptolaemus* predator in controlling the mealybug. At this writing, it is difficult to locate. When you do find a mail-order supplier that has it, it will be expensive until it becomes more commonly available.

PRAYING MANTIS
Biotype: General predator.
Description: Adult: resembles walking stick; large, up to 5 inches (13 cm) long; brown to green. Triangle-shaped head; large forearms to catch prey. Young: resembles an adult, only much smaller—1/8 inch (.3 cm) and larger. Looks almost like a large mosquito. Eggs: born from an egg case (up to 200

Praying mantis

eggs per case). The case resembles a wad of rigid brown foam about 1 1/2 inches (3.8 cm) in diameter.
Controls: While young, they feed on many soft-bodied insects, but not aphids. As they grow, they feed on larger insects, including each other.
How to acquire: Usually through the mail. In warmer climates, egg cases may be collected from outside in late fall and winter. Look for egg cases on branches of trees and shrubs.
Comments: Hang mantis egg cases from a branch in areas with pest problems. Egg cases do not change appearance appreciably after the young have hatched, so watch closely. Cases are generally available only from January through June. When they are young, mantises do a fine job on many greenhouse pests. As they get bigger, they like to eat bigger critters such as houseflies and wasps but still may feed on the smaller, more

common greenhouse pests. Unfortunately, because they are general feeders, a mantis can occasionally be found feeding upon other beneficial insects, such as ladybugs. Mantises are fun to have around, especially if you are not used to seeing them. I love the way they can turn their head to look at you in the eye.

PREDATOR MITE
(Phytoseiulus persimilis)
Biotype: Predator.
Description: Very small, 1/64 inch (.4 mm); resembles the two-spotted mite but has longer legs, is slightly larger and is reddish in color. Hard to distinguish from other mites.
Controls: Mites only.
How to acquire: Usually obtained through a commercial supplier.
Comments: This predator mite has a healthy appetite for its pesky

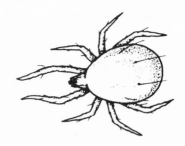

Predatory mites move much more quickly than two-spotted mites.

cousin, the two-spotted mite. It can eat up to 20 two-spots a day and multiplies fast. For these reasons, it is the fastest-acting beneficial predatory mite. It does best in temperatures between 70° and 80° F (21° and 27° C). There is a *Phytoseiulus persimilis* strain available that tolerates higher temperatures up to 100°F (38° C) and higher humidity. You will need a minimum of 10 mites per square foot (.09 sq. m) of infested area or 300 predator mites per 20 to 30 lightly infested plants. Release the mite immediately upon its arrival in areas of mite infestation. Keep a close watch on its progress (you must use a hand lens or magnifying glass). After it kills off all the harmful mites, it often starves and disappears. This requires that you release more if the two-spotted spider mite returns in high numbers. Predatory mites are decimated by the use of sulfur-based sprays and most pesticides. Avoid using these after a release has been made. Predatory mites often have a resting stage in winter and are not as effective. Fortunately, most two-spotted spider mites also are slower at infesting plants in winter when the temperatures are cooler. Positive results are usually seen in 2 to 3 weeks.

Other spider mites available for special situations include *Amblyseius californicus*, a good choice for cooler greenhouses between 65° and 85° F (18° and 29° C). It survives lower humidity situations better than the *Phytoseiulus*. Even more important, it is better suited to survive the absence of prey longer. It is slower at control of the two-spotted spider mite. Still, it is a good backup to the *Phytoseiulus*. I have found that the two together can make a good combination.

Phytoseiulus longipes is a good choice for lower humidity and temperatures between 70° and 90° F (21° and 32° C). *Galendromus occidentalis* is the best choice for hot situations with temperatures over 90° F (32°C). A selected strain of this mite, known as the photoperiod neutral strain, does not have a winter resting stage and keeps on eating the bad mites as long as the winter temperatures are on the warm side. For this reason, the *Galendromus* is another good mite to use in tandem with the *Phytoseiulus persimilis*. Check with your supplier.

SPIDERS

Biotype: General predator.
Description: Four pairs of segmented legs. Often found in webs. Abdomen strongly constricted at the base.
Controls: Spiders feed on many

small insects, including winged aphids and whiteflies. They also feed on other crawling insects.

How to acquire: Not available commercially. Spiders can be found outside and brought in or will arise naturally as you resist the spraying of pesticides. Smaller spiders seem more active and better at controlling greenhouse pests. Besides, they're not so scary to people!

Comments: Spiders are an important general predator that you should make friends with in a greenhouse. I know some of you are

Spider

thinking, "Are you kidding or crazy?" I am not kidding, although I have found a bit of craziness helpful in running greenhouses. The main point is: If you can get over your arachnophobia, spiders can become great helpers. Very few will sting and poison people— most are quite harmless and very helpful (just don't make friends with black widows). I have seen whole greenhouses cleaned of aphids in just a week by a healthy spider population. Besides, they usually make every effort to stay out of your way by hiding under leaves and benches and in dark corners.

Syrphid or hover fly

SYRPHID FLY OR HOVER FLY

Biotype: Predator.

Description: Adult: 3/8 to 1/2 inch (1 to 1.3 cm). Resembles a wasp but is really a fly. It has yellow or orange rings on a black body. Has the ability to hover like a hummingbird or bee (usually around flowers). Young: 1/16 to 3/8 inch (1.6 mm to 1 cm). Looks like a small gray or brown maggot. Eggs: laid singly, oval, white and 1/32 inch (.8 mm) in size.

Controls: Usually only young are predaceous and have a good appetite for aphids.

How to acquire: Only from the outside. They fly in, or if you are adept at identifying and catching flying bugs, you can hand collect them (no, they don't sting). It is too bad this bug is not currently for sale. If you happen to see it in your greenhouse or garden, consider yourself lucky. Flowers attract the adults into your yard and green-house. They look much like a wasp, except that their body is not segmented. You can tell you have a syrphid or hover fly by its superb flying ability and the way it hovers in the air around flowers.

THRIPS PREDATOR
(Amblyseius cucumeris
or *Amblyseius barkeri)*
Biotype: Predator mite.
Description: Almost microscopic; look for small brown speck.
Controls: Thrips.
How to acquire: Only through commercial supply houses.
Comments: These critters can provide good summer control of thrips. They need to be applied at the first thrips sighting. When winter days are short and temperatures low, their effectiveness decreases considerably.

TOADS, CHAMELEONS, LIZARDS,
SALAMANDERS AND SNAKES
Biotype: Predators.
Description: Reptiles.

Salamander

Controls: Slugs and assorted flying insects.
How to acquire: Pet shops or the outside.
Comments: Chameleons and toads seem to feed on flying insects. They position themselves on the tops of plants in search of food. Lizards, salamanders and snakes will feed on many bugs, as well as slugs. There is a lot of room for experimentation. Be sure to put away the mouse poison because it may also kill the reptiles. If food gets low for these predators, you may have to supplement with food such as mealworms, available at pet stores. Reptile predators are not recommended for the squea-mish or the commercial green-house, because these great little creatures often scare the heck out of people. Otherwise, give them a try—you may find a good friend under the scales.

WHITEFLY EGG PREDATOR
(*Delphastus pusillus*)
Biotype: Predator.
Description: A tiny black lady beetle about 1/32 inch (.8 mm).
Controls: Whitefly, sweet potato whitefly.
How to acquire: Mail order. Very experimental and expensive.
Comments: This beetle is a relative newcomer to the whitefly control

field. Currently, I have found it only in the IPM Laboratories and Praxis catalogs (see Mail-Order Bugs appendix). It is still somewhat experimental. I have not had a chance to try it. Application is recommended at one beetle every 15 to 50 square feet (1.4 to 4.6 sq. m), depending upon the level of infestation. The great advantage this critter has is that, unlike the *Encarsia formosa*, it has a good appetite for the sweet potato whitefly.

DISEASES

A disease may cause the death of a whole plant, death to part of a plant, a cancerous overgrowth of plant tissue, and dwarfing or slow growth. Not all diseases are caused by organisms. From the plant's point of view, many are the result of an adverse environment. Nonorganism-caused troubles may resemble problems caused by an organism and may be just as destructive. Conversely, some diseases resemble a plant nutrient deficiency. Your plants may be afflicted with a combination of both. Insect pests are a major contributor when it comes to spreading diseases. When you add it all up, understanding diseases can be confusing. Let's make some sense of it.

The greenhouse environment is not a sterile place; it is full of life at all times, and sometimes it will seem as if insects and diseases appear out of thin air. But the reality is that they have been in progress for some time. Upon the discovery of a pest or disease problem, people all too often overreact, and the supposed cure turns out to be worse than the disease itself.

The hardest reality that a greenhouse gardener must face is that there is rarely an all-out cure for plant diseases. This doesn't mean plants can't get well, but it is usually a slow reaction. It is not like a bug problem for which you can just kill the bug and be done with it. So where does that leave the gardener? Well, we still have some good options. First, we have the ability to control the environment. By altering the environment, sometimes even slightly, we can often control a disease problem. For example, by just providing better ventilation we can reduce many diseases that afflict plants.

We also have measures of prevention to keep the disease from ever occurring. This can be as simple as keeping the plant at a level of optimum health by giving it the proper environment and preventing infestations of bugs. Any stress from the environment will promote the occurrence of a disease. Diseases can be prevented by growing varieties that are resistant or tolerant to a given disease (as described in Chapter 4, Selecting the Right Plants). Resistance can vary from totally solving the problem to a slight decrease in the disease. Either way, it is worth growing a resistant variety whenever possible. Sometimes the resistance is listed in a catalog. More often, you'll just have to be observant and test different varieties of a given plant to find which performs better when a disease is present.

It is rare that a spray formulated for disease control will quickly cure the disease. In fact, most sprays for controlling diseases are not designed to be a cure but rather to prevent further infection. They are the type of thing that must be applied on a regular basis prior to your seeing any sign of disease. That is why I regard preventative spraying with fungicides as a big headache. When that's what is required to keep a plant alive, I usually opt to let the plant succumb to the disease.

What it all comes down to is that diseases are hard to get rid of and usually much easier to prevent.

Prevention of Disease

The old adage "An ounce of prevention is worth a pound of cure" also applies in the greenhouse. Here are some guidelines:

1. *Maintain plant health.* Avoid overcrowding, and provide a healthy growing environment with proper levels of ventilation, humidity, water, light, nutrition and so forth. This also involves proper scheduling and maintaining soil health.

2. *Keep your greenhouse clean.* Remove diseased plants. Keep the hose nozzle off the soil. Before reusing old pots, clean with hot water, soap and diluted bleach, and rinse well. Keep dead leaves off of the soil surface.

3. *Start seedlings in new potting soil* (usually sterile soil). See Chapter 5, Plant Propagation and Chapter 9, Getting to the Roots.

4. *Use compost from greenhouse plants only in an outside garden.* Outside garden plants may be composted for greenhouse use.

Running two parallel compost piles helps to break potential disease cycles because often indoor and outdoor diseases are different.

5. *Avoid taking on gift plants.* These are the gift horse that one should look in the mouth very carefully before even considering acceptance. Also, try not to baby-sit or nurse other people's plants in your greenhouse. This is a great way to get new and different bugs and diseases.

6. *Keep the air moving.* Diseases, like insects, love stagnant air, especially during the day. Try to have a small fan moving the air during the day, even when the greenhouse needs no ventilation.

7. *Rotate the crops to break disease cycles.* Keep a map of your planting layout from season to season, and be sure you are rotating your crops. Avoid following crops with their relatives (this often occurs within the large cabbage family or tomato family of plants). See Chapter 3, Plant Layout, for family lists.

8. *Interplant by mixing up the plantings in an area or a bed.* Rather than growing a solid bed of radishes here and a bed of lettuce there, try mixing them both in a bed. See Chapter 3, Plant Layout, for more information on interplanting.

Environmentally Caused Diseases

A number of plant maladies common in greenhouses are solely the result of the environment. Environmentally caused symptoms usually occur on plants of different species in a broad area of your greenhouse, rather than affecting an individual plant. Disease organisms, in contrast, usually affect only one plant species or family of plants. Rarely do organism-caused diseases afflict different plants of different families. By looking at what is affected, you can discern the problem that caused the disease. For instance, if brown blotches are affecting flowers, herbs, tomatoes and more, then you probably have an environmentally caused problem. If you see a problem on only one type of plant or a couple of related plants, such as yellowing of leaves on tomatoes and peppers (which are in the same plant family), then you probably have a problem with an organism-caused disease. Let's look at some of the common environmentally caused diseases.

SYMPTOMS OF COMMON ENVIRONMENTALLY CAUSED DISEASES

Ammonia. When high amounts of ammonia are in the air, leaves may have a cooked appearance, with brown to red splotches. Damage may also appear as tan and white spots on cabbage family plants, and leaves may drop off. Some people believe small amounts of ammonia may actually help plants, but there is debate on this. I once saw ammonia toxicity in a greenhouse attached to a chicken coop. The ammonia came in from the coop's large amount of chicken droppings.

Cold damage. Dark green, wilted or dry leaves can occur on plants nearest glazing or vents with air leaks. Also look for misshapen fruit, poor fruit set and blossom drop.

Ethylene. Ethylene is a by-product of the combustion of fossil fuels or leaks of propane or natural gas. Look for growth reduction; leaf buds and flower may fall off; also leaf deformities may occur.

Finger blight. Dead green areas on the leaves may result from too much handling. Occurs most often on unusual plants, scented herbs and other plants located at eye level. Also, smokers transmit tobacco mosaic virus to tomatoes and peppers by touching the leaves.

Lack of light. Wherever there is shade, look for plants with stems becoming elongated and spindly. This can be helped by the addition of more overhead windows or skylights and by painting walls white to increase the reflective light that enters the greenhouse.

Nitrogen oxides. The symptoms are the same as for smoke damage, along with growth suppression. Common in greenhouses located near manufacturing plants, refineries, the combustion of fossil fuels and busy highways.

Nutrient problems. A little fertilizer is good; more is often a disaster. If you suspect you over-fertilized, look for burned tips of leaves. Read Chapter 9, Getting to the Roots, for more guidance. Also, see the discussion on blossom-end rot in tomatoes in Chapter 8, A Closer Look at the Plants.

Pesticides. The use of pesticides results in variable symptoms. The herbicide 2,4-D causes unusual leaf and stem curling. Many pesticides cause burn spots or leaf yellowing and stunting. When using pesticides, please read the label for safety precautions. Even insecticidal soap can burn leaves when applied in stronger formulation or on the wrong plants. Spray drift from outside may enter the greenhouse through a vent in summer. Herbicides should never be used in the greenhouse. Accidental spills of herbicides in the soil can be helped somewhat by the addition of activated charcoal to absorb the chemical. Let's hope it never comes to that.

Smoke. Yellow, tan or papery blotches appear between the leaf veins, while the veins usually stay green. All ages of leaves are affected. Affects most crops, but let-

This smoke damage was caused by a wood-burning stove with poor draft.

tuce is somewhat resistant. Check wood heaters or other types of heaters for down drafting (not good for people either).

Sunscald. Areas of round or angular browning are caused by water droplets acting as magnifying glasses. Relatively rare in the greenhouse, but where there is clear single-pane glass, it is more likely. This problem may also occur in greenhouses with aluminum foil on the walls or where light is reflected by a polished surface (including mirrors).

Wind damage. In the greenhouse? Yes, particularly where plants are growing near fans, windows or vents. Look for brown, papery leaf spots, wilting, stunted growth.

Organism-Caused Diseases

Microorganisms (also known as microbes) have very complex biologies. To even begin to understand the ecology involved is a grand task. Identifying the disease symptom is easier and is essential to proceeding with the proper steps of control.

Diseases are caused primarily by three organisms: bacteria, fungus and virus. Depending upon

Management of the Environment to Prevent Diseases

The environment can often be slightly altered to help control your disease problems. The action you take depends upon the specific disease. Think about the environment when you are having a disease problem. Could one of these possibilities be creating the opportunity for disease?

1. *High humidity.* One of the most common environments that a disease needs in order to spread is high humidity. Always try to avoid overwatering, and use good ventilation practice to keep the air moving.

2. *Water management.* Old-time greenhouse operators have often told me that your watering habits will make or break you. Water in a manner that gets most of the water on the soil rather than on the leaf. Moisture on the leaf will help in the spread of many diseases. See Chapter 1, The Greenhouse Environment, for more about watering.

3. *Soil stress.* Salty, alkaline soils or highly acidic soils will help weaken plants for disease infestation. Overfertilization, especially with nitrogen, is commonly the root of a disease problem because it encourages rich, succulent growth that diseases (and bugs) seem to love.

4. *Overcrowding.* If plants are not placed properly and are growing too close, it can create stress and competition for light, which encourages diseases.

5. *Temperature.* Sometimes a disease can be controlled just by running the greenhouse a little bit cooler or warmer. If you have the ability to control the temperature, try experimenting with it. Run a few degrees warmer or cooler and see what happens.

the microbe, they survive by moving through air, water, soil and plant debris. They can also be carried by insects. In these same environments, however, there are also predator or parasitizing beneficial microbes that attack the disease-causing microbes. This is why a sterile environment doesn't always offer the best control. In fact, the more we encourage high microbial populations, especially in the soil, the less we see disease organisms taking hold. Much like beneficial insects, the harmful microbe populations are controlled to some extent by beneficial microbes. Organic matter, when added to the soil, is the bread of the microbes. That is one reason why organic matter is so important and probably why I have found that plants grown hydroponically are more susceptible to disease problems.

Before we look at specific diseases and organisms, let's first look at the options we have to control disease.

Resistant Varieties

Disease-resistant plant varieties are much more common than insect-resistant varieties. Don't be misled; seed companies use the term "resistant" much too freely. Usually the plant will be only more tolerant than other varieties. Resistant varieties may still become infested with the disease to which they are supposedly resistant. But a variety with an increased tolerance to a disease is still worth growing. Read catalogs for descriptions of resistant varieties. If none is available, do your own variety testing. You will often discover more-tolerant varieties. Whenever you see the word "resistant," replace it in your mind with "tolerant." See Chapter 4, Selecting the Right Plants, for more information on selecting resistant varieties.

Spraying for Disease

As with spraying for insect control, spraying for disease control is a last resort. In fact, it is usually much less effective than what is experienced with insect control. For that reason I don't recommend spraying fungicides for control of diseases. Please always follow the directions whenever spraying commercial fungicides on any plant. Never increase the concentration. Test the spray on one leaf and wait a day to see if there is any possibility for burning. Also, refer to the earlier discussion in this chapter on spraying procedures and safe spraying techniques.

HOMEMADE SPRAYS
FOR DISEASE CONTROL

Milk. There has been some evidence that milk can prevent tomato seedlings from picking up the tomato mosaic virus.

Vinegar. Many growers have reported that vinegar can help prevent seedling diseases during germination. Water into soil a dilution of 1 part vinegar to 10 parts water. Let the soil sit for 5 days before sowing seeds. This is not needed when you use sterile or new potting soil to germinate seedlings.

Baking soda. When diluted in water, it can provide some help in controlling powdery mildew. You may want to experiment around with the dilution rate. For starters, try mixing 4 tablespoons (60 ml) of baking soda in 1 gallon (3.8) of water. Mix well and spray on the leaves. Repeat every week. This is not a cure-all for powdery mildew. Sometimes it works great, and other times the results are less than outstanding.

Potato starch. When sprayed on the leaves, it has been shown to provide some control of powdery mildew. To prepare, try mixing 5 tablespoons of potato flour and 2 tablespoons of insecticidal soap in 1 gallon (3.8 l) of water. Stir well. Let it sit overnight prior to spraying. Spray every 5 to 7 days. This has also been seen to control aphids. Go easy on this spray, as it will leave your leaves looking very white.

Horsetail tea. Horsetail is a native plant found growing in many areas of the United States. Its scientific name is *Equisetum arvense*. It has been used for years by organic gardeners to control and prevent fungus diseases. To make your own, steep 1/4 cup (60 ml) of chopped or ground leaves in a 1/2 gallon (1.9 l) of water overnight. Strain and spray. Horsetail leaves are currently offered by Peaceful Valley Farm Supply (see Mail-Order Supplies appendix) if you can't find them growing locally.

MINERAL SPRAYS

Sulfur spray was mentioned earlier in this chapter, used in conjunction with copper as a control for spider mites. It has the added effect of keeping leaf mildews down. One type of mixture containing sulfur is the Bordeaux mixture, which comes in dust, wettable powder and prepared-liquid formulations. It works best as a preventative, when the sulfur-based fungicide is applied to the leaf prior to its getting the fungus. It works because it prevents the spore of the fungus from surviving on the leaf. If applied correctly, it can help prevent powdery mildew. It does little good when sprayed on leaf surfaces showing massive amounts of disease. Usually these types of mineral-based sprays are applied every 7 days (well before you see the infection until 20 days before harvest).

Do not use sulfur in any form if you anticipate the temperatures above 90° F (32° C), as it could cause burning of the leaves. Also, do not apply sulfur in conjunction with a summer oil spray. If an oil has been applied in the last 10 days, hold off on the sulfur for a few more days to prevent leaf burning.

Chemical Fungicides

Chemical-based fungicides are also on the market for controlling diseases. As mentioned earlier, most all fungicides will not control an existing disease but can work at preventing the infection. This requires an almost exhausting weekly schedule of spraying, yet fungicides still are not very effective. With that in mind, why go to all the trouble of spraying these poisons in your greenhouse? I rarely recommend using a chemical fungicide. I usually have better luck altering the environment (i.e., reducing watering, altering scheduling, changing varieties). Only on

rare occasions, with a special ornamental plant that is in danger, will I consider using a fungicide such as Benomyl (a.k.a. Benlate). Benomyl has a systemic action and should be used only on ornamental plants, never on edible crops.

If you want to try using one of the many chemical fungicides on the market, be sure to follow the label recommendations. Many fungicides are not labeled for use on food crops, and care should be taken to make special note of this when selecting a fungicide.

Disease Organisms and Their Characteristics

Viruses

Viruses are very small—ultra-microscopic—and very unusual life-forms. They don't even have cell walls. Symptoms of virus infections include mosaics (yellow angular mottling or spotting), brown areas and occasional leaf curling.

Viruses are commonly transmitted by insects. They can also be carried on seed and pollen. Even people can transmit a virus disease to a plant. This is the case with the disease known as tobacco mosaic on tomatoes and other plants in this family (see p. 348). It is easily spread by tobacco smokers' fingers. Tobacco users should wash their hands thoroughly before entering or handling any plants in a greenhouse.

Controlling viruses usually is a difficult task. No sprays are available to prevent virus infections. Usually control involves growing resistant varieties, being careful when handling plants, eliminating insects that transmit the disease and using disease-free cuttings for propagation.

BACTERIA

Many people think of bacteria when they think of disease but only a small percentage of bacteria cause disease. Many, in fact, are beneficial and essential to the health of the soil and the overall health of people. Bacteria that cause plant disease usually enter the plant through leaf or stem wounds or places damaged by insects. They can also enter a plant through microscopic openings in plant leaves. Bacteria need a relatively warm temperature to live and thrive. A bacterial infection is more rare in cooler greenhouses or in the winter.

Symptoms of a bacteria infection in a plant include both circular and angular leaf spots. At first, leaf spots often appear to be some shade of green in color, then gradu-

ally turn yellow, brown or black. Other symptoms include bacterial rots in which the plant tissue disintegrates and is often slimy and smelly. Control involves disposing of plants that are infected and practicing good greenhouse sanitation, such as keeping the soil surface clean and removing any dead leaves or stems from both the plant and the surface of the soil. Often, bacterial problems are associated with high humidity and overwatering in a warm greenhouse.

You can help prevent the spread of a bacterial infection by not touching or working among wet plants. If you suspect a bacterial infection on a plant and need to prune some dead parts off, try to disinfect your pruning shears or scissors by dipping them in a dilution of bleach or rubbing alcohol between every cut.

FUNGI

Fungi cause the great majority of plant diseases, but there are also beneficial species that actually control some diseases. Fungi generally reproduce by spores, which spread in the air, soil, water and plant debris. Fungi characteristically have complex life cycles with many different stages.

The symptoms of fungus diseases include leaf spots, wilting, rots, mildews (usually a white or gray growth on the leaf surface), rusts (a rust-colored growth on the leaf) and blights (a rapid withering or decay of tissue without rotting). Fungi are best controlled with good sanitation, resistant varieties, environmental management and chemical- and mineral-based (usually copper and sulfur) fungicides.

In general, fungus diseases are difficult to identify, unless you work with them on a daily basis. They are famous for mimicking each other or for deviating from the textbook symptoms. If you have a particularly major problem and need a positive identification, get it diagnosed by a plant pathologist at your nearest agricultural university, agricultural experiment station or county agricultural extension office. When you bring a sample of the diseased plant to an expert, be sure to pick it just before leaving for the office. Place it in a plastic bag and put your name and phone number in the bag in case the experts need to get back to you about the problem.

Common Greenhouse Plant Diseases

Note: Refer to Chapter 8, A Closer Look at the Plants, for a listing of specific diseases affecting tomatoes.

LEAF, FLOWER, STEM AND FRUIT ROT

Description: Leaves have wet, brownish rot. Often found on heading lettuce, cabbage and chinese cabbage. More serious in shady locations with lots of foliage where air circulation is lacking.

Cause: Usually bacteria, sometimes fungus.

Control: Try to minimize splashing the soil while watering or the problem may spread. Overwatering, high humidities and poor air circulation aggravate this problem. Try different varieties and wider plant spacing. In the case of lettuce, try switching to a leaf lettuce rather than heading types.

LEAF SPOTS

Description: Leaf is covered with spots ranging from pinpoints to quarters in size. Leaf spots are caused by a variety of insect pests, diseases and environmental conditions. You may need some expert help in identifying the exact cause.

Cause: Most commonly caused by fungus. Also may be caused by bacteria, insects and environmental conditions.

Control: Usually based upon correct identification. Avoid splashing water on leaves when watering.

Water in morning only and avoid overwatering.

Mildews, Powdery and Downy

Description: White to grayish leaf-surface growth with a powdery appearance. Downy mildew has more gray appearance, while powdery mildew is white. Both severely stunt growth and reduce yield.

Cause: Fungus.

Control: Use resistant varieties; sulfur application prior to major infection as a preventative (read earlier discussion); baking soda spray. I have had good luck with a spray commonly used to reduce transplant shock and leaf evaporation, called antitranspirants. It coats the leaves with a plasticlike coating that slows leaf evaporation and water loss and is commonly used on cut Christmas trees. I have found that it can be used to help control powdery mildew on ornamentals when sprayed at the first sign of the disease. Avoid using it on edible leafy plants. It can be found sold under such brand names as ForEverGreen and Wilt Pruf.

Root Rot

Description: Plants wilt constantly, roots rot.

Cause: Fungus and bacteria.

Control: Often caused by over-watering—unfortunately the urge people get when they see a wilting plant. Try replanting in new soil with a higher percentage of sand, or use a soil with better drainage. Water only when soil needs it. See Chapter 1, The Greenhouse Environment, for more information on watering technique.

Seedling Diseases (Damping Off)

Description: Damping off is a general term describing many different seedling diseases. They are very common but can be easily controlled. The symptoms may include: (1) stem rots near the soil surface and the seedling falls over; (2) seed decays in the soil before or after germination; and (3) root rots after plant is germinated and growing—plant first appears stunted and then dies, roots may turn a rust color at rotted location.

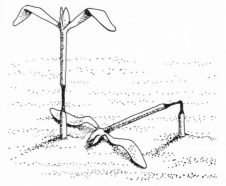

One type of damping off

Environmental Controls
of Seedling Diseases

1. *Overwatering.* Of course you should never let seedlings dry out, but overwatering and maintaining soggy soil will increase seedling diseases. Keep the soil moist, but not dripping wet.

2. *Fertilization.* The higher the level of nitrogen in the germinating soil, the softer the plant growth will be. Soft growth is particularly susceptible to seedling diseases.

3. *Light.* Seedlings grown in ample light are more resistant to seedling diseases. If your seedlings are showing signs of a light deficiency (elongated, lanky growth; light green leaves), they will also be more susceptible to seedling diseases.

4. *Soil salinity.* If your soil test shows a high concentration of salts in the soil or an unusually high pH (7.5 or more), you'll see more damping off.

5. *Temperature.* Seeds germinate best at temperatures between 65° and 80° F (18° and 27° C), depending on the specific requirements of each crop. When seeds are grown at higher or lower temperatures than optimum, they'll be more susceptible to diseases.

6. *Poorly aerated soil.* A great place for seedling diseases to grow is in poorly aerated soil. Add extra amounts of sand to your soil, or better yet, use a good commercially available potting soil.

7. *Old, infested soil.* Using soil that previously had seedlings or other plants growing in it will increase the incidence of seedling diseases. Such soil tends to be infested with the diseases that cause seedling death. Use either sterilized soil (See Chapter 5, Plant Propagation, for more information) or virgin commercial potting soil, which is already sterilized.

8. *Depth of planting.* Planting seeds too deep delays emergence and allows for more seedling diseases to occur. (See Chapter 5, Plant Propagation, for more information on planting depths.)

9. *Age of seed*. Older seeds tend to be weaker, and as a result, they may have more problems with seedling diseases. Use new seeds (within a year or two in age), especially if you are experiencing any problems with germination. Always store seeds in dark, cool airtight containers (see Chapter 5, Plant Propagation, for more information).

10. *Crowded seedlings*. Thickly planted seedlings compete for light, water and nutrients. This creates a stress situation for the seedlings, which in turn makes it easier for them to be attacked by seedling diseases. Give each seed plenty of room to grow, so that adjacent seedling leaves don't touch each other. When starting seeds in flats or containers, it is better to sow them in rows rather than just scattering them.

Cause: Fungus and environmental causes.

Control: Control the environment. One of the best controls is to use sterile soil for seed germination. Most store-bought potting soil is sterile and suitable for seedlings. See Chapter 5, Plant Propagation, for more information. In order to control seedling diseases, we must first understand the environment that fosters these problems.

Sooty Mold

Description: Black, sticky, dirty dustylike growth usually on lower leaves. You may first see a shiny cast to the leaf before it grows the mold.

Cause: Insect drippings (honeydew) from above the affected leaf trigger the growth of this black fungus.

Control: Control aphids, whiteflies and other sucking insects.

Diseases: When All Else Fails You

Sometimes figuring out the cause and control of a disease can be very frustrating. To further the frustration, all too often the root of the problem is something you did to the growing environment. When frustration sets in, the number one thing to do is to get a positive identification from an expert, such as a master gardener or county agricultural extension agent. It may also be time to bite the bullet and consider tossing out the plant. Diseases are usually not the problem in a greenhouse that bugs are. The learning curve for gardeners is quick, and you will find that a few preventative measures will handily take care of the problem.

WEEDS

A weed is defined as a plant growing out of place. A greenhouse weed could even be a tomato that sprouted in the wrong spot from a fruit that fell on the soil last season. Weeds can also come from manures or composts that contain viable seeds or from mint plants or dill seed that have the secret desire to proliferate the earth. I have rarely seen a weed pose any serious problem in a greenhouse or sunspace that could not be easily controlled by a few minutes spent weeding. Avoid any consideration of using herbicides, as it is overkill in such a small growing environment. Besides, there are too many things that can go wrong when using herbicides in the confined environment of a greenhouse.

*The
Future*

EPILOGUE

The Future

*Time present and time past
Are both perhaps present in time future,
time future contained in time past.*
—T. S. Eliot

U nless you are a time traveler, predicting the future is usually an inaccurate endeavor. The predictions of futurists are sometimes close but rarely right. Still, reading their predictions can be entertaining. The exercise of thinking about the future requires that we look at the past to see if the road behind might help us prepare for the future. Imagining what the future may bring may even alter it for the better.

For these reasons, I can't pass up the opportunity to take on the inaccurate role of futurist and look into the crystal ball of the home greenhouse. What is the future for greenhouses and sunspaces, and where are we going with these wonderful sun catchers?

NEW PURPOSES FOR THE GREENHOUSE

More and more greenhouses are being used for purposes other than growing plants; this may become a trend. Many people have successfully shown that greenhouses can be incredible fish growers, producing edible fish in clear fiberglass tanks contained in the structure. Greenhouses are also being used as a more environmentally oriented alternative to processing sewage. For instance, in New England, John Todd (who founded New Alchemy Institute) and other researchers have been working on greenhouses that can imitate the recycling processes of a marsh in nature. They call it solar aquatics. The purpose is to provide an efficient and economic means of purifying and restoring fresh water. In a greenhouse they have created an intensive man-made marsh. Here they run a stream of unprocessed sewage through a series of large fiberglass tanks filled with a diversity of bacteria, algae, microscopic plants and animals, snails, fish and higher plants. After being filtered through the tanks, the once-polluted water is transformed into clean, clear water. An intensive environmental filter is created using the recycling and purifying powers of natural eco-systems created in a greenhouse. Such incredible possibilities! If you are interested in this project, write to Ocean Arks International, 1 Locust St., Falmouth, MA 02540.

FUTURE PEST CONTROL

The reduction of spraying pesticides is a trend that will continue in the future. Greenhouse biological pest controls came on the scene back in the mid-seventies. The availability of beneficial critters used to control greenhouse pests has increased considerably since then. Every year there is a new good bug on the market to control a greenhouse pest. This trend will improve in the future, hopefully making the use of pesticides obsolete in the future home greenhouse.

In the meantime, we will be seeing many new classes of less-toxic pesticides that do not affect beneficial insects while knocking out target pests. Pesticides will be made from naturally occurring by-products of microbial agents or plants, which will be easier on the environment.

THE FUTURE GREENHOUSE IN THE PRESENT

Many people view the epitome of a future-world greenhouse as what they have viewed from a boat at Epcot at Walt Disney World in Orlando, Florida. Those of you who haven't visited Epcot have not seen the large hydroponic greenhouse producing a variety of fruits, vegetables and edible fish. The plants are grown in what is known as an aeroponics type of hydroponic system in which nutrient solutions are sprayed on the roots. Some plants are on conveyor systems that move them in and out of spray boxes. The plants always look incredibly healthy and the yields impressive.

Most people, after having seen Epcot's greenhouses, are sold on the idea that hydroponics is the way to go in the future. During our ride through the greenhouse, the tour guide told me that the bugs were controlled by the introduction of beneficial insects that prey upon or parasitize the bad insects. We were also told that much of the food produced in the greenhouses was served at the restaurants in the same pavilion. Being one who wanted to see the future up close, I went on an in-depth walking tour of the Epcot greenhouses. Upon closer inspection, I saw a few areas with a noticeable balance of good and bad bugs. However, there were large areas where I failed to see beneficial insects, or any insects for that matter. That was highly unusual for biological pest control. When I asked the tour guide about this, I was told that certain crops were not working out for that type of bug control. "Well, then," I asked, "how do you control the bugs on those crops?" The guide looked uncomfortable. "We spray them with Orthene," he replied. "But Orthene isn't rated for use on food crops!" I exclaimed. "That's right," he said. "We throw those crops out so they never get consumed." I couldn't pin the guide down on exactly how many square feet of greenhouse were regularly sprayed and what percentage of the crop was tossed out, but from what I could tell, both were substantial.

I walked away from that Epcot exhibit feeling that I had just witnessed an illusion—the greenhouse as amusement park—an illusion that people easily believed. An illusion of a food-producing greenhouse where no one gets dirty hands and everything works perfectly. Is this illusion bad? Not necessarily. Epcot's greenhouse does a good job of getting people excited about plants and greenhouses. However, what makes a home greenhouse gratifying is that you touch and work with plants and get your hands dirty while creating beautiful and edible things. It can't be boiled down to a sterile recipe in which everything happens as we wish. Automation of growing plants, as is done in the Epcot greenhouse, removes the fun parts of growing plants. What remains are the mundane tasks of growing. Automation, however, is a fact of life for commercial growers who must reduce labor costs. In contrast, a little physical work in a home greenhouse might feel good. To paraphrase writer Wendell Berry, "Gardening restores usefulness to the body." He goes on to say that other forms of exercise, such as jogging or aerobics, treat your body like a pet, taking it out for exercise. Gardening meshes the mind and the body in a wholly creative pursuit in a way that few activities can accomplish.

A more down-to-earth, but highly controversial, version of the greenhouse future is a project known as Biosphere II. Located in the desert of Arizona, it houses humans in a large self-contained greenhouse environment for long periods with (supposedly) no outside necessities such as food, water or oxygen. The greenhouse is designed to produce its own food and oxygen and recycle all of the water, nutrients and wastes.

At this writing, controversy surrounds the Biosphere project with accusations of cheating by letting in oxygen and allowing one of the people out of the sealed space for medical attention. Many people question whether the greenhouse space is truly sealed. Still, the approach taken by the biosphere experiment has stimulated a new interest in greenhouse ecology and could be helpful in teaching us about planet earth as well as potential space applications. It is a far cry from the assumption that in space we will be eating only dehydrated foods and space-food sticks and washing it all down with Tang. Rather, we see an attempt in Biosphere II to establish an ecology with little worry about conserving square footage. After all, out in the vastness of space, there is plenty of … space. Even with all the controversy, the Biosphere project takes a more sensible view of the future than does the Epcot greenhouses, which tell us our food will be grown in sterile-looking laboratory-like greenhouses.

GREENHOUSES AND HUNGER

Many have hoped and pursued the idea of realizing greenhouses for underdeveloped Third World countries as a solution to hunger. Unfortunately, hunger is usually more a matter of politics and distribution, which is not something that a greenhouse can solve. In work that I have done in high-altitude villages in Mexico, I have found the best results occur when good solid gardening information is provided with an ear toward problems before any solutions are offered. The use of indigenous materials is of prime importance in providing solutions. The materials required to construct a greenhouse are often lacking in areas where hunger problems occur. Making a simple miniature greenhouse known as a cold frame out of an old tire and a piece of plastic can work horticultural wonders. It is both more appropriate and more realistic than the idea of constructing grandiose greenhouses from which to feed the masses.

HIGH TECHNOLOGY AND THE GREENHOUSE

High technology is affecting the future of greenhouses, especially in terms of glazing materials. As computers and high-tech ideas merge with glass and plastics, we will see incredible changes. Already we are seeing smart glazings, which change with the environment. By changing, I mean they provide shading when the temperature is too hot. They become clearer in cloudy situations, thus increasing the incoming light. We are also seeing on the horizon glazings that will have amazing insulating abilities. There have been glazings developed that let in more net heat than heat lost, even when placed on a vertical north wall that receives no direct sun. Purchasing a glazing will soon be similar to purchasing a computer. The day you purchase it is the day it is outmoded.

What will glazings be like in the future? We will see glazings that store and reradiate winter heat. We will see glazings that generate electricity while transmitting light. We will see glazings that can change in characteristics by simply applying an electrical current to them. Some materials that pass light will also someday be able to pass certain gases, such as carbon dioxide. They may also be permeable to water while keeping the cold out. Lighter and stronger glazing materials will enable larger greenhouse areas to be covered with less supporting structure. With all of this potential technology applied to glazings, the design of greenhouses will change radically while the energy consumption will be almost nothing. In fact, we may be plugging our house into the greenhouse for our electricity and other energy needs.

BIOTECHNOLOGY IN THE GREENHOUSE

As people tinker more and more with the genes of plants, who knows where this engineering will lead in all fields of agriculture. They are even mixing animal genes with those of plants (can you imagine?). Breeding of plants has always been slow work, taking years and sometimes decades to develop small increments of change in a plant. With the techniques developed with biotechnology, changes in a plant's characteristics could become very rapid. This might enable us to develop a profusion of varieties specific to the greenhouse or sunspace. I must admit to having mixed feelings when I think of the potential. When changes occur slowly, there is more of a chance to develop wisdom needed to deal with them. I hope we will have the wisdom needed to deal with the fast-coming changes. It could become a biological potluck. We could all wake up in a science-fiction world with science-fiction greenhouses. I won't get any further carried away with that line of speculation.

THE GREENHOUSE AS A HOME-PRODUCTION UNIT

I see a future in which people will become more concerned with the quality of their food supply as the production of our food moves farther and farther away from home in our global economy. I will never forget the phone calls I received after the Chernobyl nuclear disaster. Worries of radiation pollution abounded halfway around the planet to concern people in my own hometown: "Is food safer when grown under glass?" "Can I purchase some fresh greens from you, please?"

There is a daily concern about the safety of food found in supermarkets, with worries of processing chemicals, artificial additives and pesticides. All the while, there is a great rise in the popularity of outside gardening. Many people like you have discovered the luxury of growing their own year-round cut flowers in their home greenhouses. The ability to grow both food and flowers in a home greenhouse will further contribute to the interest in sunspaces and greenhouses.

The advent of high energy costs in the late seventies helped people to discover the ability of a simple attached solar greenhouse to heat itself and the home. Solar-heated greenhouses spurred a rebirth of the home greenhouse/sunspace. Even though interest in energy conservation has since waned (but will rise again), the popularity of the home greenhouse has continued to rise consistently over the past 10 years. The interest in a greenhouse that also provides heat to the home will continue to increase as our dependence on foreign oil grows.

When greenhouses were first developed, they were usually the toys of the rich and royalty. Now it is common to see home green-houses in wealthy, middle-class and poor neighborhoods alike. In the lower-income neighborhoods, I have seen solar-heated green-houses built from recycled storm windows, recycled plastic and old wooden timbers. These cheap homemade structures grow plants as well as the expensive green-houses. I hope that there is never an illusion created that greenhouses are only for the wealthy. Hopefully there will continue to be kit green-houses or information on how to build simple greenhouses for both caviar and tuna-fish tastes. Maybe I should say both artichoke and turnip tastes!

Instead of greenhouses being attached onto homes, I foresee homes attached onto greenhouses. The greenhouse could well be-come the main focus of the house. In fact, two or more homes could be attached onto one greenhouse. This especially makes sense using solar-heated greenhouses in cold winter climates. Why not let the traditional living spaces spill into the greenhouse? Imagine cooking dinner in a kitchen that is partially in a greenhouse, picking fresh herbs, greens and fruits for the meal. Why not a bedroom that opens into a room with fragrant vining plants that create the walls.

Nearby would be edible fruits al-ways within reach. Think of the possibilities with bathrooms, fam-ily rooms and dens.

THE COMMUNITY GREENHOUSE CONCEPT

The idea of attaching homes onto greenhouses could also work for apartments and multiunit dwell-ings. I have often thought about transforming the south face of a small apartment building with an attached solar-heated greenhouse. This would provide free solar heat to the building and could create some interesting possibilities in marketing the rental of the units. Of course, the people living in this situation would be those with an interest in gardening, each tending a plot of the greenhouse. It would make for more neighborly interac-tion as opposed to most apartment situations, in which people rarely speak to each other or even know each other. It could have some positive social implications while providing heat, food, flowers and clean air.

Speaking of social implications and the greenhouse, I must discuss a unique botanic garden that I have been intimately involved with since 1977 in Cheyenne, Wyoming.

The Cheyenne Botanic Gardens

The Cheyenne Botanic Gardens differs from traditional botanic gardens in that its primary purpose is social. It has one of the more unusual histories among public gardens. The project began in 1976 as part of a private nonprofit, antipoverty, human service agency. Initial federal grants for construction and operating expenses resulted in building the first conservatory, a 5,000-square-foot (465-square-meter), 100 percent passively solar-heated building. It was the nation's first large-scale solar-heated greenhouse designed to provide food and meaningful activity to senior citizens year-round, even through the cold, harsh winters of the High Plains. It was built primarily with volunteer labor, and to everyone's surprise, the structure continued to stand and function for 9 years. At that point, having proved its worth to the community, we proposed and were awarded state block grant funds for a new state-of-the-art conservatory. In 1986 we moved into a new conservatory and became a division under the Cheyenne Parks and Recreation Department.

Cheyenne Botanic Gardens

The real success story is the evolution and meshing of human services with a botanic garden. In the early days, as word of our project spread throughout the community, we were approached by other human service agencies requesting that the physically and mentally challenged and youth at risk be involved in our project. These people were included with great success. Thus was formed the basis of a triad of volunteers composed of seniors, the handicapped and youth at risk. This triad represents three groups commonly isolated from the mainstream of society, hidden away in nursing homes and senior housing, sheltered workshops and detention centers. These people are working together much like an extended family.

Our volunteers provide 95 percent of all the physical work at the gardens, averaging more than 900 volunteer hours per month. In return, these same volunteers receive fresh food that they helped grow, a sense of worth and self-esteem from doing meaningful activities and a feeling of being needed (which they are!).

The Cheyenne Botanic Gardens supports its human/social services by providing to the public the traditional services of a public garden. Included are demonstration gardens, community gardens, classes and various educational plant displays both inside and outside the conservatory. In addition, the Cheyenne Botanic Gardens serves as a municipal nursery, producing all the bedding plants for city plantings. The greatest cost of operating a public greenhouse is heating and labor. Because of the great dependence upon volunteers and the use of solar heating, the project has proved to be extremely cost-effective. The project stabilizes human services and enables a small city to have a botanic garden, when previously the community did not have the resources to provide either.

The most important crops grown at the Cheyenne Botanic Gardens are pride and self-esteem of the seniors, the youth and the handicapped who work there. Self-esteem is the best therapy ever developed. These people know that they are important to the project. Their work is not the make-work type of activity common to many therapeutic programs. Rather, they do real work that is so essential to this botanic garden.

The 6,800-square-foot (632-square-meter) conservatory built in 1986 includes a kitchen–gathering room for classes, meetings and

activities; a small library/confer-
ence room; offices and a basement
root cellar. The three sections to
the conservatory include demonstration gardens, herbs, cacti, orchids, subtropicals, food crops, a
water garden and more. Surplus
food is donated to low-income
feeding programs.

The Cheyenne Botanic Gar-
dens was recognized by President
Ronald Reagan with a citation for
exemplary voluntary achievements.
More recently, President George
Bush awarded the Cheyenne
Botanic Gardens his 83d Point-of-
Light award for volunteerism. This
success is the result of two key
things: a large base of ardent community supporters aiding the
project through difficult political
and financial times, and a highly
devoted volunteer force and staff
throughout its history.

Public conservatories and
greenhouses are always a stimulation of the senses, but they can also
be a vehicle for social progress. To
paraphrase Japanese horticulturist
Masanobu Fukuoka, "Gardening is
not just the cultivation of plants, it
is also the cultivation of human
beings."

Community-oriented green-
houses such as the one in Cheyenne could be easily adapted to
the needs of different neighborhoods, cultures, ages and abilities.
I sincerely believe that through
projects of this type and similar
community gardening programs,
potentially positive effects can occur. The therapeutic benefits alone
are worth the investment, but there
are other social, educational and
nutritional rewards. Many univer-
sities offer degrees and study programs in the field of horticultural
therapy. For more information on
horticultural therapy, call the American Horticultural Therapy Association at 1-800-634-1603. For more
information on the Cheyenne
Botanic Gardens, send a request
along with a suggested donation of
$2 (cash or check) to help defray
mailing costs to the Cheyenne
Botanic Gardens, 710 S. Lions Park
Dr., Cheyenne, WY 82001. For
consulting assistance, contact
Seedpeople Associates. This is a
consulting cooperative involved in
the many related areas of commu-
nity-based gardening, greenhouse
project design, operation and horticultural therapy. Write to
Seedpeople, Attn. Shane Smith,
c/o Fulcrum Publishing, 350 Indiana
Street, Suite 350, Golden, CO 80401.

IN CONCLUSION

If we hope to live and survive
successfully in a healthy manner

on the earth, then our habitat (homes and other buildings) must mesh with the outside environment while maintaining comfort. The materials used in building must be sensitive to the finite resources of the planet. We need to be better neighbors to each other and caretakers to Mother Earth. The greenhouse is not the total solution, but it can hold many important keys to the future.

Rather than being a tourist to the plant world, where we visit them in the wild, in the grocery store or on our salad plates, we can grow a greenhouse garden that enables plants to truly enrich our lives. With thanks to the bountiful earth, the result is having fun, good health and a sense of well-being.

The greenhouse is a metaphor for our endangered planet. It can and will teach us many lessons. This is true even for a greenhouse in our own backyard.

Appendices

HELPFUL ASSOCIATIONS

The following is a short list of associations that may be of help. If you are interested in a particular plant, chances are good that there is a society or association organized for that plant. For more information, check with your nearest botanical garden, garden club or county agricultural extension agent. The ones listed here have a broader appeal or are doing interesting things. *Note:* Dues may be subject to change.

American Orchid Society, 6000 S. Olive Ave., West Palm Beach, FL 33045.
Members receive monthly bulletin. Dues are $30 a year, which includes orchid handbook, yearbook, growers directory and more.

The Hobby Greenhouse Association, 8 Glen Terra, Bedford MA 01730-2048.

An excellent organization that produces a wonderful newsletter and quarterly magazine. Membership is $12 per year.

Hydroponic Society of America, P.O. Box 60, Concord, CA 94524. For those new to or experienced with hydroponics. Publishes a bimonthly newsletter and directory of books, equipment and supplies for hydroponics. Dues are $30.

Indoor Garden Society of America, Inc., 5305 S.W. Hamilton St., Portland, OR 97221.
Publishes a bimonthly journal. Seed exchange for members. Good information on plant care that would help greenhouse growers. Dues are $15.

International Geranium Society, P.O. Box 92734, Pasadena, CA 91109-2734.
Produces a quarterly journal. Opportunity to order seeds and cuttings. A great source for unusual varieties. Dues are $12.50.

HELPFUL ASSOCIATIONS (CONTINUED)
Seed Savers Exchange, Rt. 3, Box 239, Decorah, IA 52101.
This organization works to preserve heirloom seeds, and is responsible for saving many rare vegetable varieties from extinction. The exchange allows home gardeners to help in preserving heirloom seeds and facilitates the exchanging of seeds with others. Write for dues information.

HELPFUL BOOKS

The Bountiful Solar Greenhouse, by Shane Smith, John Muir Press, 1982 (out of print).

Chemical-Free Yard and Garden, by Anna Carr, Miranda Smith, Linda A. Gilkeson, Joseph Smillie and Bill Wolf, Rodale Press, 1991.

The Essence of Paradise: Fragrant Plants for Indoor Gardens, by Tovah Martin, Little Brown, 1991.

The Food and Heat-Producing Solar Greenhouse: Design, Construction, Operation, by Rick Fisher and Bill Yanda, John Muir Press, 1976.

Greenhouse Gardening, by Miranda Smith, Rodale Press, 1985.

Greenhouse Plants, Ortho, 1990.

Greenhouses, Ortho, 1991.

Greenhouses and Garden Rooms, Brooklyn Botanic Gardens, 1988.

The Homeowner's Complete Handbook for Add-On Solar Greenhouses and Sunspaces, by Andrew Shapiro, Rodale Press, 1985.

Low-Cost Passive Solar Greenhouses, a Design and Construction Guide, by Ron Alward and Andy Shapiro, National Center for Appropriate Technology, 1980.

Organic Gardening under Glass, by George "Doc" Abraham and Katy Abraham, Rodale Press, 1975.

Pests of the West, by Whitney Cranshaw, Fulcrum Publishing, 1992.

Secrets of Plant Propagation, by Lewis Hill, Garden Way Publishing, 1985.

Plants Plus, by George Seddon and Andrew Dicknell, Rodale Press, 1987.

Rodale's Garden Insect, Disease and Weed Identification Guide, by Miranda Smith and Anna Carr, Rodale Press, 1988.

The Salad Garden, by Joy Larkcom, Viking Press, 1984.

Sun Spaces: New Vistas for Living and Growing, by Peter Clegg and Derry deWatkins, Garden Way Publishing, 1987.

MAIL-ORDER SUPPLIES

Most every seed or plant catalog carries a few supplies, but these catalogs specialize in a good selection of things you may need in a greenhouse. Catalogs are free unless otherwise noted.

The Alsto Company, P.O. Box 1267, Galesburg, IL 61401, 1-800-447-0048. Carries furniture, potting benches, tools, plant supports, watering supplies, pots and composters.

ARBICO, P.O. Box 4247 CRB, Tucson, AZ 85738. Known mostly for beneficial insects but also has a selection of fertilizers, pest traps and sustainable agricultural supplies.

Charley's Greenhouse Supplies, 1569 Memorial Highway, Mt. Vernon, WA 98273, 1-800-322-4707. One of the best sources of supplies and accessories. Good selection of products specifically for the home greenhouse. Informative catalog is $2 and worth it.

CropKing, Inc., Hydroponic Gardening Catalog, P.O. Box 310, Medina, OH 44258. Carries indoor hydroponic kits, lights, growing media, books and more. Catalog is $3, refunded with first order.

Florist Products, Inc., 2242 N. Palmer Dr., Schaumburg, IL 60173, 1-800-828-2242, 1-800-777-2242 (in Illinois). Carries fertilizers, pots and growing chemicals.

The Gardener's Eye, P.O. Box 100963, Denver, CO 80250. Supplies are mostly for the outside gardener but carries tools, furniture, books and posters of interest to greenhouse gardeners.

Gardener's Supply Company, 128 Intervale Rd., Burlington, VT 05401. Carries tools, greenhouses, watering supplies, hose winders, propagation systems and sprayers (Polyspray 2).

Hydrofarm-West, 3135 Kerner Blvd., San Rafael, CA 94901, 1-800-634-9999. Specializes in hobby hydroponic supplies and equipment.

Hydro-Gardens, Inc., P.O. Box 9707, Colorado Springs, CO 80932, 1-800-634-6362. Carries a complete collection of supplies for growing; specializes in hydroponic vegetable production and sells to commercial growers as well as hobbyists.

Kinsman Company, River Rd., Point Pleasant, PA 18950, 1-800-733-5613. Carries tools, plant supports, watering supplies, planters, plant labels, soil test kits and arbors.

MAIL-ORDER SUPPLIES
(CONTINUED)

Langenbach, P.O. Box 453, Blairstown, NJ 07825, 1-800-362-1991. Carries tools, watering supplies, potting benches, hammocks and planters.

A. M. Leonard, Inc., 6665 Spiker Rd., Piqua, OH 45456, 1-800-543-8955. Specializes in tools; also carries grafting supplies, shade cloth and glazing materials. Catalog is $1.

Mellinger's, 2310 W. South Range Rd., North Lima, OH 44452-9731, 1-800-321-7444. Carries a wide variety of seeds, plants, herbs, tools, supplies, fertilizers and pots.

The Natural Gardening Company, 217 San Anselmo Ave., San Anselmo, CA 94960. Carries tools, seed-tray heaters, books and watering cans.

Necessary Trading Company, P.O. Box 305, Main St., New Castle, VA 24127. Specializes in organic fertilizers and pest controls; carries books and kitchen supplies.

Walt Nicke's Garden Talk, 36 McLeod La., P.O. Box 433, Topsfield, MA 01983. Carries a wide selection of tools, propagators, propagation heat mats, solar ventilators, pots, soil-test kits and plant supports. Catalog is 50 cents.

Peaceful Valley Farm Supply, P.O. Box 2209, Grass Valley, CA 95945. Sells a variety of fertilizers, gardening equipment, natural pest controls and seeds; they also do soil tests. Catalog is $2.

Smith & Hawken, 25 Corte Madera, Mill Valley, CA 94941. Carries tools, furniture, watering cans, clothing and watering supplies.

Solar Components Corp., 121 Valley St., Manchester, NH 03103. Specialize in glazing and environmental control systems for greenhouses and sunrooms. Also carry fiberglass water containers (tubes) for thermal mass and aquaculture. Catalog is $2.

Teas Nursery—Orchid and Supply Catalog, P.O. Box 1603, Bellaire, TX 77402-1603. Growing supplies for orchids, florists equipment, fertilizers and more.

Wind and Weather, The Albion Street Water Tower, P.O. Box 2320, Mendocino, CA 95460. Everything you need to measure or predict the weather.

MAIL-ORDER PLANTS

Catalogs are free unless otherwise noted.

Alberts & Merkel, 2210 S. Federal Highway, Boynton Beach, FL 33435. Carries citrus, fig plants and a wide selection of ornamental plants.

The Banana Tree, Inc., 715 Northampton St., Easton, PA 18042. This is a favorite seed and plant catalog that has everything from a wide selection of banana starts to an incredible selection of tropical and rare seeds. The catalog is $3 and worth it!

The Bonsai Shop, 43 William St., Smithtown, NY 11787. Specializes in bonsai plants.

John Brudy Exotics, 3411 Westfield Dr., Brandon, FL 33511. Carries exotic rare seeds. Catalog is $2, returned upon first order.

Cactus by Dodie, 934 E. Mettler Rd., Lodi, CA 95242. Specializes in cactus; also carries succulents and other rare plants. Catalog is $1, refundable with first order.

Callia Forest Nursery, 125 Carolina Forest Rd., Chapel Hill, NC 27514.

Source for camellias and other interesting plants. Catalog is 50 cents.

Carman's Nursery, 16201 Mozart Ave., Los Gatos, CA 95030. Carries some subtropical plants, including feijoa and cherimoya.

Cook's Geranium Nursery, 712 N. Grand, Lyons, KS 67554. Complete selection of geraniums, including scented and rare varieties.

Davidson and Wilson Greenhouses, R.R. 2, Box 168, Crawfordsville, IN 47933. Good selection of bougainvillea plants and other ornamentals. Catalog is $1.

Exotica Seed Company and Rare Fruit Nursery, 2508 E. Vista Way, Vista, CA 92083. Carries an excellent selection of subtropical edible plants and seeds, including feijoa, citrus, avocado, fig, banana and more. Catalog is $2.

The Fig Tree Nursery, Box 124, Gulf Hammock, FL 32639. Specializes in fig trees. Catalog is 50 cents.

Forestfarm, 990 Tetherow Rd., Williams, OR 97544-9599. Offers a wide variety of seeds and plants. Most are for the outside garden, but the selection is so wide that you can find many things that

MAIL-ORDER PLANTS (CONTINUED) would be great for growing in the greenhouse. Catalog is $3.

Four Winds Growers, Box 3538, Mission San Jose District, Fremont, CA 94539. These growers specialize in dwarf citrus, standard citrus and avocado trees.

Garden of Delights, 14560 S.W. 14th St., Davie, FL 33325. Specializes in palms, rare fruit trees and horticultural curiosity.

Glasshouse Works, P.O. Box 97, Stewart, OH 45778. Contains one of the largest listings of ornamental greenhouse plants.

Highland Succulents, Eureka Star Route 133F, Gallipolis, OH 45631. Specializes in succulents. Catalog is $2.

Hollay Jungle, Box 5727, Fresno, CA 93755. Specializes in tillandsias.

K & L Cactus and Succulent Nursery, 12712 W. Stockton Blvd., Galt, CA 95632. A great source for cactus and succulents. Catalog is $2 and worth it.

Kartuz Greenhouses, 1408 Sunset Dr., Vista, CA 92083. Carries a great section of begonias as well as numerous other flowering plants for the greenhouse. Catalog is $2.

Living Stones Nursery, 6 N. Stone, Tucson, AZ 85705. Specializes in succulents and cacti. Catalog is $1.50.

Logee's Greenhouses, 55 North St., Danielson, CT 06239. Wide selection of greenhouse ornamentals and herbs; beautiful color photos. Catalog is $3.

Lychee Tree Nursery, 3151 S. Kanner Highway, Stuart, FL 33494. Carries a wide selection of subtropical edible plants.

Montrose Nursery, Box 957, Hillsborough, NC 27278. Carries a wide selection of cyclamens.

Nichols Garden Nursery, 1190 N. Pacific Highway, Albany, OR 97321. Carries a good selection of herb plants, seeds and books.

Pacific Tree Farms, 4301 Lynwood Dr., Chula Vista, CA 92010. Specializes in subtropical fruiting plants. Catalog $2.

Plant Kingdom, Box 7273, Lincoln Acres, CA 92083. Carries a variety of edible subtropicals.

MAIL-ORDER PLANTS (CONTINUED)
Plumeria People, P.O. Box 8214, Houston, TX 77282. Specializes in greenhouse plumeria and other plants. Catalog is $1.

Raintree Nursery, 391 Butts Rd., Morton, WA 98356. Carries citrus, figs and more.

Shady Hill Gardens, 821 Walnut St., Batavia, IL 60510. Has a wide selection of geraniums. Catalog is $2.

South Seas Nursery, P.O. Box 4974, Ventura, CA 93007. Carries avocado, feijoa and other subtropicals.

Teas Nursery—Orchid and Supply Catalog, P.O. Box 1603, Bellaire, TX 77402-1603. Carries orchids, tillandsias, hibiscus, growing supplies and more.

MAIL-ORDER SEEDS

There are hundreds of wonderful seed catalogs out there. I have listed just a few of note because either they carry a particular variety listed in the book or they are just good catalogs to have. I'm sure many other catalogs offer quality seeds suitable for greenhouses, but to list them all would fill many pages. This list is a good start. Catalogs are free unless otherwise noted.

The Banana Tree, Inc., 715 Northampton St., Easton, PA 18042.

Big Sky Seed Company, P.O. Box 21058, Billings, MT 59104.

Burpee Seed Company, Warminster, PA 18991.

The Cook's Garden, P.O. Box 535, Londonderry, VT 05148 ($1).

DeGiorgi Seed Company, 6011 "N" Street, Omaha, NE 68117.

Gurney's Seed and Nursery, 110 Capital St., Yankton, SD 57079.

Harris Seeds, P.O. Box 22960, Rochester, NY 14692-2960.

Johnny's Selected Seeds, Albion ME 04910.

Ledden's, P.O. Box 7, Sewell, NJ 08080-0007.

McFayden, Box 1030, Minot, ND 58702-1030.

Nichols Garden Nursery, 1190 N. Pacific Highway, Albany, OR 97321.

Park Seed Company, Cokesbury Rd., Greenwood, SC 29647-0001.

Pinetree Garden Seeds, New Gloucester, ME 04260.

Plants of the Southwest, 930 Baca St., Santa Fe, NM 87501 ($1).

Porter and Son Seedsmen, P.O. Box 104, Stephenville, TX 76401-0104.

Seeds Blüm, Idaho City Stage, Boise, ID 83706 ($3).

Shepherd's Garden Seeds, 6116 Highway 9, Felton, CA 95018.

Stokes Seeds, Inc., Box 548, Buffalo, NY 14240.

Thompson & Morgan, P.O. Box 1308, Jackson, NJ 08527.

Tomato Growers Supply Company, P.O. Box 2237, Fort Myers, FL 33902.

Twilley Seed Company, P.O. Box 65, Trevose, PA 19053.

Vermont Bean Seed Company, Garden Lane, Fair Haven, VT 05743.

MAIL-ORDER BUGS

Catalogs are free unless otherwise noted. Please note that some of these suppliers are producers of their product while others are distributors. Those that produce their own are often less expensive. Do some shopping around because prices can vary greatly.

Applied Bionomics, 11074 W. Saanich Rd., Sidney, BC, Canada V8L 3X9. Carries a wide variety of beneficial insects. You may need to get an importation permit to have bugs mailed across international borders. It is not nearly as hard as it sounds to get these permits. Canadians have more experience with using biological control in greenhouses than U.S. growers. To purchase insects from foreign countries, you must first obtain an import permit. Write to the USDA PPQ/APHIS, Federal Center Bldg., Hyattsville, MD 20782. Ask for permit number 526.

Arbico, P.O. Box 4247 CRB, Tucson, AZ 85738. Has a good selection of beneficial insects, many for the greenhouse. Also offers slug saloons, fertilizers and soil-test kits.

Biotactics, Inc., 7765 Lakeside Dr., Riverside, CA 92509. One of the best and most knowledgeable suppliers of beneficial predatory spider mites.

M.R. Durango, Inc. P.O. Box 886, Bayfield, CO 81122. Carries *Encarsia formosa,* thrips predator, spider mite predator and green lacewing.

MAIL-ORDER BUGS (CONTINUED)

Gardens Alive!, Highway 48, P.O. Box 149, Sunman, IN 47041. Informative catalog with many biorational pest controls, including beneficial insects.

Gerhart, Inc., 6346 Avon Belden Rd., North Ridgeville, OH 44039. Specializes in beneficial insects for the greenhouse.

Hydro-Gardens, Inc., P.O. Box 9707, Colorado Springs, CO 80932; 1-800-634-6362. Offers a wide variety of biological pest controls for the commercial grower but also sells in smaller amounts for the hobbyist.

IPM Laboratories, Main St., Locke, NY 13092-0099. This company produces a very informative catalog and newsletter with helpful information on using its many beneficial insects for greenhouses. Carries the hard-to-find whitefly egg predator and *Aphidius matricariae* for aphid control.

Mellinger's Nursery, 2310 W. South Range Rd., North Lima, OH 44452. Carries ladybugs and also plants and seeds.

Nature's Control, P.O. Box 35, Medford, OR 97501. Carries a wide variety of beneficial insects. Informative catalog.

Necessary Trading Co., P.O. Box 603, New Castle, VA 24127 Carries a wide variety of beneficial insects and other biorational pest-control supplies.

Organic Pest Management, P.O. Box 55267, Seattle, WA 98155. Carries a wide variety of beneficial insects. Charge for catalog.

Peaceful Valley Farm Supply, P.O. Box 2209, Grass Valley, CA 95945. Sells a variety of fertilizers, gardening equipment, natural pest controls and seeds. Also does soil tests. Catalog is $2.

Praxis, P.O. Box 134, Allegan, MI 49010. One of the few suppliers of *Debastus pusillus*, the whitefly egg predator.

Rincon-Vitova Insectaries, Inc., P.O. Box 95, Oak View, CA 93022. Carries a wide variety of beneficial insects for the greenhouse; has many years experience in the field of biological control.

Troy Hygro Systems, 4096 CTH ES, East Troy, WI 53120. Offers beneficial insects for whitefly control, as well as others.

Unique Insect Control, P.O. Box 15376, Sacramento, CA 95851. Carries lacewing, ladybug, whitefly parasite and others.

RECORD-KEEPING

To make record-keeping easier, it helps to know where each plant is growing and when. To do this, number each bed, part of a bed or area. It may help to make a map of the greenhouse and then look for a logical way to number each area. Copy these sample forms as needed.

Generic Record
This record provides a variety of uses and
general tracking of plant progress.

Date	Location	Plant	Variety Name	Comments

Date	Location	Plant	Variety Name	Comments

Planting Record

Use this record for keeping track of harvests,
schedules and general tracking.

Name of Plant	Name of Variety	Date Sown	Transplanted	Comments

Name of Plant	Name of Variety	Date Sown	Transplanted	Comments

Pest Monitoring

Pest monitoring is one of the most important activities in controlling bugs and diseases. This requires that you look throughout the greenhouse at random and/or selected places. It helps if you have a hand lens or magnifying glass to see some of the little critters such as spider mites, which are almost impossible to see with the naked eye. Above all, when you are looking for bugs, be sure to check the undersides of the leaves and the tips of plants. Take measurements every few days to see if there is a trend. Refer to Chapter 10, When Things Go Wrong, for more information on pest control.

Date	Location	Plant	Pest/Disease Observed	Level of Infesta- tion	Effects of Control (if any)

Date	Location	Plant	Pest/Disease Observed	Level of Infesta-tion	Effects of Control (if any)

AVERAGE MONTHLY PERCENTAGE OF POSSIBLE SUNSHINE FOR SELECTED LOCATIONS

Location	Jan.	Feb.	Mar.	Apr.	May	June	July	Aug.	Sept.	Oct.	Nov.	Dec.	Annual
ALABAMA													
BIRMINGHAM	43	49	56	63	66	67	62	65	66	67	58	44	59
MONTGOMERY	51	53	61	69	73	72	66	69	69	71	64	48	64
ALASKA													
ANCHORAGE	39	46	56	58	50	51	45	39	35	32	33	29	45
FAIRBANKS	34	50	61	68	55	53	45	35	31	28	38	29	44
JUNEAU	30	32	39	37	34	35	28	30	25	18	21	18	30
NOME	44	46	48	53	51	48	32	26	34	35	36	30	41
ARIZONA													
PHOENIX	76	79	83	88	93	94	84	84	89	88	84	77	85
YUMA	83	87	91	94	97	98	92	91	93	93	90	83	91
ARKANSAS													
LITTLE ROCK	44	53	57	62	67	72	71	73	71	74	58	47	62
CALIFORNIA													
EUREKA	40	44	50	53	54	56	51	46	52	48	42	39	49
FRESNO	46	63	72	83	89	94	97	97	93	87	73	47	78
LOS ANGELES	70	69	70	67	68	69	80	81	80	76	79	72	73
RED BLUFF	50	60	65	75	79	86	95	94	89	77	64	50	75
SACRAMENTO	44	57	67	76	82	90	96	95	92	82	65	44	77
SAN DIEGO	68	67	68	66	60	60	67	70	70	70	76	71	68
SAN FRANCISCO	53	57	63	69	70	75	68	63	70	70	62	54	66
COLORADO													
DENVER	67	67	65	63	61	69	68	68	71	71	67	65	67
GRAND JUNCTION	58	62	64	67	71	79	76	72	77	74	67	58	69
CONNECTICUT													
HARTFORD	46	55	56	54	57	60	62	60	57	55	46	46	56
DISTRICT OF COLUMBIA													
WASHINGTON	46	53	56	57	61	64	64	62	62	61	54	47	58
FLORIDA													
APALACHICOLA	59	62	62	71	77	70	64	63	62	74	66	53	65
JACKSONVILLE	58	69	66	71	71	63	62	63	58	58	61	53	62
KEY WEST	68	75	78	78	76	70	69	71	65	65	69	66	71
MIAMI BEACH	66	72	73	73	68	62	65	67	62	62	65	65	67
TAMPA	63	67	71	74	75	66	61	64	64	67	67	61	68
GEORGIA													
ATLANTA	48	53	57	65	68	68	62	63	65	67	60	47	60

Location	Jan.	Feb.	Mar.	Apr.	May	June	July	Aug.	Sept.	Oct.	Nov.	Dec.	Annual
HAWAII													
HILO	48	42	41	34	31	41	44	38	42	41	34	36	39
HONOLULU	62	64	60	62	64	66	67	70	70	68	63	60	65
LIHUE	48	48	48	46	51	60	58	59	67	58	51	49	54
IDAHO													
BOISE	40	48	59	67	68	75	89	86	81	66	46	37	66
POCATELLO	37	47	58	64	66	72	82	81	78	66	48	36	64
ILLINOIS													
CAIRO	46	53	59	65	71	77	82	79	75	73	56	46	65
CHICAGO	44	49	53	56	63	69	73	70	65	61	47	41	59
SPRINGFIELD	47	51	54	58	64	69	76	72	73	64	53	45	60
INDIANA													
EVANSVILLE	42	49	55	61	67	73	78	76	73	67	52	42	64
FORT WAYNE	38	44	51	55	62	69	74	69	64	58	41	38	57
INDIANAPOLIS	41	47	49	55	62	68	74	70	68	64	48	39	59
IOWA													
DES MOINES	56	56	56	59	62	66	75	70	64	64	53	48	62
DUBUQUE	48	52	52	58	60	63	73	67	61	55	44	40	57
SIOUX CITY	55	58	58	59	63	67	75	72	67	65	53	50	63
KANSAS													
CONCORDIA	60	60	62	63	65	73	79	76	72	70	64	58	67
DODGE CITY	67	66	68	68	68	74	78	78	76	75	70	67	71
WICHITA	61	63	64	64	66	73	80	77	73	69	67	59	69
KENTUCKY													
LOUISVILLE	41	47	52	57	64	68	72	69	68	64	51	39	59
LOUISIANA													
NEW ORLEANS	49	50	57	63	66	64	58	60	64	70	60	46	59
SHREVEPORT	48	54	58	60	69	78	79	80	79	77	65	60	69
MAINE													
EASTPORT	45	51	52	52	51	53	55	57	54	50	37	40	50
MASSACHUSETTS													
BOSTON	47	56	57	56	59	62	64	63	61	58	48	48	57
MICHIGAN													
ALPENA	29	43	52	56	59	64	70	64	52	44	24	22	51
DETROIT	34	42	48	52	58	65	69	66	61	54	35	29	53
GRAND RAPIDS	26	37	48	54	60	66	72	67	58	50	31	22	49
MARQUETTE	31	40	47	52	53	56	63	57	47	38	24	24	47
S. STE. MARIE	28	44	50	54	54	59	63	58	45	36	21	22	47
MINNESOTA													
DULUTH	47	55	60	58	58	60	68	63	53	47	36	40	55
MINNEAPOLIS	49	54	55	57	60	64	72	69	60	54	40	40	46

Location	Jan.	Feb.	Mar.	Apr.	May	June	July	Aug.	Sept.	Oct.	Nov.	Dec.	Annual
MISSISSIPPI													
VICKSBURG	46	50	57	64	69	73	69	72	74	71	60	45	64
MISSOURI													
KANSAS CITY	55	57	59	60	64	70	76	73	70	67	59	52	65
ST. LOUIS	48	49	56	59	64	68	72	68	67	65	54	44	61
SPRINGFIELD	48	54	57	60	53	69	77	72	71	65	58	48	63
MONTANA													
HAVRE	49	58	61	63	63	65	78	75	64	57	48	46	62
HELENA	46	55	58	60	59	63	77	74	63	57	48	43	60
KALISPELL	28	40	49	57	58	60	77	73	61	50	28	20	53
NEBRASKA													
LINCOLN	57	59	60	60	63	69	76	71	67	66	59	55	64
NORTH PLATTE	63	63	64	62	64	72	78	74	72	70	62	58	68
NEVADA													
ELY	61	64	68	65	67	79	79	81	81	73	67	62	72
LAS VEGAS	74	77	78	81	85	91	84	86	92	84	83	75	82
RENO	59	64	69	75	77	82	90	89	86	76	68	56	76
WINNEMUCCA	52	60	64	70	76	83	90	90	86	75	62	53	74
NEW HAMPSHIRE													
CONCORD	48	53	55	53	51	56	57	58	55	50	43	43	52
NEW JERSEY													
ATLANTIC CITY	51	57	58	59	62	65	67	66	65	54	58	52	60
NEW MEXICO													
ALBUQUERQUE	70	72	72	76	79	84	76	75	81	80	79	70	76
ROSWELL	69	72	75	77	76	80	76	75	74	74	74	69	74
NEW YORK													
ALBANY	43	51	53	53	57	62	63	61	58	54	39	38	53
BINGHAMTON	31	39	41	44	50	56	54	51	47	43	29	26	44
BUFFALO	32	41	49	51	59	67	70	67	60	51	31	28	53
CANTON	37	47	50	48	54	61	63	61	54	45	30	31	49
NEW YORK	49	56	57	59	62	65	66	64	64	61	53	50	59
SYRACUSE	31	38	45	50	58	64	67	63	56	47	29	26	50
NORTH CAROLINA													
ASHEVILLE	48	53	56	61	64	63	59	59	62	64	59	48	58
RALEIGH	50	56	59	64	67	65	62	62	63	64	62	52	61
NORTH DAKOTA													
BISMARCK	52	58	56	57	58	61	73	69	62	59	49	48	59
DEVILS LAKE	53	60	59	60	59	62	71	67	59	56	44	45	58
FARGO	47	55	56	58	62	63	73	69	60	57	39	46	59
WILLISTON	51	59	60	63	66	66	78	75	65	60	48	48	63

Location	Jan.	Feb.	Mar.	Apr.	May	June	July	Aug.	Sept.	Oct.	Nov.	Dec.	Annual
OHIO													
CINCINNATI	41	46	52	56	62	69	72	68	68	60	46	39	57
CLEVELAND	29	36	45	52	61	67	71	68	62	54	32	25	50
COLUMBUS	36	44	49	54	63	68	71	68	66	60	44	35	55
OKLAHOMA													
OKLAHOMA CITY	57	60	63	64	65	74	78	78	74	68	64	57	68
OREGON													
BAKER	41	49	56	61	63	67	83	81	74	62	46	37	60
PORTLAND	27	34	41	49	52	55	70	65	55	42	28	23	48
ROSEBURG	24	32	40	51	57	59	79	77	68	42	28	18	51
PENNSYLVANIA													
HARRISBURG	43	52	55	57	61	65	68	63	62	58	47	43	57
PHILADELPHIA	45	56	57	58	61	62	64	61	62	61	53	49	57
PITTSBURG	32	39	45	50	57	62	64	61	62	54	39	30	51
RHODE ISLAND													
BLOCK ISLAND	45	54	47	56	58	60	62	62	60	59	50	44	56
SOUTH CAROLINA													
CHARLESTON	58	60	65	72	73	70	66	66	67	68	68	57	66
COLUMBIA	53	57	62	68	69	68	63	65	64	68	64	51	63
SOUTH DAKOTA													
HURON	55	62	60	62	65	68	76	72	66	61	52	49	63
RAPID CITY	58	62	63	62	61	66	73	73	69	66	58	54	64
TENNESSEE													
KNOXVILLE	42	49	53	59	64	66	64	59	64	64	53	41	57
MEMPHIS	44	51	57	64	68	74	73	74	70	69	58	45	64
NASHVILLE	42	47	54	60	65	69	69	68	69	65	55	42	59
TEXAS													
ABILENE	64	68	73	66	73	86	83	85	73	71	72	66	73
AMARILLO	71	71	75	75	75	82	81	81	79	76	76	70	76
AUSTIN	46	50	57	60	62	72	76	79	70	70	57	49	63
BROWNSVILLE	44	49	51	57	65	73	78	78	67	70	54	44	61
DEL RIO	53	55	61	63	60	66	75	80	69	66	58	52	63
EL PASO	74	77	81	85	87	87	78	78	80	82	80	73	80
FORT WORTH	56	57	65	66	67	75	78	78	74	70	63	58	68
GALVESTON	50	50	55	61	69	76	72	71	70	74	62	49	63
SAN ANTONIO	48	51	56	58	60	69	74	75	69	67	55	49	62
UTAH													
SALT LAKE CITY	48	53	61	68	73	78	82	82	84	73	56	49	69
VERMONT													
BURLINGTON	34	43	48	47	53	59	62	59	51	43	25	24	46

Location	Jan.	Feb.	Mar.	Apr.	May	June	July	Aug.	Sept.	Oct.	Nov.	Dec.	Annual
VIRGINIA													
NORFOLK	50	57	60	63	67	66	66	66	63	64	60	51	62
RICHMOND	49	55	59	63	67	66	65	62	63	64	58	50	61
WASHINGTON													
NORTH HEAD	28	37	42	48	48	48	50	46	48	41	31	27	41
SEATTLE	27	34	42	48	53	48	62	56	53	36	28	24	45
SPOKANE	26	41	53	63	64	68	82	79	68	53	28	22	58
TATOOSH ISLAND	26	36	39	45	47	46	48	44	47	38	26	23	40
WALLA WALLA	24	35	51	63	67	72	86	84	72	59	33	20	60
YAKIMA	34	49	62	70	72	74	86	86	74	61	38	29	65
WEST VIRGINIA													
ELKINS	33	37	42	47	55	55	56	53	55	51	41	33	48
PARKERSBURG	30	36	42	49	56	60	63	60	60	53	37	29	48
WISCONSIN													
GREEN BAY	44	51	55	56	58	64	70	65	58	52	40	40	55
MADISON	44	49	52	53	58	64	70	66	60	56	41	38	56
MILWAUKEE	44	48	53	56	60	65	73	67	62	56	44	39	57
WYOMING													
CHEYENNE	65	66	64	61	59	68	70	68	69	60	65	63	66
LANDER	66	70	71	66	65	74	76	75	72	67	61	62	69
SHERIDAN	56	61	62	61	61	67	76	74	67	60	53	52	64
YELLOWSTONE PARK	39	51	55	57	56	63	73	71	65	57	45	38	56
PUERTO RICO													
SAN JUAN	64	69	71	66	59	62	65	67	61	63	63	65	65

Index

Note: Italicized numbers denote main entry for subject heading.

About the Author

Shane Smith is a nationally recognized lecturer on both commercial and home greenhouse operation, writes a gardening column and hosts a weekly gardening radio program. As a founder and director of the Cheyenne Botanic Gardens, he has developed a people-oriented, solar greenhouse conservatory that employs seniors, youth at risk and handicapped individuals and has received national recognition, including awards from Presidents Reagan and Bush. Smith has been involved in greenhouse gardening since 1976. He has a degree in horticultural science and served as a Loeb fellow in advanced environmental studies at Harvard. As a registered horticultural therapist (using horticulture as a mode of therapy for

the disabled), he enjoys bringing the therapeutic benefits of gardening to all.